Instructor's Resource Manual

for

Starr, Evers, and Starr's

Biology Today and Tomorrow
With Physiology

Second Edition

Larry G. Sellers
Louisiana Tech University

THOMSON
™
BROOKS/COLE

Australia • Brazil • Canada • Mexico • Singapore • Spain • United Kingdom • United States

Printed in the United States of America

1 2 3 4 5 6 7   10 09 08 07 06

Printer: Thomson/West

Cover Image: Jay Barnes

0-495-10921-5

Thomson Higher Education
10 Davis Drive
Belmont, CA 94002-3098
USA

For more information about our products,
contact us at:
Thomson Learning Academic Resource Center
1-800-423-0563

For permission to use material from this text or
product, submit a request online at
http://www.thomsonrights.com.
Any additional questions about permissions can be
submitted by email to **thomsonrights@thomson.com.**

CONTENTS

PREFACE

The material in this resource manual should be helpful to both novice instructors who are eager to establish good teaching practices and also to experienced professors. Because several instructors have contributed their ideas for this manual, it represents a consensus as to what might be most suitable.

Chapters in the manual correspond to chapters in *Biology: Today and Tomorrow* Second Edition by Cecie Starr, Christine A. Evers, and Lisa Starr. In addition, there is an appendix with suggestions for writing essays and term papers (these can be copied and handed out to students).

Each chapter of the manual has 11 sections:

- **Chapter Outline***:* An outline of the headings within the textbook's chapters to give an overview of its contents.
- **Objectives***:* General objectives that correspond to the main headings of each text chapter.
- **Key Terms***:* A complete listing of the boldface, italic, and other significant terms in the chapter.
- **Lecture Outline***:* A detailed, sequential outline of the chapter.
- **Suggestions for Presenting the Material***:* Helpful suggestions for presenting certain topics covered in the textbook. As in other sections, hints have been gathered from several classroom teachers.
- **Classroom and Laboratory Enrichment***:* A unique and useful collection of visual demonstrations to help make the lecture a lively learning experience for your students; most of the ideas utilize common laboratory or household equipment.
- *Impacts, Issues* **Classroom Discussion Ideas***:* These questions, written specifically to correlate to the opening essay of each chapter, are designed to evoke a range of responses from your students in a group setting.
- **Additional Ideas for Classroom Discussion***:* These are additional questions relating to the topics in the chapter.
- *How Would Vote?* **Classroom Discussion Ideas***:* In addition to reminding the teacher to monitor the online vote (see Media Menu at end of text chapter), this section has comments on how the vote might have gone.
- **Term Paper Topics, Library Activities, and Special Projects***:* For those instructors who want their students to "dig a little deeper" into the chapter content, a list of topics that require extra effort and research.
- **Possible Responses to** *Critical Thinking* **Questions***:* Although there is a response to each of the Critical Thinking questions at the end of each textbook chapter, this is only my response and, obviously, may neither be the "correct" response nor the only possibility.

I hope this Instructor's Resource Manual will facilitate your presentation of the fascinating subject of biology

Larry Sellers

1

INVITATION TO BIOLOGY

Chapter Outline

WHAT AM I DOING HERE?

LIFE'S LEVELS OF ORGANIZATION
    From Small to Smaller
    From Smaller to Vast

OVERVIEW OF LIFE'S UNITY
    DNA, the Basis of Inheritance
    Energy, the Basis of Metabolism
    Energy and Life's Organization
    Life's Responsiveness to Change

IF SO MUCH UNITY, WHY SO MANY SPECIES?

AN EVOLUTIONARY VIEW OF DIVERSITY

THE NATURE OF BIOLOGICAL INQUIRY
    Observations, Hypotheses, and Tests
    About the Word "Theory"

THE POWER OF EXPERIMENTAL TESTS
    An Assumption of Cause and Effect
    Example of an Experimental Design
    Example of a Field Experiment
    Bias in Reporting Results

THE SCOPE AND LIMITS OF SCIENCE

SUMMARY

SELF-QUIZ

CRITICAL THINKING

Objectives

1. List features that distinguish living organisms from nonliving matter.
2. Describe the general pattern of energy flow through Earth's life forms, and explain how Earth's resources are used again and again (cycled).
3. List the levels of organization in the living world.
4. Explain what is meant by the term *diversity*, and speculate about what caused the great diversity of lifeforms on Earth.
5. Explain how people came to believe that the populations of organisms that inhabit Earth have changed through time.
6. List as many steps of the scientific approach to understanding a problem as you can.
7. Understand as well as you can what limitations are imposed on science and scientists.

Key Terms

cell	biosphere	energy	homeostasis
organisms	DNA	metabolism	species
population	inheritance	producers	genus, genera
community	reproduction	consumers	domains
ecosystem	development	decomposers	archaea

bacteria	eubacteria	artificial selection	variable
eukarya	eukaryotic	hypotheses	control group
protists	mutations	prediction	experimental groups
fungi	adaptive traits	test	mimicry
plants	evolution	models	sampling error
animals	diversity	scientific theory	
prokaryotic	natural selection	scientific experiment	

Lecture Outline

What Am I Doing Here?
A. The world seems to be spinning out of control.
  1. Humans alter the environment in ways that affect both us and the other organisms around us.
  2. Pandemics past (bubonic plague) and present (AIDS) scare us.
B. We and our ancestors have been trying to make sense of our natural world.

1.1 Life's Levels of Organization
A. From Small to Smaller
  1. Consider what can fit across the head of a pin: 375 red blood cells; 1,200,000 fat molecules 53, 908,355 hydrogen atoms.
  2. Next, imagine how many of these are in your body.
B. From Smaller to Vast
  1. The molecules of life are: carbohydrates, lipids, proteins, DNA, and RNA.
  2. The cell, composed of "biological molecules," is the basic unit of life.
  3. Multicelled organisms have increasingly complex levels of organization that result in tissues >> organs >> organ systems >> multicelled organisms >> populations >> communities >> ecosystems >> biosphere.

1.2 Overview of Life's Unity
A. DNA, the Basis of Inheritance
  1. Living and nonliving matter are composed of the same particles, operating according to laws governing energy—the capacity to make things happen, to do work.
    a. Deoxyribonucleic acid, or DNA, is the special molecule that sets the living world apart from the nonliving by carrying the hereditary instructions for assembly of new organisms.
    b. The flow is from DNA to RNA to protein.
  2. Inheritance is the acquisition of traits through the transmission of DNA from parents to offspring.
    a. Each organism arises through reproduction—the production of offspring by one or more parents.
    b. DNA also guides development—the transformation of a new individual into a multicelled adult.
B. Energy, the Basis of Metabolism
  1. Energy, the capacity to do work, moves through the universe in a series of transfers.
  2. Metabolism is the cell's capacity to:
    a. obtain and convert energy from its surroundings,
    b. use energy for maintenance, growth, and reproduction.
  3. Energy flows from the sun.
    a. Plants ("producers") trap this energy by photosynthesis.
    b. Animals ("consumers") feed on the stored energy in plants, using aerobic respiration.
    c. Bacteria and fungi ("decomposers") break down complex molecules of other organisms to simple raw materials suitable for recycling.

C. Energy and Life's Organization
   1. The great one-way flow of energy into the world of life also flows out of it.
   2. These events organize life in the biosphere.
D. Life's Responsiveness to Change
   1. Receptors and the stimuli they receive allow controlled responses to be made to heat and cold, harmful substances, and varying food supplies.
   2. Homeostasis refers to a state in which the conditions of the "internal environment" are maintained within tolerable limits.
      a. Increased sugar causes insulin release, which stimulates cells to take up sugar.
      b. Decreased blood sugar causes another hormone to call on stored sugar reserves.

1.3   If So Much Unity, Why So Many Species?
   A. Attempts to clarify the diversity of life forms led to classification schemes.
      1. Carolus Linnaeus devised a plan whereby each organism could be identified by a genus and species name; example: *Scarus gibbus* (humphead parrotfish).
      2. A three domain system of classification has been proposed: Archaea, Bacteria, and Eukarya.
         a. Archaea and Bacteria are single-celled and prokaryotic.
         b. Eukarya are all eukaryotic—possessing a true nucleus.
   B. The Eukarya includes protists, plants, fungi, and animals.

1.4   An Evolutionary View of Diversity
   A. Mutations are heritable changes in DNA.
      1. Variations in hereditary instructions arise through mutations.
         a. Many mutations are harmful.
         b. Some may be harmless or even beneficial.
      2. The environment tests the combination of patterns expressed in each organism and may prove the trait adaptive—increasing survivability and reproduction.
   B. Evolution is heritable change in a line of descent over time.
      1. Charles Darwin reasoned that the practice of artificial selection used by pigeon breeders could serve as a model for his theory of natural selection.
      2. The key points of his theory are as follows:
         a. Members vary in form and behavior; much of the variation is heritable.
         b. Some varieties of heritable traits will improve survival and reproductive chances.
         c. Those with improved chances will be more likely to reproduce and pass the adaptive traits on with greater frequency in future generations (natural selection).

1.5   The Nature of Biological Inquiry
   A. Observations, Hypotheses, and Tests
      1. Biology, like all science, pursues a methodical search for information that reveals the secrets of the natural world.
      2. Explanations are sought using the following approach:
         a. Ask a question.
         b. Develop hypotheses (educated guesses) using all known information.
         c. Predict what the outcome would be if the hypothesis is valid (deductive, "if-then" reasoning).
         d. Test the hypothesis by experiments, models, and observations.
         e. Repeat the tests for consistency.
         f. Examine alternative hypotheses in the same manner.
         g. Report objectively on the tests and conclusions.
   B. About the Word "Theory"
      1. A theory is a related set of hypotheses that form a broad-ranging explanation of many phenomena.
      2. Theories are accepted or rejected on the basis of tests and are subject to revision.

3. Scientists must be content with relative certainty, which becomes stronger as more repetitions are made.
4. Scientists must be prepared to change their minds in light of new evidence.

1.6 The Power Of Experimental Tests
    A. An Assumption of Cause and Effect
        1. Experiments involve tests in which conditions are carefully controlled.
        2. Variables, features that differ, must be tested one at a time.
        3. Control groups are the standard for comparison with the experimental group.
        4. The experimental group experiences all of the same conditions as the control except for the variable being studied.
    B. Example of an Experimental Approach
        1. Hypothesis: Olestra® causes intestinal cramps.
        2. Prediction: people who eat potato chips made with Olestra will be more likely to get cramps.
        3. Experiment: control group eats regular chips; experimental group eats Olestra chips.
        4. Results: 17.6 percent of control gets cramps; 15.8 percent of experimental group do.
        5. Conclusion: the results do NOT support the hypothesis since the percentages are nearly equal.
    C. Example of a Field Experiment
        1. Durrell Kapan tested a hypothesis involving mimicry.
        2. He released two forms of a bad-tasting butterfly (*H. cydno*), one with white markings and one with yellow, into an area where another bad-tasting butterfly (*H. eleuchia*) with markings similar to the yellow *H. cydno* was already being avoided by birds who had "learned their lesson."
        3. He discovered that the birds avoided the yellow *H. cydno* just because it resembled the yellow *H. eleuchia*, but the birds ate (ugh!) the white group because they had no prior experience with it.
    D. Bias in Reporting the Results
        1. Scientists prefer quantitative reports of experimental tests to guard against bias.
        2. Changing one's mind in the light of new evidence is a strength in science.

1.7 The Scope and Limits of Science
    A. Subjective questions do not readily lend themselves to scientific analysis and experiments.
        1. All of human society must participate in moral, aesthetic, and other such judgments.
        2. Copernicus correctly stated that the Earth circled the sun—a heresy in his day.
    B. The external world, not internal conviction, must be the testing ground for science.

Suggestions for Presenting the Material

- Although Chapter 1 is a general introduction to biology and to this textbook, it will be viewed very differently by instructor and student. For the instructor, this chapter is more *review* rather than a *preview*. That means the instructor must take extra care not to "intimidate" the students during early lectures.

- A casual glance at the chapter contents will reveal terms unfamiliar to most students. These might include: *metabolism, homeostasis, DNA*. Individual instructors will have to decide to what extent these terms need explanation now or whether it can be deferred until later. Possibly this decision will depend on the time available.

- Obviously, it would be very easy to lose the attention and enthusiasm of newly enrolled students if *too much* is presented *too soon*.

- Figure 1.1 (levels of organization in nature) is an excellent "road map" and can be used throughout the course to guide the progression along the organizational ladder. It can also be used in the exercise listed in the Enrichment section below.

- The diagram in Figure 1.3 (energy flow) also has relevance to future lectures. When introducing it here, you should stress the *flow* of *energy* and the *recycling* of *raw materials.*
- Sometimes students think that methods of scientific investigation are used only by scientists. Show that this is not true by discussing the use of these methods in a routine investigation of "Why won't the car start?" (see the Enrichment section below).
- Explain carefully the necessity for control groups in scientific investigations. Point out the difficulty of determining which groups of human patients will *not* receive a valuable drug (the controls) and who will receive a possibly life-saving medication.
- Having introduced one of the great organizing principles in biology—evolution—the authors proceed to the methods by which principles are derived—scientific method.
- Although additional details will be added later in the book, the basic concept of biological evolution can, and should be, introduced early in the course.
- Students rarely hear about Darwin's life other than his famous journey. Present his biography before his theory to spark interest. Perhaps the videotape could be used. You can then proceed to *natural selection* by first explaining *artificial selection* (maybe using dogs rather than the pigeons that Darwin used in his book).

Classroom and Laboratory Enrichment

- Bring several organisms into the classroom or lab. Ask your students to name characteristics that identify each item as living or nonliving (for some organisms, this may be difficult to do without specialized equipment, such as a microscope). Ask the students to identify equipment or experiments that would help to determine if an item is a living organism.
- Obtain an overhead transparency of levels of organization in nature (Figure 1.1). With the labels of the figure covered, ask your students to help you name each higher level, going from simple to complex.
- Using various media, show a representative variety of plants, animals, and decomposers. Ask students to characterize them as *producer, consumer,* or *decomposer.*
- Show the videotape "Life on Earth" by David Attenborough (available at retail outlets) as a general introduction to biological diversity.
- In the Presentation section above, Figure 1.1 was referred to as a "road map" for the text. With an overhead transparency of that figure in view, have the students mark the chapters in the Contents in Brief page of their text that amplify each level of organization.
- Give examples of several scientific names for local plants and animals that are well known to the students. Interpret the meanings of each Latin specific epithet.
- Show a phylogenetic tree of vertebrates (or any other group of organisms for which a phylogenetic tree is available) to demonstrate the phylogenetic system of classification. Present students with a set of diverse organisms; ask them how they would classify these organisms.
- Present fossil evidence showing how a group of related organisms or a single genus (for example, *Equus*) has evolved and changed through time.
- Show a film describing Charles Darwin's voyage on the HMS *Beagle* and his thoughts as he traveled.
- Generate interest in Darwin's theory by bringing a copy of *Origin of Species* to class. Read selected chapter titles and portions of the text. Point out the lack of illustrations in the original edition.
- Briefly list the steps of the scientific method in the wrong order. Ask the class to place them, one by one, in the correct order.

- Show how we use the scientific method in everyday problem solving as illustrated by this example:

Event	Method Step
a. Auto will not start	a. Observation
b. Battery dead	b. Hypothesis
Ignition problem	Hypothesis
Out of gas	Hypothesis
c. Turn on headlights	c. Experiment
Check spark at plug	Experiment
Check gas gauge	Experiment
Dip long stick into gas tank	Experiment
d. Headlights burn brightly (battery OK)	d. Analyze results
Strong ignition spark	Analyze results
Gauge says half tank but no gas on stick	Analyze results
e. Gas gauge is not accurate; car needs gas to run	e. Generalize; form principle

Impacts, Issues Classroom Discussion Ideas

- Humans are able to manipulate certain aspects of nature for their own benefit. However, it is often said that "humans are the only animals that engineer their own destruction." Give examples to support this allegation.

- Death and decay are considered by religious fundamentalists as part of God's curse on mankind. What would the Earth be like without these two processes?

Additional Ideas for Classroom Discussion

- During your first lecture, ask students to name as many characteristics of living things as possible. While this may at first seem like an obvious and overly simple exercise, students will be surprised at some of the less obvious characteristics, such as homeostasis.

- How does our modern definition of life differ from the definition of life that a seventeenth-century biologist might have used?

- What is metabolism? What metabolic steps in humans are different from those found in green plants? What metabolic steps in humans are the same as those found in green plants?

- What are some examples of homeostasis? Why must living organisms be able to perform it?

- Present a list of 10 random organisms (or, better yet, let your students do this). Identify ways in which all of the organisms are similar, then ways in which all of the organisms are different. How would you classify (that is, place into meaningful groups) these organisms?

- Why is it important for a species to be able to change? Wouldn't a species be more successful if it could be assured of remaining the same from one generation to the next?

- Name some organisms you might find in a grassy area nearby. Using arrows, arrange the organisms in a diagram depicting energy flow and the cycling of materials (for help, see Figure 1.3). What are some organisms that may be invisible to the eye but are essential for the recycling of nutrients during decomposition?

- An animal carcass infested with insect larvae is not an attractive sight. Yet it is a biological necessity. Explore the role of these and other "recyclers."

- Is there such a concept as the "balance of nature"?

- How is a principle different from a belief?

- Why is the term *scientific creationism* an oxymoron? Describe why this body of thought cannot be considered as science.

- Does belief in the principle of evolution exclude belief in religion? Why or why not?

- What is artificial selection? How does it differ from natural selection?
- Why is it difficult to obtain a control group when selecting volunteers to test a new anticancer drug?
- Those who wish to berate certain scientific principles sometimes say "it's only a theory." This statement is used by creationists when referring to evolution. Does the use of "theory" in biology mean the concept is in doubt? Explain using examples.
- If you took a sidewalk survey, what do you think the responses would be to this statement? "Darwin wrote a very famous book on the origin of _____."

How Would You Vote? Classroom Discussion Ideas

- Monitor the voting for the online question. Ask your students to discuss their reasons for voting for or against the United States providing funding to help preserve the coral reefs.

Term Paper Topics, Library Activities, and Special Projects

- Discover more about how the first cells are thought to have evolved. How do biologists "draw the line" between that which is living and that which is nonliving?
- Outline ways in which biologists attempted to explain inheritance of particular characteristics prior to the discovery of the role of DNA in heredity.
- Describe how any one of several modern scientific investigative tools (such as electron microscopy, radioactive labeling, gas chromatography, or gel electrophoresis) has made it possible to discover similarities and differences among living organisms.
- The pupal stage of insect metamorphosis is erroneously called the "resting stage." Actually there is a complete transformation of larval tissues to adult tissues. Consult several entomology and biochemistry texts to learn the current status of our knowledge concerning these transformations.
- The origin of life on this planet has always fascinated humankind. Several explanations have been advanced. Search for the principal ones that are still in contention today.
- The supply of easily obtainable energy sources is a matter of debate today. Some persons see a bleak future; others are optimistic. What are the issues that each of these camps see?
- How do today's biologists reconcile their personal faith in an organized religion with their belief in evolution? Research the viewpoints of some famous scientists on this issue.
- Can we see evolution actually happening? Find examples of natural occurrences in the wild or experimental situations in the laboratory in which we can observe evolution occurring.
- Learn more about the discovery of fossils of *Archaeopteryx* and the reactions of the scientific community to them.
- Describe how Darwin's development of his principle of evolution was an example of the scientific method in action.

Possible Responses to *Critical Thinking* Questions

1. Actually there is more danger in using just any *one* of these phrases:
   a. "Truth" can be the truth as you see it;
   b. You could tell a *portion* of the truth but leave out some *other portions* of the truth;
   c. "Nothing but the truth" means that nothing in your narrative can be a falsehood.

So I guess that is why the question is seemingly redundant; but as an alternative maybe these:
a. Is *anything* you are about to say a lie?
b. Is there *anything* false in your testimony?
But neither of these has the ring that we are so accustomed to hearing from the bailiff.

2. Let's consider the television ads for weight loss and fitness products. They portray a few dramatic examples of smiling, satisfied "customers." What they do NOT show are the many frowning, dissatisfied customers. What they *should* show are statistics for ALL of the users, which would allow the viewer to evaluate the percent success of the product.

    You can get a hint that not everyone achieves success because there is a disclaimer that appears briefly, in very small print, at the bottom of the screen: "*Results not typical*." Translation? "IT DOESN'T WORK, FOLKS!"

3. A double-blind study keeps the subjects and the researchers "in the dark" so to speak. If either group knew which bags of chips were Olestra or which were not, they would have a tendency, albeit subtle and non-obvious, to give a prejudicial nod to the experimental group or the control. For this reason, the chips are coded by technicians so that neither group will have a clue until the results are tabulated. Sometimes this is difficult to control if stringent safeguards are not in place, especially when computer files may be shared.

4. One of the obvious problems with a prayer experiment, and ones like it, is the subjective evaluation of the patients after their regimen of treatment and prayer. If the experiment were to be conducted by strict scientific method, patients would be randomly assigned to two groups: (1) treatment by accepted medical care, and (2) only prayer. Of course, it would irresponsible, by generally accepted standards of medical practice, to assign anyone to group (2) except the truly strong believers. For this and other reasons, this type of research remains "interesting" but open to strong criticism.

5. "Facts change." That is true in scientific research because science is open to new data and new interpretations of old data, which can lead to discarding or modifying formerly-held tenets. This is a strength of science, not a weakness. It is this willingness to accept *change* that makes the phrase "scientific creationism" meaningless. Creationists have accepted as fact a set of immutable ideas that are then supported by carefully chosen facts from the realm of science.

2

MOLECULES OF LIFE

Chapter Outline

Objectives

1. Understand how protons, electrons, and neutrons are arranged into atoms and ions.
2. Explain how the distribution of electrons in an atom or ion determines the number and kinds of chemical bonds that can be formed.
3. Know the various types of chemical bonds, the circumstances under which each forms, and the relative strengths of each type.
4. Understand the essential chemistry of water and of some common substances dissolved in it.
5. Be able to distinguish: acid, base, salt, and buffer.
6. Understand how small organic molecules can be assembled into large macromolecules by condensation. Understand how large macromolecules can be broken apart into their basic subunits by hydrolysis.
7. Learn the functional groups presented and know the properties they confer when attached to other molecules.
8. Know the general structure of a monosaccharide with six carbon atoms, a fatty acid, an amino acid, and a nucleotide.
9. Know the macromolecules into which these essential building blocks can be assembled by condensation.
10. Know where these carbon compounds tend to be located in cells or organelles and the activities in which they participate.

Key Terms

atoms
protons
neutrons
electrons
element
isotopes
radioisotope
tracer
orbital
shell model
chemical bonding
molecule
compounds
mixture
ion
ionic bond
covalent bond
nonpolar covalent bond
polar covalent bond
hydrogen bond
hydrophilic substances
hydrophobic substances
temperature
evaporation
solvent

solutes
cohesion
hydrogen ions, H$^+$
hydroxide ions, OH$^-$
pH scale
acids
bases
acid rain
salt
buffer system
acute respiratory acidosis
alkalosis
tetany
organic compounds
functional groups
hydroxyl
functional-group transfer
electron transfer
rearrangement
condensation
cleavage
condensation reaction
hydrolysis

carbohydrates
monosaccharides
ribose
deoxyribose
glucose
glycerol
oligosaccharides
disaccharide
lactose
sucrose
glycolipids
polysaccharides
cellulose
starch
glycogen
chitin
lipids
fats
fatty acids
unsaturated
saturated
triglycerides
phospholipid
sterols
cholesterol

testosterone
estrogen
waxes
proteins
amino acid
R group
peptide bond
polypeptide chain
primary structure
secondary structure
domain
tertiary structure
quaternary structure
glycoproteins
lipoproteins
hemoglobin
sickle-cell anemia
denaturation
nucleotides
ATP
coenzymes
NAD$^+$, FAD
nucleic acids
DNA, RNA

Lecture Outline

Science or Supernatural?
A. The ancient Greeks thought that the oracle of Delphi delivered prophecies from Apollo.
B. Scientists have discovered that the gases methane, ethane, and ethylene seeped into Delphi's cave and caused the hallucinatory messages.

2.1 Atoms and Their Interactions
  A. Atoms and Isotopes
    1. Elements are forms of matter that can't be degraded to something else.
    2. Atoms of each element are composed of three primary subatomic particles:
      a. *Protons* (p^+) are part of the atomic nucleus and have a positive charge.
      b. *Neutrons* are also a part of the nucleus; they are neutral.
      c. *Electrons* (e^-) have a negative charge. Their quantity is equal to that of the protons. They move around the nucleus.
    3. Each element has its own unique number of protons in its atoms.
    4. Isotopes are atoms with the same number of protons (for example, carbon with six) but a different number of neutrons (carbon can have six, seven, or eight).
    5. Some radioisotopes are unstable and tend to decay into more stable atoms.
      a. They can be used to date rocks and fossils.
      b. Some can be used as tracers to follow the path of an atom in a series of reactions or to diagnose disease.
  B. Electrons and Energy Levels
    1. Electrons are attracted to protons but are repelled by other electrons.
    2. Orbitals (visualized as shells), each of which contains one or two electrons, permit electrons to stay as close to the nucleus and as far from each other as possible.
      a. The shell closest to the nucleus has one orbital holding a maximum of two electrons.
      b. The next shell can have four orbitals with two electrons each, for a total of eight electrons.
      c. Atoms with "unfilled" orbitals in their outermost shell tend to be reactive with other atoms.
    3. A chemical bond is a union between atoms, formed when they give up, gain, or share electrons.
      a. A *molecule* is a bonded unit of two or more (same or different) atoms.
      b. *Compounds* are substances in which two or more different elements are combined in fixed proportions.
      c. A *mixture* contains two or more elements in intermingled proportions that can vary.

2.2 Bonds in Biological Molecules
  A. Ion Formation and Ionic Bonding
    1. When an atom loses or gains one or more electrons, it becomes positively or negatively charged—an ion.
    2. In an *ionic bond*, (+) and (−) ions are linked by mutual attraction of opposite charges, for example, NaCl.
  B. Covalent Bonding
    1. A *covalent bond* holds together two atoms that share one or more pairs of electrons.
    2. In a *nonpolar covalent bond*, atoms share electrons equally.
    3. In a *polar covalent bond*, because atoms share the electron unequally, there is a slight difference in charge between the two poles of the bond; water is an example.

C. Hydrogen Bonding
   1. In a *hydrogen bond,* an atom or a molecule interacts weakly with a hydrogen atom already taking part in a polar covalent bond.
   2. These bonds impart structure to liquid water and stabilize nucleic acids and other large molecules.

2.3   Water's Life-Giving Properties
   A. Polarity of the Water Molecule
      1. Because of the electron arrangements in the water molecule, a polarity results that allows water to form hydrogen bonds with one another and other polar substances.
      2. Polar substances are hydrophilic (water-loving); nonpolar ones are hydrophobic (water-dreading) and are repelled by water.
   B. Water's Temperature-Stabilizing Effects
      1. Water tends to *stabilize* temperature because it can absorb considerable heat before its temperature changes.
      2. This is an important property in evaporative and freezing processes.
   C. Water's Solvent Properties
      1. Water is an excellent solvent because ions and polar molecules (solutes) dissolve in it.
      2. The *solvent properties* of water are greatest with respect to polar molecules because "spheres of hydration" are formed around the solute molecules.
   D. Water's Cohesion
      1. Hydrogen bonding of water molecules provides *cohesion* (capacity to resist rupturing).
      2. Cohesion imparts surface tension and helps pull water through plants, for example.

2.4   Acids and Bases
   A. The pH Scale
      1. pH is a measure of the H^+ concentration in a solution; the greater the H^+ the lower the pH scale.
         a. The scale extends from 0 (acidic) to 7 (neutral) to 14 (basic).
         b. The interior of living cells is near pH = 7.
      2. Acids and bases differ.
         a. A substance that releases hydrogen ions (H^+) in solution is an *acid*; for example, HCl.
         b. Substances that release ions such as OH^- (hydroxide ions) and can combine with hydrogen ions are called *bases.*
      3. Salts in Water
         a. A salt is an ionic compound formed when an acid reacts with a base; example: NaOH + HCl → NaCl + H_2O.
         b. Many salts dissolve into ions that serve key functions in cells; nerve function, for example, is dependent on ions of sodium, potassium, and calcium.
      4. Buffers Against Shifts in pH
         a. A buffer system is a partnership between a weak acid and the base that forms when it dissolves in water.
         b. Buffer molecules combine with, or release, H^+ to prevent drastic changes in pH.
         c. Carbonic acid is one of the body's major buffers.

2.5 The Molecules of Life—From Structure to Function
    A. What Is an Organic Compound?
        1. Only living cells can synthesize carbohydrates, lipids, proteins, and nucleic acids.
        2. These molecules are organic compounds consisting of carbon and one or more additional elements, covalently bonded to one another.
    B. It All Starts With Carbon's Bonding Behavior
        1. Oxygen, hydrogen, and carbon are the most abundant elements in living matter.
        2. Much of the H and O are linked as water.
        3. Carbon can share pairs of electrons with as many as four other atoms to form organic molecules of several configurations.
            a. A ball-and-stick model depicts bonding of atoms; space-filling models convey a molecule's size and surfaces.
            b. Larger molecules are best visualized using ribbon models, such as those generated by computer programs.
    C. Functional groups are atoms or groups of atoms covalently bonded to a carbon backbone; they convey distinct properties, such as solubility and chemical reactivity, to the complete molecule.
    D. How Do Cells Build Organic Compounds?
        1. Simple sugars, fatty acids, amino acids, and nucleotides are the four major families of small building blocks from which larger polymers can be formed.
        2. Enzymes are a special class of proteins that mediate five categories of reactions:
            a. *functional-group transfer* from one molecule to another,
            b. *electron transfer* electrons are stripped from one molecule and given to another,
            c. *rearrangement* of internal bonds converts one type of organic molecule to another,
            d. *condensation* of two molecules into one,
            e. *cleavage* of one molecule into two.
        3. In a condensation reaction, one molecule is stripped of its H^+, another is stripped of its OH^-; then the two molecule fragments join to form a new compound, and the H^+ and OH^- form water.
        4. Hydrolysis is the reverse: one molecule is split by the addition of H^+ and OH^- (from water) to the components.

2.6 The Truly Abundant Carbohydrates
    A. The Simple Sugars
        1. Monosaccharides—one sugar unit—are the simplest carbohydrates.
        2. They are characterized by solubility in water, sweet taste, and several –OH groups.
        3. Ribose and deoxyribose (five-carbon backbones) are building blocks for nucleic acids.
        4. Glucose and fructose (six-carbon backbones) are used in assembling larger carbohydrates.
        5. Other important molecules derived from sugar monomers include glycerol and vitamin C.
    B. Short-Chain Carbohydrates
        1. An oligosaccharide is a short chain of just a few sugar monomers.
        2. Disaccharides—two sugar units—are the simplest.
            a. Lactose (glucose + galactose) is present in milk.
            b. Sucrose (glucose + fructose) is a transport form of sugar used by plants and harvested by humans for use in food.
        3. Oligosaccharides, with three or more sugar monomers, are attached as short side chains to proteins or lipids.

C. Complex Carbohydrates
1. A polysaccharide is a straight or branched chain of hundreds or thousands of sugar monomers.
2. Starch is a plant storage form of energy, arranged as unbranched coiled chains, easily hydrolyzed to glucose units.
3. Cellulose is a fiberlike structural material—tough, insoluble—used in plant cell walls.
4. Glycogen is a highly-branched chain used by animals to store energy in muscles and liver.
5. Chitin is a specialized polysaccharide with nitrogen attached to the glucose units; it is used as a structural material in arthropod exoskeletons and fungal cell walls.

2.7 Greasy, Fatty—Must Be Lipids
A. Fats and Fatty Acids
1. Lipids are greasy or oily compounds with little tendency to dissolve in water.
2. Fats are formed by the attachment of one (mono-), two (di-), or three (tri-) fatty acids to a glycerol.
3. A fatty acid is a long chain of mostly carbon and hydrogen atoms with a —COOH group at one end.
    a. *Unsaturated* fats are liquids (oils) at room temperature because one or more double bonds between the carbons in the fatty acids permit "kinks" in the tails.
    b. *Saturated* fats have only single C—C bonds in their fatty acid tails and are solids at room temperature.
4. "Neutral" fats are mostly triglycerides.
    a. They are a rich source of energy, yielding more than twice the energy per weight basis as carbohydrates.
    b. They also provide an insulation blanket for animals that must endure cold, harsh temperatures.
B. Phospholipids
1. These are formed by attachment of two fatty acids plus a phosphate group to a glycerol.
2. They are the main structural material of membranes, where they arrange in bilayers.
C. Cholesterol and Other Sterols
1. Sterols have a backbone of four carbon rings but no fatty acid tails.
2. Cholesterol is a component of cell membranes in animals and can be modified to form sex hormones (testosterone and estrogen) and vitamin D.
D. Waxes
1. These are formed by attachment of long-chain fatty acids to long-chain alcohols or carbon rings.
2. They serve as coatings for plant parts and as animal coverings.

2.8 Proteins—Diversity in Structure and Function
A. Proteins function as enzymes, in cell movements, as storage and transport agents, as hormones, as antibodies, and as structural material.
B. What Is an Amino Acid?
1. Amino acids are small organic molecules with an amino group, a carboxyl group, and one of 20 varying R groups.
2. All of the parts of an amino acid molecule are covalently bonded to a central carbon atom.
C. Levels of Protein Structure
1. *Primary structure* is defined as ordered sequences of amino acids, each linked together by peptide bonds to form polypeptide chains.

a. There are 20 kinds of amino acids available in nature.

b. The sequence of the amino acids is determined by DNA and is unique for each kind of protein.

2. *Secondary structure* refers to the helical coil (as in hemoglobin) or sheetlike array (as in silk) that results from hydrogen bonding of side groups on the amino acid chains.

3. *Tertiary structure* is the result of folding due to interactions among R groups along the polypeptide chain forming "domains."

4. *Quaternary structure* describes the complexing of two of more polypeptide chains.

a. Hemoglobin is a good example of four interacting chains that form a globular protein; keratin and collagen are complex fibrous proteins.

b. Glycoproteins consist of oligosaccharides covalently bonded to proteins; they are abundant on the exterior of animal cells, as cell products, and in the blood.

c. Lipoproteins have both lipid and protein components; they transport fats and cholesterol in the blood.

2.9   Why Is Protein Structure So Important?

A. Just One Wrong Amino Acid...

1. Alteration of a cell's DNA can result in the wrong amino acid insertion in a polypeptide chain.

2. If valine is substituted for glutamate in hemoglobin, the result is called HbS.

a. HbS molecules form large, rod-shaped aggregates that distort the red blood cells (in which they reside) into sickle-shaped cells that clog tiny blood vessels.

b. Persons who inherit two mutated genes for the beta chain of hemoglobin can only make HbS and thus suffer from sickle-cell anemia.

B. Proteins Undone—Denaturation

1. High temperatures or changes in pH can cause a loss of a protein's normal three-dimensional shape (denaturation).

2. Normal functioning is lost upon denaturation, which is often irreversible (for example, a cooked egg).

2.10   Nucleotides and the Nucleic Acids

A. Nucleotides are involved in metabolism, survival, and reproduction.

1. Each nucleotide consists of a five-carbon sugar (ribose or deoxyribose), a nitrogen-containing base, and a phosphate group.

a. Adenosine phosphates are chemical messengers (cAMP) or energy carriers (ATP).

b. Nucleotide coenzymes transport hydrogen atoms and electrons (examples: NAD^+ and FAD).

2. Nucleotides also serve as building blocks for nucleic acids.

B. Some nucleotides store and retrieve heritable information in cells.

1. Nucleic acids are polymers of nucleotides.

a. Four different kinds of nucleotides are strung together to form large single or double-stranded molecules.

b. Each strand's backbone consists of joined sugars and phosphates with nucleotide bases projecting toward the interior.

2. The two most important nucleic acids are DNA and RNA.

a. DNA is a double-stranded helix carrying encoded hereditary instructions.

b. RNA is single stranded and functions in translating the code to build proteins.

Suggestions for Presenting the Material

- There is no escaping the fact that Chapter 2 contains chemistry. And chemistry is intimidating— especially to any nonscience majors in your classes. The material in the book is elementary and written in a lucid manner, but the quality of presentation is up to the individual instructor.

- Perhaps a quick survey of those class members who have and have not had high school chemistry will aid in adjusting your level of presentation.

- One approach that might help your students in organizing this material is to write it in outline form on an overhead transparency. This may work especially well for this chapter because a large portion of the material consists of definitions.

- The use of ball-and-stick models (see the "Enrichment" section below) is very helpful. If the lecture room is large, you may have to "tour" the room with the models for better viewing. There are excellent 3-D computer animations that may be available from your chemistry faculty.

- If students become discouraged, assure them that several of these topics will be reinforced in future chapters (hopefully before the next exam).

- The text gives careful attention to useful examples of isotopes, electron excitation, bonding, buffers, and water.

- Using Figure 2.7 (pH scale) as your visual reference will help in explaining acid, base, and pH scale. Note particularly the pH values of common household products. Emphasize that acids and bases are not necessarily terms that describe *corrosive* substances!

- The properties of water are important to life on Earth. Describe the polarity of water molecules; then proceed to the influence that water molecules have on cells and cellular environments.

- The second half of this chapter is also "chemistry" but is more applicable to daily lives because it discusses the molecules of life such as *carbohydrates, lipids,* and *proteins.*

- It is valuable to point out that carbon, hydrogen, and oxygen are the principal atoms in the "molecules of life." Sulfur and nitrogen also participate in proteins and nucleotides.

- Your students will of course recognize the molecules of life as major food groups. You can capitalize on this to generate student interest.

- The extent to which each instructor requires the learning of molecular structure will vary. Perhaps you would like your students to be able to draw the molecules, but recognition will usually suffice for the student who is a nonscience major.

- Make extensive use of the excellent overhead transparencies and CD ROM images available for this chapter. Soon your students will be able to recognize these molecules on sight.

- Carbohydrates are easy to describe because they are built by assembling monomers into polymers. Lipids are a more diverse group and will need to be defined according to *solubility* rather than *common structural features.*

- Proteins are complex because of: (a) the quantity of amino acid subunits and (b) the levels of structure, that is, primary to quaternary. Use a string of beads and a Slinky to help here (see the Enrichment section below).

- You can preview the future lecture(s) on protein synthesis by stating: "Amino acids are in a precisely defined sequence from one end of a protein to the other as dictated by the instructions in DNA." How does the cell select from the 20 amino acid choices the proper one at the proper time?

- The *nucleotide* and *nucleic acid* section is obviously only a preview of more extensive information found in Chapters 9 and 10.

- Some instructors may also want to include two more of the molecules of life, namely *vitamins* and *minerals*. If so, these are discussed in Chapter 24.
- Stress the importance of Table 2.1 as a useful summary of biological molecules.

Classroom and Laboratory Enrichment

- Students often approach even basic chemistry with considerable trepidation, especially if they lack sufficient high school background in this area or have been out of school for several years. Emphasize the biological significance of chemistry; stress that an elemental knowledge of chemistry is essential to understanding the structure and function of living things. Give students frequent opportunities to use new terms. Use overheads or diagrams; pause often and interject questions to gauge their level of understanding.
- Use as many models and diagrams as possible. If you wish to emphasize electron orbitals, use foam-and-stick models of the orbitals to make this concept seem clearer.
- Students frequently have trouble visualizing atoms and molecules as real entities. To help them get a clearer mental picture of some of the basic atoms and molecules, use ball-and-stick models that are very large and easy to see from the back of the room. These models will help students to understand the size relationships among molecules. Overhead transparencies of ball-and-stick diagrams will also help. Such models and diagrams will be especially useful when covering the larger carbon compounds.
- Present sketches of a polar covalent molecule and a nonpolar covalent molecule. Ask students to identify which molecule is polar and which is nonpolar and to explain their choices.
- Ball-and-stick models are also useful for demonstrating the hydrogen bonding that occurs between water molecules and the latticework structure of ice.
- Fill a large jar with water, then add salad oil. Shake the bottle, then allow it to sit on the front desk. Ask students to explain what has happened. Add a few drops of methylene blue (a polar dye) and sudan III fat stain (a nonpolar dye) to the jar and shake. Students will note that the water layer is blue and the oil layer is red; ask them why this is so.
- Draw a pH scale on the board (or use an overhead transparency of Figure 2.7), and discuss pH values of familiar substances.
- If your class is small, demonstrate the use of a pH meter. For larger groups, pH paper can be used to give each student a chance to quickly determine the pH of some sample solutions.
- If you are teaching in a room with a periodic table of the elements hanging on the wall, point out the major elements, or use an overhead transparency to show the same items.
- Prepare a glass of iced tea (instant mix) with added sugar and lemon. Which ingredients are compounds? What are the components of the mixture?
- Bring a package of "buffered" and "regular" aspirin to class. Ask students to discover the difference(s) in ingredients.
- Using the names of the active ingredients on an antacid package, explain how they act as *buffers* to stomach acid.
- Use ball-and-stick models that are very large and easy to see to illustrate some of the basic carbon compounds. Overhead transparencies of ball-and-stick diagrams or "straight-stick" line drawings will also help students get a mental picture of each molecule.

- Use models, diagrams, or transparencies to demonstrate the functional groups you wish to emphasize. Stress the importance of knowing several characteristic functional groups by identifying those functional groups present in diagrams or models of real molecules.

- To illustrate amino acid structure, draw a generalized amino acid stem (as shown in Figure 2.23 but with an empty spot at the R-group location) on an overhead transparency. Create different amino acids by changing the R groups, each sketched on a small piece of transparency material.

- Use models or overhead transparencies to show condensation and hydrolysis. Show an example (such as the formation of a polypeptide in Figure 2.22), and ask students to state whether it is condensation or hydrolysis.

- Show a ball-and-stick diagram or three-dimensional model of any protein. An enzyme would be a good example; ball-and-stick diagrams of enzymes are readily available. Students will be amazed at the large size of proteins when compared to carbohydrates and lipids.

- Help students to understand nucleotide structure with models or diagrams. If students can get a good grasp of nucleotides now, they will have a better understanding of ATP and nucleic acids when these topics are covered in later chapters.

- Protein *primary structure* can be demonstrated by a string of beads or a Christmas tree garland. Individual beads can be colored with felt-tip markers for greater clarity and distinction. Secondary structure (alpha helix) is adequately illustrated by use of a Slinky®. You can even demonstrate tertiary structure by *carefully* folding a portion of the expanded Slinky®.

- Students have been exposed to many words related to those in this chapter, whether in print or broadcast media. Use this opportunity to explain complex carbohydrates, polyunsaturates, cholesterol, fiber, high-fructose syrup, dextrose, and anabolic steroids.

- Select a variety of food products from your pantry and bring them to class. Ask students to check the ingredients list for forms of sugar. Can you find it in some very unlikely places, such as table salt?

Impacts, Issues Classroom Discussion Ideas

- How will your knowledge of carbohydrates, fatty acids, proteins, and nucleic acids help you in your study of biology? How will such information help you with personal health and diet issues?

- What is a steroid? What steroids are sometimes taken by athletes? What are the obvious and hidden effects of these steroids on the body?

- "The human body uses a lot of protein in its construction and function. Therefore, you should eat massive quantities to be even healthier." Right or wrong? What could be some of the complications of a "high protein diet"?

Additional Ideas for Classroom Discussion

- Distinguish between a compound and a mixture, and an atom and a molecule.

- What chemicals are in the human body? Ask students to name as many as they can; help them complete their list.

- Discuss the role of electron excitation in photosynthesis.

- What is the difference between polar and nonpolar covalent bonds?

- Why do soft drinks have such a low pH? What ingredient is responsible for this low pH?

- What is acid precipitation? What chemical reaction is responsible for the mildly acidic pH of normal rainwater? What chemicals are responsible for acid precipitation?

- What is a calorie? What are we measuring when we determine the calorie content of different foods?

- What would happen to aquatic organisms living in temperate climates if water sank when it froze instead of floated?

- What is meant by the phrase *lipid bilayer*? Where would you find lipid bilayers inside a living organism?

- What is the difference between the composition of a *molecule* of a substance and an *atom* of that substance?

- If atoms are beyond the reach of visualization even by "super" electron microscopes, how then do we know so much about their structure?

- Water is the "universal solvent" for Earth. Do you know of any other compound that would serve as well, or better?

- Some pain relievers are advertised as "tribuffered." Is this a real advantage or just a sales gimmick?

- Television commercials portray the "acid stomach" as needing immediate R-O-L-A-I-D-S. Is the stomach *normally* acid? How do you know when there is too much acid down there?

- Compare the calorie contents of carbohydrates, lipids, and proteins.

- Why do alcohols dissolve in water?

- What is the difference between methyl alcohol and ethyl alcohol? How is each of these alcohols processed by the human body?

- What is a complex carbohydrate?

- Why don't animal cells contain cellulose? Can you think of at least one reason why cellulose in an animal cell could be considered a drawback?

- Why are saturated fatty acids solid at room temperature while unsaturated fatty acids are liquid?

- What is the difference between a globular protein and a fibrous protein?

- Why is sugar (in various forms) so prevalent as an additive in our packaged food products?

- Which yields more energy, a pound of carbohydrate or a pound of fat?

- Cellulose and starch both consist of chains of glucose units. One is a useful source of energy to humans, the other is not. Identify which is which and why they differ.

- Where is glycogen stored in the human body? What regulates interconversions of glucose and glycogen?

- Television advertising implies that the ideal diet would include *zero* cholesterol. Is this feasible? Would it even be *desirable*?

How Would You Vote? Classroom Discussion Ideas

- Monitor the voting for the online question. Have the students participate in a lively debate on the positive and negative aspects of tapping the natural gas reserves under the ocean floor.

Term Paper Topics, Library Activities, and Special Projects

- How are hydrophobic substances such as fats broken down in the human digestive tract? What chemicals are released by the body to assist with fat breakdown?

- Why are the cells lining the stomach able to withstand pH ranges between one and three?

- How does the body measure blood pH? What are the homeostatic mechanisms that help the human body to regulate blood pH?

- Discuss strategies currently being considered by the United States and other nations to remedy acid precipitation. What suggestions would you make to help solve this problem?

- Describe some of the roles played by ions in the human body.

- Many elements have radioactive isotopes that are useful as tracers in biological systems. Show how $^{14}CO_2$ can be used to follow the fate of carbon as it is incorporated into carbohydrate.

- The structure of atoms can be deduced using nuclear magnetic resonance (NMR) and mass spectrometer machines. Report on the principles underlying the performance of each of these instruments.

- Using a pH meter, test the degree of acidity/alkalinity of common household products. If the substance is not a liquid, mix it with water according to package directions before testing.

- Most of the content of human blood is water. However, synthetic blood has been made and tested. What is the base in this fluid? Is it a feasible substitute? Report on its advantages and disadvantages.

- Describe the effects of alcohol on the human body.

- How are termites able to digest wood products?

- What is aspartame? How is it processed by the body? Describe studies that have been done regarding its safety as a food additive.

- What is dietary fiber? Describe its possible role as an anti-carcinogen.

- Learn more about the recently synthesized artificial fats that can be used to replace fats in foods.

- Why do women have a higher percentage of body fat than men? Can you think of any adaptive value for this characteristic?

- Discuss the role of cholesterol in diet.

- Describe how scientists discovered the structure of hemoglobin.

- Search the body building magazines currently available for diet supplement advertising that might be misleading or outright false. Report on the distortions you find.

- Prepare a historical report on the cultivation and use of plant fibers (cellulose) from various sources in the construction of clothing.

- After searching for background information on the extent and variety of steroid use by athletes, interview persons who can give a local and inside perspective. Can you document any damage to heavy users?

Possible Responses to *Critical Thinking* Questions

1. Hydrogen is possibly the most abundant element in the universe because it is the stuff of stars and planets.

2. To change lead (atomic number 82) into gold (atomic number 79) would necessitate a change in the number of protons. This is not possible, for the very definition of an element tells us that this is a form of substance that is unchangeable.

3. The explanation for why water in the pan heats more slowly than the metal of the pan can be complicated and explained in detail by a physicist. It can also be simple: water heats more slowly and cools more slowly because of the hydrogen bonds in the water molecules (see section 2.3 in the text). The extensive hydrogen bonding both within the water molecules and between the water molecules confers this and many other unique properties that make life and all of nature possible.

4. The identification of the molecules are as follows:
    a) amino acid (see figure 2.23)
    b) carbohydrate (specifically glucose)
    c) polypeptide (glycine repeated 20 times)
    d) fatty acid (note the long chain of 16 CH_2s)

5. "Natural" vitamin C and synthetic vitamin C differ in one major way—COST! Chemicals are chemicals. Let's look at simpler comparison. I go into the lab and react the following:

    $$HCl + NaOH \rightarrow NaCl + H_2O$$

    After I evaporate off the water, I gingerly dip my finger into the beaker and taste my *synthetic* sodium chloride—salty! Alternatively, I go the ocean, collect some water, heat it, and crystallize out some *natural* sodium chloride—salty!

    Now there may be subtle differences, but in reality they are both salt. Similarly, vitamin C is ascorbic acid no matter how you obtain it.

    You could devise an experiment by choosing an organism that requires vitamin C in its diet for growth (perhaps a yeast mutant or such). Set up at least three trials: 1) no vitamin C; 2) natural vitamin C; and 3) synthetic vitamin C. Record the growth results.

6. *Trans* unsaturated fatty acids have more double bonds in the *trans* configuration; that is, the hydrogens adjacent to the double bonds are on opposite sides of the molecule. This puts zigzags or "kinks" in the tails of the fatty acids. Much research has shown that the trans fatty acids are not healthy. Just exactly why this is so is not entirely clear. It is known that they elevate harmful LDLs and lower beneficial HDLs. Furthermore, the *trans* fatty acids reduce the fluidity of the cell membranes and thus decrease functionality. As a speculation it may also be possible that the metabolic enzymes have been selected to deal with the *cis* form more efficiently than the *trans* form.

3

HOW CELLS ARE PUT TOGETHER

Chapter Outline

Objectives

1. Be able to cite the key features of the cell theory.
2. Contrast the general features of prokaryotic and eukaryotic cells.
3. Describe the nucleus of eukaryotes with respect to structure and function.
4. Describe the organelles associated with the endomembrane system, and tell the general function of each.
5. Contrast the structure and function of mitochondria and chloroplasts.
6. Describe the cytoskeleton of eukaryotes and distinguish it from the endomembrane system.
7. List several surface structures of cells and tell how they help cells survive.

Key Terms

cell theory
cell
plasma membrane
nucleus
nucleoid
cytoplasm
ribosomes
prokaryotic cells
eukaryotic cells
transmission electron
  microscope
scanning electron
  microscope
surface-to-volume ratio
phospholipid

lipid bilayer
fluid mosaic model
pili
organelles
secretory pathways
endocytic pathway
chromosome
chromatin
nuclear envelope
nucleolus
endomembrane system
endoplasmic reticulum
rough ER
smooth ER
Golgi bodies

vesicles
lysosomes
peroxisomes
central vacuole
mitochondria
plastids
chloroplasts
stroma
thylakoids
endosymbiosis
cytoskeleton
microtubules
microfilaments
cell cortex
motor proteins

intermediate filaments
flagella, flagellum
cilia, cilium
pseudopods
cell wall
primary wall
secondary wall
cell junctions
plasmodesmata
tight junctions
adhering junctions
gap junctions

Lecture Outline

Animalcules and Cells Fill'd With Juices
A. Nearly all cells, prokaryotic and eukaryotic, are invisible to the naked eye.
1. Robert Hooke used a simple microscope to view slices of cork in which he saw tiny compartments he called "cells."
2. Anton van Leeuwenhoek made exceptional lenses capable of revealing sperm, protists, and even bacteria.
3. By the 1800s, Matthias Schleiden and Theodor Schwann proposed the idea that all organisms are composed of cells; Rudolf Virchow went even further to say that all cells come from preexisting cells.
B. Thus, the beginnings of the fascinating study of the cell, basic unit of life, was begun.

3.1   What Is "a Cell"?
A. These are the three points of the cell theory:
1. All organisms are composed of one or more cells.
2. The cell is the smallest unit having the properties of life.
3. The continuity of life arises directly from the growth and division of single cells.
B. All cells have three features in common:
1. A *plasma membrane* separates each cell from the environment, permits the flow of molecules across the membrane, and contains receptors that can affect the cell's activities.
2. A *nucleus* or *nucleoid* localizes the hereditary material, which can be copied and read.
3. The *cytoplasm* contains membrane systems, particles (including ribosomes), filaments (the cytoskeleton), and a semifluid substance.
C. There are basically two kinds of cells in nature:
1. *Prokaryotic* cells (archaea and bacteria) have no nucleus.
2. *Eukaryotic* cells contain distinctive arrays of organelles, including a membrane-bound nucleus.

3.2   Most Cells Are *Really Small*
   A. Types of Microscopes
      1. Most cells are too small to be seen without a microscope.
      2. Light microscopes are useful to enlarge cells up to 2,000 times.
      3. Transmission and scanning electron microscopes can achieve magnifications many thousands of times greater, enabling us to see the fine detail in cell structure.
   B. Why Aren't All Cells Big?
      1. The surface-to-volume ratio constrains increases in cell size.
      2. As the surface area of a cell increases by the square of the diameter, the volume increases by the cube of the diameter.
      3. Therefore, small cell size permits efficient diffusion across the plasma membrane and within the cell.

3.3   The Structure of Cell Membranes
   A. Cell membranes form a continuous boundary layer around the cell.
      1. Phospholipids are the most abundant components of the cell membrane.
         a. Each molecule has a phosphate-containing head and two fatty acids attached to a glycerol backbone.
         b. The head is hydrophilic and the tails are hydrophobic, causing phospholipids to spontaneously form a lipid bilayer when exposed to an aquatic environment.
      2. The fluid mosaic model describes a cell membrane of mixed composition:
         a. The *mosaic* consists of phospholipids, glycolipids, sterols, and proteins.
         b. The *fluid* aspects of the model refer to the motions and interactions of its components, which allow the membrane to remain very flexible.
   B. Proteins interspersed in the lipid bilayer serve many functions:
      1. Some are receptors for chemical signals.
      2. Others transport solutes across the bilayer.
      3. Still others participate in cell identification, defense, and communication.

3.4   A Closer Look at Prokaryotic Cells
   A. Prokaryotes are the smallest known cells.
      1. The term *prokaryotic* ("before the nucleus") indicates the existence of bacteria before evolution of cells with a nucleus.
         a. A somewhat rigid cell wall supports the cell and surrounds the plasma membrane, regulating transport into and out of the cell.
         b. Sticky polysaccharides help cells attach to surfaces, such as teeth.
         c. Ribosomes, protein assembly sites, are dispersed throughout the cytoplasm.
         d. The bacterial chromosome is a single, circular DNA molecule.
      2. Bacterial flagella project from the membrane and permit rapid movement; pili filaments aid in attachment to surfaces.
   B. Two major groups of prokaryotes exist: Archaea and Bacteria.

3.5   A Closer Look at Eukaryotic Cells
   A. Eukaryotic cells are larger and generally more complex.
      1. Organelles form compartmentalized portions within the cytoplasm, allowing reactions to be separated with respect to time (allowing proper sequencing) and space (allowing incompatible reactions to occur in close proximity).
      2. Secretory and endocytic pathways allow substances to move through the cytoplasm in vesicles.

B. The Nucleus
  1. The nucleus isolates the DNA from dangerous reactions in the cytoplasm and controls access to DNA.
      a. Each *chromosome* is a single molecule of DNA and its associated proteins; it may take on different appearances depending on the events currently happening within the cell.
      b. *Chromatin* refers to the total collection of DNA and proteins.
  2. The nuclear envelope consists of <u>two</u> lipid bilayers with pores and transport proteins.
  3. The nucleolus appears as a dense, globular mass of material within the nucleus where RNA subunits of ribosomes are prefabricated before shipment out of the nucleus.
C. The Endomembrane System
  1. The endomembrane system is a series of organelles in which lipids are assembled and new polypeptide chains are modified into final proteins.
  2. The endoplasmic reticulum is a collection of interconnected tubes and flattened sacs that begins at the nucleus and winds its way through the cytoplasm.
      a. *Rough ER* consists of stacked, flattened sacs with many ribosomes attached; oligosaccharide groups are attached to polypeptides as they pass through on their way to other organelles or to secretory vesicles.
      b. *Smooth ER* has no ribosomes; it is the area from which vesicles carrying proteins and lipids are budded; it also inactivates harmful chemicals.
  3. Golgi bodies consist of flattened sacs—resembling a stack of pancakes—where proteins and lipids undergo final processing, sorting, and packaging before being enclosed in break-away secretory vesicles.
  4. Vesicles that break away include the organelles of intracellular digestion:
      a. *Lysosomes* are vesicles that bud from Golgi bodies; they carry powerful enzymes that can digest the contents of other vesicles, worn-out cell parts, or bacteria and foreign particles.
      b. *Peroxisomes* are small vesicles that contain enzymes using oxygen to degrade fatty acids and amino acids, forming a harmful byproduct, hydrogen peroxide, which is then converted to water.
  5. The central vacuole of mature plant cells accumulates ions, amino acids, sugars, and even toxic substances.
D. Mitochondria
  1. Mitochondria are the primary organelles for transferring the energy in carbohydrates to ATP under oxygen-plentiful conditions.
  2. Each mitochondrion has an outer membrane and an inner folded membrane (cristae).
      a. Two compartments are formed by the membranes.
      b. Hydrogen ions and electrons move between the compartments during ATP formation.
  3. Mitochondria have their own DNA and ribosomes, a fact which points to their origination from ancient bacteria engulfed by predatory cells.
E. Chloroplasts
  1. Chloroplasts are oval or disk shaped, bounded by a double membrane, and are critical to the process of photosynthesis.
      a. In the stacked disks (thylakoids), pigments and enzymes trap sunlight energy to form ATP and NADPH.
      b. Sugars are formed in the fluid substance (stroma) surrounding the stacks.
      c. Pigments such as chlorophyll (green) confer distinctive colors to the chloroplasts.
  2. Chloroplasts may have evolved from photosynthetic bacteria by way of endosymbiosis.

F. Summary of Major Organelles
   1. Organelles typical of plant cells are depicted in Figure 3.12.
   2. Organelles typical of animal cells are depicted in Figure 3.13.

3.6   Where Did Organelles Come From?
   A. Origin of the Nucleus and ER
       1. The infoldings of prokaryotic plasma membranes may have been the forerunners of eukaryotic organelles.
       2. The infoldings around DNA and the ER may have protected the contents from foreign materials.
   B. Theory of Endosymbiosis
       1. Prokaryotic cells may have been invaded by other prokaryotic cells, which evolved into mitochondria, chloroplasts, and other organelles.
       2. The invaders had developed aerobic metabolic pathways which were now of benefit to their unwitting hosts.
   C. Evidence of Endosymbiosis
       1. Jeon Kwang observed *Amoeba* cultures that engulfed bacteria and developed dependence on them.
       2. Mitochondria are like bacteria in size and structure, even possessing their own DNA and protein synthesizing machinery.
       3. Chloroplasts also resemble some eubacteria, displaying similar metabolism, DNA, and cell division.

3.7   The Dynamic Cytoskeleton
   A. The cytoskeleton gives cells their internal organization, shape, and capacity to move.
       1. It forms an interconnected system of bundled fibers, slender threads, and lattices that extends from the nucleus to the plasma membrane.
       2. The main components are microtubules, microfilaments, and intermediate filaments—all assembled from protein subunits.
           a. Microtubules are used in chromosome movement during cell division.
           b. Microfilaments are particularly important in movements that take place at the cell surface; they also contribute to the shapes of animal cells by forming the cell cortex.
           c. Intermediate filaments, the most stable of the cytoskeleton elements, occur only in animal cells of specific tissues.
   B. Moving Along With Motor Proteins
       1. Microtubules and microfilaments function as tracks, while motor proteins are the freight engines.
       2. Some motor proteins move chromosomes; others slide microtubules over one another (mitosis); still others are critical to muscle movement in animals.
   C. Cilia, Flagella, and False Feet
       1. Microtubular extensions of the plasma membrane and associated motor proteins can move parts of cells.
           a. Flagella are quite long and not usually numerous; they are found on one-celled protistans and animal sperm cells.
           b. Cilia are shorter, more numerous, and can provide locomotion for free-living cells, or they may move surrounding water and particles if the ciliated cell is anchored.
       2. Pseudopods are temporary lobes that project from the cell, used in locomotion and food capture.

3.8   Cell Surface Specializations
    A. Eukaryotic Cell Walls
       1. Cell walls are carbohydrate frameworks for mechanical support in bacteria, protistans, fungi, and plants; cell walls are not found in animals.
          a. In growing plant parts, bundles of cellulose strands form a primary cell wall that is pliable enough to allow enlargement under pressure.
          b. Later, more layers are deposited on the inside of the primary wall to form the secondary wall.
       2. Lignin composes up to 25 percent of the secondary wall in woody plants; it makes plant parts stronger, more waterproof, and less inviting to insects.
       3. Waxes form a cuticle on the outer surfaces of plants to restrict water loss.
    B. Matrixes Between Animal Cells
       1. A matrix forms between animals cells made from surrounding materials and secretions.
       2. For example, cartilage consists of scattered cells and collagen embedded in a "ground substance" of modified polysaccharides; bone is similarly constructed.
    C. Cell Junctions
       1. In plants, tiny channels called plasmodesmata cross the primary walls to interconnect the adjacent cytoplasms.
       2. Animal cells display three types of junctions:
          a. *Tight junctions* occur between cells of epithelial tissues in which cytoskeletal strands of one cell fuse with strands of neighboring cells, causing an effective seal.
          b. *Adhering junctions* are like spot welds at the plasma membranes of two adjacent cells that need to be held together during stretching, as in the skin and heart.
          c. *Gap junctions* are small, open channels that directly link the cytoplasm of adjacent cells.

Suggestions for Presenting the Material

- For many readers, Chapter 3 represents the real entry into the realm of biology. Indeed, a discussion of the cell is fundamental to all future lectures.

- Because of the extent of knowledge concerning the cell, it is impossible to include all of it in one chapter. Therefore, Chapter 3 presents an overview that includes a fair amount of cell part description and a glimpse of functions, the details of which are explained in several successive chapters.

- Discussing the *cell theory* presents an excellent time to review the use of the word *theory* as explained in Chapter 1.

- A clear distinction between prokaryotic and eukaryotic cells should be made (see the Enrichment section below for visual aid suggestion).

- As you begin the litany of cell organelles, use the overhead of Figure 1.1 (the "road map") to remind students of the progress they are making.

- Although the descriptions and diagrams of the cell organelles occupy only a small number of textbook pages, it is best to proceed carefully and deliberately. There is a dizzying array of unfamiliar terms here.

- When describing each cell structure, a visual representation of some type should be constantly in view of the students. Each time a new cell part is introduced, the cell diagrams of Figures 3.12 and 3.13 should be shown for reference purposes.

- Stress the fact that several cell parts are so complex in function that greater detail will follow in future lectures.
- Table 3.2 contains a wealth of information about cell components and functions that is conformable to your needs. If you choose *not* to stress the difference between prokaryotic and eukaryotic cells with respect to structure (the right-hand columns), then the table is reduced to one that lists cell structure and function (the two left-hand columns). It still remains a very useful table.

Classroom and Laboratory Enrichment

- Use sketches or models drawn to scale to demonstrate the size difference between prokaryotic and eukaryotic cells.
- Show an overhead transparency of a diagram, or an electron micrograph, of any cell. Ask if the cell is prokaryotic or eukaryotic. Is it an animal cell? A plant cell? Some other type of cell?
- Arrange for students to see an electron microscope and learn about specimen preparation and the operation of the microscope.
- Use a Hoberman sphere to demonstrate the decrease of surface area to volume as the sphere is expanded from its condensed to expanded states.
- Ask students to match "organelle" with "cellular task" at the board or on an overhead (Table 3.2).
- If you present the historical sketch of the cell theory, include slides of the researchers you are discussing. These photos can usually be found in a variety of introductory biology texts or special texts on the history of biology.
- Construct a table (overhead or handout) listing side-by-side comparisons of prokaryotic and eukaryotic cells.
- Most departments possess some type of cell model. These are especially helpful in perception of the 3-D aspects of cell structure. They can also be useful in oral quizzing.
- If you have access to electron micrographs generated by your colleagues, bring some to class to pass around, or prepare 2 x 2 transparencies. Students will be impressed by the "home-grown" aspect of these micrographs.

Impacts, Issues Classroom Discussion Ideas

- What is the largest example of a single cell that you can think of?
- How do photosynthetic prokaryotes perform photosynthesis without plastids?
- Where in your body would you find cells with the highest concentrations of mitochondria?

Additional Ideas for Classroom Discussion

- List the tasks that a cell must do.
- Why are there no unicellular creatures that are 12 inches in diameter?
- Discuss some of the methods by which single cells overcome surface-to-volume constraints. (Possibilities include: thin, flat cell shapes; invaginations to increase cell surface area; cellular

extensions of the plasma membrane.) Describe ways in which multicellular organisms solve this problem (some examples: thin or sheetlike body plans, transport systems).

- Distinguish between a nucleus and a nucleoid.
- Why must bacteria have ribosomes when they lack other organelles?
- What is the difference between scanning electron microscopy and transmission electron microscopy?
- Why do you think most plant cells have a central vacuole while animal cells lack this organelle?
- What is the significance of the word *theory* in reference to the basic properties of the cell?
- Does the cytoplasm have any functions of its own, or is it just a "filler" matrix in which other organelles float?
- Why is the term *nucleus* used to describe the center of an atom and the organelle at the center of the cell, when these are such different entities?
- In measurement of length, what are the largest cells (when mature) in the human body? [neurons] What fundamental property of all cells is denied to these cells? [mitosis]
- What feature makes a eukaryotic cell a "true" cell?
- What organelle could be compared to the control center of an assembly line in a factory?
- Describe the interrelationship(s) of the individual members comprising the *endomembrane system* (see Figure 3.9).
- Compare the functions of mitochondria and chloroplasts.

How Would You Vote? Classroom Discussion Ideas

- Monitor the voting for the online question. Perhaps you could spark some discussion by asking the students to give reasons why they think, or do not think, this research is necessary for the betterment of science; or is it just being done "for interest's sake"?

Term Paper Topics, Library Activities, and Special Projects

- Who first coined the term *organelle*? When did biologists discover that eukaryotic cells contained organelles?
- Learn more about plant tissue culture. What mechanisms govern cell differentiation in vitro?
- Discuss the development of electron microscopy. What are some of the advances in cell biology that electron microscopy has made possible? How are biological specimens prepared for examination with an electron microscope?
- How do antibiotics such as penicillin stop bacterial growth?
- Design a hypothetical cell that would function with maximum efficiency in extreme drought.
- Describe the function of smooth ER in the metabolism of drugs and alcohol in the liver. How might the liver cells of an alcoholic differ from those of a moderate consumer of alcohol or a nondrinker?
- Prepare brief biographies of the researchers who are credited with early discoveries of cell structure and function.
- Search the library shelves for biology texts of 20, 30, 40, and 50 years ago. Find the diagrams of cell structure. Prepare a sequential composite of these, and compare each to the others and to your

present text. What instrument allowed for the increasing detail that you observe in more recent drawings?

- Using a special dictionary of Latin and Greek root words, search for the literal meanings for each of the cell parts listed in Table 3.2. (Be careful with Golgi—it is a man's name!)

Possible Responses to *Critical Thinking* Questions

1. The idea of a gigantic cell of any kind, or a gigantic creature of any kind, has fascinated Hollywood movie-makers for decades. Movie-goers love this sort of thing. But wet-blanket scientists have to spoil the fun by pointing out the impossibility of gigantic cells based on that surface-to-volume ratio thing. Simply put, a huge cell would have so much volume that the distance from the deepest reaches of the interior of the cell would be too far for nutrients and oxygen to diffuse in and carbon dioxide and metabolic waste to diffuse out, not to mention the woefully inadequate surface area for all that diffusion to take place.

2. A cell with lots of mitochondria, Golgi bodies, and endoplasmic reticulum would be in the business of generating ATP and synthesizing proteins. The micrograph being shown to the students might well be of a *muscle cell*.

3. The most easily seen feature that Peggy could use to characterize the mystery organism would be the presence (protist) or absence (bacteria) of a membrane-bound *nucleus*.

4. The evidence would indicate that there is nothing wrong with the chromosomes in the head of the sperm because the microinjection technique has resulted in a successful fertilization. However, the lack of dynein arms on the microtubules of the flagella of the sperm has resulted in lowered motility of the sperm, preventing their travel up the oviduct to meet the egg during normal intercourse.

4

HOW CELLS WORK

Chapter Outline

Objectives

1. Know two laws that govern the way energy is transferred from one substance to another.
2. Provide an example of a metabolic pathway and explain what kinds of substances regulate activity of the pathway.
3. Tell exactly what enzymes do and how they do it.
4. Explain how a molecule can "carry" energy.
5. Know the forces that cause water and solutes to move across membranes passively (that is, without expending energy).
6. Understand which types of substances move by simple diffusion and which by bulk flow.
7. Understand the importance of osmosis to all cells.
8. Know the mechanisms by which substances are moved across membranes against a concentration gradient (actively, with energy expenditure).

9. Understand how material can be imported into or exported from a cell by being wrapped in membranes.

Key Terms

energy	products	antioxidants	tonicity
first law of thermodynamics	energy carriers	free radicals	hypotonic solution
	enzymes	allosteric site	hypertonic solution
second law of thermodynamics	cofactors	feedback inhibition	isotonic solution
	transport proteins	selective permeability	hydrostatic pressure
ATP	chemical equilibrium	concentration gradient	turgor pressure
phosphorylations	metabolic pathways	diffusion	osmotic pressure
ADP	biosynthetic	electric gradient	exocytosis
ATP/ADP cycle	degradative	pressure gradient	endocytosis
endergonic reaction	substrates	passive transport	receptor-mediated endocytosis
exergonic reaction	activation energy	active transport	
oxidation-reduction reaction	active site	calcium pump	phagocytosis
	transition state	sodium-potassium pump	bulk-phase endocytosis
electron transfer chains	binding energy		
reactants	cofactors	bulk flow	
intermediate	coenzymes	osmosis	

Lecture Outline

Beer, Enzymes, and Your Liver
A. The liver is your body's detoxification center.
  1. Beverage alcohol is degraded to non-toxic acetate.
  2. Excessive amounts of alcohol over a lifetime can lead to liver disease and failure.
B. Your liver performs other functions relative to food utilization including synthesis of plasma proteins.

4.1 Inputs and Outputs of Energy
A. The One-Way Flow of Energy
  1. Energy is the capacity to do work.
    a. *First law of thermodynamics* states that the total amount of energy in the universe is constant; it cannot be created nor destroyed; it can only change form.
    b. Energy from the sun or from organic substances becomes coupled to thousands of energy-requiring processes in cells.
  2. *Second law of thermodynamics* states that the spontaneous direction of energy flow is from high- to low-quality forms.
    a. Each conversion produces energy (usually heat) that is unavailable for work.
    b. Energy transfers are never entirely efficient.
  3. The world of life (plant and animal) maintains a high degree of organization only because it is being resupplied with energy from the sun.
B. ATP—The Cell's Energy Currency
  1. ATP's role is like currency in an economy: earning ATP during energy-releasing reactions and spending it during energy-requiring ones.

2. ATP is composed of adenine, ribose, and three phosphate groups.
   a. Energy input links phosphate to ADP to produce ATP (process called phosphorylation).
   b. ATP can in turn donate a phosphate group to another molecule, which then becomes primed and energized for specific reactions.
3. ADP can be recycled to ATP very rapidly in the ATP/ADP cycle.
C. Up and Down the Energy Hills
   1. When cells convert one form of energy to another, they change the amount of usable energy available to them.
      a. In plant cells sunlight energy drives electrons from water molecules to initiate the endergonic reactions that will eventually produce carbohydrates.
      b. In aerobic respiration, the degradation of glucose releases energy (exergonic) that can be transferred to ATP.
   2. Energy release occurs by efficient oxidation-reduction reactions.
   3. Electron transfer chains are arrays of molecules in cell membranes that accept and give up electrons in a sequence to harness energy for use in the formation of ATP.

4.2   Inputs and Outputs of Substances
A. What Are Metabolic Pathways?
   1. Metabolic pathways form a series of reactions that regulate the concentration of substances within cells by enzyme-mediated linear and circular sequences.
   2. In *biosynthetic* pathways, small molecules are assembled into large molecules; for example, simple sugars are assembled into complex carbohydrates.
   3. In *degradative* pathways, large molecules such as carbohydrates, lipids, and proteins are broken down to form products of lower energy. Released energy can be used for cellular work.
B. The Nature of Metabolic Reactions
   1. The participants in metabolism are as follows:
      a. *Reactants* are substances that enter reactions.
      b. *Intermediates* are the compounds formed between the start and the end of a pathway.
      c. *Products* are the substances present at the conclusion of a pathway.
      d. *Energy carriers* are mainly ATP.
      e. *Enzymes* are proteins that catalyze (speed up) reactions.
      f. *Cofactors* are small molecules and metal ions that help enzymes by carrying atoms or electrons.
      g. *Transport proteins* are membrane-bound proteins that participate in adjusting concentration gradients that will influence the direction of metabolic reactions.
   2. When a reaction approaches chemical equilibrium, the forward and reverse reactions proceed at equal rates.
      a. There is no *net* change in concentrations.
      b. Every reaction has its own ratio of products to reactants at equilibrium.

4.3   How Enzymes Make Substances React
A. Enzymes are catalytic molecules that speed up the rate of chemical reactions.
B. Lowering the Energy Hill
   1. Activation energy is the amount of energy needed to get a reaction going.
      a. Enzymes increase the rate of reaction by creating a microenvironment that is energetically more favorable for the reaction.

b. Each enzyme molecule has an active site where the (smaller) substrate binds to the (larger) enzyme during a reaction.
   2. Binding energy helps bring about the transition state by four mechanisms:
      a. Helping substrates get together;
      b. Orienting substrates in positions favoring reaction;
      c. Shutting out water;
      d. Inducing changes in enzyme shape (induced-fit model).
   C. Help From Cofactors
      1. Cofactors are nonprotein groups that bind to many enzymes and make them more reactive.
      2. Inorganic metal ions such as Fe^{++} also serve as cofactors when assisting membrane cytochrome proteins in their electron transfers in chloroplasts and mitochondria.
   D. How Is Enzyme Activity Controlled?
      1. Some controls regulate the number of enzyme molecules available by speeding up/slowing down their synthesis.
      2. Allosteric enzymes have (in addition to active sites) regulatory sites where control substances can bind to alter enzyme activity; if this control substance is the end product in the enzyme's metabolic pathway, feedback inhibition occurs.
   E. Effects of Temperature, pH, and Salinity
      1. Because enzymes operate best within defined temperature ranges, high temperatures decrease reaction rate by disrupting the bonds that maintain three-dimensional shape (denaturation occurs).
      2. Most enzymes function best at a pH near 7 (pepsin in the stomach is an exception); higher or lower values disrupt enzyme shape and halt function.
      3. Most enzymes do not work well when fluids are saltier than their usual range of tolerance.

4.4   Diffusion and Metabolism
   A. All cell membranes show selective permeability, that is, some substances can cross, others cannot.
      1. Gases and small electrically-neutral molecules can readily cross the lipid bilayer.
      2. Glucose and other large, polar molecules cannot pass through the bilayer directly but must rely on passage through the interior of transport proteins.
   B. What Is a Concentration Gradient?
      1. Concentration gradient refers to the number of molecules (or ions) per unit volume of a substance between two regions.
      2. The thermal energy of the molecules drives the movement of molecules.
         a. Molecules constantly collide and tend to move down a *concentration gradient* (high to low).
         b. The net movement of like molecules down a concentration gradient is called *diffusion*; each substance diffuses independently of other substances present, as illustrated by dye molecules in water.
   C. What Determines Diffusion Rates?
      1. Several factors influence the rate and direction of diffusion: *concentration differences, temperature* (higher = faster), *molecular size* (smaller = faster), *electric gradients* (a difference in charge), and *pressure gradients*.
      2. When gradients no longer exist, there is no *net* movement (dynamic equilibrium is reached).

4.5 Working With and Against Diffusion
   A. When water-soluble molecules bind to transport proteins, they trigger changes in shape that "ease" the solute through the protein and hence through the membrane.
   B. Passive Transport
      1. A carrier protein that functions in passive transport (also called "facilitated diffusion") tends to move molecules to the side of the membrane where they are less concentrated.
      2. Passive transport will continue until solute concentrations are equal on both sides of the membrane or other factors intervene.
   C. Active Transport
      1. To move ions and large molecules across a membrane against a concentration gradient, special proteins are induced to change shape (in a series), but only with an energy boost from ATP.
      2. An example of active transport is the sodium-potassium pump of the neuron membrane, and the calcium pump of most cells.

4.6 Which Way Will Water Move?
   A. Osmosis
      1. Bulk flow is the tendency of different substances in a fluid to move together in the same direction due to a pressure gradient (as in animal circulatory systems).
      2. Osmosis is the passive movement of water across a differentially permeable membrane in response to solute concentration gradients, pressure gradients, or both.
      3. For example, if a bag containing a sugar solution is placed in pure water, the water will diffuse *inward* (higher to lower).
   B. Effects of Tonicity
      1. Tonicity denotes the relative concentration of solutes in two fluids—extracellular fluid and cytoplasmic fluid, for example.
      2. Three conditions are possible:
         a. A *hypotonic* fluid has a lower concentration of solutes than the fluid in the cell; cells immersed in it may swell.
         b. A *hypertonic* fluid has a greater concentration of solutes than the fluid in the cell; cells in it may shrivel.
         c. An *isotonic* fluid has the same concentration of solutes as the fluid in the cell; immersion in it causes no net movement of water.
      3. Cells either are dependent on relatively constant (isotonic) environments or are adapted to hypotonic and hypertonic ones.
   C. Effects of Fluid Pressure
      1. Hydrostatic pressure is a force directed against a membrane by a fluid; the greater the solute concentration, the greater will be the hydrostatic pressure it exerts.
      2. This force is countered by osmotic pressure, which prevents any further increase in the volume of the solution.
      3. When plants lose water, there is a shrinkage of the cytoplasm called plasmolysis.

4.7 Cell Burps and Gulps
   A. In exocytosis, a cytoplasmic vesicle moves substances from cytoplasm to plasma membrane where the membranes of the vesicle and cell fuse.
   B. Endocytosis encloses particles in small portions of plasma membrane to form vesicles that then move into the cytoplasm.
      1. In *receptor-mediated* endocytosis, specific molecules are brought into the cell by specialized regions of the plasma membranes that form coated pits, which sink into the cytoplasm.

2. *Phagocytosis* is an active form of endocytosis by which a cell engulfs microorganisms, particles, or other debris; this is seen in protistans and white blood cells.
3. In *bulk-phase* endocytosis, a vesicle forms around a small volume of extracellular fluid without regard to what substances might be dissolved in it.

Suggestions for Presenting the Material

- Because students may be unfamiliar with the first and second laws of thermodynamics, it is important to distinguish clearly between the two laws; emphasize the central role of the sun in sustaining life on Earth.

- Acknowledge that this chapter speaks in *generalities* and defines terms that will be used to describe *specific* metabolic reactions in subsequent chapters.

- If you prefer to teach from specific examples, you may want to choose a specific metabolic pathway (of your own or from elsewhere in the book), draw it on an overhead transparency, and use it to explain the various terms found in this chapter.

- After presentation of the various capabilities of enzymes, students may think of them as "miracle workers." Remind the students that these are nonliving molecules—albeit, amazing ones. Also emphasize the limitations and vulnerability of enzymes, including causes and effects of denaturation.

- Encourage students to bring their textbook to class and refer frequently to the excellent figures in it.

- This chapter provides a good opportunity to introduce the idea that oxidations release energy, reductions require energy.

- The various methods by which molecules move, either through space or through membranes, can be confusing to students because of the subtle differences that distinguish each method. Perhaps you could begin with general, nonmembrane-associated phenomena such as diffusion and bulk flow. Then proceed to membrane-associated mechanisms such as osmosis, facilitated diffusion, active transport, and vesicle formation.

- Note that each of the transport phenomena topics is accompanied by an illustration, which should be used to reduce the "abstract quality" of the mechanism.

Classroom and Laboratory Enrichment

- The action of an enzyme (salivary amylase) can be easily demonstrated by the following procedure:
  a. Prepare a 6 percent starch solution in water and confirm its identity by a spot plate test with iodine solution (produces blue-black color).
  b. Collect saliva from a volunteer by having the person chew a small piece of Parafilm and expectorate into a test tube.
  c. Place diluted saliva and the starch solution in a test tube and mix.
  d. At suitable intervals, remove samples of the digestion mixture and test with iodine on the spot plate. (Lack of dark color indicates conversion of starch to maltose.)
  e. Variations can include: heating the saliva to destroy the enzyme; adding acid or alkali; adding cyanide.

- The effect of ATP on a reaction can be demonstrated by use of bioluminescence kits available from biological supply houses.

- Show a videotape or slide/sound set depicting the role and function of enzymes.

- Show a film about energy transformations in cells.
- Demonstrate the two models of enzyme-substrate interactions in the following ways:
  a. *Rigid "lock and key" model:* Use preschool-size jigsaw puzzle pieces or giant-size Lego blocks.
  b. *Induced-fit model:* Use a flexible fabric or latex glove to show how the insertion of a hand (substrate) induces change in the shape of the glove (active site).
- The relationship between ATP, ADP, energy, enzymes, and phosphorylation may be illustrated by the use of a toy dart gun with rubber suction cup-tipped darts. It is helpful to have acetate transparencies of ADP and ATP structures that can be projected on a screen as the following demonstration is performed:
  a. Tell the students that the unloaded dart gun represents ADP and the dart represents inorganic phosphate (P). Show the structure of ADP on the screen.
  b. As you insert the dart into the gun, emphasize the need for the expenditure of energy to do this. Tell the students that the addition of P to ADP is, therefore, an endergonic reaction; it is also called a phosphorylation reaction. At this time show the structure of ATP on the screen. Also point out that the spring inside the dart gun is under much tension and as such has a great deal of potential energy. The same can be said for the P group that has been added to ADP.
  c. Next, demonstrate the hydrolysis of ATP. The trigger finger represents the necessary enzyme. Aim the gun at some vertical smooth surface (window or aquarium works well) and depress the trigger. Hopefully the dart will adhere to the surface (a substrate molecule being energized by phosphorylation). The reaction is thus exergonic and some of the energy has been transferred to the substrate molecule.
- Discuss the terms *isotonic, hypotonic,* and *hypertonic* by showing students three sketches (Figure 4.16) of semipermeable bags in beakers of distilled water. (These can be drawn ahead of time on an overhead transparency if you wish.) Vary the concentrations of the sugar solutions shown in the bags. Ask students what the direction of water movement would be in each case. Then ask what direction the sugar molecules will move in. Many students will believe that the sugar molecules will move across the membrane, even though they previously learned these sugar molecules are too large to cross the plasma membrane.
- To demonstrate that some molecules will pass through membranes and some will not, prepare two test tubes as follows: In one tube pour dilute Lugol's iodine solution until it is about nine-tenths full; in another tube pour 1 percent starch paste until it is about nine-tenths full. Cover the mouth of each test tube with a wet goldbeater's membrane; then secure it tightly by tying with thread or a tight rubber band. Invert the starch-paste test tube into a beaker about one-half full of dilute Lugol's solution; invert the test tube containing dilute Lugol's solution into a beaker containing a 1 percent starch paste. Ask students why the well-known blue-black color appears in the starch solution and not in the Lugol's solution. Students may decide that the starch requires digestion to a more soluble form before it can pass through the membrane.
- Set up two or more osmometer tubes (glass or plastic thistle tubes covered with a selectively permeable membrane) at the front of the room. Compare rates of osmosis by filling each tube with a colored sugar (you may use corn syrup) or salt solution (vary the concentrations) and placing the base of the tube into a beaker of distilled water.
- Living cells can be used to demonstrate the osmotic water passage through semipermeable membranes. Use an apple corer to remove a center cylinder of a raw white potato; leave about one-half inch of potato tissue at the bottom. Carefully pour a concentrated sucrose solution into the core; seal the opening with a one-hole rubber stopper through which a piece of glass tubing has been inserted. Pour melted paraffin around the stopper as a seal to avoid leakage. Place the potato in a beaker of water; use a clamp on a ringstand to support the glass tube.

- To show how molecules move from points of greater concentration to regions of lower concentration, pour red ink or dye along one side of a container of water. The liquid will diffuse through a liquid.

- Use models or overhead transparencies to show how channel proteins and transport proteins function during passive transport and active transport, respectively.

- Open a bottle of perfume and place it on the desk early in the lecture period. Discuss principles involved later in the lecture.

- Demonstrate the diffusion of a liquid in a solid. Prepare three petri dishes, each filled with a layer of plain agar. Use a cork borer to carefully make three equidistant holes in the agar. Turn the dish over and number each hole. Put three or four drops of the following solutions in each of the appropriately numbered holes: (1) 0.02M potassium dichromate in the first hole, (2) 0.02M potassium permanganate, (3) 0.02M methylene blue. View results after at least one hour. Because the solutions have identical molarities, the rate of diffusion depends upon the molecular weight of each compound. Methylene blue (MW = 373) diffuses at the slowest rate, while potassium permanganate diffuses fastest (MW = 158). Potassium dichromate (MW = 294) diffuses at an intermediate rate.

- At least one day before lecture, dissolve gelatin in water and pour into a screw-top test tube; leave a small space between the top of the gelatin and the top edge of the test tube. Cool the tube in the refrigerator until the gelatin solidifies. At the beginning of the lecture, pour in a small amount of a bright-colored dye on top of the gelatin; replace and tighten the screw top. Allow the dye to diffuse through the gelatin until it reaches the bottom of the glass thread area of the test tube. At this time, turn the test tube to a horizontal position and place it so that students can observe progress of the dye through the gelatin. If one wishes to time the progress of the dye, begin timing when the tube is turned to the horizontal position.

- The diffusion of a gas through other gases (air) can be demonstrated easily as follows: Wet a circle of filter paper with phenolphthalein and insert it into the bottom of a large test tube. Next, invert the test tube over an open bottle of ammonium hydroxide. Ask students to explain the rather rapid color change of the filter paper to red. Set up a control with filter paper soaked in water.

- Demonstrate the diffusion of a gas in a gas using a glass tube at least one-half inch wide and eighteen inches in length. Plug one end of the tube with a cotton wad saturated with HCl (hydrochloric acid); plug the opposite end with a cotton wad saturated with NH_4OH (ammonium hydroxide). Label each end appropriately. Hydrochloric acid and ammonium hydroxide react together to produce ammonium chloride and water. Students will be able to see a ring of ammonium chloride that has formed closest to the HCl end of the tube; the ammonium ion (NH_4^+) has a smaller molecular weight than the chloride ion (Cl^-) and thus diffuses faster, meeting the Cl^- ion about two-thirds of the way down the tube.

- Bring a can of room deodorizer spray to class to demonstrate diffusion (in this case, a liquid in a gas) as a general example of how concentration gradients operate.

Impacts, Issues Classroom Discussion Ideas

- Pose several "what if" questions concerning enzyme action such as: What if the body temperature of humans mutated to 105°? Or body pH rose to 9.5?

- What the limiting factors that allow an enzyme to process only a certain amount of substrate in a given time period?

- *Exactly* what causes the liver of a heavy alcohol drinker to diminish in its capacity to metabolize alcohol over a lifetime of drinking?

Additional Ideas for Classroom Discussion

- The second law of thermodynamics is often used by creationists as the basis for an argument against evolution. According to their view, the second law depicts a world that must become more disordered. This is in contrast to evolution, which depicts a world that is becoming more ordered. Evaluate the creationists' argument. Is it valid?
- Compare the energy "hill" that an enzyme must overcome to a ski slope. Does an enzyme act more like a chair lift or a bulldozer?
- Discuss what would happen to life on Earth if the flow of sunlight energy stopped.
- Name some of the different forms of energy. Are they interconvertible? Give some examples of interconversions. For example, trace the energy interconversions involved in cooking your breakfast on an electric stove. Begin with the dam over a hydroelectric plant.
- What would happen to freshwater unicellular organisms if suddenly released in a saltwater environment?
- Distinguish between diffusion and osmosis.
- Why do unicellular protists (such as *Paramecium*) not burst even though their cell interiors are hypertonic to their freshwater environments?
- What is physiological saline solution? (Hint: It is used to dilute samples of red blood cells in the laboratory.)
- How do exocytosis and endocytosis differ from passive transport and active transport?
- What is "fertilizer burn"? What can be done to correct it?
- What would be the result on blood cells of a substitution of pure water for physiological saline in an IV bottle?
- In some cases, a 5 percent glucose solution is given intravenously to persons after surgery. If you were the doctor on such a case, would you order the glucose solution to be isotonic, hypertonic, or hypotonic to blood? Explain your decision.
- Ask students what the prefixes *hyper-* and *hypo-* refer to in the text discussions. If they do not understand that these terms refer to solute concentration (not water), they will have difficulty with the concept.
- Plant cells have a rather rigid wall enclosing their plasma membranes; animal cells do not. Ask students to think about a comparison of consequences when plant and animal cells are placed in isotonic, hypertonic, and hypotonic solutions.

How Would You Vote? Classroom Discussion Ideas

- Monitor the voting for the online question. The question of who should be eligible for a liver (or any organ for that matter) transplant is a controversy that sparks many ethical debates. Ask groups of students to defend allocation on the basis of: (1) medical need, (2) first-come, first-served; (3) lifestyle; (4) ability to pay, etc.

Term Paper Topics, Library Activities, and Special Projects

- Research the basis for the first and second laws of thermodynamics. On the basis of what observations did scientists formulate these laws? What experiments can be done in the laboratory to confirm the laws?

- Explain the defect in the metabolic pathway that results in the condition known as phenylketonuria (PKU). How can this condition be treated? Is it curable?

- Construct clay models depicting an enzyme, a substrate, the enzyme-substrate complex, and induced fit.

- Explain the role of the B vitamins in human metabolism.

- Discuss some of the ways that coenzymes and inorganic cofactors participate in enzymatic reactions.

- Learn more about the discovery and function of the sodium-potassium pump and the calcium pump.

- How are saltwater fish species able to cope with their extremely salty surroundings?

- Look up the composition of "physiological saline." Are there different varieties of this preparation for different animal species?

- The diffusion and transport phenomena discussed in the chapter are based on a property called Brownian movement that is demonstrated by all molecules, whether alive or not. What is the physical manifestation of this property, and what is the derivation of its name?

Possible Responses to *Critical Thinking* Questions

1. The phrases "You can't win" and "You can't break even," as applied to thermodynamics, both indicate that when energy conversions occur there are going to be losses as stated by the second law of thermodynamics. The first law is a bit more forgiving when it states that you can't create energy or destroy it, but its form can change. In other words, you won't gain any energy but you can be content that you at least changed into some other form, perhaps even more useful.

2. Because the *Paramecium* is taking on water, its surroundings must be <u>hypotonic</u>. The reasoning goes like this: first, we are told that water is moving INTO the cell, so the concentration of water must be **higher** on the outside of the cell. Correspondingly, the solute concentration must be **lower** than on the inside. By definition, a solution (or environment) with a lower solute concentration is <u>hypotonic</u>.

3. Plant enzymes would probably not be expected to perform in the human digestive tract because the environment would not be of the proper pH. This of course assumes that they would survive attack by the human digestive enzymes, which is highly unlikely.

4. Lemon juice is acidic and would inhibit the enzymes responsible for the reactions that normally turn apple slices to turn brown when exposed to air.

5. Hydrogen peroxide bubbles when placed on an open cut because it is reacting with enzymes of the blood and tissues. This would not occur on the rather inert and hydrophobic intact skin.

6. Irrigation water has small amounts of dissolved salt, which will accumulate in the soil as the water evaporates day after day, year after year. Although very minimal at first, the *increased* salt content (hyper) in the water available to plants would necessarily cause a *decrease* in the water content (hypo). As we know from our textbook, water will move from an area of higher concentration to one of lower concentration. In this instance the area outside the plant roots is decreasing in water concentration, thus reducing the tendency for the water to move into the root cells—with obvious detriment to the plants.

7. The proposed canal from the lake to the estuary will, depending on elevation, most likely add fresh water to the mix. This will make the conditions more hypotonic and could lead to excessive uptake of water by the shrimp—a condition they are not equipped to handle. Even though shrimp have excretory organs, they are not selected for dealing with excessive amounts of freshwater.

5

WHERE IT STARTS— PHOTOSYNTHESIS

Chapter Outline

SUNLIGHT AND SURVIVAL

THE RAINBOW CATCHERS
 Light and Pigments
 Two Stages of Reactions

LIGHT-DEPENDENT REACTIONS

LIGHT-INDEPENDENT REACTIONS
 The Sugar Factory
 Different Plants, Different Pathways

PASTURES OF THE SEAS

SUMMARY

SELF-QUIZ

CRITICAL THINKING

Objectives

1. Understand the main pathways by which energy from the sun or from specific chemical reactions enters organisms and passes from organism to organism, and/or back into the environment.
2. Know the steps of the light-dependent and light-independent reactions. Know the raw materials needed to start each phase and know the products made by each phase.
3. Explain how autotrophs use the intermediates as well as the products of photosynthesis in their own metabolism.

Key Terms

photosynthesis
wavelength
pigments
chlorophyll a
chlorophyll b
carotenoids
xanthophylls
anthocyanins
phycobilins

light-dependent
 reactions
ATP
$NADP^+$; NADPH
light-independent
 reactions
chloroplast
stroma
thylakoid membrane

photon
photosystems, I and II
electron transfer chain
ATP synthases
cyclic pathway of ATP
 formation
noncyclic pathway of
 ATP formation
Calvin-Benson cycle

rubisco
RuBP
carbon fixation
PGA
PGAL
stomata
C3 plants
C4 plants
CAM plants
photoautotroph

Lecture Outline

Sunlight and Survival
A. Plants are autotrophic ("self-nourishing") because their cells can get energy from the sun and carbon from the environment to make nutrients.
   1. Photoautotrophs such as plants, some prokaryotic cells, and protistans use sunlight as the energy source.
   2. Chemoautotrophs, such as prokaryotic cells at deep ocean hydrothermal vents, use energy and carbon from methane and hydrogen sulfide.
B. With the advent of photosynthesis on the planet, free oxygen was available for aerobic respiration pathways.

5.1 The Rainbow Catchers
A. Light and Pigments
   1. Light moves in waves, with the distance between them measured in wavelengths of varying energy levels.
   2. Pigments absorb photons of specific energies boosting electrons to a higher energy level, from which they can quickly return *releasing* energy for cellular work.
      a. Chlorophylls are the main pigments in plants, green algae, and some bacteria.
         1) Chlorophyll *a* (green) is the main pigment inside chloroplasts.
         2) Chlorophyll *b* (bluish-green) absorbs wavelengths that chlorophyll *a* misses.
      b. Carotenoid pigments absorb blue-violet wavelengths but reflect yellow, orange, and red.
      c. Xanthophylls may be yellow, brown, purple, or blue.
      d. Anthocyanins are pigments of red and purple in many leaves, flowers, and fruits.
      e. Phycobilins are the red and blue pigments of the red algae and cyanobacteria.
B. Two Stages of Reactions
   1. Light-dependent reactions occur in the thylakoid membrane system inside the chloroplasts.
      a. The light-catching pigments located in the membranes of the thylakoids absorb sunlight energy and give up excited electrons, leading to ATP formation.
      b. Water is split to release oxygen.
      c. NADP+ picks up electrons to become NADPH to be used later.
   2. The light-independent reactions occur in the stroma, where sugars and other carbohydrates are assembled using ATP, NADPH, and CO_2.
   3. Overall, the equation for glucose formation is written:

$$12H_2O + 6CO_2 \xrightarrow{\text{sunlight}} 6O_2 + C_6H_{12}O_6 + 6H_2O$$

5.2 Light-Dependent Reactions
A. A photosystem is an array of hundreds of pigment molecules.
   1. The pigments "harvest" photon energy from sunlight.
      a. Absorbed photons of energy boost electrons to a higher level.
      b. The electrons quickly return to the lower level and release energy.
      c. Released energy is trapped by chlorophylls located in the photosystem's reaction center.
      d. The trapped energy is then used to transfer a chlorophyll electron to an acceptor molecule, eventually leading to the production of ATP and NADPH.

2. As the electrons are transferred through the electron transfer chain from photosystem II, hydrogen ions are pumped from the stroma into the thylakoid space.
   a. Large numbers of hydrogen ions accumulate inside the thylakoid compartment.
   b. As the hydrogen ions flow out through channels into the stroma, ATP synthase enzymes link P_i to ADP to form ATP.
   c. The "hole" created in photosystem II when the electron left is filled when water is split into hydrogen ions and oxygen.
3. The electrons from photosystem II eventually end up filling a hole in photosystem I, created when it also was hit by sunlight to boost an electron that would be used in making NADPH.

5.3   Light-Independent Reactions
   A. The Sugar Factory
      1. The Calvin-Benson cycle uses carbon dioxide, ATP, and NADPH to make sugars.
         a. Carbon fixation occurs when the carbon atom of CO_2 becomes attached to ribulose bisphosphate (RuBP) to form a six-carbon intermediate; the enzyme responsible is rubisco.
         b. The six-carbon intermediate splits at once to form two PGA (phosphoglycerate) molecules.
         c. Each PGA then receives a phosphate group from ATP plus H^+ and electrons from NADPH to form PGAL (phosphoglyceraldehyde).
         d. Most of the PGAL molecules continue in the cycle to fix more carbon dioxide, but two PGAL join to form a sugar phosphate, which will be modified to glucose.
      2. Most of the glucose is converted to sucrose (transportable within the plant) or starch (for longer-term storage).
   B. Different Plants, Different Pathways
      1. Plants in hot, dry environments close their stomata to conserve water, but in so doing retard carbon dioxide entry and permit oxygen buildup inside the leaves.
         a. Thus, oxygen—not carbon dioxide—becomes attached to RuBP to yield one PGA (instead of two) and one phosphoglycolate (not useful).
         b. This is why C3 plants such as beans do not grow well without irrigation in hot, dry climates.
      2. To overcome this fate, crabgrass, sugarcane, corn, and other C4 plants fix carbon twice (in mesophyll cells then in bundle-sheath cells) to produce oxaloacetate (a four-carbon) compound, which can then donate the carbon dioxide to the Calvin-Benson cycle.
      3. CAM plants such as cacti open their stomata and fix CO_2 only at night, storing the intermediate product for use in photosynthesis the next day.

5.4   Pastures of the Seas
   A. Green leaves and blades of grass are readily recognized as photoautotrophic, but the photoautotrophs of the sea are not so easily seen.
      1. These bacteria and protists are the beginning of the complex ocean food webs.
      2. They are eaten by enormous numbers of crustaceans, known as krill, which in turn are food for fishes, penguins, seabirds, and whales.
   B. Not only do these photosynthetic cells form the "pastures of the seas," but they also shape the global climate by sponging up carbon dioxide molecules.

Suggestions for Presenting the Material

- Students may have previously learned to refer to the two divisions of photosynthesis as the "light" and "dark" reactions. The author uses the more accurate and currently acceptable terms *light-dependent* and *light-independent,* respectively. You may wish to explain why "dark reactions" is a poor designator and no longer used (the reactions can occur in both the dark and the light).

- ATP and NADPH are "carrier molecules." Their connection between the light-dependent and light-independent reactions is an excellent opportunity for reinforcement of these molecules as "bridges."

- Photosynthesis is much more complicated than the usual simple equation that a student may have seen in a previous course. Perhaps the best approach to presenting this topic is to follow a stepwise outline and rely heavily on Figures 5.4d, 5.7, 5.8, and 5.11.

- The numbering of the photosystems (I and II) also is done with reference to their evolution; when the noncyclic pathway is operating, the sunlight is *initially* absorbed by photosystem II.

- You may wish to note the similarities and differences between the chemiosmotic mechanism in chloroplasts (Chapter 5) and mitochondria (Chapter 6), or defer this comparison until mitochondria are discussed.

- Although the diagram of the Calvin-Benson cycle (Figure 5.8) is a bit complicated by the inclusion of the intermediates (PGA and PGAL), the most important features are the entry of *carbon dioxide* and the production of *glucose,* driven by *ATP* and *NADPH* from the light-dependent reactions.

- The emphasis on C3, C4, and CAM plants can be moderated according to the interests of the instructor. Omitting it will not affect future discussions in the book.

- A discussion of why colored objects appear the color they do may facilitate the students' understanding of why, for example, green light is ineffective for photosynthesis.

- Show a diagram of the electromagnetic spectrum and discuss how the wavelength of the radiation is related to its energy content.

Classroom and Laboratory Enrichment

- You can demonstrate the production of oxygen by plants with the following:
  a. Place *Elodea* (an aquarium plant) in a bowl and expose it to bright light.
  b. Invert a test tube over the plant and collect the bubbles.
  c. Remove the tube and immediately thrust a glowing wood splint into the tube.
  d. Result: The splint burns brightly in the high-oxygen air.

- Separate the pigments in green leaves by using paper chromatography. (Consult a botany laboratory manual for the correct procedure.)

- Many students have never seen the action of a prism in separating white light into its component colors; a demonstration would most likely be appreciated.

- If a greenhouse facility is readily accessible, a brief tour and explanation of the devices used to control light, water, air, heat, etc., is very instructive.

- Show a video on photosynthesis.

- Provide a model of a chloroplast.

- Show an electron micrograph of a chloroplast and indicate where light-dependent reactions, light-independent reactions, and chemiosmosis occur.

- Cut out separated leaf pigments from a paper chromatogram and elute each pigment from the paper with a small amount of alcohol. Using a spectrophotometer, determine the absorption spectrum for each pigment and graph the results. (Consult a biology or botany laboratory manual for the procedure.)

Impacts, Issues Classroom Discussion Ideas

- Evaluate the truth of this statement: "In reality we all drive *solar powered* cars."
- What if oxygen had never appeared on Earth as a by-product of photosynthesis?
- Usually we think of photosynthesis as *producing* carbohydrate and oxygen, but what important role does photosynthesis perform as a consumer?

Additional Ideas for Classroom Discussion

- In what ways could the "greenhouse effect" hurt agriculture? In what ways could it possibly *help*, especially in Canada and the former USSR?
- Suppose you could purchase light bulbs that emitted only certain wavelengths of visible light. What wavelengths would promote the most photosynthesis? The least?
- Assume you have supernatural powers and can stop and start the two sets of photosynthesis reactions. Will stopping the light-independent affect the light-dependent, or vice versa?
- What conflicting needs confront a plant living in a hot, dry environment? What is the frequent result in C3 plants? How is the problem avoided in C4 plants?
- What colors of the visible spectrum are absorbed by objects that are black? What about white objects?

How Would You Vote? Classroom Discussion Ideas

- Monitor the voting for the online question. There are many types of scientific research, and each researcher thinks his or hers is most important. However, many financially-struggling Americans would probably balk at spending their hard-earned cash on projects to determine the oxygen levels on distant planets. How did the vote turn out?

Term Paper Topics, Library Activities, and Special Projects

- How did the unusually hot and dry summer of 1988 affect the production of food and grain crops in North America? Prepare an analysis of the effect(s) of that summer's drought on future food availability and its cost to the consumer.
- Consult a biochemistry or advanced plant physiology text to learn of a laboratory technique that would clearly indicate whether the oxygen produced by plants is derived from water or from carbon dioxide.
- Prepare a detailed diagram of the Calvin-Benson cycle showing the introduction of radioactively labeled carbon dioxide and its subsequent journey through several "turns" of the cycle.

- Of the total amount of sunlight energy impinging on a green plant, what percentage of the energy is actually converted into glucose?
- Compare the mechanisms of C3 and C4 photosynthesis and give examples of plants that fit into each category.
- Discuss why radiation with greater or lesser wavelengths than visible light is not generally used in biological processes.

Possible Responses to *Critical Thinking* Questions

1. Both the C3 and C4 plants were exposed to radiolabeled carbon dioxide, which was absorbed. The C3 plant uses rubisco to combine the CO_2 and RuBP to form PGA (see Figure 5.8). However, the C4 plants use a slightly different approach because their stomata close in the heat of the day, reducing the supply of CO_2. In this case the CO_2 is fixed into oxaloacetate in mesophyll cells. This compound is in turn decarboxylated in the bundle sheath cells to enter the Calvin-Benson cycle in the usual way.

2. Let's look at the possibilities. The gain in weight of the tree could have been unchanged water simply absorbed through the roots and retained in the plant tissues, but not *164 pounds of it*! Furthermore, we know that the water molecules are not going to combine *directly* with any other molecules in the tree. Of course, we now know much more about the reactions of photosynthesis than van Helmont did, so we can conclude that the gain in weight was from the synthesis of carbohydrate (specifically, cellulose) in the chloroplasts of the leaf cells from the reacting of carbon dioxide from the air and water from the soil.

3. Pigments must be selected by nature to perform under the conditions existing, but their cell hosts must be selected as well. The chlorophylls (green) that worked in the shallow waters were sufficient to allow their owners to survive. Other pigments evolved that allowed absorption in dim light and permitted their owners to survive in new environments.

6

HOW CELLS RELEASE CHEMICAL ENERGY

Chapter Outline

WHEN MITOCHONDRIA SPIN THEIR WHEELS

OVERVIEW OF ENERGY-RELEASING PATHWAYS

GLYCOLYSIS—GLUCOSE BREAKDOWN STARTS

SECOND AND THIRD STAGES OF AEROBIC RESPIRATION

    Acetyl-CoA Formation and the Krebs Cycle

    Electron Transfer Phosphorylation

ANAEROBIC ENERGY-RELEASING PATHWAYS

    Alcoholic Fermentation

    Lactate Fermentation

ALTERNATIVE ENERGY SOURCES IN THE BODY

    The Fate of Glucose at Mealtime and In Between Meals

    Energy From Fats

    Energy From Proteins

CONNECTIONS WITH PHOTOSYNTHESIS

SUMMARY

SELF-QUIZ

CRITICAL THINKING

Objectives

1. Understand what kinds of molecules can serve as food molecules.
2. Know the relationship of food molecules to glucose and thus to glycolysis.
3. Understand the fundamental differences between glycolysis leading to fermentation and glycolysis leading to aerobic respiration.
4. Know the factors that determine whether an organism will carry on fermentation or aerobic respiration.
5. Know the input materials and output products of each of these processes: glycolysis, fermentation, the Krebs cycle, and electron transfer phosphorylation.

Key Terms

anaerobic pathways
fermentation
aerobic respiration
glycolysis
pyruvate
Krebs cycle

NAD$^+$, NADH
FAD, FADH
electron transfer
  phosphorylation

substrate-level
  phosphorylation
mitochondrion
acetyl-CoA
ATP synthases
fermentation pathways

alcoholic fermentation
lactate fermentation
insulin
glucagon

Lecture Outline

When Mitochondria Spin Their Wheels
A. Mitochondria are the organelles responsible for releasing the energy stored in foods.
   1. In Luft's syndrome, the mitochondria are active in oxygen consumption, but with little ATP formation to show for it.
   2. In Friedreich's ataxia, too much iron in the mitochondria causes an accumulation of free radicals that attack valuable molecules of life.
B. Proper, or improper, functioning of mitochondria is the difference between health and disease.

6.1   Overview of Energy-Releasing Pathways
A. Aerobic respiration (with oxygen) is the main pathway for energy release from carbohydrate to ATP.
   1. All energy-releasing pathways start with glycolysis.
     a. Glucose is split into two pyruvate molecules.
     b. Glycolysis reactions occur in the cytoplasm without the use of oxygen.
   2. Aerobic respiration yields 36 ATPs; fermentation yields merely two.
   3. The aerobic route is summarized:

$$C_6H_{12}O_6 + 6O_2 \ ---> \ 6CO_2 + 6H_2O$$

B. Three series of reactions are required for aerobic respiration:
   1. *Glycolysis* is the breakdown of glucose to pyruvate; small amounts of ATP are generated.
   2. *Krebs cycle* degrades pyruvate to carbon dioxide, water, ATP, H$^+$ ions, and electrons (accepted by NAD$^+$ and FAD).
   3. *Electron transfer phosphorylation* processes the H$^+$ ions and electrons to generate high yields of ATP; oxygen is the final electron acceptor.

6.2   Glycolysis—Glucose Breakdown Begins
A. Enzymes in the cytoplasm catalyze several steps in glucose breakdown.
   1. Glucose is first phosphorylated in steps requiring two ATP, then the six-carbon intermediate is split to form two molecules of PGAL.
   2. Enzymes remove H$^+$ and electrons from PGAL and transfer them to NAD$^+$, which becomes NADH (used later in electron transfer).
   3. By substrate-level phosphorylation, four ATP are produced.
B. The end products of glycolysis are: two pyruvates, two ATP (net gain), and two NADH for each glucose molecule degraded.

6.3 Second and Third Stages of Aerobic Respiration
   A. Acetyl Co-A Formation and the Krebs Cycle
      1. Pyruvate enters the mitochondria and is converted to acetyl-CoA, which then joins oxaloacetate already present from a previous "turn" of the cycle.
      2. During two turns of the cycle, six carbon atoms enter (as pyruvate) and six leave as six carbon dioxide molecules.
      3. The results of the Krebs cycle are:
         a. H^+ and e^- are transferred to NAD^+ and FAD to produce 8 NADH and 2 $FADH_2$, respectively.
         b. Two molecules of ATP are produced by substrate-level phosphorylation.
         c. Most of the molecules are recycled to conserve oxaloacetate for continuous processing of acetyl-CoA.
         d. Carbon dioxide is produced as a by-product.
   B. Electron Transfer Phosphorylation
      1. NADH and $FADH_2$ give up their electrons to transfer (enzyme) systems embedded in the mitochondrial inner membrane.
         a. The energy is used to pump hydrogen ions out of the inner compartment.
         b. When hydrogen ions flow back through ATP synthase in the channels, the coupling of P_i to ADP yields ATP.
         c. At the end of the electron transfer chains, electrons are passed to oxygen to form water.
      2. Electron transfer yields 32 ATP; glycolysis yields two ATP; Krebs yields two ATP, for a grand total of 36 ATP per glucose molecule.

6.4 Anaerobic Energy-Releasing Pathways
   A. Anaerobic pathways operate when oxygen is absent (or limited); pyruvate from glycolysis is metabolized to produce molecules *other than* acetyl-CoA.
      1. With an energy yield of only two ATPs, fermentation is restricted to single-celled organisms and the cells of multicelled organisms only at certain limited times.
      2. Glycolysis serves as the first stage, just as it does in aerobic respiration
   B. Alcoholic Fermentation
      1. Fermentation begins with glucose degradation to pyruvate.
      2. Cellular enzymes convert pyruvate to acetaldehyde, which then accepts electrons from NADH to become alcohol.
      3 Yeasts are valuable in the baking industry (carbon dioxide byproduct makes dough rise) and in alcoholic beverage production.
   C. Lactate Fermentation
      1. Certain bacteria (as in milk) and muscle cells have the enzymes capable of converting pyruvate to lactate.
      2. No additional ATP beyond the net two from glycolysis is produced, but NAD^+ is regenerated.

6.5 Alternative Energy Sources in the Body
   A. The Fate of Glucose at Mealtime and In Between Meals
      1. After eating a meal glucose is absorbed into the blood.
         a. Insulin levels rise, causing greater uptake of glucose by cells for entry into glycolysis.
         b. Excess glucose is converted into glycogen for storage in muscles and the liver.

2. Between meals blood glucose levels fall.
    a. The hormone glucagon prompts liver cells to convert glycogen back to glucose.
    b. Glycogen levels are adequate but can be depleted in about 12 hours.
  B. Energy from Fats
    1. Excess fats (including those made from carbohydrates) are stored away in cells of adipose tissue.
    2. Fats are digested into glycerol, which enters glycolysis, and fatty acids, which enter the Krebs cycle.
    3. Because fatty acids have many more carbon and hydrogen atoms, they are degraded more slowly and yield greater amounts of ATP.
  C. Energy from Proteins
    1. Amino acids are released by digestion and travel in the blood.
    2. After the amino group is removed, the amino acid remnant enters the Krebs cycle.

6.6 Connections with Photosynthesis
  A. Aerobic respiration arose after the noncyclic pathway of photosynthesis had enriched the atmosphere with oxygen.
  B. Photosynthesizers use the carbon dioxide products of aerobic respiration when building organic compounds, and most organisms now depend on the oxygen released by photosynthesis.

Suggestions for Presenting the Material

- Assuming that photosynthesis has already been presented, Chapter 6 can be even more intimidating when students view the diagrams of complicated pathways. It would be helpful to your students if you could spend a few minutes presenting an *overview* based on Figures 6.1, 6.5, and 6.8)

- The critical role of ATP must be emphasized. Distinguish clearly between the *transfer* of energy from carbohydrates to ATP and the *synthesis* of the ATP molecule.

- The material in the chapter is most easily and logically presented by skillful use of the figures.
  a. Begin with Figure 6.1, which interrelates the three series of reactions: glycolysis, Krebs cycle, and electron transfer. Point out the entry molecules, exit molecules, and key intermediates as well as the total energy yield (36 ATP).
  b. For some instructors, Figure 6.1 may be of sufficient detail; however, if you choose, Figure 6.2 gives the individual steps of glycolysis; Figure 6.3 details the steps of Krebs; Figure 6.5 depicts electron transfer.

- As you progress deeper into the pathway discussions, it is advisable to refer frequently to Figure 6.1 to maintain an overview.

- Summing up the total energy yield using Figure 6.1 is important and should be included in your summary.

- You can emphasize the roles of other foods (proteins and lipids) and their relationship to carbohydrates by following the arrows of Figure 6.8. This especially appeals to students interested in nutrition (as they all should be!).

- A superb wrap-up to this unit on energy conversions is the "balance of nature" diagram in section 6.6, which depicts the interdependence of chloroplasts (photosynthesis) and mitochondria (aerobic respiration).

- It should be stated that plants, as well as animals, carry on aerobic respiration, albeit to a lesser extent. Many students have the mistaken idea that plants perform photosynthesis *only*.
- Emphasize the *processes* taking place rather than requiring students to memorize the various *reactions*.
- Although the focus in this chapter is the harvest of energy into ATP, you may wish to explain to your students that another major function of respiration is the production of intermediates for biosynthetic reactions.

Classroom and Laboratory Enrichment

- Show a video on cellular respiration.
- Demonstrate a computer simulation whereby basal metabolism rate (BMR) is calculated by measuring oxygen consumption.
- Select several persons who differ in physical stature and exercise conditioning. Allow them to exercise vigorously for several minutes, then determine heart rate and the length of time before breathing rate returns to normal (indicates extent of oxygen debt).
- Ask an exercise physiologist to talk to the class about the effect(s) of exercise on body metabolic rate.
- Show an electron micrograph of a mitochondrion and point out the matrix (inner compartment), cristae (inner membranes), and outer compartment. Relate this to the drawings in the text.
- If there is a brewery or winery nearby, arrange for a field trip. Brewmasters and winemakers generally are happy to conduct a tour through the facilities and explain the processes involved.

Impacts, Issues Classroom Discussion Ideas

- Tell how the measurement of oxygen consumption by a human patient is related to metabolic rate.
- In *Luft's syndrome* the mitochondria are not producing sufficient amounts of ATP. What series of reactions could be most responsible for the deficiency?
- Mitochondria are critical for normal metabolism, but from which parent did each human being's original mitochondria come at conception?

Additional Ideas for Classroom Discussion

- Table wines, that is, those that have NOT been fortified, have an alcoholic content of about 10–12 percent. What factors could limit the production of alcohol during fermentation? Is it self-limiting, or do the vintners have to stop it with some additive?
- Your text lists two types of fermentation: one leads to alcohol, the other to lactate. Which occurs in yeasts, and why? Which pathway is reversible? What would be the consequences of nonreversible lactate formation in muscle cells?
- Yeast is added to a mixture of malt, hops, and water to brew beer—a product in which alcohol and carbon dioxide are desirable! Why is yeast added to bread dough?

- Analyze the simple equation for cellular respiration shown in the Overview of Aerobic Respiration section by telling exactly at what place in the aerobic metabolism of glucose each item in the equation is a participant.
- What is "metabolic water"?
- Why is fermentation necessary under anaerobic conditions? That is, why does the cell convert pyruvate to some fermentation product when it does not result in any additional ATP production?

How Would You Vote? **Classroom Discussion Ideas**

- Monitor the voting for the online question. One's response to this question depends on whether you have great compassion for humankind or are more interested in successful business ventures. Obviously, pharmaceutical companies are in business to make money—lots of money. Therefore, they cannot profitably invest time and money in developing a drug/treatment for a small number of persons who will be grateful, but not make the company rich. The only alternative is for the government to give the company(ies) some financial incentives, such as tax breaks, to pursue such research.

Term Paper Topics, Library Activities, and Special Projects

- Rotenone is a fish poison and insecticide. Its mode of action is listed on container labels as "respiratory poison." Exactly where and how does it disrupt cellular respiration?
- Prepare a fermentation vat with grape juice and yeast (don't seal it!). Allow the process to proceed for a few days, then strain the fluid into a flask and distill it. What gas is produced during fermentation? What product distills at 78.5°C?
- Certain flour beetles and clothes moths can live in environments where exogenous water is virtually unobtainable, yet they thrive. What mechanisms do they use for the synthesis and retention of water?
- Use diagrams to show how radioactive carbon 14 in glucose fed to rats could end up in body fat and proteins.
- Because ATP is the direct source of energy for body cells, why not bypass the lengthy digestion and cellular metabolism processes necessary for carbohydrate breakdown and eat ATP directly?
- Your textbook says that the net energy yield from one molecule of glucose is 36 ATPs. Some textbooks say it can be either 36 or 38. Investigate these numbers and see who is correct; maybe both.
- Investigate the "set-point theory" of metabolism; discuss how it relates to people who are trying to lose or gain weight.
- Hydrogen cyanide is the lethal gas used in gas chambers. How does it cause death?

Possible Responses to *Critical Thinking* Questions

1. The body can use the following for energy in this order: carbohydrate, fats, protein. However, nucleic acids are not used as an energy source because these macromolecules are necessary for critical information storage and retrieval applications.

   Using up these molecules would be like using up the central memory of your computer.

2. Consuming extra proteins in one's diet is usually recommended for building additional muscle mass. However, users should follow the label directions on protein supplement products very carefully to ensure sufficient water intake to flush any unincorporated proteins from their system.

3. The muscle cells of the rabbit's legs would be using glucose via the glycolysis → Krebs cycle → ETP pathway. As long as oxygen supplies are sufficient, this should supply ample amounts of ATP needed for the short, quick sprints the rabbit must make to elude the coyote.

   The Canada geese on the other hand must generate ATP over much longer periods of time with a steady, albeit slow, generation of ATP from the breakdown of fatty acids. Because these fatty acids are quite lengthy molecules, many carbon units can be cleaved off and converted to acetyl-CoA for entry into the Krebs cycle. This allows for many more ATPs to be generated *per fatty acid* (see Figure 6.8 in the textbook). This pathway would not serve the rabbit well at all, unless the coyote was very old and very slow on his paws.

4. Altitude sickness results from a lack of oxygen, but more specifically it results from the deficiency of oxygen needed to "pull" the train of electrons along the electron transfer chain, which provides the energy necessary to produce ATP. This would explain why the symptoms of altitude sickness would mimic those of cyanide poisoning, namely, the inability to produce enough ATP to power the muscle cells necessary for breathing and pumping blood.

7

HOW CELLS REPRODUCE

Chapter Outline

Objectives

1. Understand the factors that cause cells to reproduce.
2. Compare mitosis and meiosis; cite similarities and differences.
3. Explain the necessity of maintaining the same number of chromosomes per cell after cell division.
4. Understand what is meant by *cell cycle* and be able to visualize where mitosis fits into the cell cycle.
5. Be able to characterize each phase of mitosis.
6. Explain how the cytoplasm is apportioned to plant and animal daughter cells following mitosis.
7. Describe the mechanisms that keep chromosomes organized within the cell.
8. Contrast asexual and sexual types of reproduction that occur on the cellular and multicellular organism levels.
9. Understand the effect that meiosis has on chromosome number.
10. Describe the events that occur in each meiotic phase.

Key Terms

mitosis

meiosis

somatic cells

gametes

germ cells

chromosome

sister chromatids

histone proteins

nucleosome

centromere

cell cycle

interphase

G_1, S, G_2, M

chromosome number

diploid number

mitotic spindle

prophase

metaphase

anaphase

telophase

centromere

centrioles

centrosomes

microtubules

cleavage furrow

actin filaments

cell plate formation

asexual reproduction

clones

sexual reproduction

haploid number

homologous
  chromosomes

gene

alleles

meiosis I

meiosis II

prophase I

crossing over

nonsister chromatids

metaphase I

maternal chromosomes

paternal chromosomes

gametes

spores

gametophytes

sporophytes

primary spermatocyte

spermatids

sperm

oocyte

secondary oocyte

polar body

ovum, egg

fertilization

growth factors

neoplasms

benign

cancers

malignant

metastasis

HeLa cells

Lecture Outline

Henrietta's Immortal Cells
A. Researchers at Johns Hopkins cultured a line of immortal cells in 1951.
   1. They are referred to as HeLa cells after their source—a woman named Henrietta Lacks.
   2. Her cells continue to provide for research around the world.
B. Understanding cell division starts with three questions:
   1. What kind of information guides inheritance?
   2. How is the information copied in a parent cell before being distributed into daughter cells?
   3. What kinds of mechanisms actually parcel out the information to daughter cells?

7.1   Overview of Cell Division Mechanisms
A. Mitosis and Meiosis
   1. Before cells are able to reproduce, there must be a division of the nucleus and its DNA.
   2. Mitosis and meiosis are eukaryotic nuclear division mechanisms that lead to the distribution of DNA to new nuclei in forthcoming daughter cells.
      a. Mitosis is used by multicelled organisms for growth by repeated divisions of somatic cells.
      b. Meiosis occurs only in reproductive (germ) cells that divide to form gametes.
   3. Prokaryotic cells reproduce asexually by an entirely different mechanism, called prokaryotic fission.
B. Key Points about Chromosome Structure
   1. Each chromosome is a molecule of DNA complexed with proteins.
   2. Prior to division, each threadlike chromosome is duplicated to form two sister chromatids held together by a centromere.
   3. Proteins called histones tightly bind to DNA and cause spooling into structural units called nucleosomes.

7.2　Introducing the Cell Cycle
　　A. The cell cycle is a recurring sequence of events that extends from the time of a cell's formation until each division is completed.
　　B. Most of a cell's existence is spent in interphase; mitosis occupies only a small part.
　　　　1. During interphase the cell's mass increases, the cytoplasmic components approximately double in number, *and the DNA is duplicated*.
　　　　　　a. In G1, most of the carbohydrates, lipids, and proteins for a cell's own use and for export are assembled.
　　　　　　b. In the S phase, the cell copies its DNA and synthesizes proteins used in organizing the condensed chromosomes.
　　　　　　c. In G2, the proteins that will drive mitosis to completion are produced.
　　　　2. Some cells are arrested in G1 of interphase and never divide again (example: brain cells).
　　　　3. The cell cycle has built-in checkpoints where proteins can advance, delay, or block forward progress of the cycle.

7.3　Mitosis Maintains the Chromosome Number
　　A. Each species has a characteristic chromosome number (for example: human somatic cells contain 46 chromosomes).
　　　　1. Body cells have a diploid number (2*n*) of chromosomes.
　　　　　　a. Chromosomes exist as pairs: one member of each pair from each parent.
　　　　　　b. Mitosis produces two daughter cells, both diploid, and each containing 23 *pairs* of chromosomes.
　　　　2. The mitotic spindle assures correct separation of the chromosomes.
　　　　　　a. The spindle apparatus is composed of two sets of microtubules.
　　　　　　b. Microtubules (components of the cytoskeleton) extend from the two "poles" of the cell and overlap at the cell equator.
　　　　　　c. Because each chromosome was duplicated *before* mitosis began, each new cell now can have one of each chromosome, thus restoring its diploid number.
　　　　3. The four sequential stages of mitosis are: prophase, metaphase, anaphase, and telophase.
　　B. Prophase: Mitosis Begins
　　　　1. Chromosomes become visible as rodlike units, each consisting of two sister chromatids.
　　　　2. Two centrioles next to the nucleus duplicate before prophase begins.
　　　　　　a. One centriole moves to the opposite side of the nucleus.
　　　　　　b. Microtubules extend from each centriole to form the mitotic spindle.
　　C. Transition to Metaphase
　　　　1. The nuclear membrane now breaks up in the transition between pro- and metaphase.
　　　　2. Sister chromatids, each attached to microtubules, become oriented toward opposite poles of the cell.
　　　　3. Metaphase is defined by the alignment of the chromosomes at the cell's equator, halfway between the poles.
　　D. From Anaphase Through Telophase
　　　　1. Sister chromatids separate and move toward opposite poles.
　　　　　　a. Microtubules attached to the centromeres *shorten* and pull the chromosomes toward the poles.
　　　　　　b. Other microtubules at the spindle poles *ratchet* past each other to push the two spindle poles apart.
　　　　　　c. Once separated, each chromatid is now an independent chromosome.

2. Telophase begins when the two daughter chromosomes of each original pair of chromatids arrive at opposite poles.
   a. Chromosomes return to the threadlike form typical of interphase.
   b. The nuclear envelope reforms from the fusion of small vesicles
   c. Each daughter cell has the same number of chromosomes as the parent cell; mitosis is complete.

7.4   Division of the Cytoplasm
   A. Cytoplasmic division in animals is by means of a cleavage furrow.
      1. The flexible plasma membrane of animal cells can be squeezed in the middle to separate the two daughter cells—a process called cleavage.
      2. Parallel arrays of contractile microfilaments slide past one another at the cleavage furrow, pulling the plasma membrane inward.
   B. Plant cells separate by constructing a new cell wall.
      1. Because of the rather rigid cell wall, the cytoplasm of plant cells cannot just be pinched in two.
      2. Instead, vesicles containing remnants of the microtubular spindle form a disk-like structure during cell plate formation.

7.5   Meiosis and Sexual Reproduction
   A. Asexual Versus Sexual Reproduction
      1. In asexual reproduction, all offspring inherit the same DNA from a single parent.
         a. This DNA contains all the heritable information necessary to make a new individual.
         b. Asexually produced individuals can only be genetically identical clones of the parent.
      2. In sexual reproduction, each parent contributes one gene for each trait.
         a. Meiosis reduces the chromosome number in each gamete by one-half (humans = 23).
         b. Each gamete has *one of each pair* of homologous chromosomes.
         c. During fertilization, egg and sperm will join to restore the diploid chromosome number; each pair of chromosomes has one member from mother and one from father.
      3. Each pair of look-alike chromosomes is called a homologous chromosome.
         a. A gene is a section of chromosomal DNA with instructions for building some aspect of the organism.
         b. The genes on each of the homologous chromosomes are not identical; different molecular forms of the same gene are called alleles.
      4. Sexual reproduction shuffles the alleles during gamete formation and fertilization, thus producing offspring with unique combinations of alleles.
   B. Two Divisions, Not One
      1. In some ways meiosis resembles mitosis:
         a. The chromosomes are duplicated during interphase to form sister chromatids held together at the centromere.
         b. Chromosomes are moved by the microtubules of the spindle apparatus.
      2. Unlike mitosis, meiosis has two series of divisions—meiosis I and II.
         a. During meiosis I, homologous chromosomes pair and cytokinesis follows.
            1) Each of the two daughter cells receives a haploid number of chromosomes.
            2) BUT…each chromosome *is still duplicated*.
         b. In meiosis II, the sister chromatids of each chromosome separate; cytokinesis follows, resulting in four haploid cells.

7.6   How Meiosis Puts Variation in Traits
   A. Crossing Over in Prophase I
      1. Homologous chromosomes pair up and lie very close to each other.
         a. Nonsister chromatids exchange segments in a process called *crossing over*.
         b. Because alleles for the same trait can vary, new combinations of genes in each chromosome can result; this is one source of genetic variation.
      2. After crossing over, the nonsister chromatids begin to partially separate.
   B. Metaphase I Alignments
      1. During metaphase I, homologous chromosomes randomly line up at the spindle equator.
      2. During anaphase I, homologous chromosomes (still duplicated) separate into two haploid cells, each of which has a *random* mix of maternal and paternal chromosomes.

7.7   From Gametes to Offspring
   A. Gamete Formation in Plants
      1. Germ cells within the tissues of a plant (sporophyte stage) produce haploid spores by meiosis.
         a. In a suitable habitat a spore will germinate and undergo mitosis to produce a haploid gametophyte.
         b. Gametophytes produce haploid cells—eggs or sperm.
      2. Fertilization results in a new diploid sporophyte (example: pine tree).
   B. Gamete Formation in Animals
      1. The life cycle of multicelled animals proceeds from meiosis to gamete formation >>> fertilization >>> growth by mitosis.
      2. In males, meiosis and gamete formation are called *spermatogenesis*.
         a. Germ cell ($2n$) >>> primary spermatocyte ($2n$) >>> MEIOSIS I >>> two secondary spermatocytes (n) >>> MEIOSIS II >>> four spermatids (n).
         b. Spermatids change in form; each develops a tail to become mature sperm.
      3. In females, meiosis and gamete formation are called *oogenesis*.
         a. Germ cell ($2n$) >>> primary oocyte ($2n$) >>> MEIOSIS I >>> secondary oocyte (n, and large in size) plus polar body (n, and small in size) >>> MEIOSIS II >>> one large ovum (n) plus three polar bodies (n, small).
         b. The single ovum is the only cell capable of being fertilized by a sperm; the polar bodies wither and die.
   C. More Gene Shufflings at Fertilization
      1. The diploid chromosome number is restored at fertilization when two very different gamete nuclei fuse to form the zygote.
      2. The variation present at fertilization is from three sources:
         a. Crossing over occurs during prophase I.
         b. Random alignments at metaphase I lead to millions of combinations of maternal and paternal chromosomes in each gamete.
         c. Of all the genetically diverse gametes produced, chance will determine which two will meet.

7.8   The Cell Cycle and Cancer
   A. The Cell Cycle Revisited
      1. Many mechanisms control cell growth, DNA replication, and division to replace worn-out cells.
         a. Sometimes however, one daughter cell may end up with too many chromosomes, the other too few.

   b. Chromosomes may be attacked by free radicals or radiation.

  2. The cell cycle has built-in checkpoints to keep errors from getting out of hand.

   a. Growth factors promote transcription of genes that help the body grow.

   b. If chromosomal DNA is damaged, mitosis can be halted until it is repaired.

  3. Neoplasms are abnormal masses of cells that have lost controls over their growth and cell division.

   a. Benign growths pose no threat to the body.

   b. Cancers are abnormally growing and dividing cells of a malignant neoplasm.

 B. Characteristics of Cancer

  1. All cancer cells display four characteristics:

   a. They grow and divide abnormally.

   b. The cell membrane is leaky and the cytoskeleton is disorganized.

   c. Cells have a weakened capacity for adhesion and may break away to move to other sites in the body (metastasis).

   d. Cancer cells have lethal effects.

  2. Researchers have identified many of the mutated genes that contribute to the multistep process of cancer.

Suggestions for Presenting the Material

- This chapter covers both types of cell reproduction: (1) mitosis—division in which the number of chromosomes remains the same in the identical daughter cells, and (2) meiosis—a more complicated type of cell division in which the number of chromosomes is reduced during the production of cells destined to become gametes.

- Remind students again of the differences between prokaryotic cells and eukaryotic cells. When students remember the differences that distinguish these two kinds of cells, it will be easier for them to understand why prokaryotes use a simple division technique called fission and eukaryotes use the more complex process of mitosis.

- Make sure that students can distinguish between such terms as *centromere* and *chromatid,* which at first glance can appear very similar.

- Emphasize the cell cycle, stressing that most cells are not dividing *all of the time*. Students should be aware of the fact that the steps of cell division are part of a continuum. Our separation of the process into four stages is an artificial one, and it may be hard to say where one stage ends and the next begins when looking at a dividing cell. You may compare it to the showing of a game tape that athletes watch to see the errors committed in the big game.

- Students often have trouble following the number of chromosomes throughout the stages of mitosis. To help them, remind them that each chromosome has one centromere, and it is not until the centromere divides in anaphase that each "sister chromatid" can be considered a chromosome in its own right. Make certain that students understand where and when mitosis occurs in any organism.

- The confusion in quantifying the number of chromosomes at any one point in cell division comes from the various designations of the chromosome at different times in the cell cycle. One convenient way to avoid this pitfall entirely is to keep track of the *number of DNA molecules*. For example, in mitosis of a human skin cell the number of DNAs goes from 46 to 92 during S phase and then back to 46 and 46 during anaphase. Similarly, during meiosis the number goes from 46 to 92 during S; then is halved at anaphase I (i.e. 46 and 46), then halved again in anaphase II to 23, 23, 23, and 23. All the while we are thinking of bits of DNA rather than chromosomes, chromatids, and daughter chromosomes.

- Reduction division of chromosomes is an important topic for beginning biology students. Students must have a good understanding of meiosis to comprehend the workings of inheritance explained later.

- The events of meiosis can be confusing. Emphasize that meiosis makes it possible for organisms to undergo sexual reproduction. Remind students of the benefits of sexual reproduction; this helps them to understand why a process as complex as meiosis has evolved.

- Students often find it hard to understand when and how the chromosome number changes during meiosis, so be sure they understand that the two chromatids of one chromosome are each considered a chromosome after the centromere splits during meiotic anaphase II.

- Meiosis will be easier to grasp if students can become thoroughly acquainted with a typical plant life cycle (Figure 7.12a) and a typical animal life cycle (Figure 7.12b). Before finishing with this chapter, be sure to question the students about the events of meiosis and its consequences to the organism.

Classroom and Laboratory Enrichment

- Show a video presentation using time-lapse photography of cells undergoing actual cell division.

- Ask students (working individually or in small groups) to use chromosome kits (available from biological supply houses) to demonstrate chromosome replication during the stages of mitosis. If kits are unavailable, make your own chromosomes using pop-it beads for each chromatid and a magnet for each centromere.

- View ready-made squashes of mitotic material, such as onion root tip, on visual media. Ask students to estimate the length of each mitotic phase after counting the number of cells in each phase in several fields of view.

- Perhaps the following analogy can help students visualize chromosomes during mitosis:

2 chromatids	=	2 matched red socks
1 centromere	=	1 clothespin
spindle fiber	=	clothesline

(Hint: This analogy can be extended during meiosis to include one pair of red socks and one pair of blue—a tetrad!)

- Prepare an overhead transparency of your own sketch, or use one from Chapter 9, to explain how one DNA molecule (that is, one chromosome) becomes two identical DNA molecules (that is, two daughter chromosomes).

- Show students a karyotype of a normal man or woman to introduce the concept of homologous pairs of chromosomes.

- Show overhead transparencies of adult plants or animals, and ask students to point out where meiosis occurs in each organism.

- Illustrate crossing over by using lengths of different colored string. Snip and tie the ends to create the products of a crossover (see Figure 7.10).

- Place Figure 7.9 on the screen and have students indicate the number of *human* chromosomes present at each stage (note how conveniently the *four* chromosomes in the diagram convert to *46* human ones). Use the centromere hint in the Discussion section below. You many want to use the number of DNA idea presented in the Suggestions for Presenting Materials section above.

- If you can locate a segment of film depicting the union of gametes and subsequent cleavage, it will provide visual presentation of what mitosis and meiosis accomplish in a living cell.

Impacts, Issues Classroom Discussion Ideas

- Loosely speaking, the process of one cell becoming two cells may be referred to as mitosis, but to be completely accurate, what does mitosis *specifically* refer to?

- How can the mathematically impossible become the biologically possible—namely, a cell with 46 chromosomes splits to form two cells *each* with 46 chromosomes? This means 46 divided by 2 equals 46 and 46. What event during the cell cycle makes this possible?

- Why do cells undergoing mitosis require one set of divisions but cells undergoing meiosis need two sets of divisions?

Additional Ideas for Classroom Discussion

- Bacteria divide by prokaryotic fission, and their cell cycle is much shorter than that of eukaryotes. Ask students to think of reasons why this might be so.

- Using a generation time of 20 minutes, calculate the size of a bacterial population that has arisen from a single bacterium growing under optimum conditions (for example, *Salmonella* in a bowl of unrefrigerated potato salad at a picnic on a warm summer day) for eight hours.

- Many of the drugs used in chemotherapy cause loss of hair in the individual being treated. Ask students if they can figure out why such drugs affect hair growth.

- Biologists used to believe that interphase was a "resting period" during the life cycle of the cell. Why did this appear to be so?

- Ask students how cell division in plant cells differs from that in animal cells.

- How can there be 46 chromosomes in a human cell at metaphase and also 46 chromosomes after the centromere splits in anaphase? Hint: Focus on the name change of chromatids to daughter chromosomes.

- What is there about the composition of an animal cell versus a plant cell that necessitates different methods of cleavage?

- Do more advanced organisms have more chromosomes than primitive organisms? Review chromosome numbers of some common plants and animals.

- All but the most primitive species of organisms have the ability to reproduce sexually. Can you explain why sexual reproduction is considered a hallmark of evolutionary advancement? What are the advantages over asexual reproduction?

- Division of the cell cytoplasm is equal during spermatogenesis but unequal during oogenesis. Can you think of at least one reason why this might be necessary?

- The generalized life cycle of complex land plants is often described as "alternation of generations." Describe the meaning of this phrase.

- An old-fashioned name for meiosis II is "reduction division." Why?

- What would happen if meiosis did not halve the chromosome number?

- Ask students to compare an animal life cycle to a complex land-plant life cycle. How is the life cycle of a human different from that of a plant?

- Why does crossing over occur in prophase of *meiosis* and not *mitosis*?

- One of the meiotic series is very much like mitosis. Is it meiosis I or II?

- Does the reduction in chromosome number occur in meiosis I or II? Hint: To conveniently count the number of chromosomes (whether doubled as chromatids or newly formed daughter chromosomes) simply count the number of centromeres (or portions thereof) present in any particular stage.

- When do the processes of human spermatogenesis and oogenesis begin? Are they the same in males and females?

- What is the derivation of the prefix "chrom-" as used in describing the carriers of heredity?

How Would You Vote? Classroom Discussion Ideas

- Monitor the voting for the online question. The very question of whether a person (or his relatives) should be compensated for being the source of human body tissue for research is very much in debate today. Various court cases have decided the issue both for and against. However, in a strictly ethical sense, it would seem only the right thing to do, that is, to compensate the family of Henrietta Lacks for the contribution she has made to science even in her death.

Term Paper Topics, Library Activities, and Special Projects

- Much progress in studying human disease has been made using the research technique of tissue culture. Describe techniques of tissue culture, explaining how cells can be induced to grow and divide in vitro.

- Explore diseases (such as cancer) that involve cell growth gone wrong. How do such diseases affect the mechanism of cell division? What drugs are used to halt runaway cell growth? How do these drugs work, and what are their side effects?

- Why do some cells of the human body (for example, epithelial cells) continue to divide, yet other cells (for example, nerve cells) lose their ability to replicate once they are mature? Describe some of the latest research efforts to induce cell division in nerve cells.

- Colchicine is a chemical used to treat dividing plant cells to ensure that chromosomes of cells undergoing mitosis will be visible. How does colchicine achieve this effect? What is the natural source of colchicine?

- The 1956 edition of the high school biology text *Modern Biology* by Moon, Mann, and Otto was the last to state the human chromosome number as *48*. This was not a misprint! Why was the number reported incorrectly and what investigations resulted in assigning the correct number of *46* to humans? [Incidentally, this was the last edition of this famous text to NOT mention DNA.]

- The preparation of a karyotype (picture of chromosomes) is a simple but multistep procedure. Provide a procedural outline for making such a preparation of chromosomes for publication in a book.

- There is some question as to exactly how chromosomes move to opposite ends of the cell in concert with the spindle fibers. Investigate the various theories, and report on their strengths and weaknesses.

- How are human karyotypes prepared? Discover the laboratory steps required in this procedure.

- Trace the increasing dominance of the sporophyte in the life histories of land plants beginning with the bryophytes and ending with the angiosperms.

- Use the karyotypes of related species (for example, primates) to describe evolutionary relationships, if any, between the species.
- Meiosis precisely reduces the chromosome number so that union of several gametes restores the diploid number. How many extra or fewer chromosomes can a human body cell have and survive? Are there consequences? Does the same hold true for plants?
- What are the latest theories and evidence relative to the blockage of entry into the egg of all sperm subsequent to the first one?
- Select from the library shelves several biology texts from the past 50 years. Compare the formal definitions of "gene," and prepare a historical resumé of the changes.

Possible Responses to *Critical Thinking* Questions

1. Because Taxol interferes with microtubule disassembly, this drug would halt mitosis. Since cancer cells are dividing uncontrollably, this would serve the goal of cancer treatment.

2. Radiation has the greatest effect on cells with high rates of mitosis, such as those in hair follicles and the lining of the gut. Cancer cells can be killed by disrupting their mitosis using radiation.

3. Meiosis produces recombination of genes, leading to genetic differences by: 1) crossing over during prophase I, and 2) independent assortment of the chromosomes during metaphase I.

4. Reproduction without sexual union and fertilization is a great time saver and allows the production of numerous offspring. In the case of aphids, things are even better because the asexual offspring are all females, who can in turn generate more females. This is an especially good mechanism to increase numbers of aphids when many predators are picking them off. In the fall and winter when predation declines, the females can be more leisurely about reproduction, seeking males for a source of genetic variation as they produce fewer offspring.

5. All the bdelloid rotifers were female? Wow! That seems nearly impossible for a multicellular animal. Certainly we would expect male and female for the diversity that accompanies sexual reproduction. Researchers would want to examine the sex organs and reproductive lives of these creatures, but perhaps they are too reclusive. Of course, there could be a very simple explanation: the males just don't want to be found!

8

OBSERVING PATTERNS IN INHERITED TRAITS

Chapter Outline

Objectives

1. Know Mendel's principles of dominance, segregation, and independent assortment.
2. Understand how to solve genetics problems that involve monohybrid and dihybrid crosses.
3. Understand and provide an explanation for the variations that can occur in observable patterns of inheritance.
4. Describe how an understanding of chromosomes helps to account for events that compose mitosis and meiosis.
5. Name some ordinary and extraordinary chromosomal events that can create new phenotypes (outward appearances).
6. Understand how changes in chromosome structure and number can affect the outward appearance of organisms.
7. Distinguish *autosomal recessive inheritance* from *sex-linked recessive inheritance*.
8. Give examples of each of the above types of inheritance.
9. Explain how changes in chromosomal number can occur and present an example of such a change.
10. List examples of phenotypic defects and describe how each can be treated.
11. Explain how knowing about modern methods of genetic screening can minimize potentially tragic events.

Key Terms

genes
locus
alleles
hybrids
homozygous
heterozygous
dominant allele
recessive allele
homozygous dominant
homozygous recessive
gene expression
genotype
phenotype
P, F$_1$, F$_2$
monohybrid cross
homologous
  chromosomes
probability
Punnett-square method
Mendel's theory of
  segregation
dihybrid crosses

Mendel's theory of
  independent
  assortment
codominance
ABO blood typing
multiple allele system
incomplete dominance
albinism
pleiotropy
Marfan syndrome
camptodactyly
continuous variation
bell curves
wild-type allele
mutant allele
crossing over
sex chromosomes
autosomes
X chromosome
Y chromosome
Punnett square
SRY gene
linkage group

pedigrees
genetic abnormality
genetic disorder
syndrome
disease
autosomal dominant
  inheritance
Huntington disease
achondroplasia
autosomal recessive
  inheritance
galactosemia
X-linked recessive
  inheritance
color blindness
Duchenne muscular
  dystrophy
hemophilia A
duplications
deletion
inversion
translocation
cri-du-chat

aneuploidy
polyploidy
nondisjunction
Down syndrome
trisomy 21
Turner syndrome
XO
XXX condition
Klinefelter syndrome
XXY
XYY condition
abortion
genetic counseling
prenatal diagnosis
embryo
fetus
amniocentesis
chorionic villi sampling
  (CVS)
fetoscopy
in-vitro fertilization
"test-tube" babies
phenylketonuria

Lecture Outline

Menacing Mucus

A. Cystic fibrosis is a debilitating genetic disorder.
 1. Persons with two recessive genes will suffer from excessive accumulations of mucus in their lungs.
 2. The location of the defective gene was identified in 1989.
B. A campaign for mass screening of prospective parents was initiated in 2001 but it has met with mixed success.

8.1 Tracking Traits with Hybrid Crosses

A. Terms Used in Modern Genetics
 1. *Genes* are units of information about specific traits, each located at a particular *locus* on a chromosome.
 2. Diploid cells have two genes (a gene pair) for each trait—each on a *homologous chromosome*.
 3. *Alleles* are various molecular forms of a gene for the same trait.
 4. *True-breeding lineage* occurs when offspring inherit identical alleles, generation after generation; non-identical alleles produce *hybrid offspring*.
 5. When both alleles are the same, the condition is called the *homozygous* condition; if the alleles differ, then it is the *heterozygous* condition.
 6. When heterozygous, one allele is *dominant* (A), the other is *recessive* (a).
 7. Homozygous dominant = AA, homozygous recessive = aa, and heterozygous = Aa.
 8. *Gene expression* is the process by which information coded in a gene is converted to structural or functional parts of a cell.
 9. *Genotype* is the sum of the genes, and *phenotype* is how the genes are expressed (what you observe).
 10. P = parental generation; F_1 = first-generation offspring; F_2 = second-generation offspring.
B. Mendel's Experimental Approach
 1. Gregor Mendel used experiments in plant breeding and a knowledge of mathematics to form his hypotheses.
 2. Mendel used the garden pea in his experiments.
    a. This plant can fertilize itself; true-breeding varieties were available to Mendel.
    b. Peas can also be cross-fertilized by human manipulation of the pollen.
 3. Mendel cross-fertilized true-breeding garden pea plants having clearly contrasting traits (example: white vs. purple flowers).
C. Mendel's Theory of Segregation
 1. Mendel suspected that every plant inherits two "units" (now called genes) of information for each trait, one from each parent.
 2. Mendel's first experiments were monohybrid crosses.
    a. Monohybrid crosses have two parents that are true-breeding for contrasting forms of a trait (white vs. purple flowers).
    b. One form of the trait (white) disappears in the first generation offspring (F_1), only to show up in the second generation (F_2).
    c. We now know that all members of the F_1 offspring are heterozygous because one parent could produce only an A gamete and the other could produce only an a gamete.

3. In the F_2 generation the white flowers reappeared.
  a. The numerical ratios of crosses suggested that genes do not blend.
  b. For example, the F_2 offspring showed a 3:1 phenotypic ratio of purple to white.
  c. Mendel assumed that each sperm has an equal probability of fertilizing an egg. This can be seen most easily by using the Punnett square.
  d. Thus, each new plant has three chances in four of having at least one dominant allele.
4. Mendel's theory of segregation states that diploid organisms inherit two genes per trait, located on pairs of homologous chromosomes. During meiosis the two genes segregate from each other such that each gamete will receive only one gene per trait.
D. Mendel's Theory of Independent Assortment
  1. Mendel also performed experiments involving two traits—a dihybrid cross.
    a. Mendel correctly predicted that all F_1 plants would show both of the dominant alleles (example: all with purple flowers and all tall).
    b. Mendel wondered if the genes for flower color and plant height would travel together when two F_1 plants were crossed.
  2. We now know that genes located on *non*homologous chromosomes segregate independently of each other and give the same phenotypic ratio as Mendel observed—9:3:3:1.
  3. Mendel's theory of independent assortment states that during meiosis each gene of a pair tends to assort into gametes independently of other gene pairs located on nonhomologous chromosomes.

8.2   Not-So-Straightforward Phenotypes
A. ABO Blood Types: A Case of Codominance
  1. In codominance, both alleles are expressed in heterozygotes (for example, humans with both glycolipids on their red blood cells are designated with blood type AB).
  2. Whenever more than two forms of alleles exist at a given locus, it is called a *multiple allele system*. In this instance it results in four blood types: A, B, AB, and O.
B. Incomplete Dominance
  1. In *incomplete dominance*, a dominant allele cannot completely mask the expression of another.
  2. For example, a true-breeding red-flowered snapdragon crossed with a white-flowered snapdragon will produce *pink* flowers because there is not enough red pigment (produced by the dominant allele) to completely mask the effects of the white allele.
C. When Products of Two or More Gene Pairs Interact
  1. One gene pair can influence other gene pairs, with their combined activities producing some effect on phenotype.
  2. In Labrador retrievers, one gene pair codes for the *quantity* of melanin produced while another codes for melanin *deposition.*
  3. Still another gene locus determines whether melanin will be produced at all—lack of any produces an albino (recessive).
  4. Comb shape in chickens is of at least four types depending on the interactions of two gene pairs (R and P).
D. Single Genes with a Wide Reach
  1. Sometimes the expression of alleles at one location can have effects on two or more traits; this is termed pleiotropy.
  2. Marfan syndrome is characterized by these effects: lanky skeleton, leaky heart valves and weakened blood vessels, deformed air sacs in lungs, pain, and lens displacement in the eyes.

8.3 Complex Variations in Traits
   A. Regarding the Unexpected Phenotype
      1. Tracking even a single gene through several generations may produce results that are different than expected.
      2. Camptodactyly (immobile, bent fingers) can express itself on one hand, both hands, or neither due to the possibility that a gene product is missing in one of the several steps along the metabolic pathway.
   B. Continuous Variation in Populations
      1. A given phenotype can vary by different degrees from one individual to the next in a population.
         a. This is the result of interactions with other genes, and environmental influences.
         b. In humans, eye color and height are examples.
      2. Most traits are not qualitative but show continuous variation, as illustrated by bell curves, and are transmitted by quantitative inheritance.
   C. Environmental Effects on Phenotype
      1. Fur on the extremities of certain animals will be darker because the enzyme for melanin production will operate at cooler temperatures but is sensitive to heat on the rest of the body.
      2. The color of the floral clusters on *Hydrangea* plants will vary depending on the acidity of the soil.

8.4 The Chromosomal Basis of Inheritance
   A. A Rest Stop on Our Conceptual Road
      1. *Genes* are units of information about heritable traits.
      2. Diploid organisms possess pairs of *homologous chromosomes*, which are alike in length, shape, and gene sequence.
      3. *Alleles* are slightly different molecular forms of the same gene, which are shuffled during meiosis.
      4. *Crossing over* between homologous chromosomes results in *genetic recombination*.
      5. *Independent assortment* refers to the random alignment of each pair of homologous chromosomes at metaphase I of mitosis, which results in new combinations of genes in offspring.
      6. A chromosome's structure may change during mitosis or meiosis, as can the parental chromosome number (quantity).
   B. Karyotyping
      1. Karyotyping reveals an image of a cell's diploid chromosomes.
      2. The chromosomes are arrested in the metaphase stage of mitosis.
      3. The cell is placed in a hypotonic solution, causing the chromosomes to move apart.
      4. The chromosomes are viewed with a microscope and arranged for numbering and observation.
   C. Autosomes and Sex Chromosomes
      1. *Sex chromosomes* determine gender.
         a. Human females have two X chromosomes.
         b. Males have one X and one Y.
      2. Most of the chromosomes are of the same quantity and type in both sexes and are called *autosomes* (44 in humans).
      3. Each human egg will contain 22 autosomes plus one X; but sperm will carry 22 autosomes plus *either* an X or a Y.
         a. X-bearing egg plus X-bearing sperm produces female offspring.

b. X-bearing egg plus Y-bearing sperm produces male offspring.
4. The Y chromosome carries a male-determining *(SRY)* gene, which leads to formation of the testes. Absence of the male gene in females results in formation of ovaries.
5. The X chromosome obviously codes for sexual traits, but it also carries many genes for nonsexual traits.

8.5 Impact of Crossing Over on Inheritance
A. Linked genes on specific chromosomes are referred to as linkage groups.
1. Linkage can be disrupted by crossing over—the exchange of parts of homologous chromosomes.
a. Certain alleles that are linked on the same chromosome tend to remain together during meiosis because they are positioned closer together on the chromosome.
b. This eventually led to the generalization that the probability that a cross over will disrupt the linkage of two genes is proportional to the distance that separates them.
B. Careful analysis of recombination patterns in experimental crosses has resulted in linkage mapping of gene locations.

8.6 Human Genetic Analysis
A. Constructing Pedigrees
1. Human genetics is difficult to study
a. We live under variable conditions in diverse environments.
b. Humans mate by chance and may, or may not, choose to reproduce.
c. Humans live as long as those who study them.
d. The small family size characteristic of human beings is not sufficient for meaningful statistical analysis.
2. A pedigree is a chart that shows genetic connections among individuals.
a. The analysis of family pedigrees provides data on inheritance patterns through several generations.
b. Knowledge of probability and Mendelian inheritance patterns is used in analysis of pedigrees to yield clues to a trait's genetic basis.
B. Some traits are deviations from the average.
1. *Genetic abnormality* is a term applied to a genetic condition that is a deviation from the usual, or average, and is not life-threatening.
2. *Genetic disorder* is more appropriately used to describe conditions that cause medical problems.
3. *Syndrome* is a recognized set of symptoms that characterize an abnormality or disorder.
4. *Genetic disease* is applied to those instances where a person's genes increase susceptibility to infection or weaken the response to it.

8.7 Examples of Human Inheritance Patterns
A. Autosomal Dominant Inheritance
1. The dominant allele is nearly always expressed even in heterozygotes.
2. If one parent is heterozygous and the other homozygous recessive, there is a 50 percent chance that any child will be heterozygous.
3. If the gene (and its resulting disorder) reduces the chance of surviving or reproducing, its frequency should decrease; but this may not happen due to mutations, nonreproductive effects, and post-reproductive onset.

- a. *Huntington disease* is serious degeneration of the nervous system with an onset from age 40 onward, by which time the gene has (usually) been passed from parent to offspring unknowingly.
- b. *Achondroplasia* (dwarfism) is a benign abnormality that does not affect persons to the point that reproduction is impossible, so the gene is passed on.
- B. Autosomal Recessive Inheritance
  1. The characteristics of this condition are:
     - a. Either parent can carry the recessive allele on an autosome.
     - b. Heterozygotes are symptom-free; homozygotes are affected.
     - c. Two heterozygous parents have a 50 percent chance of producing heterozygous children and a 25 percent chance of producing a homozygous recessive child. When both parents are homozygous, all children can be affected.
  2. *Galactosemia* (the inability to metabolize lactose) is an example of autosomal recessive inheritance in which a single gene mutation prevents manufacture of an enzyme needed in the conversion pathway.
- C. X-Linked Recessive Inheritance
  1. The characteristics of this condition are:
     - a. The mutated gene occurs only on the X chromosome.
     - b. Heterozygous females are phenotypically normal; males are more often affected because the single recessive allele (on the X chromosome) is not masked by a dominant gene on any other chromosome.
     - c. A normal male mated with a female heterozygote have a 50 percent chance of producing carrier daughters and a 50 percent chance of producing affected sons. In the case of a homozygous recessive female and a normal male, all daughters will be carriers and all sons affected.
  2. Two examples of X-linked inheritance are:
     - a. *Color blindness* is the inability to distinguish colors; mutated genes change the light-absorbing capacity of sensory receptors of the eyes.
     - b. *Duchenne muscular dystrophy* is a disorder characterized by rapid degeneration of muscles, starting early in life.
     - c. A serious X-linked recessive condition is *hemophilia A*, (affecting 1/7,000 males), which is the inability of the blood to clot because the genes do not code for the necessary clotting agent(s).

8.8 Structural Changes in Chromosomes
  - A. Major Categories of Structural Change
    1. *Duplication* occurs when a gene sequence is in excess of the normal amount.
    2. A *deletion* is the loss of a chromosome; an example is the loss of a portion of chromosome 5, causing a disorder called cri-du-chat with its symptoms of crying and mental retardation.
    3. An *inversion* alters the position and sequence of the genes so that gene order is reversed.
    4. A *translocation* occurs when a part of one chromosome is transferred to a nonhomologous chromosome.
  - B. Does Chromosome Structure Evolve?
    1. Changes in chromosome structure tend to be selected against rather than conserved over evolutionary time.
    2. However, gene regions for the polypeptide chains of hemoglobin have duplicated to produce different hemoglobins with different oxygen transporting efficiencies.

8.9   Change in the Number of Chromosomes
   A. Abnormal events occur before or during cell division, causing a change in the chromosome number.
      1. Aneuploidy is a condition in which the gametes or cells of an affected individual end up with *one extra* or *one less* chromosome than is normal.
      2. Polyploidy is the presence of *three or more* of each type of chromosome in gametes or cells. It is common in plants but fatal in humans.
         a. A chromosome number can change during mitotic or meiotic cell division or during the fertilization process.
         b. Tetraploid germ cells can result if cytoplasmic division does *not* follow normal DNA replication and mitosis.
      3. *Nondisjunction* at anaphase I or anaphase II frequently results in a change in chromosome number.
         a. If a gamete with an extra chromosome ($n + 1$) joins a normal gamete at fertilization, the diploid cell will be $2n + 1$; this condition is called *trisomy*.
         b. If an abnormal gamete is missing a chromosome, the zygote will be $2n - 1$; this condition is called *monosomy*.
   B. An Autosomal Change and Down Syndrome
      1. Down syndrome results from trisomy 21; about 1 in 1000 liveborns in North America are affected.
      2. Most children with Down syndrome show mental retardation, heart defects, and skeletal deformation.
      3. Down syndrome occurs more frequently in children born to women over age 35.
   C. Changes in the Sex Chromosome Number
      1. Female Sex Chromosome Abnormalities
         a. *Turner syndrome* involves females whose cells have only one X chromosome (designated XO).
            1) Affected individuals (1/2,500 to 10,000 girls) are infertile and have other phenotypic problems such as premature aging and shorter life expectancy.
            2) About 75 percent of the cases are due to nondisjunction in the father; furthermore, about 98 percent of all XO zygotes spontaneously abort.
         b. The XXX condition is an inheritance of multiple X chromosomes.
            1) About 1 in 1,000 females inherits 3, 4, or 5 X chromosomes.
            2) Most of these girls are taller and slimmer than average, but are fertile and fall within the normal range of appearance and social behavior.
      2. Male Sex Chromosome Abnormalities
         a. Klinefelter syndrome is caused by a nondisjunction that results in an extra X chromosome in the cells (XXY) of these affected males (1/500 to 2,000 liveborn males)
            1) About 67 percent of these result from nondisjunction in the mother.
            2) Sterility, slight mental retardation, and body feminization are symptoms.
         b. In the XYY condition the extra Y chromosome in these males (1/1,000) does not affect fertility, but they are taller than average and are slightly mentally retarded.

8.10   Some Prospects in Human Genetics
   A. Bioethical Questions
      1. Should we institute programs to identify people who may carry harmful alleles and recommend they not pass them on?
      2. Who decides which alleles are bad?

3. Should society bear the cost of treating genetic disorders, or have a say in whether an affected embryo should be aborted?

B. Choices Available

   1. Genetic Counseling

      a. Genetic counseling includes diagnosis of parental genotypes, pedigrees, and genetic testing for many metabolic disorders.

      b. Counselors help prospective parents evaluate risks in bringing a child into the world.

   2. Prenatal Diagnosis

      a. Amniocentesis is a procedure in which small amounts of fluid from inside the amnion sac are removed and analyzed for the presence of abnormal cells that have been shed from the fetus.

      b. Chorionic villi sampling (CVS) is also a sampling of cells from the fetus but in this case from the chorion; it can be done weeks earlier than amniocentesis.

      c. Fetoscopy uses a fiber-optic device with pulsed sound waves that scans the contents of the uterus.

   3. Preimplantation Diagnosis

      a. Relying on in-vitro fertilization for conception, couples may ask for an analysis to be done on the embryos before insertion into the female for implantation.

      b. Embryos with no detectable genetic defects are implanted; those with defects are discarded; again some may consider this a type of abortion.

   4. Phenotypic Treatments

      a. The symptoms of genetic disorders can be minimized by controlling the diet, adjusting to the environment, surgery, and hormone replacement therapy.

      b. Phenylketonuria can be controlled by restricting the intake of the amino acid phenylalanine.

   5. Regarding Abortion

      a. Ethical considerations arise when prenatal diagnosis reveals a serious problem. Will the parents consider induced abortion?

      b. They must weigh the severity of the disorder against their own strongly-held beliefs, plus face possible judgment from a polarized community.

Suggestions for Presenting the Material

- Students are usually naturally curious and interested in genetics. Start first with the simple examples of Mendel's monohybrid and dihybrid crosses before fielding questions on human traits such as height or eye color. Emphasize the remarkable nature of Mendel's work; remind the students that he knew nothing of chromosomes and their behavior, and that the term *gene* was not used until many years after Mendel's death.

- Use Mendel's experiments and his conclusions as real-life examples of the scientific method at work. Ask questions to make sure students understand monohybrid and dihybrid crosses.

- Use Figure 8.1 to ensure that students can visualize: homologous chromosomes, gene locus, alleles, and gene pairs.

- Students should be able to relate the events of meiosis to the concepts of segregation and independent assortment; if their understanding of meiosis is weak, they will have trouble doing this.

- Beginning with this chapter, students will be quick to ask questions about human traits, many of which are governed by mechanisms more complex than those postulated by Mendel. Answer questions in this area during (or after) the discussions of variations on Mendel's themes are presented in section 8.2.

- Students should be well grounded in their understanding of chromosomal structure before attempting to tackle the material in section 8.4 and beyond. The use of sketches, diagrams, and overhead transparencies will greatly assist in making this material as clear as possible.

- Students also must understand the events of meiosis or they will have difficulty comprehending crossing over and changes in chromosome number resulting from nondisjunction.

- Remind students that crossing over and genetic recombination create variability among sexually reproducing organisms; encourage students to think about the role this plays in evolution.

- To reduce the difficulty that students often have when learning about *sex-linked* genes, remind them that more precise terms for genes on either sex chromosome are *X-linked* or *Y-linked*. You may wish to look up information on how Thomas Hunt Morgan discovered sex linkage in fruit flies. Ask students to solve the genetics problems that deal with sex-linked genes at the end of the chapter. To assess how well students understand this material, work on as many of these problems together in class as time allows.

- Linkage is a concept that is sometimes confusing. Use as many drawings and diagrams as possible to show students what linkage means and how genes can be separated by crossing over. Include, if possible, gene maps of human chromosomes; students will be fascinated by them.

- Explain how karyotypes are prepared before showing a human karyotype; otherwise, students might think that human chromosomes naturally occur paired up as shown in Figure 8.18

- Students need practice to learn how the different types of inheritance (autosomal recessive, autosomal dominant, and X-linked recessive) actually influence the inheritance of a trait in real-life examples. Review, if necessary, basic genetic terms such as *homozygous, heterozygous, dominant,* and *recessive.* To see how well students understand these types of inheritance, begin by working through some simple examples of autosomal dominant inheritance (Figure 8.24), autosomal recessive inheritance (Figure 8.25), and X-linked recessive inheritance (Figure 8.26) at the blackboard; ask students to predict the possible phenotypic outcomes in each example.

- During lectures, use the genetics problems at the end of the chapter as they apply, working through one or two examples at the blackboard with your class as a whole and then asking students to complete the rest in class (possibly as part of a quiz) or on their own time. Students will enjoy the puzzle-solving aspects of pedigree analysis, while at the same time it will measure their level of understanding of the different types of inheritance.

- Many of the genetic disorders and abnormalities mentioned in this chapter are ones whose names students have heard but whose mechanisms of inheritance were unknown to them before reading this chapter. To lend more meaning to the conditions described here, ask students to think about the social and ethical problems associated with some of the diseases mentioned in this chapter.

Classroom and Laboratory Enrichment

- Ask groups of students to conduct coin tosses. Demonstrate the importance of large sample size by having the students vary the number of tosses before calculating variation from expected ratios.

- Distribute PTC tasting paper to your students, and calculate the number of tasters and nontasters in the classroom. Or use easily seen physical traits such as tongue rollers versus nontongue rollers or attached earlobes versus unattached earlobes to demonstrate traits governed by simple dominance/recessiveness.

- Prepare a biographical sketch of Mendel, including his education and practice as a monk. Enliven your presentation with as many slides of photos as you can find.

- Select a portion of the class to reenact the photo in Figure 8.15 (continuous variation in human height). If the quantity of students chosen does not provide the same distributions as in the photos in the text, use this as an illustration of how a greater number of trials/subjects/experiments tends to increase probability.

- Ask students (working individually or in small groups) to use chromosome kits (available from biological supply houses) to review chromosome structure, homologous pairing, crossing over, and independent assortment during gamete formation. If kits are unavailable, make your own chromosomes using a pop-it bead (or bead and cord) for each chromatid and a magnet for each centromere.

- Show karyotypes of males and females of different species without revealing the sex of the individual. Ask students to identify the sex.

- Discuss gene mapping in humans using an overhead transparency showing some of the known locations of particular genes.

- Use large, transparent chromosomes with labeled gene sequences to demonstrate deletions, duplications, inversions, and translocations on the overhead projector.

- If you have not done it previously, you may wish to demonstrate crossing over by using the colored string as explained in the Enrichment section for Chapter 7 (this manual).

- To dramatize independent assortment, use the following simulation of a cocktail party. Have several students pair off and line up as couples. Next, allow all participants to intermingle, but ask a few couples to switch partners and form new couples. (Explanatory comments: Those couples that did not switch but remained together represent genes linked together on the same chromosome; they travel together. Those that did switch were not linked and could independently assort themselves.)

- Ask a local health unit or testing lab if you can copy (anonymously of course) some karyotypes that show chromosomal defects. Show transparencies of these to the class, and ask if the students can spot the defect before it is revealed to them.

- Prepare a hand-drawn transparency to present the equivalency of the DNA molecule to a chromosome, which is subdivided into regions called genes.

- Prepare unlabeled overhead transparencies of karyotypes of normal individuals and individuals with chromosomal abnormalities such as Turner syndrome, Klinefelter syndrome, or Down syndrome. Ask students if the karyotype appears normal; if not, what is wrong?

- Ask a genetic counselor to speak to your class about his/her job.

- Hand out a partially completed pedigree, and show students how to assign squares and circles for their family. Then ask them to select a trait and complete the pedigree after surveying the family members for presence/absence of the trait.

- Draw a pedigree for an unnamed genetic condition. Ask students if the disorder is autosomal dominant, autosomal recessive, sex-linked dominant, or sex-linked recessive.

- Obtain from your local health unit several brochures that explain the various genetic problems that can be inherited. Make projection transparencies and show these to the class for their evaluation and information.

- From the same source mentioned above you may be able to obtain a list of those genetic diseases for which there is mandatory testing (usually of newborns) in your state. What voluntary testing programs are available?

Impacts, Issues Classroom Discussion Ideas

- Why do harmful genes remain in the human population?

- Can you think of some of the ethical questions involved in performing genetic research on humans? As our society learns more about genetic diseases, do you think couples who plan to have children should be forced to have genetic counseling or undergo amniocentesis?

- Your text refers to *phenotypic* treatments for genetic diseases. What are the hindrances to the perfecting of *genotypic* cures?

- Do you have any idea why the incidence of Down syndrome should increase with the mother's age?

- What is the difference between *genetic screening* and *genetic counseling*?

Additional Ideas for Classroom Discussion

- Describe the behavior of a particular trait with regard to its inheritance in a particular cross; then ask students to identify the genetic mechanism at work (simple dominance/recessiveness, incomplete dominance, codominance, environmental effects, epistasis, pleiotropy, continuous variation).

- List some human traits that you would guess are each governed by a single gene.

- Give several reasons why Mendel's pea plants were a good choice for an experimental organism in genetics. Give an example of an organism that would be a poor choice for genetic research and explain your choice.

- Describe several different crosses using organisms such as Mendel's pea plants. Then ask students to calculate phenotypic and genotypic ratios for each cross.

- Discuss the significance of Mendel's use of mathematical analysis in his research.

- Why do you think Mendel was not immediately recognized and given credit as the discoverer of a new area of biology—genetics?

- What conclusions would Mendel have come to if he had chosen *snapdragons* instead of *peas* for his study material?

- Why are the traits of (a) human skin color and (b) human height not suitable for explaining the concept of simple dominance?

- There are four possible blood types in the ABO system. But how many *different* alleles are in the human population for this marker? Be sure students can distinguish between the number of alleles in *each* human body cell and the number of alleles in the *entire* human population.

- What is the subtle difference between *incomplete dominance* and *codominance*?

- What is the significance of using upper- and lowercase versions of the same letter (for example, A and a) for the dominant and recessive trait, respectively, rather than a capital A for dominant and a B (or b) for recessive?

- If it becomes possible to easily and inexpensively choose the sex of your child, how will this change the male:female ratio among newborns in the United States? China? The world? Do you think it is ethically correct to select the sex of your children?

- Do you think that any of the traits Mendel followed in the garden pea were linked? Why or why not?

- If male and female offspring are born in a ratio of approximately 50:50, why do some couples have only boys or only girls?
- What is the distinction between the terms *gene* and *allele*?
- Why do individual chromosomes present at the conclusion of meiosis not have the same genetic constituency as they did before meiosis?
- If one sex of offspring tends to exhibit a trait more frequently than the other sex, this is an indication of what?
- What is the physical relationship of *genes* to *chromosomes* to *DNA*?
- What is the difference between a *translocation* of chromosomal segments and *crossing over*?
- Discuss the risks and benefits of amniocentesis. Would you elect to undergo this procedure (or urge your spouse to do so) if you had a history of genetic abnormalities in your family, or you or your spouse were over 35? Why or why not?
- Why is hemophilia more threatening to the life of a female sufferer than to a male?
- Why do so many people insist that girls cannot be red-green color blind (an X-linked inherited condition)?

How Would You Vote? Classroom Discussion Ideas

- Monitor the voting for the online question. As more options become available for parents to select the genetic makeup of their offspring, it is inevitable that many will chose to do so. Whether this is "right" or ethical will be debated even as the selection process proceeds. Some persons say that we should be allowed to be as selective of our children as we are about fruit at the grocery. Others draw the line and prefer to let nature or God be in control. What does your class say?

Term Paper Topics, Library Activities, and Special Projects

- What organisms are used most frequently in modern genetic research, and why?
- Describe the legal role now played by blood type evidence in paternity cases. Are other aspects of blood genetics (besides the ABO series) now used in deciding such cases?
- How do you think Charles Darwin's writings on his theory of evolution might have changed had he known of Mendel's work?
- Describe examples of how modern knowledge of genetics has led to improved agricultural strains of plants and animals.
- Search for details of Mendel's life and work. Seek answers to the allegations that his results may have been "too good."
- When studying genetics, it is easy to discover variations in plants and animals that result in organisms that, even though related, are very different in appearance. How does a researcher prove whether or not the variants are/are not the "same species"?
- Prepare an update on the extent of Marfan syndrome in the United States and the world. Include in your report the consequences to those persons who are recessive and those who are carriers.
- Sickle-cell anemia is another example of pleiotropy. This disease results from an abnormal hemoglobin in which valine is substituted for glutamate. Is this substitution random, or does it occur under the direction of the DNA that directs protein synthesis? Explain the mechanism.

- How do the sex chromosomes actually determine the sex of the individual? What are some of the characteristics governed by genes of the X and Y chromosomes?

- What human genes have been mapped?

- Because the sex of an individual is determined by the sperm at the moment of conception, is it possible to select the sex of a child by separating sperm with X chromosomes from those with Y chromosomes? Discuss recent experimental techniques that attempt to do this.

- How are human karyotypes prepared? Discover the laboratory steps required in this procedure (briefly described in Figure 8.18).

- Find specific examples of how irradiation, chemical action, or viral attack can cause chromosome breakage.

- Are any human traits Y-linked?

- Describe how (and why) artificially induced changes in chromosome number have been used to create new varieties of fruits and vegetables.

- As indicated above, the predicted ratio of newborns should show a 50:50 sex ratio. Ask a local hospital to provide statistics on the sex ratio in order to confirm or deny this prediction.

- Report on the progress being made on the Human Genome Project.

- Prepare a protocol for rearing *Drosophila* in the lab and making simple crosses.

- Construct a pedigree for your own family using a trait governed by simple Mendelian inheritance.

- Describe the history of the discovery and treatment of victims of any one of the human genetic abnormalities or disorders described in your text.

- Discover information about some of the tests now available for some genetic diseases (for example, Huntington's disorder) to determine if one is a carrier for that disease. What are some of the ethical questions raised by such tests?

- Learn more about hemophilia: Discuss its history, its role in the downfall of the Russian monarchy, and modern treatments for the disease.

- Contact your local health unit for statistics on the incidence of Down syndrome and other genetic disorders whose causes are known.

- Research the current treatment for hemophilia. Is there a difference in the regimen for males and females?

9

DNA STRUCTURE AND FUNCTION

Chapter Outline

Objectives

1. Understand how experiments using bacteria and viruses demonstrated that instructions for producing heritable traits are encoded in DNA.
2. Know the parts of a nucleotide and know how they are linked together to make DNA.
3. Understand how DNA is replicated and what materials are needed for replication.
4. How can mammals be cloned?

Key Terms

deoxyribonucleic acid, DNA	guanine	base pairing	DNA repair
bacteriophages	thymine	DNA replication	cloning
nucleotide	cytosine	DNA polymerases	artificial twinning
deoxyribose	pyrimidines	DNA ligases	
adenine	purines	semiconservative replication	
	x-ray diffraction images		

Lecture Outline

Here Kitty, Kitty, Kitty, Kitty, Kitty

A. Dolly was the first cloned mammal.
   1. A nucleus from a sheep udder cell was placed in an unfertilized egg that had its own nucleus gently removed.
   2. The embryo was gestated and produced a lamb, named Dolly, that was identical to the one from which the donor cell had been taken; she had no father's contribution of genes.
B. Cloning mammals is difficult.
   1. Not many nuclear transfers are successful; most individuals die before birth or shortly thereafter.
   2. Those that do survive have many problems with individual organs.
C. Cloning is controversial but it may be beneficial for producing desirable livestock, and for producing replacement cells and organs for people with degenerative diseases.

9.1   The Hunt for Fame, Fortune, and DNA
A. Early and Puzzling Clues
   1. Johann Miescher is credited with the discovery of DNA in the late 1800s.
   2. In 1928, Fred Griffith was working with S (pathogenic) and R (nonpathogenic) strains of a pneumonia-causing bacterium.
   3. He performed four experiments summarized here:
      a. Inject mice with R cells; mice lived.
      b. Inject mice with S cells; mice died; blood samples contained many live S cells.
      c. S cells were heat-killed then injected into mice; mice lived.
      d. Live R cells plus heat-killed S cells were injected into mice; mice died; live S cells were found in the blood.
   4. Some substance from the S cells had transformed the R cells.
      a. Both proteins and nucleic acids were candidates.
      b. In 1944, Oswald Avery showed that the substance was DNA.
B. Confirmation of DNA Function
   1. Viruses called bacteriophages use bacterial cells for reproduction.
   2. Because they consist of only a protein coat and a nucleic acid core, these viruses were used in experiments by Hershey and Chase to prove which of these constituents was the hereditary material (It was the nucleic acid).
      a. ^{35}S-labeled proteins in the bacteriophage coat *did not* enter the bacteria and thus were not participating in providing directions for new virus assembly.
      b. ^{32}P-labeled DNA in the viral core *did* enter the bacteria and direct new virus assembly.
C. Enter Watson and Crick
   1. Watson and Crick used numerous sources of data to build various models of DNA.
   2. In 1953 they discovered the double-helix structure of DNA.

9.2   DNA Structure and Function
A. How Are Nucleotides Arranged in DNA?
   1. DNA is composed of four kinds of nucleotides, each of which consists of:
      a. a five-carbon sugar—deoxyribose;
      b. a phosphate group;
      c. one of four bases—adenine (A), guanine (G), thymine (T), cytosine (C).

2. The nucleotides are similar, but T and C are single-ring pyrimidines; A and G are double-ring purines.
3. Edwin Chargaff, in 1949, noted two critical bits of data.
   a. The four kinds of nucleotide bases making up a DNA molecule differ in relative amounts from species to species.
   b. The amount of A = T, and the amount of G = C.
4. Rosalind Franklin used X-ray diffraction techniques to produce images of DNA molecules.
   a. DNA exists as a long, thin molecule of uniform diameter.
   b. The structure is highly repetitive.
   c. DNA is helical.
B. Fame and Glory
   1. Rosalind Franklin used techniques that directed x-rays at molecules to obtain x-ray diffraction images.
   2. She obtained many images of DNA and theorized about its structure but was not aggressive in publishing her results.
   3. Her coworker, Maurice Wilkins, passed some of her images to Watson and Crick and "the rest is history."
C. Patterns of Base Pairing
   1. The following features were incorporated into the Watson and Crick models.
      a. Single-ringed thymine was hydrogen bonded with double-ringed adenine, and single-ringed cytosine with double-ringed guanine, along the entire length of the molecule.
      b. The backbone was made of chains of sugar-phosphate linkages.
      c. The molecule was double stranded and looked like a ladder with a twist, forming a double helix.
   2. The base pairing is constant for all species but the sequence of base pairs in a nucleotide strand is different from one species to the next.

9.3   DNA Replication and Repair
A. How Is a DNA Molecule Duplicated?
   1. First, the two strands of DNA unwind and expose their bases.
      a. Then unattached nucleotides pair with exposed bases.
      b. Thus, replication results in DNA molecules that consist of one "old" strand and one "new" strand; this is designated "semiconservative replication."
   2. Several enzymes participate in replication:
      a. One kind of enzyme unwinds the two nucleotide strands.
      b. DNA polymerases attach free nucleotides to the growing strand.
      c. DNA ligases seal new short stretches of nucleotides into one continuous strand.
B. Monitoring and Fixing the DNA
   1. DNA polymerases, DNA ligases and other enzymes engage in DNA repair.
   2. DNA polymerases "proofread" the new bases for mismatched pairs, which are replaced with correct bases.
   3. Sometimes repair processes fail and a mutation results.

9.4   Using DNA to Clone Mammals
A. Geneticists have been cloning large animals by artificial twinning for some time.
   1. The embryos are produced by in vitro fertilization, allowed to develop to the eight-cell stage, and then separated.

2. Small clusters of cells are implanted into surrogate mothers, where they grow into identical clones.
    B. Cloning with a differentiated cell from an adult, whose traits are already known, is more difficult.
        1. The nucleus from a differentiated cell, say liver, replaces an unfertilized egg's nucleus by microinjection.
        2. The cell is induced to divide by chemicals or electric shock.
        3. Soon a cluster of embryonic cells is implanted into a surrogate mother.

Suggestions for Presenting the Material

- This chapter amplifies the information on nucleic acids presented at the close of Chapter 2. Depending on the amount of information you presented in your lectures at that time, some of this chapter could be repetitious.

- For best success in presenting this chapter, use diagrams, models, and overhead transparencies when discussing the structure and replication of DNA.

- Students find it hard to understand and identify the components of DNA, so begin this section of the text by making sure that they have clear mental pictures of deoxyribose (the five-carbon sugar in DNA), phosphate groups, and the four nitrogen-containing bases. Briefly show overheads of the molecular structures of each of these three major players, and then introduce the term *nucleotide*.

- Ask students to think about the benefits and drawbacks of DNA as a genetic material.

Classroom and Laboratory Enrichment

- Use large three-dimensional models to show DNA structure.

- Ask students to work in teams of two. Give each student a set of labeled paper shapes representing the sugars, phosphate groups, and each of the four bases present in DNA. Ask each student to construct a short segment of a DNA strand while their partner builds the complementary strand of the DNA double helix. Then ask students to demonstrate the semiconservative replication of DNA.

- Use a video to demonstrate the semiconservative nature of DNA replication.

- DNA is described as a "double helix" or "twisted ladder." An inexpensive device that can show this structure very well is a plastic parakeet ladder that is flexible enough to be twisted from "ladder" configuration to "helix."

- Prepare a chronological listing of the dates, people, and significant contributions to the discovery of the structure of DNA.

- In the Term Paper Topics, Library Activities, and Special Projects section for Chapter 7 of this manual, mention is made of a glaring error in the popular high school text *Modern Biology* by Moon, Mann, and Otto. Another distinction in that 1956 edition was the complete absence of any mention of DNA. Use this as a dramatic example of how much we know now compared to then.

- Redraw Figure 9.5 ("exploded" DNA structure) so that each component is on separate acetate sheets bound at the edge. To use, simply lay down each sheet as you "assemble" DNA. (You can probably make this visual aid by some clever use of a copy machine.) Perhaps you can find an animation of this also.

Impacts, Issues Classroom Discussion Ideas

- Why are so many nuclear transfers in cloning experiments not successful?
- Why don't the *different species* of single-celled and multicellular organisms have *different nucleic acids* for coding hereditary information? Why do they all use DNA as the hereditary material?
- Is cloning necessary? Is it desirable? Is it unethical? Is it just "cool"?

Additional Ideas for Classroom Discussion

- What are some reasons why DNA is double-stranded instead of single-stranded?
- When during the cell cycle does DNA replication occur?
- What are some advantages of semiconservative replication?
- What experiments done before the structure of DNA was known showed that nucleic acid was the carrier of heredity?
- How did the Hershey and Chase experiment settle the question of which molecule—DNA or protein—carries heredity?
- Why should the term *DNA relative* replace the more popular term *blood relative* when referring to human kinship?
- Which of the following is a more likely source of altered DNA sequences?
  a. New copy has error made during replication from correct original.
  b. New copy has error faithfully copied from incorrect original.
- A *casual* reading of any one of a number of biology texts would imply that Fred Griffith was a pioneer in DNA research. Is this an accurate assessment?
- What would the shape of a DNA molecule be like if purines paired with purines and pyrimidines paired with pyrimidines?

How Would You Vote? Classroom Discussion Ideas

- Monitor the voting for the online question. Have the students explore the ramifications of banning research on animal cloning. Can the ban be enforced by a new "cloning police"? How would scientists get around the ban?

Term Paper Topics, Library Activities, and Special Projects

- What happens if DNA is damaged? How does a cell "recognize" an error in base pairing? Does an organism have ways of repairing such damage?
- Describe the research tools (such as radioactive labeling) that have been used in the past and are being used today to learn about DNA structure and function.
- Describe how the semiconservative nature of DNA replication was discovered.
- Learn more about the collaborative nature of scientific discovery using the discovery of DNA as an example. Could such a discovery have been made at the time by only one individual working alone?

- The shape and structure of bacteriophages is reminiscent of a piece of hardware designed for outer space exploration. To make it more visually appealing, construct a model from inexpensive materials.
- Prepare a synopsis of James Watson's account of the discovery of DNA as recorded in the book *The Double Helix*, published by Atheneum.
- Rosalind Franklin collected data critical to the elucidation of DNA structure. However, she is hardly mentioned in some textbook accounts. Locate a biography of her, and speculate on why she is lesser known than her collaborators.
- Using the diagram in Figure 9.7 as a starting point, show how copies of DNA from your great-grandparents are present in you.

Possible Responses to *Critical Thinking* Questions

1. The replication would look like this (dark lines = ^{15}N; light lines = ^{14}N)

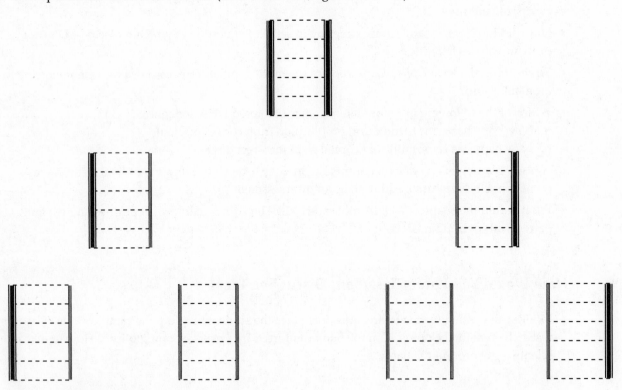

2. When DNA is replicated, the DNA strands separate at a replication fork. One strand is designated the "leading strand," the other the "lagging strand." The leading strand has a 3' end opposite the fork and is copied sequentially from 5' to 3' in a straightforward manner. However, on the lagging strand the direction of copying appears to be *reversed*, but indeed it is proceeding in the required 5' to 3' also, *but in small sections*. Eventually, the segments will be linked by DNA ligase to form a complete strand.

3. While it is true that cells have repair mechanisms to fix structurally altered of discontinuous DNA, these may not be 100 percent fail-safe. Perhaps the repair enzymes might come upon a mistake that they have not encountered before and therefore have no workable repair mechanism. Or perhaps the repair enzymes themselves have been produced from mutated genes and are therefore mutants.

4. Cloning an extinct animal sounds like a dream, but it may become a reality. Perhaps the greatest benefit would be to see a living, functioning wooly mammoth rather than some dry bones. We could fill in all the details about its life that are now only speculations. Technically, it would be a challenge. Ethically, I don't know if we should be tampering with animals that have been so long gone.

10

GENE EXPRESSION AND CONTROL

Chapter Outline

Objectives

1. Know how the structure and behavior of DNA determine the structure and behavior of the three forms of RNA during transcription.
2. Know how the structure and behavior of the three forms of RNA determine the primary structure of polypeptide chains during translation.
3. Know that there are exceptions to the universality of the genetic code and know how geneticists try to account for their existence.
4. Know the various ways that gene activity (replication and transcription) are turned on (activated) and off (inactivated).
5. Understand how operon controls regulate gene expression in prokaryotes.
6. Understand how differentiation proceeds by selective gene expression during development.
7. Be able to list and explain the levels of control in eukaryotes.

Key Terms

genes

transcription

translation

messenger RNA

ribosomal RNA

ribosomes

transfer RNA

ribose

uracil

RNA polymerases

promoter

mRNA transcripts

introns

exons

codons

genetic code

anticodon

wobble effect

initiation

elongation

termination

polysome

gene mutations

base-pair substitution

frameshift mutation

insertions

deletions

transposons

ionizing radiation

nonionizing radiation

alkylating agents

regulatory proteins

negative control

positive control

promoter

enhancers

methylation

operator

repressor

lac operon

lactose intolerance

cell differentiation

homeotic genes

antennapedia

X chromosome

 inactivation

Barr body

mosaic tissue effect

anhidrotic ectodermal

 dysplasia

dosage compensation

Lecture Outline

Ricin and Your Ribosomes

A. Ricin could be a biochemical weapon.

 1. It is most concentrated in the seeds of the castor oil plant.

 2. It is very poisonous and is a product of castor oil production.

B. Ricin inactivates ribosomes.

 1. It takes adenine bases off the RNA on the ribosome.

 2. The ribosome "workbenches" are destroyed and protein synthesis stops; death!

10.1 Making and Controlling the Cell's Proteins

A. DNA is like a book of instructions in each cell.

 1. The instructions are written in the alphabet of A, T, G, and C. But merely knowing the letters does not tell us how the genes work.

 2. DNA consists of two strands of nucleotides twisted together in a double helix.

 a. All DNA is composed of nucleotide subunits utilizing the same four bases, but the base sequence differs from species to species.

 b. Genetic information is coded in the sequence itself as sets of three bases.

 3. Each gene is a linear stretch of DNA nucleotides that codes for the assembly of amino acids into a polypeptide chain.

B. Proteins are built according to precise instructions.

 1. The path from genes to proteins has two steps:

 a. In *transcription,* molecules of RNA are produced on the DNA templates in the nucleus.

 b. In *translation,* RNA molecules shipped from the nucleus to the cytoplasm are used as templates for polypeptide assembly.

 2. The overall plan is expressed thus:

transcription   *translation*

DNA — — — — — — —> **RNA** — — — — — —> **proteins**

10.2　How Is RNA Transcribed from DNA?
   A. Three Classes of RNA
      1. *Messenger RNA* (mRNA) carries the "blueprint" for protein assembly to the ribosome.
      2. *Ribosomal RNA* (rRNA) combines with proteins to form ribosomes upon which polypeptides are assembled.
      3. *Transfer RNA* (tRNA) brings the correct amino acid to the ribosome and pairs up with an mRNA code for that amino acid.
   B. The Nature of Transcription
      1. RNA differs from DNA in two ways:
         a. RNA uses ribose sugar, not deoxyribose.
         b. RNA bases are A, G, C, and URACIL (U).
      2. Transcription differs from replication in three ways:
         a. Only *one* region of *one* DNA strand is used as a template.
         b. RNA polymerase is used instead of DNA polymerase.
         c. RNA is single stranded; DNA is double.
      3. Transcription begins when RNA polymerase binds to a promoter region (a base sequence at the start of a gene) and then moves along to the end of a gene; an RNA transcript is the result.
   C. Finishing Touches on mRNA Transcripts
      1. Newly formed mRNA is an unfinished molecule, not yet ready for use.
      2. mRNA transcripts are modified before leaving the nucleus.
         a. Noncoding portions (*introns*) are snipped out, and actual coding regions (*exons*) are spliced together to produce the mature transcript.
         b. The 5' end is *capped* with a special nucleotide that may serve as a "start" signal for translation.
         c. A "poly-A tail" of about 100–200 adenines is added to the 3' end.

10.3　Deciphering mRNA
   A. Like a sentence, an mRNA is a linear sequence of genetic words spelled out with an alphabet of four nucleotides.
      1. Both DNA and its RNA transcript are linear sequences of nucleotides carrying the hereditary code.
      2. Every three bases (a triplet) specifies an amino acid to be included into a growing polypeptide chain; the complete set of triplets is called the *genetic code.*
         a. Each base triplet in RNA is called a *codon.*
         b. The genetic code consists of 61 triplets that specify amino acids and three that serve to stop protein synthesis.
         c. AUG (specifies methionine) is the "start" codon.
         d. With few exceptions, the genetic code is universal for all forms of life.
   B. Other RNAs help in translating the genetic code into a polypeptide chain.
      1. Each kind of tRNA has an *anticodon* that is complementary to a specific mRNA codon; each tRNA also carries one specific amino acid.
      2. After the mRNA arrives in the cytoplasm, an anticodon on a tRNA bonds to the codon on the mRNA; thus a correct amino acid is brought into place.
      3. The first two bases of the anticodon must pair up with the codon by the usual rules of base pairing (A with U and G with C), but there is some latitude in the pairing of the third base (called the "wobble effect").
      4. A ribosome has two subunits (each composed of rRNA and proteins) that perform together only during translation.

10.4   From mRNA to Protein
    A. Translation proceeds through three stages:
        1. In *initiation,* a complex forms in this sequence: initiator tRNA + small ribosomal subunit + mRNA + large ribosomal subunit.
        2. In *elongation,* a start codon on mRNA defines the reading frame; a series of tRNAs deliver amino acids in sequence by codon-anticodon matching; a peptide bond joins each amino acid to the next in sequence.
        3. In *termination,* a stop codon is reached and the polypeptide chain is released into the cytoplasm or enters the cytomembrane system for further processing.
    B. What happens to the new polypeptides?
        1. The three steps just outlined can be repeated many times on the same mRNA because several ribosomes may be moving along the mRNA at the same time (polysome).
        2. Some polypeptides join the cytoplasm's pool of free proteins; others enter the rough ER of the cytomembrane system.

10.5   Mutated Genes and Their Protein Products
    A. A gene mutation is a change in one to several bases in the nucleotide sequence of DNA, which can result in a change in the protein synthesized.
    B. Common Mutations
        1. Mutations can result from base-pair substitutions, insertions ("frameshift mutation"), and deletions.
        2. They can also result when DNA regions (called transposons) move from one location to another in the same DNA molecule of a different one.
    C. How Do Mutations Arise?
        1. Mutations are rare, chance events, but fortunately special enzymes correct most of the mistakes.
        2. Mutations can be caused by mutagens such as ionizing radiation (gamma and X-rays), ultraviolet radiation, and chemicals such as alkylating agents, which act as carcinogens.
    D. The Proof Is in the Protein
        1. If a mutation arises in a somatic cell, it will affect only the owner of that cell and will not be passed on to offspring.
        2. If however the mutation arises in a gamete, it may be passed on and thus enter the evolutionary arena.
        3. Either kind of mutation may prove to be harmful, beneficial, or neutral in its effects.

10.6   Controls Over Gene Expression
    A. Common Controls
        1. Even though all body cells have the same genetic instructions, only a small number of genes will be active at any given time depending on responses to chemical signals and built-in control systems.
        2. Regulatory proteins interact with DNA, RNA, or actual gene products.
            a. In *negative control,* a regulatory protein binds to the DNA to block transcription; it can be removed by an inducer.
            b. In *positive control,* a regulatory protein binds to the DNA and promotes initiation of transcription.
            c. In chemical modification, regions of newly replicated DNA can be shut down by methylation and access to genes can be controlled by acetylation of histone proteins that organize DNA.

B. Bacterial Control of the Lactose Operon
1. *E. coli* bacteria (common in the human digestive tract) can metabolize lactose because of a series of genes that code for lactose-digesting enzymes.
    a. The three genes that code for these enzymes are preceded by a promoter and an operator—all together called an operon.
    b. A regulator gene nearby codes for a repressor protein that binds to the operator when lactose concentrations are low and effectively blocks RNA polymerase's access to the promoter.
2. When milk is consumed the lactose binds to the repressor, changing its shape and effectively removing its blockage of the promoter; thus RNA polymerase can now initiate transcription of the genes.
C. Eukaryotic Gene Controls
1. Controls over gene expression allow cells to respond to changing environmental conditions.
    a. Gene expression controls also govern cell differentiation in complex eukaryotes.
    b. Cells become more specialized when they start using a unique fraction of their genes.
2. Here are two examples of eukaryotic gene controls:
    a. Homeotic Genes and Body Plans
        1) Homeotic genes interact with one another and with control elements to bring about the formation of tissues and organs in accordance with the basic body plan.
        2) These genes code for regulatory proteins that can bind to promoters and enhancers to control transcription.
    b. X Chromosome Inactivation
        1) In mammalian females, the gene products of only one X chromosome are needed; the other is condensed and inactive—called a Barr body.
        2) Because in some cells the paternal X chromosome is inactivated, while in other cells the maternal X chromosome is inactivated, each adult female is a mosaic of X-linked traits, called mosaic tissue effect.
        3) This mosaic effect is seen in human females affected by anhidrotic ectodermal dysplasia in which a mutant gene on one X chromosome results in patches of skin with no sweat glands.
        4) Dosage compensation is the name for the process that shuts down one X of the female so that the overall expression of the remaining X of the female is equivalent to the lone X of the male.

Suggestions for Presenting the Material

- The subject of protein synthesis, which begins this chapter, is a difficult one even when presented on an introductory level. Begin by very briefly summarizing the process using the same linear sequence used by Francis Crick in 1956 (known as the "Central Dogma" and shown in section 10.1). You may also want to review protein structure (Chapter 2).

- Students should be able to achieve a good understanding of protein synthesis if they begin by visualizing it as two major steps, *transcription* and *translation*, rather than getting lost in complex details. The events of protein synthesis can be effectively presented with visual aids such as overhead transparencies, videos, and models. Students need to have some kind of mental picture in order to understand what happens during the making of a protein.

- The chapter continues with discussions of the expression of genes and gene products, assuming a firm grasp of the protein synthesis mechanisms. Terms such as *DNA, mRNA, transcription,* and *translation* must be familiar before continuing.

- Emphasize to the students that the control of gene expression is an extremely complex subject area, one which is best approached by first studying some fairly simple and well-understood examples in prokaryotes.

- Give students opportunities to learn and use new words such as *promoter, operator,* and *operon.* Gene control among eukaryotes will be easier to understand if students view it as a series of levels (Figure 10.14).

Classroom and Laboratory Enrichment

- Use models, transparencies, and videos to show protein synthesis.

- Give students a "dictionary" of the genetic code (Figure 10.4) either as a handout or as an overhead transparency. Then ask them to identify the codons within a linear stretch of mRNA and tell what amino acid each codon will specify (see Figure 10.2). This can also be part of a quiz.

- Using the overhead transparency of Figure 10.8, cover several of the labels and ask students to review the steps of protein synthesis aloud in class.

- The following items may help your students remember the difference between "transcription" and "translation":
  a. *Transcription* involves the transfer of information from one form to another *in the same* language, for example, an office memo in shorthand transcribed into typed copy but both in English; likewise a section of genetic code in DNA is copied to RNA (both nucleic acids).
  b. *Translation* is the transfer of information in *one language* to *another language,* for example, a story in French translated into English; likewise genetic code in RNA (nucleic acid) is transferred to amino acids (protein).

- As an aid to the understanding of protein synthesis, the following analogy in which the process is compared to the construction of a building may be useful.
  a. DNA "sealed" in the nucleus................................. a. Master blueprints that never leave the architect's office
  b. mRNA that leaves nucleus to go to ribosome ..... b. Blueprint copies that are taken to the job site
  c. Ribosomes and rRNA..c. The construction site
  d. Enzymes...d. Construction workers
  e. tRNA carrying amino acids......................................e. Trucks carrying materials
  f. Amino acids...f. Building materials

- Use visual aids such as overhead transparencies to illustrate the lactose operon (Figure 10.13).

- Modify the overhead transparency of Figure 10.13 (lactose operon) by obscuring the labels. Ask students to identify each item on the figure.

Impacts, Issues Classroom Discussion Ideas

- Why are ribosomes essential to protein synthesis?
- How might alterations in DNA structure be harmful to a species? How might such alterations be beneficial? What type of genetic change is most important for evolution?

Additional Ideas for Classroom Discussion

- Ask students to compare and contrast: transcription and translation; codons and anticodons; rRNA, mRNA, and tRNA.
- Why is transcription necessary? Why don't cells use their DNA as a direct model for protein synthesis?
- Describe the three stages of translation.
- In what ways are the instructions encoded in DNA sometimes altered?
- In most species, mutation is usually not considered an important evolutionary force. Why?
- Using the blackboard or overhead transparency, demonstrate how gene mutations such as a base-pair substitution, a frameshift, or a transposition will produce abnormal proteins.
- In what ways does RNA differ from DNA?
- Which of the RNAs is "reusable"?
- Why do you think DNA has *introns,* which are transcribed but removed before translation begins?
- If all DNA is made of the same basic building units (sugar, phosphate, and nitrogenous bases), then how can DNA differ in, say, a human and a bacterium?
- This chapter refers to the participants and process involved in protein synthesis as if they have been *seen* doing their work; have they? How then do we know all of this information is accurate?
- How can you explain the occurrence of birth defects (caused by altered genes) in children and grandchildren of the victims of the atomic bombs that destroyed Hiroshima and Nagasaki, Japan, when the victims themselves were only mildly affected?
- Scientists know much more about controls over gene expression among prokaryotes than among eukaryotes. What are some reasons why research in this area is more difficult among eukaryotic species than it is among prokaryotic species?
- Distinguish between negative gene control and positive gene control.
- What is the role of gene control in causing cancer? How are some viruses known to be linked to cancer?
- Do you think cancer-causing genes could someday be repaired?
- What would be the hypothetical effect on the lactose operon of a modified lactose molecule? Do you think it would still bind to the repressor?
- What is the "economic" advantage to a prokaryotic cell of possessing inducible enzymes?
- There is far more DNA in eukaryotic cells than scientists can label as "necessary." Why do *you* think it is there? Do you think its function is eluding us for now?
- Why do eukaryotic cells "need" *histones, nucleosomes,* and *looped domains*?

How Would You Vote? Classroom Discussion Ideas

- Monitor the voting for the online question. Invite your students to consider the value of any mass immunization versus the risks. Remind them that even with a long history of successful immunization for such common diseases as measles, there are still minimal risks. What greater challenges face programs that do not have such a long history?

Term Paper Topics, Library Activities, and Special Projects

- Describe experiments performed by Khorana, Nirenberg, Ochoa, Holley, and others to decipher the genetic code.

- Discover why repeated applications of a single drug or pesticide can result in resistance among bacterial strains and species of insects. Why does this pose a problem? What steps can be taken to avoid resistant strains of pathogenic bacteria and disease-carrying insects?

- What kinds of substances act as chemical mutagens? What are some of the effects mutagenic substances can have? What kinds of mutagenic agents might be found in industrial waste?

- Prepare a visual aid chart that graphically depicts the series of errors (in DNA, mRNA, tRNA, amino acids) that lead to the production of the abnormal hemoglobin in sickle-cell anemia.

- The progress in molecular biology has proceeded from deciphering genetic codes to the construction of man-made genes by machine. Report on the construction and use applications of such devices.

- Investigate reports of "gene replacement" as a preventative against possible genetic abnormalities. In what organism has it been tried? Was it successful? What are the difficulties of this procedure?

- Learn more about current research efforts attempting to uncover the mysteries of differentiation.

- Describe the operon and its function.

- Learn more about oncogenes and cancer.

- Discover more about the discovery and diagnostic uses of the Barr body in female mammalian cells.

- What are some common substances that act as mutagens? How are some of these mutagens known to cause cancer? Are there substances that will block the effects of mutagens?

- Learn more about tumor cell lines used to study cancerous cell growth in vitro in the laboratory.

- Locate the original article by Francois Jacob and Jacques Monod proposing the lac operon. How have the details changed?

- Likewise, see if you can locate the original research publications of Murray Barr and Mary Lyon. Notice the dates of these publications. Were they before or after the publication of DNA structure by Watson and Crick in 1953?

Possible Responses to *Critical Thinking* Questions

1. This is the given DNA segment (hyphens have been added for easier reading):

    5'-GGT-TTC-TTC-AAG-AGA-3'

    First, we must transcribe the DNA to mRNA:

    5'-CCA-AAG-AAG-UUC-UCU-3'

    Next, we consult Figure 10.4 (genetic code) to see which amino acid matches each codon to produce the finished amino acid sequence of the polypeptide:

    proline-lysine-lysine-phenylalanine-serine

2. Antisense RNA is a molecule of RNA that is complementary to mRNA and will bind to it. When this happens, the double-stranded RNA hybrid inhibits translation of the mRNA to protein. This could be used to prevent the production of the protein coats for SARS viruses.

3. Perhaps binding of carcinogenic products of cigarette smoke can cause an error in transcription to mRNA. We know that incorrect codons will match with incorrect anticodons of tRNA, leading to an incorrect sequence in the finished protein. Perhaps one or more of these proteins, either structural or enzymatic, could trigger cancerous growth.

4. The parents had nonmutated genes, so we know that they did not pass the defect to their children. Therefore, the mutation had to have occurred either in one of the gametes or possibly in the cells of the early embryo. The transposon would have moved a gene from one chromosome to another, where it was transcribed and translated differently than it normally would be.

5. Because cc is a clone from one cell of Rainbow, the particular cell used happened to have the allele for black color active, but not orange. Perhaps another cell would produce a cc.2 with brown fur.

11

STUDYING AND MANIPULATING GENOMES

Chapter Outline

Objectives

1. Explain the types of genetics experiments that nature has been performing for billions of years.
2. Understand what plasmids are and how they may be used to insert new genes into recombinant DNA molecules.
3. Know how DNA can be cleaved, spliced, cloned, and sequenced.
4. Understand how one organism can produce the products of another.
5. Be aware of several limits and possibilities for future research in genetic engineering.

Key Terms

restriction enzyme
"sticky" end
DNA ligase
recombinant DNA
plasmids
cloning vector
reverse transcriptase
cDNA

library
genomic library
cDNA library
probe
nucleic acid
 hybridization
polymerase chain
 reaction, PCR

primers
DNA sequencing
gel electrophoresis
DNA fingerprint
tandem repeats
recombinant DNA
Human Genome Project

automated DNA
 sequencing
genomics
human gene therapy
transgenic
eugenic engineering
xenotransplantation

Lecture Outline

Golden Rice or Frankenfood?
A. Many of the world's children suffer from vitamin A deficiency.
 1. Three genes have been transferred into rice plants that direct the plants to make beta-carotene.
 2. Eating just 300 grams of this "golden rice" will prevent vitamin A deficiency.
B. Not everyone is pleased and many are protesting.
 1. Humans have been experimenting with new breeds of organisms for thousands of years.
 2. Nature has been doing so too by mutation, crossing over, and gene transfers between species.
 3. Maybe it is the speed and scope of the new genetic engineering work that arrests our attention.

11.1 A Molecular Toolkit
 A. The Scissors: Restriction Enzymes
 1. Bacteria possess restriction enzymes whose usual function is to cut apart foreign DNA molecules.
 2. Each enzyme cuts only at sites that possess a specific base sequence.
 3. The wide variety of restriction enzymes and their specificity makes it possible to study the genome of a particular species.
 a. Many times the "sticky end" that results from the cut will pair up with another DNA fragment cut by the same enzyme.
 b. DNA fragments produced by restriction enzymes are treated with DNA ligase to splice the DNA fragments (from same or different species) together to form a recombinant DNA molecule.
 B. Cloning Vectors
 1. Plasmids are circular DNA molecules in bacteria that carry only a few genes and can replicate independently of the single "main" chromosome.
 2. Modified plasmids that are capable of accepting, replicating, and delivering DNA to another host cell are called cloning vectors.
 3. When the plasmid is replicated, any foreign DNA that might have become incorporated into it is also replicated, producing a *DNA clone*.
 C. cDNA Cloning
 1. Even after a desired gene has been isolated and amplified, it may not be translated into functional protein by the bacteria because introns (noncoding regions) are still present.

2. Researchers minimize this problem by using cDNA, which is made from "mature" mRNA transcripts.
   a. The cDNA is made from mRNA by reverse transcriptase.
   b. The cDNA can be inserted into a plasmid for amplification.

11.2   Haystacks to Needles
   A. Isolating Genes
      1. A library is a collection of cells that host fragments of DNA from a particular organism.
         a. Cells in a genomic library contain the organism's entire set of genetic material.
         b. A cDNA library is derived from mRNA, so it is free of introns.
      2. The library will contain some DNA clones with a particular gene of interest along side many other clones that do not. How can we identify the one we want?
         a. DNA probes, short DNA sequences assembled from radioactive nucleotides, can pair with parts of the gene to be studied.
         b. This nucleic acid hybridization technique can be used with other procedures to select cells and their DNA, which may be of interest to the researcher.
   B. PCR
      1. The polymerase chain reaction (PCR) can be used to make millions of copies of cDNA.
      2. What is needed for the reaction?
         a. Primers are short nucleotide sequences that are made in the laboratory.
         b. They are recognized by DNA polymerases as the START tags for building complementary sequences of DNA dictated by computer programs stored in the machines.
      3. What are the reaction steps?
         a. Researchers mix primers, DNA polymerase, cellular DNA from an organism, and free nucleotides.
         b. Precise temperature cycles cause the DNA strands to separate, exposing the bases.
         c. Primers become positioned on the exposed nucleotides to form new copies of the original DNA.
         d. Each round of reactions doubles the number of DNA molecules to eventually produce billions of molecules from very tiny amounts of original DNA.

11.3   DNA Sequencing
   A. Currently, laboratories use automated DNA sequencing to determine the unknown sequence of bases in a DNA sample.
      1. The machine builds DNA molecules but uses eight kinds of bases: four normal and four that are modified to fluoresce in laser light.
      2. When a modified base is incorporated, DNA synthesis is halted, producing tagged fragments of different lengths.
   B. The automated DNA sequencer separates the sets of fragments by gel electrophoresis.
      1. The "tag" base at the end of each fragment in the set is identified by the laser beam.
      2. The computer program in the machine assembles the information from all the nucleotides in the sample to reveal the entire DNA sequence.

11.4   First Just Fingerprints, Now DNA Fingerprints
   A. A DNA fingerprint is a unique array of base sequences in each organism that is slightly different form the DNA in other organisms—even close relatives.
      1. The technique focuses on tandem repeats, copies of the same short DNA sequences, which are highly variable in their repetition from one person to the next.

2. The differences can be detected by gel electrophoresis, a technique that pulls molecules through a block of gelatin by electric current; different size molecules travel at different speeds.

B. DNA fingerprinting is now a widely accepted and valuable tool to either prove or disprove guilt in criminal cases.

11.5   Tinkering With the Molecules of Life
A. Emergence of Molecular Biology
1. Watson and Crick revealed the structure of DNA and how it could replicate, but more tools were needed to discover the full story of DNA's function.
2. In 1972, Paul Berg made recombinant DNA by fusing genetic material from different species, a technique that allowed the isolation of subsets of DNA for study.
   a. Could super pathogens be created by accident?
   b. Could a new form of life be created?
   c. Extensive laboratory precautions were put into place.
3. In 1977 a method for sequencing cloned DNA fragments was developed.
B. The Human Genome Project
1. Determining the sequence of bases in all of a human's DNA seemed a daunting task, but automated (robotic) sequencing and PCR came to the rescue.
2. In 1988, NIH launched the federal effort to complete the sequencing.
3. In 1998, Craig Venter declared his company could sequence the genome faster and cheaper, and he did.
4. Sequencing the 21,000 genes of the human genome was officially completed in 2003.
C. Genomics
1. *Structural* genomics deals with the actual mapping and sequencing of genomes of individuals.
2. *Comparative* genomics is concerned with finding evolutionary relationships among groups of organisms.
3. Genomics has the potential for human gene therapy—the transfer of modified genes into a person's body cells to correct a genetic defect.

11.6   Practical Genetics
A. Designer Plants
1. Farmers are turning to genetically engineering crop plants to produce more food at reduced cost.
   a. Many plant species can be regenerated from cultured cells; some can be hybridized to make transgenic plants with enhanced pesticide resistance.
   b. Genetically modified plants also yield more crop per acre; certain transgenic tomato plants can be grown in salty soils typical in high irrigation plots.
2. An early experiment showed that a plasmid from a bacterium that normally causes tumors in plants could be modified by replacing the tumor gene with desirable genes.
   a. Such modified bacteria have been injected into plant cells where they expressed their "foreign" genes.
   b. Genetically modified crop plants could increase food production or grow with greater resistance to pest attack.
B. Genetically Engineered Bacteria
1. Microorganisms can produce useful substances such as human insulin and blood-clotting factors.
2. Genetically engineered bacteria can clean up messes such as oil spills.

3. Knowing about genes may help us devise counterattacks against rapidly mutating pathogens.
   C. Barnyard Biotech
      1. In 1982, the rat gene for somatotropin production was introduced into mouse eggs; the mice that subsequently expressed the rat gene grew larger than their littermates.
      2. Transgenic animals are used for research, as in the case of "knock out" mice, in which targeted genes are inactivated by using recombination techniques to give clues as to the usual gene function.
      3. Genetically engineered animals are also sources of pharmacological products.
         a. Rabbits produce interleukin-2; cattle produce collagen used to repair the skeleton; goats produce antithrombin used to treat blood clotting disorders.
         b. Although there are ethical concerns, most scientists believe that the present research is simply an extension of thousands of years of acceptable barnyard breeding practices.

11.7   Weighing the Benefits and Risks
   A. More than 15,500 genetic disorders affect newborns.
      1. In 1998 a virus was used to insert replacement copies of a gene that would cure a child of severe immune deficiency.
      2. Ten of the 11 children had a positive outcome, but cancer and one death also resulted.
   B. Correcting genetic disorders seems like a socially acceptable goal.
      1. Eugenic engineering is the idea of being able to select desirable human traits, including behaviors.
      2. How much would potential parents pay to engineer tall, blue-eyed, fair-skinned children of super intelligence and athleticism?
   C. Knockout Cells and Organ Factories
      1. Xenotransplantation is the transferring of an organ from one species to another.
      2. Pigs can be engineered to lack certain genes that would cause rejection problems when their organs are transplanted to humans.
   D. Regarding "Frankenfood"
      1. Genetically engineered foods are widespread in the United States.
      2. In 2003, 81 percent of soybeans and 40 percent of corn were modified to withstand weedkillers.
      3. At least 70 percent of processed foods may contain ingredients from genetically engineered plants.

Suggestions for Presenting the Material

- Help students to see the relevance of the topics in this chapter by telling them about some of the products (such as insulin) that are produced as a result of genetic engineering.

- Begin by reminding students that genetic recombination occurs naturally in all organisms during meiosis. Emphasize that even though examples of genetic research in bacteria may seem obscure and of little relationship to more complex eukaryotic genomes, such experimentation yields results of great value to humans.

- Ask questions to ensure that students are indeed knowledgeable about the use of *plasmids* and restriction enzymes. Visuals are very helpful with this rather abstract and unseen procedure.

Classroom and Laboratory Enrichment

- Illustrate the cleavage and splicing steps of recombinant DNA formation using overhead transparencies or models.

- Use overhead transparencies to show the exchange of F plasmids among bacteria.

- Demonstrate transfer of a plasmid for antibiotic resistance from one strain of bacteria to another using selected strains of *E. coli.* (Laboratory kits containing all necessary materials are available.)

- Fabricate workable models of the recombination that occurs in the formation of a DNA library as depicted in Figure 11.3

- Prepare a summary table of the recombination methods listed in this chapter. Include the following information:
  a. Natural versus man-made
  b. Examples of organisms
  c. Usefulness

- Ask two groups of students to prepare brief arguments *for* and *against* the continuation of genetic engineering research and development.

Impacts, Issues Classroom Discussion Ideas

- Where (and when) does genetic recombination naturally occur?

- What are some characteristics of an organism ideally suited for research in genetic engineering?

- Discuss the benefits of genetic engineering versus potential risks.

- What do you think may happen in areas of the world where different antibiotics are being used in ever-increasing amounts?

Additional Ideas for Classroom Discussion

- Why are restriction enzymes useful tools for genetic engineering? How is DNA ligase used in genetic engineering?

- Do you think that new genomes resulting from genetic engineering should be patented? Who should receive monetary benefits from such discoveries—the research scientists performing the work or their academic institutions?

- What advantages would insulin produced by genetic engineering have over preparations from animal sources in the treatment of human diabetes mellitus?

- Is genetic engineering a new concept in nature or just the human application of a natural mechanism already in operation? Explain with examples.

- How is the movement of a portion of DNA in the process called *transposition* different from *translocation*?

How Would You Vote? Classroom Discussion Ideas

- Monitor the voting for the online question. Although it may at first sound like a good idea to label all foods that are genetically modified, I can foresee a squabble as to the exact wording, the size of the lettering, the location on the label, etc. This will be because the food producer will want to downplay the label and the concerned consumers will want to make it plainly visible.

Term Paper Topics, Library Activities, and Special Projects

- Compile a history of research efforts in genetic engineering.
- Describe problems that have resulted from the standard prophylactic use of antibiotics among farm animals such as poultry, pigs, and cattle.
- Describe the safeguards currently followed in labs doing work in genetic engineering.
- List and describe companies currently doing research in genetic engineering. Investigate the current financial worth of some of these companies.
- Discuss the growing problem of antibiotic resistance among the different species of bacteria responsible for causing diseases such as gonorrhea, typhoid, and meningitis.
- Trace the history of the development and production of interferon, insulin, or any other substance produced using techniques of genetic engineering.
- In the early days of genetic recombination research, fears of creating "monster" bacteria that could run amok in the human population were quite real. However, after careful evaluation of all laboratory procedures used in thousands of experiments, these fears seem exaggerated. Why do *you* feel this thinking has changed?
- It is known that the HIV that causes AIDS can delay its deadly effects for some time. Search the literature to find out if this is an instance of the virus entering a latent state before resuming its attack.

Possible Responses to *Critical Thinking* Questions

1. I think one's choice of tomatoes would depend on your opinion of scientific research and development. Those persons who take their concept of science and scientists from Hollywood movies or the tabloids may picture scientists as perverters of nature. Therefore, they would view the tomatoes—however attractive to the eye and tastebuds—as a scheme to alter nature and eventually harm its inhabitants.

   Persons who realize that virtually all organisms are hybrids and not genetically "pure" would see the genetically modified tomatoes as simply better. Furthermore, these persons tend to have trust in the scientific community and its pledge to work for the betterment of humankind.

2. Most persons believe that it is only a matter of time until foreign genes are inserted into human embryos—for good or evil intent. It may have already happened. Of course, those in the scientific community would be more sympathetic to such transfers if they were based on a reasonably plausible prospect of effecting a cure for some genetic malady or conferring immunity against some catastrophic disease. As in the case of the tomatoes (see #1 above), the general public may not accept such work with similar enthusiasm.

3. At first glance, the reconstruction of the A-H1N1 virus is a very scary thing. However, the arguments for doing so are persuasive; that is, the more we know about the virus, the more we can do to protect ourselves from another pandemic.

Upon reflection though, the assurances for containment fall on skeptical ears. Haven't we heard the same arguments before? And haven't there been breeches?

12

PROCESSES OF EVOLUTION

Chapter Outline

Objectives

1. Explain how people came to believe that the populations of organisms that inhabit Earth have changed through time.
2. Understand as well as you can the ideas and evidence that biologists use to explain how life might have changed through time.
3. Compare and contrast the differing views on how species might have changed and emerged.

4. Explain the origin and eventual articulation of the views Darwin had on evolution.
5. Understand how variation occurs in populations and how changes in allele frequencies can be measured.
6. Know how mutations, gene flow, and population size can influence the rate and direction of population change.
7. Define natural selection in terms of differential survival and reproduction.
8. Describe the kinds of selection mechanisms that help shape populations.

Key Terms

evolution	adaptation	mutation rate	sexual selection
Chain of Being	population	lethal mutation	balancing selection
species	morphological traits	neutral mutation	balanced polymorphism
biogeography	physiological traits	beneficial mutation	sickle-cell anemia
comparative	behavioral traits	Hardy-Weinberg rule	genetic drift
morphology	qualitative differences	directional selection	probability
fossils	polymorphism	rock pocket mice	fixation
catastrophism	quantitative differences	pesticide resistance	bottleneck
inheritance of acquired	gene pool	pest resurgence	founder effect
characteristics	alleles	antibiotic resistance	inbreeding
Beagle	phenotype	antibiotics	emigration
theory of uniformity	allele frequencies	stabilizing selection	immigration
glyptodonts	genetic equilibrium	disruptive selection	gene flow
natural selection	microevolution	sexual dimorphism	

Lecture Outline

Rise of the Super Rats
A. Rats are one of the most notorious pests of all time.
   1. The rodenticide Warfarin was very effective when it was first introduced in the 1950s.
   2. Within a few years, rats developed resistance—the chemical would no longer kill.
B. The resistant rats happened to inherit a gene that made the chemical ineffective.
   1. The survivors passed on the gene to their offspring; soon resistant rats were the normal population.
   2. This is an example of evolution.

12.1 Early Beliefs, Confounding Discoveries
A. Questions from Biogeography
   1. By the fourteenth century, the ancient view of gradual levels of organization from lifeless matter to the most complex organisms had been formalized into the great Chain of Being.
      a. The Chain extended from lowest forms to spiritual beings.
      b. Each being (*species*) had its fixed place in the divine order—unchanged and unchanging since creation.
   2. When global voyages of the sixteenth century revealed unusual species not known in Europe, the students of biogeography began to question, "Where do all these species 'fit' in the great Chain?"

3. Furthermore, if all species had been created at the same time and place, "Why were certain species found in only some parts of the world but not others?" and "How did so many species get from the cradle of creation to islands and isolated places?"

B. Questions from Comparative Morphology
1. Studies of the comparative morphology of seemingly unrelated animals led to questions of why certain structures should be so similar.
2. One explanation: Some body parts were so perfect at the time of creation there was no need for any variation; but what about bones still present but without function (ankle bones in whales, tail bones in humans)?

C. Questions about Fossils
1. Studies of sedimentary beds revealed that deposits had been laid down slowly, one above the other.
   a. The layers held recognizable remains or impressions of organisms—fossils.
   b. The arrangement of the layers suggested that different organisms had lived at different times.
2. Perhaps species originated in more than one place, and perhaps species became modified over time—evolution!

D. Squeezing New Evidence into Old Beliefs
1. Georges Cuvier believed in an original creation of all species.
2. Cuvier further suggested that the abrupt changes seen in the fossil record in different rock strata reflected the concept of catastrophism.
   a. After each catastrophe, fewer species remained.
   b. The survivors were not new species; it was just that their ancestors' fossils had not been found.
3. Lamarck formulated a theory of inheritance of acquired characteristics—the idea that simple forms had changed into more complex ones by a built-in drive for perfection up the Chain of Being; for instance, a giraffe stretching its neck to reach higher branches would result in offspring with longer necks.

E. Voyage of the *Beagle*
1. As a child (early 1800s), Charles Darwin was curious about nature, but in college he first pursued premedicine, and finally received a degree in theology.
2. Botanist John Henslow arranged for Darwin (at age 22) to sail around the world as a ship's naturalist.
   a. Throughout the trip, Darwin studied and collected a variety of plants and animals.
   b. He was also reading Lyell's *Principles of Geology*, which proposed a theory of uniformity—the notion of a gradual, lengthy molding of the earth's geologic structure.
   c. Thus, the earth was not thousands, but possibly millions of years old—enough time for evolution.

F. Old Bones and Armadillos
1. Darwin returned after five years at sea and began pondering the "species problem"—what could explain the remarkable diversity among organisms?
2. In Argentina, Darwin had observed extinct glyptodonts that bore suspicious resemblance to living armadillos; Darwin wondered if the present species had evolved from the extinct one.

G. A Key Insight—Variation in Traits
1. Thomas Malthus had suggested that as a population outgrows its resources, its members must compete for what is available; some will not make it.

2. Darwin felt that if some normally variant members of a population bore traits that increased their survival, then nature would select those same individuals to survive, reproduce, and possibly change future populations' traits.
   a. On the Galapagos Islands, the dozen or so species of finches all varied from one another to some extent but resembled the mainland finches to some degree also; perhaps they had descended from common ancestors.
   b. Darwin reasoned that a population is evolving when its heritable traits are changing through successive generations.
3. The major points of Darwin's theory of natural selection as published in *On the Origin of Species* in 1859 are:
   a. *Observation:* All populations have the reproductive capacity to increase in numbers over generations.
   b. *Observation:* No population is able to increase indefinitely, for its individuals will run out of food, living space, and other resources.
   c. *Inference:* Sooner or later, individuals will end up competing for dwindling resources.
   d. *Observation:* All the individuals have the same genes, which represent a pool of heritable information.
   e. *Observation:* Most genes occur in different molecular forms (alleles), which give rise to differences in phenotypic details.
   f. *Inferences:* Because adaptive traits promote survival and reproduction, they must increase in frequency over the generations, and less adaptive traits must decrease in frequency or disappear.
   g. *Conclusions:* A population can evolve by natural selection, that is, the traits characterizing the population can change over time when its individuals differ in one or more heritable traits that are responsible for differences in survival and reproduction.

12.2   The Nature of Adaptation
   A. Adaptation is defined variously:
      1. Short-term adaptations, such as an individual plant's stunted growth on a windy plain, last only as long as the individual does.
      2. Long-term adaptations have some heritable aspect that improves the odds for surviving and reproducing.
   B. Salt-Tolerant Tomatoes
      1. Tomatoes originated in South American soils with a high salt content; they were adapted to these conditions.
      2. Commercial tomatoes in today's markets will not tolerate salt.
      3. However, gene transfers can yield a salt-tolerant tomato that will grow in irrigated plots.
   C. Adaptation to What?
      1. You can safely assume that a polar bear is well adapted to the Arctic environment and would not do well in the desert.
      2. The environment in which a trait evolved may be very different from the one prevailing now.
      3. For example, llamas are well adapted to high altitudes because of their hemoglobin; however, their close relative the camel has the same capability and lives in low altitude deserts.

12.3   Individuals Don't Evolve, Populations Do
   A. Variation in Populations
       1. Populations evolve, not individuals.
       2. A population is a group of individuals belonging to the same species, occupying the same given area.
       3. A population exhibits variation among the individual members, but they also hold certain morphological, physiological, and behavioral traits in common.
           a. Qualitative variation is called polymorphism.
           b. Quantitative differences result in a continuous range of differences.
   B. The "Gene Pool"
       1. Individuals of the same population generally have the same number and kinds of genes.
           a. All of the genes in the entire population constitute the gene pool.
           b. Each gene exists in two or more slightly different molecular forms called alleles, which offspring inherit and express as phenotype.
       2. Each particular mix of alleles depends on these five factors:
           a. Gene mutations create new alleles.
           b. Crossing over at meiosis I results in novel recombinations of alleles in chromosomes.
           c. Independent assortment of chromosomes in meiosis mixes maternal and paternal chromosomes in gametes.
           d. Fertilization combines alleles from two parents.
           e. Changes in chromosome structure or number leads to loss, duplication, or repositioning of genes.
   C. Stability and Change in Allele Frequencies
       1. Allele frequencies are a measure of the abundance of each kind of allele in the entire population.
       2. Evolution can be detected by a change in allele frequencies from the genetic equilibrium.
       3. Because these five conditions are rarely fulfilled in natural populations, any deviation from the reference point established by the "rule" will indicate evolution.
       4. Microevolution is the change in allele frequencies brought about by mutation, natural selection, gene flow, and genetic drift.
   D. Mutations Revisited
       1. Mutations are heritable changes in DNA that can alter gene expression.
       2. Mutations are random and the phenotypic outcome may be neutral, beneficial, harmful, or even lethal to the individual depending on other interactions.
           a. A *lethal mutation* is an expression of a gene that results in death.
           b. *Neutral mutations*, whether or not they are expressed in phenotype, have no effect on survival and reproduction.
           c. *Beneficial mutations* are those that bestow survival advantages.
       3. Mutations are the only source of new alleles—the genetic foundation for biological diversity.

12.4   When Is a Population *Not* Evolving?
   A. These five conditions are necessary for a stable population:
       1. No mutations are occurring.
       2. The population is very, very large.
       3. The population is isolated from other populations of the same species.
       4. All members survive, mate, and reproduce (no selection).
       5. Mating is random.

B. The assumptions listed above are the basis for the Hardy-Weinberg rule.
   1. Any exceptions will indicate that change in gene frequencies is occurring—evolution.
   2. If the frequencies of certain alleles are known, the quadratic equation can be used to calculate the genotypes to see if any frequency changes (evolution) have occurred.

12.5   Natural Selection Revisited
   A. Directional Selection
      1. Directional selection shifts allele frequencies in a consistent direction, which may be in response to environmental pressures or occur as a new mutation appears and is proved adaptive.
      2. Rock Pocket Mice
         a. The larger population of rock pocket mice in the Arizona desert survives well because of its genetically-determined lighter fur color that blends in with the granite; predator birds cannot spot them easily.
         b. A smaller population of mice has darker coats, which allow them to blend in with the dark basalt (from lava) and avoid being seen by predators.
      3. Pesticide Resistance
         a. When insecticides are first applied, susceptible insects (most of the population) die, but the few that have the adaptation that affords survival will live and pass the heritable characteristic on; eventually most of the population will become resistant.
         b. In addition to pest species, pesticides kill natural enemies thus allowing pests to multiply even more abundantly—pest resurgence.
      4. Antibiotic Resistance
         a. Antibiotics are wonderful drugs that have proven very effective in treating bacterial-induced diseases.
         b. However, overuse of antibiotics has led to the selection of resistant strains that are no longer susceptible to the drug.
   B. Selection Against or in Favor of Extreme Phenotypes
      1. Stabilizing Selection
         a. Stabilizing selection favors the most common phenotype in the population.
         b. It counters the effects of mutation, genetic drift, and gene flow.
         c. Human birth weight that averages around 7 pounds is favored.
      2. Disruptive Selection
         a. Disruptive selection favors forms at the extremes of the phenotypic range of variation and selects against the intermediate forms.
         b. Thomas Smith discovered African finches in which the bill size was either large or small, no in-between.

12.6   Maintaining Variation in a Population
   A. Sexual Selection
      1. Most species have distinctively male and female phenotypes—sexual dimorphism.
      2. Sexual selection is based on any trait that gives the individual a competitive edge in mating and producing offspring.
      3. Usually it is the females that are the agents of selection when they pick their mates.
   B. Sickle-Cell Anemia–Lesser of Two Evils?
      1. Humans that are homozygous for sickle-cell anemia (Hb^S/Hb^S) develop the disease and die at an early age.
      2. However, individuals with alleles for both normal hemoglobin (Hb^A) and sickle-cell hemoglobin (Hb^S) have the greatest chances of surviving malaria.

12.7   Genetic Drift—The Chance Changes
  A. Chance Events and Population Size
     1. Genetic drift is the random fluctuation in allele frequencies over time, due to chance occurrences alone.
     2. It is more significant in small populations; sampling error helps explain the difference.
     3. Genetic drift increases the chance of any given allele becoming more or less prevalent when the number of individuals in a population is small.
  B. Bottlenecks and the Founder Effect
     1. In *bottlenecks,* some stressful situation greatly reduces the size of a population leaving a few (typical or atypical?) individuals to reestablish the population.
     2. In the *founder effect,* a few individuals (carrying genes that may/may not be typical of the whole population) leave the original population to establish a new one.
  C. Genetic Drift and Inbred Populations
     1. Inbreeding refers to nonrandom mating among closely related individuals.
     2. It tends to increase the homozygous condition, thus leading to lower fitness and survival rates.

12.8   Gene Flow—Keeping Populations Alike
  A. Genes move with individuals when they move out of (emigration), or into (immigration), a population.
  B. The physical flow (and resultant shuffling) tends to minimize genetic variation between populations.

Suggestions for Presenting the Material

- This chapter begins with a historical perspective that can be enlivened by the use of visual material such as slides of world explorers and drawings of the great Chain of Being. Students' attention tends to become unfocused without concrete visuals of some sort.

- The textbook authors enumerate three areas (biogeography, comparative anatomy, and fossils) that were puzzling to early scientists. Your lectures could take the same approach as you introduce the material by asking for student response to those same questions.

- Before proceeding to the men who proposed a changing biological world, point out that the prevailing thought 200 years ago was "fixity of species." Because of the belief that species did not change, it was incumbent on humans to classify all living things. Although Linnaeus believed in this "fixity," his system is nevertheless still very valid and useful.

- One way to present the historical development of evolutionary thought is to chronicle the contributions of persons such as de Lamarck, Lyell, Malthus, Wallace, and of course, Darwin.

- Students rarely hear about Darwin's life other than his famous journey. Present his biography *before* his theory to spark interest. Perhaps the videotape listed in the Enrichment section could be used. You can then proceed to *natural selection* by first recalling *artificial selection* (maybe using dogs rather than pigeons as Darwin did in his book).

- The main points of the chapter concerning variability and evolution are as follows:

    Variation is the result of several factors.

    The Hardy-Weinberg equation provides a baseline for calculating gene frequencies under unrealistic conditions.

Several factors yield change in the real world:

mutation

> genetic drift (founder, bottleneck)
>
> gene flow
>
> natural selection (stabilizing, directional, disruptive)

- Work a Hardy-Weinberg problem in the manner suggested in the Enrichment section below.

- A few of the topics in the chapter may not have enough visual material in the textbook. Check other texts for photo examples of founder effects, bottlenecks, isolating mechanisms, and so on.

- Pesticide resistance in insects is perhaps one of the best examples of natural selection. It should be presented clearly!

Classroom and Laboratory Enrichment

- Show a video describing Charles Darwin's voyage on the HMS *Beagle* and his thoughts as he traveled.

- Present fossil evidence (or 35 mm transparencies, filmstrips, or films of fossils) showing how a group of related organisms or a single genus (for example, *Equus*) has evolved and changed through time.

- Whales, like snakes, have pelvic girdles. Show an overhead diagram of this portion of the whale skeleton.

- Generate interest in Darwin's theory by bringing a copy of *On the Origin of Species* to class. Read selected chapter titles and portions of the text. Point out the lack of illustrations in the original edition.

- Choose an easy-to-see trait governed by one gene with two alleles such as tongue-rolling (the ability to roll one's tongue into a U-shape) or free earlobes (earlobes whose bases are not attached to the jawline), and ask students to determine their own phenotype. Determine the number of homozygous recessive individuals in the class (those who are non-tongue-rollers or have attached earlobes). Use the Hardy-Weinberg principle to calculate the frequencies of the dominant allele and the recessive allele.

- Demonstrate genetic drift by tracing changes in allele frequency throughout time. In small hypothetical populations, select a trait governed by two alleles and calculate the frequency of each allele. Different groups of students could be assigned populations of different sizes. Follow each population throughout several generations as some of its members (selected by coin tosses) succumb to disease, predation, and other random causes of early death. How does population size affect genetic variation over time?

- Show 35 mm slides or films about endangered species that are threatened by sharp reductions in population size and subsequent loss of genetic variability.

- What happens to the genetic variability of small, isolated populations of laboratory organisms after many generations without the introduction of new organisms? Design and implement an experiment using any organism with a short generation time and several easy-to-see traits that can be followed from one generation to the next.

- How does artificial selection by humans affect gene frequencies of domestic plants and animals? Pursue this question with experiments or demonstrations.

- Prepare an overhead transparency on which you have written the solution to a Hardy-Weinberg problem (check a genetics or majors biology text). This method is more convenient than blackboard presentation, and you will feel more confident. Don't disclose the entire page at once. Instead, arrange the problem stems and solutions in such a way that one can be uncovered while the other is hidden.

- Select a well-known example of the founder effect in a human population, perhaps a religious group. Using slides, show how a phenotypic characteristic (for example, polydactyly) "spreads" from one generation to the next.

- Explain the development of insect resistance to DDT as a modern-day example of natural selection. Point out that DDT was introduced to the world in the early 1940s and in just 10 years resistant strains were reported in many countries. By the time it was banned in the United States in 1973, virtually every housefly was resistant to its effects.

Impacts, Issues Classroom Discussion Ideas

- How could the results of various scientific experiments be influenced by using strains of laboratory mice that are continuously inbred?

- In the instance of resistance to insecticides, it was pointed out that the resistant strains gradually replaced the susceptible ones. Are these two strains different species? How could you prove/disprove your answer?

- What is artificial selection? How does it differ from natural selection?

- How does sexual selection benefit a species? Would the introduction of alleles from a similar but different species introduce variety and thus help the species? Why or why not?

Additional Ideas for Classroom Discussion

- What was Jean-Baptiste Lamarck's contribution to our modern understanding of evolutionary theory?

- Why is the term *scientific creationism* an oxymoron? Describe why this body of thought cannot be considered a science.

- What steps did Lamarck fail to perform before setting forth his hypothesis of inherited characteristics?

- How did the widespread discoveries of fossils in the nineteenth century help to support Darwin's views on evolution?

- Does belief in the principle of evolution exclude belief in religion? Why or why not?

- Why was extensive travel a key ingredient in the development of Darwin's evolutionary thought?

- Can you think of any ideas commonly expressed today that are similar to Lamarck's understanding of evolution?

- How did the work of geologists such as Charles Lyell, who were Darwin's contemporaries, help Darwin to create his principle of evolution?

- Those who wish to berate certain scientific principles sometimes say "It's only a theory." This statement is used by creationists when referring to evolution. Does the use of "theory" in biology mean the concept is in doubt? Explain using examples.

- If you asked the following question in a sidewalk survey, what do you think the responses would be? "Darwin wrote a very famous book on the origin of _____."

- Compare and contrast the principles of "uniformitarianism" and "catastrophism." Evaluate the physical evidence for each.

- How did Darwin's observation of variation among species help him to develop his principle of evolution?

- What is the difference between a theory and a principle? Why does your text refer to the principle of evolution rather than the theory of evolution?

- How does phenotypic variation arise? Ask students to list as many sources of phenotypic variation as they can. They should be able to remember how genetic variation comes about from their earlier study of genetics.

- What is the difference between natural selection and artificial selection?

- How are new alleles created? Is the creation of new alleles an important source of genetic change? Why or why not?

- What are some phenotypic variations that might have assisted the success of *Homo sapiens*? Ask your students to think of some imaginative examples of variations that might be useful in the future evolution of our species.

- How representative of the human population is your class? Discuss the importance of sample size with reference to determining allele frequencies. Ask your students to think about gene pool size and the founder effect if they were stranded forever on an uninhabited island. Would certain alleles be over- or underrepresented? What would happen to allele frequencies after many generations?

- Think of examples of human alleles whose frequencies vary from one global region to the next.

- What did Darwin's study of the different finch species among the Galapagos Islands tell him about speciation? What conclusions can you make about the evolutionary histories of the different species of Galapagos finches, given what you now know about the process of speciation?

- Why are conservationists concerned when the genetic variation within a population of rare or endangered organisms begins to decrease?

- How do reproductive isolating mechanisms help a species?

- Why is the statement "She has evolved into a fine pianist" not biologically accurate?

- Of the five sources of phenotypic variation, why is mutation the only one that creates new alleles? How do the others yield variation?

- Which of the factors that cause changes in allelic frequencies could be under conscious human control?

How Would You Vote? Classroom Discussion Ideas

- Monitor the voting for the online question. The banning of antibiotics in animal feed has been discussed for some years, and there is progress. Perhaps the first effort should be a voluntary move to limit the antibiotics that are of value to humans from those animals most likely to pass it on to humans. This could be monitored to see if it is making a difference in the quantities transferred. If not, then an outright ban may be necessary.

Term Paper Topics, Library Activities, and Special Projects

- Describe how a trip through the Grand Canyon with a paleontologist would reinforce our modern understanding of evolution.

- How do today's biologists reconcile their personal faith in an organized religion with their belief in evolution? Research the viewpoints of some famous scientists on this issue.

- Can we see evolution actually happening? Find examples of natural occurrences in the wild or experimental situations in the laboratory in which we can observe evolution occurring.

- Learn more about the discovery of fossils of *Archaeopteryx* and the reactions of the scientific community to them.

- Write a short biography of Linnaeus.

- Describe how Darwin's development of his principle of evolution was an example of the scientific method in action.

- From time to time, Lamarck's hypothesis of "inheritance of acquired characteristics" is revived as an explanation for certain events. Is the idea totally without merit, or could this be the explanation for the inheritance patterns in certain microorganisms? (See *Scientific American*, Nov. 1988, p. 34.)

- The great "catastrophe" that dominated Cuvier's thinking was the flood of Noah as recorded in the Book of Genesis. This is still the cornerstone of creationist thinking. Investigate creationist writings to see how this event is critical to their theories.

- Darwin's emerging ideas on natural selection were not welcomed by the *Beagle* captain. Investigate how this challenge to his views strengthened Darwin's hypotheses.

- It is ironic that Darwin and Wallace would arrive independently at so important a concept as natural selection. Investigate the path each took.

- Read about research of the founder effect in human populations isolated by geography or custom.

- What is the frequency of the allele for Tay-Sachs disease among Ashkenazic Jews? How do scientists explain the high frequency of this allele in this segment of the population?

- How has the loss of genetic diversity (possibly resulting from a population bottleneck at some time in the past) affected cheetahs? Report on recent research efforts in this area.

- Describe how artificial selection in the genus Brassica has resulted in several very different vegetable varieties.

- What is the frequency of the allele for cystic fibrosis in the United States? Does the frequency of this allele differ among different segments of the population? Is the allele frequency changing over time?

- How do commercial plant breeders and agricultural biologists maintain genetic variability among the plants they raise?

- Why is inbreeding harmful to a species? Select a species or a group of organisms (a dog breed, for example), and discuss the results of inbreeding.

- Examine the role of geographic barriers (such as high elevations, mountaintops, isolated stream drainages, islands) in the development of a group of closely related regional species or genera.

- Prepare brief biographies of G. H. Hardy and W. Weinberg. How is it that they discovered their principle "independently"? Did they ever collaborate?

- Among invertebrates there are several hermaphroditic (both sexes in the same animal) species such as the common earthworm. How is self-fertilization avoided when these animals reproduce? (Answer: anatomical features and differential timing of gamete maturation)

- It is known that Hb^S/Hb^A (sickle-cell heterozygote) persons in Africa are more likely to survive a malarial infection. Is the percentage of heterozygous individuals in nonmalaria areas (such as the United States) different from that in malaria areas?

Possible Responses to *Critical Thinking* Questions

1. What is needed in the proposed experiment is to give the female bird a choice—flamboyant male bird versus dull geek bird. Ideally, both types of living birds would be available and would differ <u>only</u> in coloration. Even if both types were available, it is doubtful that they would have similar courtship behaviors; hey—look at humans!

   So perhaps the female could be given a choice between flamboyant and geek *decoys*, which can be very lifelike looking and acting (robotics). Human observers would then record how many approaches and "interests" the female showed.

2. Although *Tonight Show* host Jay Leno probably exploits the "incestuous hillbilly" for comic purposes a bit too much, it is known that there is higher percentage of cousin marriages in remote areas of Appalachia. As the scenario indicates, this skin condition is caused by a recessive gene that, if single, causes no effect because it is masked by the dominant gene. Only if the recessive is double will the condition appear in the phenotype—a *possibility* that increases in *probability* when persons who are closely related [by DNA] reproduce.

3. It is widely recognized that Darwin was led to his development of *natural* selection by observing the breeding practices of *artificial* selection. In this item it is dogs that are described, but of course the genes of many other plants and animals have been artificially manipulated for the good or ill of humankind. Let us compare the points of natural selection as found on page 180 of the textbook to see how they would compare with artificial selection. #1: both natural populations and domestic populations have "inherent capacity to increase in numbers"; #2: "no population can indefinitely grow in size" could be *more* applicable to natural populations because domestic populations would probably have their needs met by human caretakers; #3: "sooner or later individuals will end up competing for limited resources" is more true of natural populations for the reason just listed; #4: "individuals share a pool of heritable information about traits" is true of natural and domestic groups; #5: "mutations give rise to different forms of genes" is the basis for the breeds that we see in artificial selection; of course, in dog breeding we are looking for these mutations and mate different animals at a rate that will encourage the traits to show up as quickly as possible; #6: "some phenotypes are better than others in helping an individual compete for survival and reproduction" is more true in the wild of natural populations than in domestic situations where the "desirable" trait may actually *reduce* the animal's chances; #7 the resulting selection, whether it be natural or artificial, results in differences that are notable and, for the breeder, profitable.

13

EVOLUTIONARY PATTERNS, RATES, AND TRENDS

Chapter Outline

Objectives

1. Be able to cite what biologists generally accept as evidence that supports evolution.
2. Be able to explain the difference between microevolution and macroevolution.
3. Explain how observations from fossils, comparative morphology, and comparative biochemistry are used to reconstruct the past.
4. Be able to define *species* in terms of population interbreeding.
5. Explain under what circumstances species will, and will not, change.
6. Distinguish the various types of isolating mechanisms that can lead to speciation.
7. Describe the process of speciation, with reference to allopatric, parapatric, and sympatric modes.
8. Be able to explain how biological systematics show patterns of diversity in the distribution of organisms in space and over evolutionary time.
9. Distinguish taxonomy, phylogenetic reconstruction, and classification.
10. Characterize the six kingdoms and three domains.

Key Terms

fossils
fossil record
trace fossils
fossilization
stratification
lineage
radiometric dating
half-life
geologic time scale
macroevolution
theory of uniformity
Pangea
continental drift
plate tectonics theory
Gondwana
comparative
  morphology
homologous structures
morphological
  divergence

morphological
  convergence
analogous structures
patterns of development
transposons
protein comparisons
cytochrome *c*
nucleic acid
  hybridization
mitochondrial DNA
neutral mutations
molecular clock
species
biological species
  concept
gene flow
genetic divergence
speciation
reproductive isolating
  mechanisms
mechanical isolation

temporal isolation
behavioral isolation
ecological isolation
gamete mortality
postzygote isolating
  mechanisms
allopatric speciation
archipelago
sympatric speciation
polyploidy
parapatric speciation
hybrid zone
cladogenesis
anagenesis
evolutionary trees
gradual model of
  speciation
punctuation model of
  speciation
adaptive radiation
adaptive zones

key innovations
extinction
mass extinction
taxonomy
genus
specific epithet
classification systems
higher taxa
family
order
class
phylum
kingdom
six-kingdom system
three-domain system
monophyletic group
clade
derived trait
cladograms

Lecture Outline

Measuring Time
A. Geologic time requires time measured in almost incomprehensible lengths
B. We have dated asteroid impacts and their consequences, such as dinosaur extinctions.
C. More recently we have documented the rise of modern humans and their effects on the planet.

13.1   Fossils—Evidence of Ancient Life
    A. Fossils are recognizable, physical evidence of organisms that lived long ago.
        1. Many years ago, fossils were interpreted through the prism of cultural beliefs.
        2. The most convenient explanation for the layering of fossil in rocks was the Great Flood as recorded in the Holy Bible.
    B. How Do Fossils Form?
        1. Most fossils are skeletons, shells, leaves, seeds, imprints of leaves and tracks (trace fossils), and even fossilized feces.
        2. Fossilization is a slow process.
            a. Body parts or impressions must be buried in rock before decomposition.
            b. Over time, chemical changes and pressure transform living structures into stony hardness.
        3. Preservation is favored when organisms are buried rapidly in the absence of oxygen and the burial site is left undisturbed.
    C. Fossils in Sedimentary Rock Layers
        1. Stratification, the layering of sedimentary deposits bearing fossils, is quite similar from continent to continent.
        2. Deepest rock strata are assumed to be the oldest, surface layers the youngest.
    D. Interpreting the Fossil Record
        1. Fossil records vary according to type of organism (hard parts preserve well, soft parts do not), stability of the geographical region (sea floor vs. eroding hill), and quality of the specimen.
        2. The fossil record is far from complete, but some lineages are extensive.

13.2   Dating Pieces of the Macroevolutionary Puzzle
    A. Radiometric Dating
        1. Radiometric dating is a way to measure the proportions of daughter/parent isotopes in ancient rocks or other objects.
        2. Because the decay of the isotopes is constant, the rate (half-life) can determined and the time since it formation can be calculated back in time.
    B. Placing Fossils in Geologic Time
        1. Abrupt changes in the fossils in the layers were the basis for dividing Earth history into great eras, which formed a "geologic time scale" to which actual dates were added later.
        2. The current geologic time scale has been correlated with macroevolution—major patterns, trends, and rates of change among lineages.

13.3   Evidence From Biogeography
    A. According to the theory of uniformity, mountain building and erosion had repeatedly changed the surface of the Earth in exactly the same ways through time.
    B. An Outrageous Hypothesis
        1. A model was proposed in which there was a single world continent, named Pangea, that at one time extended from pole to pole surrounded by a single huge ocean.
            a. The idea of continental drift explains the separation of the continents and the formation of great mountain ranges as the continents collided.
            b. Sea-floor spreading and plate tectonics also show that the Earth's crust is moving
        2. Gondwana was an early continent that drifted southward from the tropics, across the south polar region and northward until it crunched into other land masses to form Pangea.

C. A Big Connection
  1. Huge land masses collided to form supercontinents and split to form new land masses.
  2. These changes in the land, oceans, and atmosphere profoundly influenced the evolution of life.

13.4   More Evidence from Comparative Morphology
  A. Comparative morphology provides evidence of evolution by comparing anatomical features to reveal similarities and differences in homologous structures.
  B. Morphological Divergence
    1. In morphological divergence, features have departed in appearance and/or function from the ancestral form.
    2. These are body features that resemble one another in form or patterning due to descent through common ancestors.
    3. A good example of homology is the similarity of the structure of the bones in forelimbs of birds, bats, and humans.
  C. Morphological Convergence
    1. *Morphological convergence* is the adoption of similar function over periods of time in animals of evolutionary remote lineages.
    2. Analogous body parts perform similar functions in dissimilar and distantly related species.
    3. A good example of analogy is the similarity of function, but not structure, of the forelimbs of birds, bats, and insects.

13.5   Evidence From Patterns of Development
  A. Different organisms may show similarities in morphology during their embryonic stages that often indicate evolutionary relationships.
    1. The early embryos of vertebrates strongly resemble one another because they have inherited the same ancient plan for development.
    2. Some of the variation seen in adult vertebrates is due to mutations in genes that control the rates of growth of different body parts.
  B. One illustration of changes occurring in the timing of development is the similarity in size of the skull bones of humans and chimps at birth, which becomes dramatically different as these two animals age.
    1. About 99 percent of human and chimp DNA is identical.
    2. But the *Alu* transposon, which makes up more than 5 percent of the human genome, could affect the expression of certain genes in developing tissues.

13.6   Evidence from DNA, RNA, and Proteins
  A. Protein Comparisons
    1. Because genes dictate the sequence of amino acids in proteins, analysis of proteins can determine the similarity of genes between species.
    2. For example: The amino acid sequence of cytochrome *c*, a crucial part of electron transfer chains, shows similarities in species ranging from aerobic bacteria to humans.
  B. Nucleic Acid Comparisons
    1. The degree of similarity of nucleotide sequences of DNA reveals information about evolutionary relationships.
    2. If a single strand of DNA from one species is allowed to recombine with a single strand of DNA from another species (nucleic acid hybridization), the degree to which they match up is a measure of similarity.

3. Computer programs based on DNA sequencing are used to construct evolutionary trees.
C. Molecular Clocks
   1. Neutral mutations have no more measurable effect on survival and reproduction rates than do other alleles for the trait.
   2. These mutations accumulate in the DNA and can be used as a "molecular clock" for (back)dating times of divergence of species.

13.7 Reproductive Isolation, Maybe New Species
A. Speciation begins with reproductive isolation and ends with a new species.
   1. The morphological species concept expresses the following:
      a. *Species*, in its simplest interpretation, means "kind."
      b. Attempting to determine whether similar, yet different, animals are the same species by appearance (phenotype) is not reliable due to the subtle variations that are displayed.
   2. The biological species concept relies on reproduction to define relatedness of species.
      a. Ernst Mayer says, "Species are groups of interbreeding natural populations that are reproductively isolated from other such groups."
      b. As good as it is, this definition is troublesome for organisms that are non-sexually reproducing and those known only from fossils.
B. Reproductive Isolating Mechanisms
   1. Gene flow, the movement of genes into and out of a population, maintains diversity.
      a. Genetic divergence is the process whereby local units of a population become reproductively isolated from other units and thus experience changes in gene frequencies between them.
      b. Speciation is the attainment of reproductive isolation.
   2. Reproductive isolating mechanisms are any heritable features of body form, functioning, or behavior that prevent interbreeding between genetically divergent populations.
      a. *Mechanical isolation:* two populations are mechanically isolated when differences in reproductive organs prevent successful interbreeding (for example: floral arrangements in sage plants discriminate between different bee pollinators).
      b. *Temporal isolation:* different groups may not be reproductively mature at the same season, or month, or year (for example: periodical cicadas).
      c. *Behavioral isolation:* patterns of courtship may be altered to the extent that sexual union is not achieved (for example: albatross courtship rituals).
      d. *Ecological isolation:* potential mates may be in the same general area by not in the same habitat where they are likely to meet (for example: different species of manzanita shrubs live at different altitudes and habitats).
      e. *Gamete mortality:* incompatibilities between egg and sperm prevent fertilization (for example: signals to pollen grains to begin growing toward the egg).
   3. Postzygote mechanisms take effect after fertilization.
      a. Sometimes fertilization does occur between different species, but the hybrid embryo is weak and dies.
      b. In some instances the hybrids are vigorous but sterile (example: mule produced by a male donkey and a female horse).

13.8 Interpreting the Evidence: Models for Speciation
A. Geographic Isolation
   1. Physical separation prevents gene flow between populations.
      a. Allopatric refers to the "different lands" the two species occupy.

   b. Reproductive isolating mechanisms evolve in the genetically diverging populations and will result in complete speciation when the two species can no longer interbreed.

  2. Geographic isolation usually occurs over vast periods of time.

   a. Glaciers may produce conditions that cut off plants and animals from one another.

   b. Studies of enzymes from fishes on the Atlantic and Pacific sides of the Isthmus of Panama reveal molecular differences.

 B. The Inviting Archipelagos

  1. An archipelago is an island chain some distance away from a continent.

  2. The finches of the Galápagos Islands are evidently ancestors of mainland finches that invaded first a few islands and then spread to others, diverging as time progressed.

 C. Sympatric Speciation

  1. In this model, species may form within the home range of an existing species, in the absence of a physical barrier.

  2. Evidence From Cichlids in Africa

   a. In two crater lakes of East Africa exist small fish called cichlids.

   b. The species in each lake are alike in their mitochondrial DNA and unlike the species in neighboring lakes and streams.

   c. The lakes are small so the fish must live in sympatry.

  3. Polyploidy's Impact

   a. Polyploidy is the inheritance of three or more of each type of chromosome due to improper separation of chromosomes during meiosis or mitosis.

   b. Speciation is instantaneous for plants that are polyploid.

 D. Parapatric Speciation

  1. Daughter species form from a small proportion of individuals along a common border between two populations.

  2. Literally means "near another homeland."

  3. Interbreeding individuals produce hybrid offspring in this region, called a hybrid zone.

13.9 Patterns of Speciation and Extinctions

 A. Branching and Unbranched Evolution

  1. *Cladogenesis* applies to populations that become isolated from one another and subsequently diverge in different directions.

  2. *Anagenesis* is a pattern of descent in which species form within a single, unbranched line.

 B. Evolutionary Trees and Rates of Change

  1. *Evolutionary trees* summarize information about the continuity of relationship among species.

  2. The *gradual model* of speciation is represented by tree diagrams with branches at slight angles to each other to show slow change over time.

  3. The *punctuation model* of speciation is drawn with short, horizontal branches that represent abrupt periods of speciation followed by stable periods.

 C. Adaptive Radiations

  1. An adaptive radiation is a burst of microevolutionary activity that results in the formation of new species in a wide range of habitats.

  2. The presence of adaptive zones presents new ways of life by physical, evolutionary, or ecological access.

 D. Extinctions—End of the Line

  1. Extinction is the rather inevitable loss of species as local conditions change over periods (usually long) of time.

  2. Mass extinctions are abrupt disappearances due to catastrophic, global events.

13.10 Organizing Information About Species
    A. Naming, Identifying, and Classifying Species
        1. Taxonomists attempt to identify, name, and classify species.
            a. The first part of the scientific name is the *genus* (always capitalized and italicized) and signifies very closely related organisms.
            b. The second part is the *specific epithet* (never capitalized but always italicized) and signifies an even closer, interbreeding relationship.
            c. The language used for scientific names is Latin for universal recognizability.
        2. Classification schemes are organized ways of retrieving information about particular species.
            a. The main taxa of the hierarchy from most to least inclusive are: kingdom >>> phylum >>> class >>> order >>> family >>> genus >>> species.
            b. In time, the traditional classification schemes became modified to reflect phylogeny—the evolutionary relationships among species.
            c. A six-kingdom system (Bacteria, Archaea, Protista, Fungi, Plantae, and Animalia) is one way to organize living things; a three-domain system (Bacteria, Archaea, and Eukarya) is another.
    B. What's in a Name? A Cladistic View
        1. In *cladistic* taxonomy, groups are arranged by branch points in an evolutionary tree diagram.
            a. Only species that share *derived traits*—novel features that evolved only once and are shared only by descendants of the ancestral species from which they evolved—are grouped past a given branch point, which represents the last shared common ancestor.
            b. Diagrams, called cladograms, do not convey direct information about ancestors and descendants, but rather, portray <u>relative</u> relationships by placing taxa closer together that share a more recent common ancestor.
        2. Cladograms reflect findings from morphological and biochemical comparisons.

Suggestions for Presenting the Material

- This chapter contains three main topics: (1) macroevolution, which continues the discussion of microevolution begun in Chapter 12, (2) speciation, and (3) classification of life's diversity.

- Stress the tenuous conclusions that are in constant revision when scientists attempt to reconstruct the past. Just as a good medical diagnosis is not based on one examination or one lab test, a good analysis of past evolutionary history is not based on any one line of evidence, but rather, several lines of corroborating evidence.

- You may wish to include a brief discussion of how radioisotopes are used to date fossils (section 13.2). Certainly, emphasis should be placed on how these calculations are *used* rather than the actual calculations.

- The distinction between *homologous* and *analogous* structures is a subtle one for beginning students. Careful discussion, coupled with the use of diagrams and slides, should help.

- Evidence of shared ancestry from comparative biochemistry (protein and nucleic acid comparisons) is very current and should be of interest to your students, especially the comparisons of humans to chimps (almost guaranteed to offend creationists).

- Defining a species in terms of ability to interbreed may not seem as obvious to students as just saying two organisms look alike. Perhaps the existence of various dog breeds is a good example of how individuals can look very different yet all be *Canis familiaris*.

- It would helpful if you could locate additional photos, slides, or videos of the isolating mechanisms presented in this chapter.

  You will also note the listing of six kingdoms, details of which are contained in the chapters 15 and 16.

- Emphasize that humans construct classification schemes and therefore these systems are subject to change and interpretation.

- Note the inclusion of a very recently devised evolutionary tree in Figure 13.27.

- Table 13.1 is a concise summary of microevolutionary and macroevolutionary processes of evolution.

Classroom and Laboratory Enrichment

- Discuss methods of fossil preservation. Examine actual fossils or films, videos, or slides of fossils. Visit collections of fossils in nearby museums.

- Ask a geology teacher how to prepare some "instant" fossils.

- Prepare a summary table of the "tools" used in "reconstructing the past." For each tool, list the procedure, reliability, advantages/disadvantages, accuracy, and so forth.

- Show actual fossils or photographs of fossils representing some of the life forms prevalent during the Paleozoic, Mesozoic, and Cenozoic eras.

- See if you can obtain some electrophoresis patterns of protein comparisons (starch gel, or photos of same) that show actual "runs." Interpret the similarities and differences in the proteins from different sources (see the Discussion section below). If you can arrange for a researcher to present this information, so much the better.

- Present some examples of the names that were given to plants and animals BEFORE Linnaeus got the idea of binominal nomenclature.

- Use data from protein or DNA hybridization studies to reconstruct the phylogenetic branch points during the evolutionary history of a group of organisms.

- Present the results of a study where gene frequencies were determined by analyzing the proteins of an organism by gel electrophoresis.

- Explain why the analysis of proteins can be an indicator of gene variability.

- What happens to the genetic variability of small, isolated populations of laboratory organisms after many generations without the introduction of new organisms? Design and implement an experiment using any organism with a short generation time and several easy-to-see traits that can be followed from one generation to the next.

- How does artificial selection by humans affect gene frequencies of domestic plants and animals? Pursue this question with experiments or demonstrations.

- Study a road map that shows the Mississippi River as it winds its way south. Notice the bends and turns that were once in the main channel but are no longer. Speculate as to the effect these changes might have had on speciation.

- Consider the possibility that the Isthmus of Panama never existed. What kinds of organisms might, and might not, have been affected by this?

- Show slides or films about endangered species that are threatened by sharp reductions in population size and subsequent loss of genetic variability.

- Compare the various schemes that have been proposed for the number of recognized kingdoms, including the recent three-kingdom system (see a current microbiology text).

- Perform exercises in which student groups each devise their own classification system for an array of similar objects, for example buttons or bolts. Groups should share their results when finished. Did each group invent different classification schemes? Discuss the merits and shortcomings of each system. What are the attributes of a good classification system?

- Discuss the historical background of the classification of one group of organisms. Compare early views of biologists regarding the evolutionary history of your chosen group to those of modern biologists. Discuss how new research techniques have shed new light on the group's history.

- Show overhead transparencies of phylogenetic trees of familiar organisms, such as horses, vertebrates, or mammals.

Impacts, Issues Classroom Discussion Ideas

- What kinds of organisms are well represented in the fossil record? What types of organisms have left little or nothing in the fossil record?

- How does microevolution differ from macroevolution? Can biologists actually see microevolution occurring? Give some examples.

- How do worldwide distribution patterns of fossils suggest a common evolutionary origin for many organisms?

- Could fossils be forming today for some scientists to find in the future?

- Of all the methods used to reconstruct the past, which is most conclusive? Least conclusive? Which of these was (were) not available to scientists of Darwin's time?

Additional Ideas for Classroom Discussion

- What types of conditions favor fossil formation? What conditions are poor for fossil formation?

- What information about the structure and function of animals could be learned from an analysis of fossilized feces?

- One of the methods used to show evolutionary relationships is *comparative biochemistry*. Of course it is the DNA that we wish to compare, but it is easier to compare the products of DNA, namely proteins (see the Enrichment section above). Using the knowledge gained from Chapter 10, show how the comparisons of proteins can reveal information about DNA.

- Using data on comparison of cytochrome *c* in humans and chimps, stimulate a discussion as to the significance of this to evolutionists and its problematic stance to creationists.

- Why is that body of thought known as "scientific creationism" not a science? List the types of evidence supporting the principle of evolution.

- How does phenotypic variation arise? Ask students to list as many sources of phenotypic variation as they can. They should be able to remember how genetic variation comes about from their earlier study of genetics.

- What is the difference between natural selection and artificial selection?

- Which term is more precise, *kind* or *species*? Why?

- Is it legitimate to use the concept of *species* when naming bacteria? Why or why not?

- There are examples of animals with distinct species names, such as the donkey and horse or the buffalo and Angus steer, but these animals can interbreed and produce living offspring. Are there other criteria that some authorities include in the definition of species to take care of these "exceptions"?

- What isolating mechanism(s) separates humans from other primates?

- What did Darwin's study of the different finch species among the Galapagos Islands tell him about speciation? What conclusions can you make about the evolutionary histories of the different species of Galapagos finches, given what you now know about the process of speciation?

- Why are conservationists concerned when the genetic variation within a population of rare or endangered organisms begins to decrease?

- How does sexual selection benefit a species? Would the introduction of alleles from a similar but different species introduce variety and thus help the species? Why or why not?

- How do reproductive isolating mechanisms help a species?

- What type of isolation makes allopatry "thought [of as] the main speciation route" according to your text?

- Why is polyploidy referred to in the text as creating instantaneous species?

- Which of the models of speciation (gradual or punctuation) would be more likely to incorporate the necessity for "missing links"?

- Why do many evolutionary biologists believe that the punctuation model of evolution may explain the progression of different organisms better than does the gradual model?

- Which evolutionary model is supported more fully by the fossil evidence—gradualism or punctuation?

- What was the impetus for Linnaeus to devise only two names for each organism rather than the taxonomy schemes in place during his day?

- What was the advantage afforded by Linnaeus' binominal names?

- Prior to Linnaeus, what types of names were used for plants and animals?

- Why is it important to use a "dead" language such as Latin for the scientific names? Why was Latin chosen in the first place?

- What is the difference between "taxonomy" and "classification"? How are they related?

- How does the "human factor" come into play when reconstructing the evolutionary past?

- There are only seven categories in the classification hierarchy listed in Figure 13.24. What happens if the group is so large that another category is needed, say between "order" and "family"? What if two more categories are needed?

- Discuss the merits and problems inherent in using common (local) names for plants and animals.

- Most zoos and botanical gardens place the scientific name on a little plaque near the cage or specimen. Is this of any value to the general viewing public? Do you think anybody really reads these plaques?

How Would You Vote? Classroom Discussion Ideas

- Monitor the voting for the online question. Talk about spending money for a rare event! This would be it. Ask the students to speculate on what could be done even if we knew an asteroid were about to hit us.

Term Paper Topics, Library Activities, and Special Projects

- Describe famous fossil finds. You may wish to include famous fossils that were later found to be hoaxes, such as the Piltdown man discovered in England in 1912.

- Discover what fossil evidence has revealed about the past history of your region of the United States.

- Describe radioactive dating.

- Trace the evolutionary history of one group of plants or animals throughout geologic time.

- Prepare a time line tracing the geologic and biologic history of your section of the United States.

- Collect fossils, photographs, or descriptions of fossils from your region of the United States. What do they reveal about the past history of your area?

- Discuss the formation of coal and oil. Prepare a map showing areas of coal and oil concentration in the United States.

- Discuss recent controversial studies that use human mitochondrial DNA to draw conclusions about human evolution.

- Investigate the type of names used to describe plants and animals before Linnaeus proposed his binominal nomenclature.

- Prepare a biography of Carl von Linné emphasizing the personal aspects of his life: his name change, his commissioning of expeditions, his record keeping, his collections, and so on.

- Prepare a report on the procedures required to establish the fact that an insect found in the jungles of South America is indeed a "new" species that has not been described before, even though it may have been on Earth for thousands of years.

- Humans and other primates are closely related. What isolating mechanism(s) prevent their success in interbreeding?

- How did Ernst Mayer come upon the idea of defining *species* on the basis of interbreeding?

- Consult a microbiology textbook to learn how bacteria are named and classified.

- What are the first recorded crossings of a donkey with a horse?

- What cellular mechanisms prevent mules from reproducing?

- There have been conflicting reports as to whether the squirrels on the North and South rims of the Grand Canyon are the same or different species because of geographical isolation. Research and analyze these claims.

- What are the commercial benefits of polyploidy in plants?

- Examine the role of geographic barriers (such as high elevations, mountaintops, isolated stream drainages, and islands) in the development of a group of closely related regional species or genera.

- What research led to the proposal of the punctuation model of speciation?

- Critically compare the strengths and weaknesses of the gradual and punctuation models of speciation.

- Among invertebrates there are several hermaphroditic (both sexes in the same animal) species such as the common earthworm. How is self-fertilization avoided when these animals reproduce? (Answer: anatomical features and differential timing of gamete maturation)

- What is thought to be the current rate of species extinction today? Is the rate of extinction today higher than can be accounted for by background extinction? What areas of the Earth are experiencing the highest rates of species extinction?

- When reconstructing the past evolutionary history of the Earth and its living forms, vast periods of time are necessary to account for the amount of change. How do strict creationists view the geologic time scale?
- What are the current theories for the great mass extinctions of the past? Which is (are) the most plausible?
- Research the causes of extinction *today*. Are all, or most, of the causes the result of human intervention?
- Prepare a report, preferably with photos, of classification in use at a zoo or botanical garden.

Possible Responses to *Critical Thinking* Questions

1. Traditionally, the coccyx of humans has been thought of as a "relic" of a tailbone that humans retain from their tailed ancestors. Of course, as the scenario poses, it could be the beginnings of something new—only a few million years will tell. But we could look carefully into the human and human-like lineages and attempt to determine whether the coccyx bones are getting more pronounced or are continuing to diminish in importance.

2. This question calls for quite a bit of speculation, so here goes. If global warming is a real and persistent threat to planet Earth, it would appear that we are all in for some warmer weather. Contrary to other mammals, humans have sparse body hair—the key innovation. Perhaps as the temperatures climb and heat dissipation via sweating becomes critical to survival, the lack of body hair ("fur") will prove beneficial.

3. Creating more taxonomic groups may have the advantage of more precisely identifying the members of the group based on shared characteristics. As in the scenario, domain Archaea readily identifies a group of unusual prokaryotes and distinguishes them from members of domain Bacteria. Lumping the two together would blur these differences. Conversely, the lumping of four eukaryotic kingdoms into domain Eukarya tends to hide the incredible diversity among the member organisms.

4. Rama the cama is an animal that is not supposed to be. Camels and llamas are designated as two different species because they do not interbreed. But alas, it appears as though Rama has nullified the definition. However, a more strict reading of the definition of a species may clarify things. Usually the words "naturally interbreeding" are included in the definition. Rama was the result of artificial insemination. Also, in order to be members of the same species the offspring of a pairing must be living (truly Rama is) AND fertile (Rama has yet to demonstrate his procreative ability). So, just as in the case of horse + donkey = mule, the species are separate—albeit very close.

14

EARLY LIFE

Chapter Outline

Objectives

1. Describe how life might have spontaneously arisen on Earth approximately 3.8 billion years ago.
2. Describe the factors that led to the divergence of the three major cellular lineages.
3. Describe the principal types of bacteria.
4. Describe the unique features of bacterial life processes.
5. Give examples of positive and negative impacts of bacteria on humans.

6. Describe the criteria for admission to the Kingdom Protista.
7. List the ways protists differ from bacteria.
8. Be able to compare protists with other eukaryotes.
9. Distinguish each of the major groups within the Protista.
10. Describe the various types of fungal body plans, patterns of reproduction, and natural history.
11. Name at least one specific example of each of the major groups of true fungi.
12. Provide two examples of fungi in symbiotic relationships.
13. Describe the structure and reproduction cycles of viruses.
14. List several viruses that cause human illness and describe how the viruses do their dirty work.

Key Terms

crust	Lyme disease	late blight	spores
clay templates	protists	sudden oak death	asci
metabolism	flagellated protozoans	diatoms	yeasts
RNA world	diplomonads	coccolithophores	symbiosis
proto-cells	parabasalids	brown algae	mutualism
Archean	cyst	kelps	lichen
prokaryotic cells	giardiasis	stipes	mycorrhiza
bacteria	trichomoniasis	blades	histoplasmosis
archaea	trypanosomes	holdfasts	ergotism
eukaryotic cells	African sleeping	red algae	virus
stromatolites	sickness	phycobilins	bacteriophages
cell wall	Chagas disease	agar	parvoviruses
bacterial flagella	euglenoids	carrageenan	poxviruses
pili	contractile vacuoles	green algae	AIDS
bacterial conjugation	pellicle	amoebozoans	lytic pathway
plasmid	radiolarians	amoebas	lysis
photoautotrophs	foraminiferans	slime molds	lysogenic pathway
chemoautotrophs	plankton	amoebic dysentery	cold sores
photoheterotrophs	ciliates	plasmodial slime molds	viroids
chemoheterotrophs	alveolates	cellular slime molds	prion
pathogens	binary fission	fungi	bovine spongiform
bacterial chromosome	dinoflagellates	saprobes	encephalopathy
prokaryotic fission	algal bloom	mutualism	infection
lateral gene transfer	red tide	mycelium, -lia	disease
extreme halophiles	apicomplexans	hypha, -ae	sporadic
methanogens	malaria	microsporidians	endemic
extreme thermophiles	sporozoites	chytrids	epidemic
cyanobacteria	merozoites	club fungi	pandemic
heterocysts	gametocytes	sac fungi	SARS
endospore	stramenopiles	zygomycetes	antibiotic
botulism	oomycotes	mushrooms	
tetanus	water molds	stalk	
cholera	downy mildews	cap	
gonorrhea	white rusts	gills	

Lecture Outline

Looking for Life in All the Odd Places

A. Some organisms can live in extreme environments.

    1. *Thermus aquaticus* can live in hot water at 176°F.

        a. A heat-resistant enzyme taken from this prokaryote is used in PCR.

        b. This has resulted in a new line of inquiry—bioprospecting.

    2. Some organisms can survive near hydrothermal vents on the seafloor (230°F); others in acidic springs (pH near 0); and still others cling to life on mountain glaciers.

B. "Life is a magnificent continuation of the physical and chemical evolution of the universe, and the planet Earth."

14.1   Origin of the First Living Cells

A. Conditions on the Early Earth

    1. About 4.5 billion years ago remnants of exploding stars began to condense into planets, including our own Earth.

    2. The Earth was initially very hot, but cooled to form an outer mantle and partially-molten core.

        a. The first atmosphere probably consisted of gaseous hydrogen, nitrogen, carbon monoxide, and carbon dioxide.

        b. Gaseous oxygen and water were not thought to be present.

        c. When the crust cooled the water condensed, rains began, and pools of chemicals began to form.

    3. Within 200 million years life had originated on its surface, but how?

        a. Evidence from neighboring bodies in our solar system indicates that precursors for building biological molecules must have been present on the primitive Earth.

        b. Energy in the form of sunlight, lightning, and heat from the Earth's crust was also present.

            1) Stanley Miller used a lab apparatus to demonstrate synthesis of amino acids from a mixture of hydrogen, methane, ammonia, and water under abiotic conditions.

            2) Even if molecules were formed spontaneously, they would have quickly hydrolyzed unless clay templates served to hold the molecules together for condensation reactions.

            3) Other experiments have shown that when amino acids are placed in water and heated, they spontaneously order themselves into small protein-like molecules.

        c. Another hypothesis has simple organic compounds arriving on Earth from outer space; any complex molecules that formed could have been protected from disassembly by clay templates.

        d. Yet another hypothesis says that deep-sea hydrothermal vents could have been the place where ancient biological molecules could have formed.

B. Origin of Agents of Metabolism

    1. During the early history of the Earth, enzymes, ATP, and other molecules could have assembled spontaneously.

    2. The close association of these materials would have naturally promoted chemical interactions and the beginning of metabolic pathways.

C. Origin of Self-Replicating Systems

    1. From accumulated organic compounds emerged self-replicating systems consisting of DNA, RNA, and proteins.

2. Some types of coenzymes (enzyme helpers) have a structure identical to that of RNA nucleotides; furthermore, nucleotide precursors will self-assemble under conditions similar to those on the early Earth.

3. Perhaps RNA templates set up an RNA world that preceded DNA's dominance as the main informational molecule.

4. How DNA entered the picture is not yet clear, but we do know that some reactions were more probable than others—not random.

D. Origin of Cell Membranes

1. The metabolism in living cells cannot occur without a barrier against the chemical actions on the outside.

2. Proto-cells were probably membrane-bound sacs containing nucleic acids that served as templates for proteins.

3. In one series of experiments amino acids were heated to form protein chains which, when allowed to cool, self-assembled into proteinoid spheres that were selectively permeable.

E. The First Cells and Beyond

1. The Archean eon (3.8 to 2.5 billion years ago) was the time of macromolecule synthesis plus the origin of anaerobic prokaryotes.

2. The original prokaryote line split into archaea, bacteria, and a line leading to eukaryotes.

3. Evolution of the cyclic pathway of photosynthesis in bacteria tapped a renewable source of energy—sunlight; large accumulations of these cells are seen today as fossils known as stromatolites.

4. By 2.5 billion years ago, photosynthetic machinery had become altered enough in bacteria to produce oxygen as a byproduct, which stopped further chemical evolution and allowed aerobic respiration to proceed.

14.2   What Are Existing Prokaryotes Like?

A. General Characteristics

1. Prokaryotes have no nucleus or other membrane-bound organelles.
   a. Metabolic reactions take place in the cytoplasm or at the plasma membrane.
   b. Proteins are assembled on floating ribosomes.

2. Nearly all bacteria have a cell wall, usually containing a tough mesh of peptides cross-linked with polysaccharides, overlaid with a slime layer.

3. Two kinds of filamentous structures may be attached to the cell wall:
   a. The *bacterial flagellum* rotates like a propeller to pull the cell along.
   b. *Pili* help bacteria attach to one another for plasmid transfer during bacterial conjugation, or help them attach to surfaces.

4. Prokaryotic cells have four modes of nutrition:
   a. *Photoautotrophs* synthesize their own organic compounds using sunlight as the energy source and carbon dioxide as the carbon source.
   b. *Chemoautotrophs* utilize carbon dioxide and produce organic compounds using the energy in simple inorganic substances.
   c. *Photoheterotrophs* use sunlight as an energy source, but their carbon must come from organic compounds—not CO_2.
   d. *Chemoheterotrophs* include parasitic types that draw nutrition from living hosts and saprobic types that obtain nutrition from products, wastes, or remains of others.

5. Many prokaryotes are pathogens—infectious, disease-causing agents.

B. Growth and Reproduction

1. We measure bacterial growth as an increase in the number of cells in a given population.

2. When a bacterium divides, each daughter cell inherits a single chromosome—a circular, double-stranded DNA molecule.
        3. Bacteria reproduce by *prokaryotic fission,* resulting in two genetically identical daughter cells.
   C. Prokaryotic Classification
        1. Today's classification is based on evolutionary relationships made possible by comparative biochemistry studies, especially of RNA.
        2. A recent discovery that prokaryotic genomes may contain hereditary material from more than one source by lateral gene transfer has complicated the classification effort.
   D. Examples of Archaean Diversity
        1. Extreme halophiles are "salt-lovers."
            a. These species can tolerate high salt environments such as brackish ponds, salt lakes, volcanic vents on the seafloor, and the like.
            b. Most are heterotrophic aerobes, but some can switch to a special photosynthesis, using bacteriorhodopsin, to produce ATP.
        2. Methanogens are "methane-makers."
            a. They inhabit swamps, mud, sewage, and animal guts.
            b. They make ATP anaerobically by converting carbon dioxide and hydrogen to methane.
        3. Extreme thermophiles are "heat-lovers."
            a. These bacteria live in hot springs and other very hot places such as the thermal vents of the sea floor where temperatures exceed 110o C.
            b. They use sulfur as a source of electrons for ATP formation.
   E. Examples of Bacterial Diversity
        1. Some bacteria are photoautotrophic.
            a. Cyanobacteria are photosynthetic.
            b. *Anabaena,* by means of heterocysts, can fix nitrogen.
        2. Chemoheterotrophic bacteria include gram-positive ones.
            a. *Lactobacillus* forms lactate by fermentation and is used in making yogurt and pickles.
            b. Some form resistant endospores that can survive harsh environmental conditions; examples: *Clostridium botulinum* (botulism), *Bacillus anthracis* (anthrax).
        3. Proteobacteria include: *Helicobacter* (stomach ulcers), *Vibrio* (cholera), and *Neisseria gonorrhoea* (gonorrhea).
        4. Chemoautotrophic bacteria, such as *Rhizobium,* live in the nodules of plant roots where they convert nitrogen gas into nitrates for plant, and eventually animal, use.
   F. Bacterial Behavior
        1. Bacteria may be small but they can display remarkably complex behavior.
        2. Consider *Borrelia burgdorferi* (Lyme disease), which is taken into the gut of a tick in its blood meal and spreads to the salivary glands, where it awaits transfer to the next mammalian host.

14.3   The Curiously Classified Protists
   A. Protists are most like the earliest eukaryotic cells.
        1. They have a nucleus and the usual eukaryotic organelles.
            a. The DNA of their chromosomes is wound around histones.
            b. They divide using mechanisms of meiosis, mitosis, or both.
        2. Most are single-celled but there are colonial forms and multicelled species.
        3. They can be photoautotrophs, predators, parasites, and decomposers.

B. Flagellated Protozoans and Euglenoids
1. Flagellated protozoans are heterotrophic cells with one or more flagella.
2. Among the most ancient are the diplomonads and parabasalids.
   a. *Giardia* can enter the body in cyst form from drinking feces-contaminated water, resulting in severe diarrhea.
   b. *Trichomonas vaginalis* can be transmitted during sexual intercourse and lead to damage of the urinary and reproductive tracts.
3. Trypanosomes are flagellated cells that live in a variety of hosts.
   a. *Trypanosoma brucei* is carried by the tsetse fly and causes African sleeping sickness.
   b. Chagas disease is caused by *T. cruzi,* a trypanosome carried by kissing bugs.
4. Euglenoids are free-living, flagellated, photoautotrophic cells.
   a. They have the same chlorophyll as green algae and plants.
   b. The contractile vacuole expels excess water and the pellicle provides a flexible, but stable cell covering.
C. Radiolarians and Foraminiferans
1. Both groups use pseudopods to trap and engulf prey.
2. Foraminiferans live on the sea floor; they have a shell of calcium carbonate perforated by numerous holes through which the slender pseudopods extend.
3. Radiolarians have delicate, glasslike shells of silica through which stiffened, thin pseudopods extend.
D. The Ciliates
1. Ciliated protozoans, alveolates, are characterized by their numerous cilia, which beat in synchrony on the cell surface.
   a. Other features include: a cell "mouth" for food entrance, and waiting digestive vacuoles and contractile vacuoles to get rid of excess water.
   b. There are two types of nuclei: a small micronucleus and a larger macronucleus.
2. Ciliates reproduce asexually by binary fission and may demonstrate a primitive form of sexual reproduction called conjugation in which genetic material is mutually exchanged.
E. Dinoflagellates
1. Dinoflagellates are usually single photosynthetic cells of varying colors.
   a. These marine cells display flagella located in grooves of the cellulose covering.
   b. Some are photosynthetic while others are predatory on bacteria.
2. Some forms of red-pigmented cells cause the infamous red tides and also produce a neurotoxin fatal to humans.
F. Apicomplexans and Malaria
1. Apicomplexans are parasitic alveolates equipped with a unique microtubular device that can attach to and penetrate a host cell.
2. Malaria, caused by *Plasmodium* and transmitted by mosquitoes, is a serious worldwide disease.
   a. The female *Anopheles* mosquito transmits the sporozoite to the human host during feeding.
      1) After multiplying first in the liver and then in the red blood cells, the merozoite stage breaks out into the bloodstream, causing terrific bouts of chills and fever.
      2) The gametocyte stage cannot mature in humans but must be picked up by the female mosquito during feeding to complete the life cycle.
   b. When the merozoites are released into the bloodstream, severe chills and fever result in recurring bouts.
   c. Many *Plasmodium* strains are now resistant to older drugs; vaccines are in development.

G. Diatoms, Brown Algae, and Relatives
   1. Stramenopiles are ancient flagellates named for the thin filaments that project from one of their two flagella.
   2. Oomycotes include water molds, downy mildews, and white rusts.
      a. Some are parasitic on aquatic animals, such as goldfish, or attack grapevines and fruits.
      b. They produce extensive mycelia, some of which become modified to form gamete-producing structures.
      c. One infamous member of this group was responsible for late blight, which caused a failure of the Irish potato crop in the mid-1800s, resulting in thousands of deaths.
   3. Diatoms have unique two-part silica shells, which are commercially valuable as abrasives and filtering materials.
   4. Brown algae include the large kelps of the intertidal zones.
      a. Accessory pigments provide the color.
      b. They are very plantlike in structure:
         1) Leaflike *blades* grow from a stemlike *stipe,* which may be attached to a rootlike *holdfast.*
         2) Some giant kelp have gas-filled bladders, or *floats.*
H. Red Algae
   1. These algae possess phycobilin pigments, which can trap sunlight in deep marine waters.
   2. Some forms can aid in reef building (stonelike cell walls), others yield agar, and carrageenan is used as a stabilizer in ice cream.
I. Green Algae
   1. These algae grow virtually everywhere and bear the greatest resemblance to land plants because of structure and biochemistry.
      a. They have the same pigments as land plants (chlorophylls *a* and *b,* carotenoids, and xanthophylls).
      b. They possess cellulose in the cell walls and store carbohydrates as starch.
   2. There is much diversity in this group.
      a. *Volvox* forms colonies consisting of a sphere of perhaps thousands of cells.
      b. In the rather simple *Chlamydomonas,* there is no multicelled stage, only an alternation between haploid and diploid cells.
J. Amoebozoans
   1. Amoeboid protozoans have no permanent locomotor structures but form extensions of the cytoplasm and cell membrane in the form of pseudopods.
      a. True amoebas resemble tiny blobs as their plasma membranes constantly change the shape of the cell.
      b. One species causes amoebic dysentery, a serious intestinal diarrhea.
   2. Slime molds are not fungi.
      a. These are heterotrophic, free-living, amoeba-like protists.
      b. They can assume two forms depending on the food supply:
         1) The cells are phagocytic and can aggregate to form a slimy mass that can migrate to find new food sources.
         2) Later the slime molds will produce spores released from stalklike structures.

14.4   The Fabulous Fungi
   A. Characteristics of Fungi
      1. Fungi are heterotrophs that utilize organic matter.
         a. Most are saprobes; they get their nutrients from nonliving matter and cause its decay.

        b. All fungi rely on extracellular enzymatic digestion and absorption.
        c. Some fungi are parasites; others form mutualistic relationships.
    2. Fungi have both sexual and asexual modes of reproduction.
        a. Sexual reproduction proceeds through the formation of gametes in gametangia as well as by spores.
        b. Asexual reproduction is mostly by spores produced in sporangia.
            1) Spores germinate to give rise to tubular filaments called hyphae.
            2) A mass of hyphae called a mycelium forms the nutrient-absorbing "body" of the fungus.
B. Fungal Diversity
    1. About 56,000 species of fungi have been identified and there are many more.
        a. Some fossilized forms date to 900 million years ago.
        b. Microsporidians and chytrids are considered the most evolutionarily ancient lineages.
    2. There are three major groups: club fungi, sac fungi, and zygomycetes.
C. The Club Fungi
    1. The aboveground part of the fungal body is the common mushroom consisting of a stalk and a cap.
        a. Spores are produced in the club-shaped gills of the cap.
        b. When spores land on a suitable site, they germinate to produce extensive underground mycelia that then reproduce sexually when two compatible mating strains make contact.
    2. Club fungi include mushrooms, shelf fungi, coral fungi, puffballs, and stinkhorns.
        a. Some of the saprobic species are important decomposers of plant debris.
        b. Others are symbionts that live in close association with tree roots.
        c. The edible mushroom is a multimillion-dollar business.
D. Spores and More Spores
    1. Fungi are prolific spore producers.
        a. Spores can be sexual, asexual, or both.
        b. They are small, dry, and easily dispersed by air currents.
        c. Each spore that germinates can be the start of a hypha and a mycelium.
    2. In the zygomycetes group of fungi, sexual reproduction begins when two hyphae (different mating strains) grow toward each other and fuse.
        a. Gametangia form and make haploid nuclei, which later fuse to form a zygote.
        b. A zygosporangium forms around the zygote; later it releases haploid spores.
    3. Sac fungi form sexual spores called ascospores inside sac-shaped cells called asci.
        a. Multicelled sac fungi include edible morels and truffles.
        b. Single-celled yeasts are useful in baking (carbon dioxide production makes the bread rise) and for alcoholic-beverage production.
E. Fungal Symbionts
    1. Symbiosis refers to species living together in close association; mutualism is an interaction in which both partners benefit.
    2. Lichens
        a. Lichens are mutualistic associations between fungi and cyanobacteria, green algae, or both.
            1) The fungus (mycobiont) parasitizes the photosynthetic alga (photobiont) upon which it depends entirely for its food.
            2) The algae derive very little benefit other than a protected place to survive.

b. Lichens live in inhospitable places such as bare rock and tree trunks.
   1) By their metabolic activities, lichens can change the composition of their substrate.
   2) They are unusually sensitive to air pollution
3. Mycorrhizae
   a. A mycorrhiza is a symbiotic relationship in which fungi hyphae surround roots of shrubs and trees.
   b. Because of its extensive surface area, the fungus can absorb mineral ions and facilitate their entry into the plant.
4. As Fungi Go, So Go the Forests
   a. The number and diversity of fungi are declining due to pollution.
   b. When fungi die, trees lose their support systems and become vulnerable to frost and drought.
F. The Unloved Few
   1. Fungi cause many problems for humans.
      a. Molds grow on live plants and on harvested fruits and vegetables.
      b. Spores of *Ajellomyces capsulatus* cause a respiratory disease called histoplasmosis.
   2. Fungi have even had a role in history.
      a. *Claviceps purpurea* parasitizes rye producing a toxic alkaloid that, when consumed, causes ergotism.
      b. Peter the Great's soldiers and their horses became so ill that it thwarted the effort of conquering ports along the Black Sea.

14.5   Viruses, Viroids, and Prions
A. Characteristics of Viruses
   1. A virus consists of a nucleic acid core surrounded by a protein coat.
      a. The genetic material may be either DNA or RNA.
      b. The coat, or capsid, may be rod shaped, a polyhedron, or a lipid envelope.
   2. A virus can replicate only after its nucleic acid has entered and subverted the host cell's biosynthetic apparatus to produce new viral particles.
   3. The vertebrate immune system can detect and fight viruses, but the problem for the defense mechanisms is the constantly mutating viral proteins.
   4. Bacteriophages infect bacterial cells, usually with negative effects on the cell; they have been valuable in genetic engineering research.
   5. Animal viruses infect human cells, causing such common diseases as influenza, chickenpox, and the common cold; others such as HIV can cause much more serious conditions such as AIDS.
B. Viral Multiplication Cycles
   1. There are five basic steps in the multiplication of viruses:
      a. *Attachment:* the virus recognizes and becomes attached to the host cell.
      b. *Penetration:* DNA or RNA alone (or whole virus) enters the cytoplasm.
      c. *Replication and synthesis:* viral genes direct the host cell into replicating viral nucleic acids, and synthesizing viral enzymes and capsid proteins.
      d. *Assembly:* synthesized components are put together into new infectious particles.
      e. *Release:* new virus particles are released from the infected cell.
   2. Replication can proceed by way of two pathways:
      a. In the *lytic* pathway, the virus quickly accomplishes the first four steps listed above and causes the cell to rupture (lysis), spilling its contents and the viruses.

        b. In the *lysogenic* pathways, the viral genes remain inactive inside the host cell (and its descendants); often the genes become integrated into the host DNA only to resume their destructive viral activity later.

    C. Viroids and Prions

        1. Viroids are naked snippets of RNA (no protein coat) that cause plant diseases; only one has been found in humans, contributing to hepatitis D.

        2. A prion is an infectious particle; the most studied is one that causes bovine spongiform encephalopathy ("mad cow disease") or Creutzfeld-Jacob disease in humans.

14.6   Evolution and Infectious Diseases

    A. Infection is the invasion of the body by a pathogen, or its genetic material.

        1. The outcome—disease—occurs when the body's defenses are overcome, at least temporarily.

        2. Sporadic diseases occur irregularly among very few people; endemic diseases occur rather constantly at low infection levels; an epidemic results if the disease spreads throughout the population; a pandemic is defined as an outbreak in several countries at the same time.

    B. A pathogen can explode on the scene rather quickly.

        1. SARS suddenly appeared in 2002 in China with a few reported cases.

        2. Within seven months, thousands of cases were reported around the world.

    C. Two barriers keep pathogens from achieving world dominance:

        1. The pathogen's host has usually evolved immune defenses against it.

        2. If the pathogen kills too well and too fast, it might disappear.

Suggestions for Presenting the Material

- This chapter "steps back" in time to look at the origin and early evolution of life on Earth then goes on to describe prokaryotes, protists, fungi, and viruses.

- Stress the tenuous conclusions that are in constant revision when scientists attempt to reconstruct the past. Just as a good medical diagnosis is not based on just *one* examination or one lab test, a good analysis of past evolutionary history is not based on any *one* line of evidence, but rather several lines of corroborating evidence.

- You may want to begin the topic of origin of life by surveying the class for the explanations most frequently given to account for the origin of life on planet Earth. (Responses from my classes are, in frequency order: #1: special creation, #2: arrival from distant planets, #3: "just happened.")

- Based on the above survey, you may find that your students know the *least* about *spontaneous generation* and are indeed skeptical that "life could come from nonliving matter." Be sure you include some mention of the difference in possibilities of spontaneous generation happening in the *past* and *today* (see the Enrichment section).

- Because of the rather theoretical and speculative nature of the Origin of Life section, students' minds often wander because they don't have any concrete terms to write down. Use of suitable visual material will help to retain focus.

- Students should be very interested in the bacteria and viruses covered in this chapter, especially those that are capable of causing well-known diseases.

- Most students are unfamiliar with the structure and function of the viruses and bacteria. Emphasize the nonliving nature of the viruses, a point that students often have trouble grasping.

- This chapter offers an excellent opportunity to discuss epidemiology and to show how scientists use the scientific method when attempting to find the causative agent of a disease. The recent widespread public awareness of AIDS also opens an avenue for discussion of the accuracy with which scientific stories are covered by the media.

- Table 14.3 (Comparison of Prokaryotes and Eukaryotes) is a helpful one that may escape students' notice, by its location in the Summary section, if it is not brought to their attention.

- Briefly review the six major groups of organisms, reminding students that this chapter covers organisms in the rather ill-defined phylum Protista. Ask students again to recall the differences between prokaryotic and eukaryotic cells.

- The text reports progress is being made in classifying protists based on comparative methods using molecular technology.

- It is very difficult for students to get a sense of the relative size and shape of protists unless the instructor makes liberal use of photos, especially ones that give some comparison to objects of known size.

- Because the protists are sometimes "...looked upon as the rag-bag of classification schemes..." as one text said, it is important to assure the students that water molds do in fact resemble fungi and brown algae do have plant-like parts. Rather than dwelling on the imprecision of this situation, use it to emphasize the continuum of evolution.

- To make the names of these protists more real, seek practical uses and applications for as many as you can. For example, foraminiferans seem to be just lying at the bottom of the ocean, but to a geologist exploring for oil reserves they tell a valuable story.

- Be sure to spend ample time discussing the parasitic and saprobic lifestyles found among the fungi; students will be much more familiar with the autotrophic mode of nutrition among photosynthetic green plants.

- Ask students to name examples of fungi they might know from everyday life and use these examples when discussing fungal diversity. Students will be surprised at the variety of organisms found in this group.

- Many years ago fungi were classified with the plants. Some "chronologically challenged" professors still may think of them in that way. Clearly emphasize the reasons for establishing a separate kingdom for the fungi.

Classroom and Laboratory Enrichment

- Prepare an overhead summarizing the work of Redi, Spallanzani, and Pasteur in disproving spontaneous generation under "recent" conditions on Earth.

- Assemble a replica (sans ingredients) of the apparatus Stanley Miller used in his famous experiment. Point out how really simple it was.

- Using modeling clay, make "templates" such as might have been available for molecules in the primordial Earth.

- To stimulate interest in Sidney Fox's "proto-cells," blow soap bubbles using the materials available in any store's toy section.

- Ask for a first-hand account of what it is like to be in an area where the Earth's plates are fulfilling their destiny according to the plate tectonic theory; in other words, "Who has been in an earthquake?"

- The dinosaurs may have been done-in by the biggest dust storm ever. Have someone give an account of what it is like to experience such an event in the Great Plains.

- Demonstrate the events of continental drift using an overhead transparency to represent the Earth and pieces of transparency film to represent the land masses. Films and videotapes can also be used to effectively explain continental drift.

- Use the tip of a flat toothpick to collect bacteria from sources such as plaque from the surface of a tooth or yogurt with live cultures. Prepare a simple bacterial smear, stain with crystal violet, and observe at 1000x.

- Prepare Gram stains of bacterial species of varying morphology and Gram status from cultures obtained from biological supply houses.

- Collect and examine cyanobacteria from stagnant ponds, tree trunks, and greenhouse flowerpots.

- Survey your environment for the presence of bacteria. This can be done with help from a microbiologist who can prepare media and plates. Then you and your students can: (a) take swabs of various surfaces; (b) allow dust to settle on a plate; (c) allow insects to land; (d) apply samples of food, and so on.

- Remind students of the beneficial aspects of bacteria, including their usefulness in producing products (e.g., human insulin) through genetic engineering.

- Emphasize the importance of viruses and bacteria by showing a film or video of the misery these microscopic entities bring to humans and their animals.

- Invite a health care worker to tell of experiences and precautions against pathogens in the hospital or clinic setting.

- Visit an electron microscope in a research laboratory where research on viruses is being done. Ask the technician to discuss preparation techniques for viral specimens and to demonstrate the operation of the microscope. If possible, allow students to prepare their own viral suspensions of a plant virus (such as tobacco mosaic virus) in the laboratory for subsequent examination under the electron microscope.

- Use overhead transparencies, films, or videos to show the steps of a viral infectious cycle.

- Prepare an exhibit of living organisms or portions of organisms, such as leaves, affected by viruses.

- Gather information from local health authorities about any of the diseases caused by bacteria and viruses that are found in your area. Sexually transmitted diseases such as gonorrhea, syphilis, and AIDS would be good examples. What is the number of cases per month within your city or state? Is the number of new cases rising or falling?

- Seek class members or faculty colleagues who may have traveled to a tropical area where diseases unknown in the United States are present. Ask them to report on any precautions taken before, during, and after their trip.

- Read a more expanded account of the great Irish potato famine.

- Obtain samples of water from decorative fountains, flower pots, small ponds, and the like and examine them for protists.

- You can obtain kits from biological supply houses for growing slime molds.

- Show videos of living protists.

- View protozoa in a hay infusion.

- Look for slime molds on moist logs and fallen trees in damp forest areas.

- Collect diatoms from the edges of quiet ponds and slow-moving streams.

- Gather information from local health authorities about any of the diseases caused by protists that are found in your area.

- Many protists are highly mobile creatures and fun to watch. If you have a small class, secure some cultures and allow students to make their own preparations for microscopic observation. If your class is large, use a videotape (several biological supply houses offer these).

- Present a flow chart depicting the role of fungi in the carbon cycle.

- Use overhead transparencies to show life cycles of species of fungi and plants. If the life cycle is un-labeled, you can ask your students to find the points at which meiosis and fertilization occur. Ask them which part of the life cycle is haploid and which part is diploid.

- Demonstrate variety within the fungi by growing cultures of representative fungal species or ordering them from a biological supply house. Use slides to survey the fungi. Use prepared microscope slides to look at vegetative hyphae and reproductive structures of representative fungi.

- Collect samples of plant tissues exhibiting signs of pathogenic fungi. Some examples include leaves infected with powdery mildew, rusts, or black spot, young seedlings killed by "damping off" (caused by the fungus *Pythium*), and citrus fruits covered with blue-green *Penicillium*.

- Ask the produce manager of a local supermarket to save rotting or damaged fruit for one or two days. Place the fruits on display in lab, and allow students to look at fungi with a dissecting scope or to make wet mounts and view them under the compound scope.

- Start a culture of bread mold *(Rhizopus)* by wiping a small piece of preservative-free bread across a dusty floor or cabinet top, misting with water, and placing in a covered petri dish for several days.

- Grow *Pilobolus* on extremely fresh horse manure that has been placed on filter paper in a culture dish covered with an upside-down beaker. Soon after *Pilobolus* has started to appear, sporangia ejected by *Pilobolus* stalks will appear on the inside of the beaker.

- Collect fungi from forests and fields after cool, damp weather conditions. Lichens can be collected from a wide variety of locations regardless of weather conditions.

- Prepare a yeast culture in lab by dissolving an envelope of baker's yeast and a small amount of sugar in a beaker of warm water. Keep the beaker warm. Make a wet mount and observe budding yeast cells under the microscope.

- Demonstrate the ability of yeast to perform fermentation by making beer or wine in the laboratory.

- Use fresh grocery store mushrooms *(Agaricus)* as an example of a basidiomycete. Pass them around the classroom or lab, and ask students to observe the basidiocarp, stalk, cap, and gills.

Impacts, Issues Classroom Discussion Ideas

- Describe the metabolic pathways used by the first living cells to obtain energy.

- What are the objections you could raise to the possibility of life arriving here millions of years ago from distant planets?

- In the hypothetical series of events (Figure 14.3) leading from spontaneous formation of molecules to living cells, which step is most puzzling and the one about which little is known?

- Evolutionary biologists believe that life on Earth first evolved in the absence of oxygen. So where did the oxygen in our atmosphere come from?

- Name some organisms living today that are virtually unchanged from their earliest appearances in the fossil record millions of years ago. Why do some organisms seem to fail to change significantly throughout geologic time?

- Why are the methanogens, halophiles, and thermophiles placed in the archaea?

Additional Ideas for Classroom Discussion

- Diagram the apparatus used by Stanley Miller to study the synthesis of organic compounds in an atmosphere like that of the early Earth. Ask students what they think of Miller's findings.

- Why was free oxygen (O_2) not included in Miller's experiment? What did the electrical spark simulate?

- What distinguishes a nonliving lipid-bound sphere containing nucleic acids and amino acids from a living cell?

- Why was aerobic respiration necessary for the evolution of eukaryotes?

- What are some of the advantages of multicellularity?

- Why do you think people believed as recently as 100 years ago that spontaneous generation still occurs on the Earth?

- The branching of prokaryotes during the Archean into archaea, bacteria, and eukaryotes is the basis for a new three-domain scheme of classification. Evaluate the merits of this scheme versus the more traditional five or six kingdom scheme.

- Why is that body of thought known as "scientific creationism," or its newest version "intelligent design," not a *science*? List the types of evidence supporting the principle of evolution.

- How have extinctions facilitated the development of new species?

- Do you think it is possible for scientists studying the evolution of life to also believe that a supreme being played a role in the creation of life? Why or why not?

- Are the continents still moving today?

- In much older classification schemes, bacteria were included with the plants. For what reason was this a rather poor match?

- Normally, we would think of "autotrophic" as synonymous with "green" if we were considering members of the plant kingdom. What two sources of energy are available to *bacterial* autotrophs?

- Why is the "Gram" of Gram stain written with a capital letter?

- How would you classify the viruses? Would you consider them to be nonliving? If the viruses are nonliving, why do you think they are covered in the study of biology?

- How does the human body respond to a sudden onslaught of viral invaders?

- What are viroids? How are they similar to/different from viruses?

- What is a pathogen? What is the Greek word from which this term is derived?

- What is the role of disease in limiting the growth of human and animal populations? (Remember Malthus!)

- What is epidemiology? Discuss the roles played by the World Health Organization and the Centers for Disease Control and Prevention in the study and treatment of outbreaks of disease.

- Discuss the possibility that the "age of antibiotics" may be drawing to a close.

- Why would a natural disaster such as the Irish potato famine not be a reality today? What international conditions and attitudes have changed since that tragic event?

- What makes the water in a decorative fountain turn green?

- Algae occur in tremendous quantities in nature. To what extent have they been used for human or animal food? Are there any "algae farms"?

- What would be the consequences of a worldwide kill off of protists?

- Of what ecological value are the water molds and slime molds?

- What are some steps that tropical countries can take to reduce the rate of malaria?
- Why did the effort to eradicate malaria fail? Which of Darwin's ideas was ignored in the eradication proposal?
- How is amebic dysentery transmitted to humans?
- Why do apicomplexans have such complicated life cycles? Does this complexity improve or hinder their survival chances?
- What features make *Euglena* seem like a hybrid of plant and animal?
- What causes red tides?
- Why are water molds more properly considered protists than fungi?
- Why are the red, brown, and green algae more properly considered protists than plants?
- Describe the similarities and differences between fungal spores and spores found among members of the plant kingdom.
- Wildlife biologists have occasionally observed wild bears that appear to stagger and walk unsteadily after consuming large quantities of fallen fruit in late summer and early autumn. What is happening to them?
- The relationship of the algae and fungi that compose a lichen is mutualism. What is the symbiotic relationship of the entire *lichen* to the *tree* to which it is attached?
- What body feature is the basis for classification of the fungi?
- Is it true that lichens grow only on the north side of trees? What is the basis of this? Is this also true of lichens in the Southern Hemisphere?

How Would You Vote? Classroom Discussion Ideas

- Monitor the voting for the online question. It only seems fair that if the discovery of an organism leads to a profitable venture then the source of that organism should share in the monetary profits.

Term Paper Topics, Library Activities, and Special Projects

- Discuss the history of the experiments by Stanley Miller.
- See if you can locate the original article by Miller and Urey in which they reported their famous experiment. Read it carefully to see what speculative application they made for their experiment.
- Although the idea of life originating on Earth from forms traveling from distant planets is highly imaginative, serious proposals have been advanced. Locate some of these and evaluate their merit.
- In recent years, some scientists have questioned the significance of Stanley Miller's experiment. Prepare an evaluation of their criticisms.
- What is thought to be the current rate of species extinction today? Is the rate of extinction today higher than can be accounted for by background extinction? What areas of the Earth are experiencing the highest rates of species extinction?
- Research the causes of extinction *today*. Are all, or most, of the causes the result of human intervention?
- Trace the evolutionary history of one group of plants or animals throughout geologic time.
- Collect fossils, photographs, or descriptions of fossils from your region of the United States. What do they reveal about the past history of your area?

- Discuss the formation of coal and petroleum. Prepare a map showing areas of coal and oil deposits in the United States.

- Discuss recent controversial studies that use human mitochondrial DNA to draw conclusions about human evolution.

- Describe the effects of the plate tectonic theory on organism diversity.

- The five-kingdom system of classification was proposed by Robert H. Whittaker in 1969. Locate the original article to see how much of his original version has changed much up to the present time.

- Are public swimming areas (pools, lakes, springfed ponds, rivers) in your area required to routinely check for evidence of pollution from sewage effluent? Discover the maximum *E. coli* count allowed by law before the facility must be closed to public swimming. How is this figure determined? What does it mean? Why is it unsafe to swim in waters that have a relatively large number of *E. coli* bacteria?

- How do antibiotics such as penicillin and tetracycline kill bacteria? Discuss the modes of action of several commonly used antibiotics.

- Report on the increasing resistance of pathogenic bacteria to commonly-used antibiotics.

- Explain why the phrase "bacteria are *immune* to antibiotics" is inaccurate, while the phrase "bacteria are *resistant* to antibiotics" is correct.

- Describe the role of certain species of bacteria in producing food products such as buttermilk, sour cream, yogurt, and sauerkraut.

- Describe the morphology and physiology of any one of the pathogenic genera of bacteria. Discuss the diseases caused by the members of the genus and their treatments.

- Where did viruses come from? Discover what scientists know about the evolutionary origin of the viruses.

- How are viruses destroyed? What kinds of chemicals and filters are used in the laboratory to ensure that an experimental liquid is virus-free?

- Research the history, mode of action, and treatment of several economically important viral diseases of crops.

- Discuss the role of the immune system in fighting viral outbreaks or bacterial infections. How does the immune system recognize viral strains or bacterial species that have caused disease within the individual on previous occasions?

- Discuss the worldwide Spanish flu epidemic of 1918–1920, emphasizing the fear it caused because of the tremendous death rate.

- Collect stories about AIDS from magazines and newspapers. Analyze the stories for scientific accuracy and completeness. In what areas do such stories effectively cover AIDS? In what ways do they mislead or fail to inform the reader?

- Report on the latest scientific research in the treatment of any one of the diseases caused by viruses discussed in your text.

- Your text indicated that flu epidemics (and pandemics) tend to occur in ten- to forty-year cycles. Check an epidemiology or medical textbook to locate possible explanations for this periodicity.

- How does a retrovirus differ from other viruses in its operation?

- The following are diseases caused by spirochetes and transmitted in different ways:
  a. Lyme disease by ticks
  b. Relapsing fever by lice
  c. Syphilis by human sexual contact

  Are the different spirochete species able to interchange vectors? Explain why.

- Research the details of the SARS outbreak of 2002-2003.
- Investigate the nutritional value of kelp.
- Prepare a report on the Irish potato famine.
- Diagram the complete life cycle of *Plasmodium.*
- Chronicle the rise and fall of the campaign to eradicate malaria.
- Compare the extent and severity of problems caused by viruses, bacteria, and protists.
- Discuss the geographic distribution and economic impact of red tides in the United States.
- Write a report on any one of the diseases caused by protozoans. Discuss the historical roles played by these diseases in situations such as the colonization of new lands, wars, and the building of the Panama Canal.
- Historically the multicelled algae (red, brown, green) were considered plants. Enumerate the reasons why they are more properly considered protists.
- Discuss the economic importance of fungi, both as agents of decay and disease and as organisms important in research and industry.
- Discuss the diagnosis and treatment of fungi that grow on the human skin and mucous membranes.
- Describe the role of yeasts in the making of beer and wine.
- Write a report about the use of lichen species as indicators of pollution.
- Compile a list of wild mushrooms found in your area.
- Discuss the possible future role of algae as a human food source.
- Consult a textbook on insect control methods to investigate the use of fungi as biocontrol agents for insects.
- Obtain a listing of the active ingredients in an antifungal medication for athlete's foot. Consult the Merck Index to learn how these chemicals inhibit fungal growth.
- Obtain a field guide to the edible mushrooms. What easily seen features warn us of poisonous varieties?

Possible Responses to *Critical Thinking* Questions

1. *Dictyostelium discoideum* is a desirable organism to study for several reasons. One interesting aspect of its life cycle is the formation of the fruiting body from identical slime mold cells. This is similar to the incredible differentiation that occurs in multicelled organisms when genetic programming produces the germ layers, and eventually organs from identical blastomeres. Perhaps the signals in the slime mold cells could give a clue to what is happening in more advanced creatures.

2. (a) Humans in general are a short-sighted and self-centered bunch. If pressed we give assent to preservation of wildlife, but not at the expense of food shortages for ourselves. Can't we just hear the radio call-ins shouting "PRIORITIES, man, PRIORITIES."

   (b) So runoff is a continuing problem, but haven't we always raised crops and applied fertilizers (commercial and natural)? Sure, but now we are applying massive quantities to massive fields with unhindered paths of runoff to our waterways. Can the government force a farmer to jeopardize his own livelihood and those he feeds and clothes with his crops by dictating his farming practices? This would seem to be the only way to reduce the problem because it is so pervasive.

(c) So if we limit the application of fertilizers we create an even more serious and immediate problem—hungry people! And *angry* people. In the past we have heard of implausible proposals to raise more food in the ocean, outer space, and the like. None of these have proven adequate to supply our ever-increasing needs.

(d) People have always generated wastes, as archeological digs reveal. These wastes have included fecal material, which can be decomposed and recycled, plus other wastes such as paper, pottery, metal, etc. In times past, the amount of area for disposal was large, and the number of disposers small. In other words, there were enough places to get this stuff "out of sight." With over six billion plus people on the Earth and few new disposal areas, we are having a hard time finding enough places for our trash. We've tried the ocean, landfills, and even outer space. I wish we could all generate less waste but the container industry seems to be against us; reusable makes sense but it doesn't make many profits!

3. There are several issues to be considered when the spraying of mycoherbicides into the environment is considered. Foremost is the possibility that the fungus will adversely affect a non-target plant. Initially, the developers assure the public that the fungus is very specific for the pest plant, say coca. But who really knows whether a change in the fungus will cause some ornamental or agricultural plant to be killed? During the Vietnam War we saw video of huge tanker planes dropping millions of pounds of herbicide on the jungles to "expose" the enemy. Of course the enemy still remained hidden and humans on both sides of the conflict suffered health damage.

4. Perhaps it would be an interesting mental exercise to look at the "flip side" of viruses—as *good*! Let's think of some ways. One obvious one would see viruses as agents of population control. Now of course it would be heartless to think of human deaths as a good thing for the environment but what about rodents or nuisance birds? Furthermore, most people don't even know that bacteria can be infected by viruses, but if they were aware of it, perhaps they would conclude that killing off some bacteria wouldn't necessarily be a bad thing. And then there are insects and other arthropods like ticks: my students always ask whether the viruses that these invertebrates carry (for example, Lyme disease in ticks) harm the carrier. Unfortunately, if you are hoping to reduce the insect or tick population by natural means, the answer is "No."

5. The irradiation of food is controversial mostly because the average consumer knows so little about it. Furthermore, we are reluctant to accept new methodologies because of the mistakes of the past, especially when it involves something we eat on a daily basis. The food industry makes a case for safety and health: safety of the food and the assurance that the irradiated food will protect us against pathogens. Now as to what effect seeing this symbol would have on a shopper; that would depend on previous knowledge concerning the irradiation process. If the shopper *believes* in the benefits of irradiation, then the symbol is reassuring. If the shopper *fears* the dangers of irradiation, the symbol is a deterrent to picking that product. I suspect that both of these groups are not the majority of shoppers, who frankly don't even recognize the symbol for what it means.

15

PLANT EVOLUTION

Chapter Outline

Objectives

1. Outline the evolutionary advances that converted marine algal ancestors into forms that could exist on wet land.
2. State the advances that converted primitive marsh plants into dry-land flowering plants.
3. Characterize the mosses, seedless vascular plants, gymnosperms, and angiosperms.

Key Terms

root systems	nonvascular plants	bryophytes	ferns
shoot systems	vascular plants	mosses	strobilus
xylem	seedless vascular	liverworts	rhizomes
phloem	seed-bearing vascular	hornworts	epiphytes
cuticle	plants	rhizoids	frond
stomata	heterosporous	peat bogs	sorus, sori
gametophyte	homosporous	lycophytes (club	microspores
sporophyte	pollen grains	mosses)	pollination
spores	seed	horsetails	megaspores

ovule	conifers	pollinators	monocots
cycad	cones	coevolution	fruits
ginkgos	evergreen	magnoliids	deforestation
gnetophytes	flowers	eudicots	

Lecture Outline

Beginnings, and Endings
A. Change is a way of life.
1. The earliest plants were club mosses and horsetails.
2. Then came gymnosperms followed by angiosperms.
B. Human populations have increased spectacularly.
1. Crops have been cultivated for food.
2. Confers are harvested for lumber and paper.

15.1 Pioneers in a New World
A. Roots, Stems, and Leaves
1. Underground parts of plants developed into root systems, specialized for absorption of water and minerals through extensive cylindrical tubes.
2. Plant parts above ground developed into shoot systems, adapted for exploiting sunlight and absorbing carbon dioxide from the air.
3. Vascular tissue became increasingly extensive: xylem for conducting water and minerals, phloem for products of photosynthesis.
4. Extensive growth of stems and branches became possible due to the strengthening of cell walls afforded by deposits of lignin.
5. Stems and leaves were covered by cuticle to minimize water loss; evaporation was controlled by opening and closing of stomata (openings).
B. From Haploid to Diploid Dominance
1. The life cycle of simple aquatic plants is dominated by the haploid *gametophyte* phase.
a. Gametes of some green algae are all motile and of the same size; others are differentiated into motile sperm and immotile eggs.
b. A watery environment was necessary for gametes to meet each other.
2. The life cycle of complex land plants is dominated by the large, diploid *sporophyte*.
a. Cells within the sporophyte undergo meiosis to give rise to the haploid spores.
b. The spore develops into the *gametophyte*, which produces the gametes.
3. Over time the sporophytes, while developing extensive root and shoot systems, began holding onto their spores and gametophytes—protecting and nourishing them.
C. Seeds and Pollen Grains
1. The spores of some algae and simple vascular plants are all alike—homosporous.
2. In the gymnosperm and angiosperm lineages, the spores are differentiated into two types—heterosporous.
a. The male gametophytes—pollen grains—are released from the parent plant to be carried by whatever means to the female gametophyte.
b. The female gametophytes remain in the plant and are surrounded by protective tissues, eventually producing a seed.

15.2   The Bryophytes—No Vascular Tissues
A. Bryophytes include the mosses, liverworts, and hornworts.
   1. Although they resemble more complex land plants, they do not contain xylem or phloem.
   2. Most species do have *rhizoids* that attach the gametophytes to the soil and absorb water and minerals.
B. Mosses are the most common bryophytes.
   1. Eggs and sperm develop in the *gametangia* at the shoot tips of the familiar moss plants.
   2. After fertilization, the zygote develops into a mature sporophyte, which consists of a *sporangium* in which the spores develop.
C. These nonvascular plants show three features that were adaptive during the transition to land:
   1. Above-ground parts display a cuticle with numerous stomata.
   2. A cellular protective jacket surrounds the sperm-producing and egg-producing parts of the plant to prevent drying out.
   3. The embryo sporophyte (small, dependent) begins life inside the female gametophyte (large, independent).

15.3   Seedless Vascular Plants
A. Most of the seedless vascular plants that flourished in the past are extinct.
   1. Their present-day descendants (lycophytes, horsetails, and ferns) differ from bryophytes with respect to the sporophytes, which:
      a. develop independently of the gametophytes,
      b. have well-developed vascular tissues, and
      c. are the larger, longer lived phase of the life cycle.
   2. Although the sporophytes of seedless vascular plants can live on land, their gametophytes cannot because they lack vascular tissues and because the male gametes must have water to reach the eggs.
B. Club Mosses
   1. Lycophytes were once tree-sized but now are represented by small club mosses on the forest floor.
      a. The sporophyte has true roots, stems, and small leaves containing the vascular tissue.
      b. Strobili bear spores that germinate to form small, free-living gametophytes.
   2. This group is still closely tied to an aquatic environment because the sperm must swim to the eggs.
C. Horsetails
   1. The ancient relatives of horsetails were treelike; only the moderately sized *Equisetum* has survived.
      a. The sporophytes possess underground stems called rhizomes.
      b. The scalelike leaves are arranged in whorls around the hollow, photosynthetic stem.
   2. Spores are produced inside cone-shaped clusters of leaves at the shoot tip.
D. Ferns
   1. Ferns bear underground stems (rhizomes) and aerial leaves (fronds).
   2. Sori are clusters of sporangia that release spores that develop into small heart-shaped gametophytes.

15.4   The Rise of Seed-Bearing Plants
A. The most successful of the vascular plants are the seed-bearing species, which have escaped dependency on water for fertilization, relying instead on air currents and insects.

B. Seed ferns, gymnosperms, and angiosperms are the three main groups and differ from the seedless vascular plants in three ways:
   1. They produce microspores, which develop into pollen grains that carry the sperm to the female structures to accomplish pollination.
   2. They also produce megaspores, which develop into ovules and, at maturity, produce seeds; each seed is a mature ovule consisting of the embryo sporophyte (egg cell plus sperm) plus seed coats.
   3. Compared to seedless vascular plants, these plants have thicker cuticles, stomata recessed below the surface of the leaf, and other competitive traits.

15.5   Gymnosperms—Plants with "Naked" Seeds
   A. Gymnosperm sporophyte stages are conspicuous trees and shrubs; the seeds are rather unprotected ("naked seeds") perched at the surface of reproductive parts.
      1. Cycads are palmlike trees that flourished during the Mesozoic era.
         a. Only about 130 species still exist—confined to the tropics and subtropics.
         b. They bear massive cone-shaped strobili that produce either pollen (transferred by air currents or insects) or ovules.
      2. Ginkgos have been reduced in diversity from the Mesozoic to only one surviving species today.
         a. They are unusual in being deciduous.
         b. They are remarkably hardy, showing resistance to insects, disease, and air pollutants.
      3. Gnetophytes (Gnetophyta) are the most unusual gymnosperms; they live in tropical and desert areas.
      4. Conifers (cone-bearers) are woody trees with needlelike or scalelike leaves.
         a. Most are evergreens, some are deciduous.
         b. Examples of conifers: pines, redwoods, firs, and spruces.
   B. The life cycle of the pine is typical of gymnosperms.
      1. The pine tree (sporophyte) produces two kinds of cones:
         a. Male cones produce sporangia, which yield microspores that develop into pollen grains (male gametophyte).
         b. Female cones produce ovules that yield megaspores (female gametophyte).
      2. Pollination is the arrival of a pollen grain on the female reproductive parts, after which a pollen tube grows toward the egg.
      3. Fertilization, which is delayed for up to a year, results in a zygote that develops into an embryo within the conifer seed.

15.6   Angiosperms–The Flowering Plants
   A. Only angiosperms produce specialized reproductive structures, called flowers.
      1. Of all the divisions of plants, angiosperms ("vessel seed") are the most successful and most diverse.
         a. The diploid sporophyte has extensive root and shoot systems; it also retains and nourishes the gametophyte.
         b. Embryos are nourished by the endosperm within the seeds, which are packaged inside fruits.
      2. Most flowering plants coevolved with pollinators–insects, bats, birds, etc.
   B. There are three major groups of flowering plants:
      1. Magnoliids include magnolias, avocados, nutmeg, and black pepper plants.
      2. Eudicots include familiar shrubs, trees (except conifers), and herbaceous plants.
      3. Monocots include grasses, lilies, and the major food-crop grains.

15.7   Deforestation in the Tropics
   A. Deforestation means mass removal of all trees from large tracts for logging, agriculture, and grazing.
      1. Tropical forests are in greatest peril.
      2. Deforestation is now greatest in Brazil, Indonesia, Colombia, and Mexico.
   B. Massive deforestation is a bad idea because:
      1. The soils left behind are not rich enough to sustain food-crop growth.
      2. Loss of trees reduces evaporation, increases rates of runoff, and may affect regional patterns of rainfall.
      3. Deforested land reflects more sunlight back into space.
      4. Reduced absorption of carbon dioxide for photosynthesis and increased generation of the same gas in burning may have an impact on global warming.

Suggestions for Presenting the Material

- When students think of plants, almost all of the examples that come to mind will be angiosperms. Counter this tendency by asking for examples of plants that do NOT have flowers.

- Review the evolutionary trend from gametophyte dominance to sporophyte dominance (Figure 15.3). If students still find this confusing, they will have trouble comparing one plant life cycle to another. Highlight evolutionary hallmarks (summarized in Table 15.2) such as development of vascular tissue, dominant sporophyte, heterospory, nonmotile gametes, and seeds that distinguish simple plants from those that are more complex.

- Because of the numerous classification categories included within this chapter it is easy to get lost. To alleviate this difficulty, you may wish to make a transparency of Table 15.1 and have it in view as you proceed through the different groups of plants.

- Because of their natural geographic locations, many of the plants mentioned in the earlier sections of this chapter are not familiar ones to students. Transparencies of representative species, even made from photos in the book, will help to remove the abstract quality of a ginkgo or cycad.

Classroom and Laboratory Enrichment

- Look at fossils of ancient lycopods, horsetails, ferns, and gymnosperms. Discuss how changing climates influenced the geographic distributions and the sizes of these plants.

- Prepare a small display of portions of bryophytes, lycopods, horsetails, ferns, and gymnosperms from local areas where plant collection is allowed. Prepared slides and live materials ordered from biological supply houses can supplement your collection.

- Collect reproductive structures of gymnosperms (use photos, drawings, or models to represent those taxonomic divisions for which structures are unavailable). Compare them to the reproductive structures of angiosperms (students can dissect flowers).

- Use models, photos, drawings, or overhead transparencies to discuss the life cycle of pine (a good representative gymnosperm because it is familiar to students). Compare it to the life cycle of a typical angiosperm.

- Obtain a set of slides that will provide a survey of the plant world including algae.

- Redraw several of the life cycle figures in this chapter but omit several key labels. Photocopy these and distribute as a labeling exercise.

Impacts, Issues Classroom Discussion Ideas

- What happened to the treelike lycopods and horsetails that were dominant during the Carboniferous period? How did the Carboniferous period get its name?
- What features had to evolve in plants to enable survival on land?
- What are the local and global effects of deforestation?
- Can the timber industry and good ecological conservation practices abide together?

Additional Ideas for Classroom Discussion

- What are the only land plants with a dominant, independent gametophyte and a dependent sporophyte?
- What are some differences and similarities between a pine cone and a fruit?
- Which type of pollination is more efficient—wind pollination, as seen among conifers, or insect pollination, as seen among some of the angiosperms?
- What is the status of the word *algae*? Because many algae are green and others such as the kelps (brown algae) are called "seaweeds," many people think of them as plants. But as you already know they are considered by most taxonomists as protistans.
- What major structural difference separates the bryophytes from the ferns?

How Would You Vote? Classroom Discussion Ideas

- Monitor the voting for the online question. Recycling is a laudable program, especially for paper products, which we use so much of. But getting persons and companies to do it is difficult unless incentives, such as tax breaks, are offered.

Term Paper Topics, Library Activities, and Special Projects

- Prepare a list of the vascular plant flora on your campus or some other local area.
- Find vegetation maps showing the worldwide distributions of major vegetation associations of gymnosperms and angiosperms (for example, grasslands, temperate forests, coniferous forests, and so on).
- Investigate the extent of removal of trees and small plants in your vicinity that has occurred in the past few years in preparation for commercial property development.
- Assess the balance between producing healthy, oxygen-yielding lawn plants and the fertilizers and pesticides used to keep them that way.
- Read about the "balanced terrarium" concept. Set up one and attempt to prove if the theory is workable.
- Evaluate the effects of possible global warming on the world's grain-producing regions. Will all areas be affected negatively? Some positively?
- Estimate the number of acres of land that is not available for food production because it is part of the right-of-way of the U.S. interstate highway system.

Possible Responses to *Critical Thinking* Questions

1. I happen to live in an area that grows pine trees very fast and very tall. Vast acreages are owned and managed by the national timber companies. Logging is represented to the public as a renewable enterprise; I hope it is so. There appears to be no need for nonprofit advocacy groups. I realize that this is not the case in many countries. Perhaps we would not need to replant so many trees if we could reduce our usage of them. As an example: newspapers are a big waste because we don't read but a portion of each issue. Indeed, large numbers are not sold or read at all. Everything we touch has been excessively "containerized" using cardboard and paper. I would hate to give up toilet tissue, but many cultures have never heard of it.

2. The early botanists referred to in this question were considering ferns to be in the paradigm of flowering plants, which bear seeds. They did not realize that the tiny particles they were planting were asexually-produced spores, which of course are not the result of any gamete union. This was happening in the small heart-shaped gametophyte growing on the ground.

3. Xylem, which is in reality "wood," is a very strong tissue. It allows modern trees to reach significant heights with far reaching branches. Fortunately, these heights permit the trees to have unlimited access to the sunlight that is so vitally needed for photosynthesis. Shorter trees will not be as successful as they compete for the snippets of light that filter through the forest canopy.

4. Flagellated sperm are the norm for bryophytes and ferns. The flagella permitted the sperm to swim through water to reach the egg. Cycads and ginkgos represent a "transitional" condition in which the sperm still have flagella for swimming, but instead of free water, they are swimming through the fluid around an egg. In angiosperms, the sperm are delivered directly to the egg via a sperm tube, providing the selective advantage of a more certain arrival.

16

ANIMAL EVOLUTION

Chapter Outline

Objectives

1. Describe the major advances in body structure and function that made invertebrates and vertebrates increasingly large and complex.
2. Trace the development of symmetry, body cavity, cephalization, and segmentation in the invertebrates.

3. Provide two characteristics for each invertebrate phylum that clearly distinguish it from all other such phyla.
4. List a representative animal from each phylum.
5. Be able to reproduce from memory a phylogenetic tree that expresses the relationships between the major groups of animals.
6. Describe the four characteristics that are distinctive of chordates.
7. Be able to distinguish invertebrates in general, invertebrate chordates, and vertebrate chordates.
8. Trace the trends in vertebrate evolution from fishes to mammals.
9. Understand the general physical features and behavioral patterns attributed to early primates. Know their relationship to other mammals.
10. Understand the distinction between hominoid and hominid.
11. Distinguish between *Australopithecus* and *Homo*.

Key Terms

animals
ectoderm
endoderm
mesoderm
vertebrates
invertebrates
Ediacarans
radial symmetry
bilateral symmetry
anterior
posterior
dorsal
ventral
cephalization
gut
incomplete digestive system
complete digestive system
protostomes
deuterostomes
coelom
peritoneum
thoracic cavity
abdominal cavity
pseudocoel
segmentation
sponges
spicules
collar cells
larva
cnidarians
nematocysts

medusa
polyp
epithelium
gastrodermis
epidermis
nerve net
mesoglea
hydrostatic skeleton
planula
organ
flatworms
hermaphrodites
transverse fission
turbellarians
flukes
tapeworms
definitive host
intermediate host
schistosomiasis
earthworms
annelids
leeches
polychaetes
setae
oligochaetes
polychaete
brain
nerve cord
parapods
mollusks
mantle
gastropods
snails

nudibranchs
bivalves
cephalopods
jet propulsion
roundworms
cuticle
molting
trichinosis
elephantiasis
arthropods
trilobites
chelicerates
crustaceans
insects
myriopods
exoskeleton
jointed appendages
tracheae
metamorphosis
arachnids
Lyme diseases
larvae
pupae
echinoderm
tube feet
chordates
notochord
nerve cord
pharynx
tail
tunicates
lancelets
craniates

lampreys
ostracoderms
jaws
placoderms
vertebrates
vertebrae
gill slits
fins
gills
lungs
cartilaginous fishes
bony fishes
swim bladder
ray-finned fishes
lobe-finned fishes
lungfishes
tetrapods
amphibians
amniotes
synapsids
sauropsids
"reptiles"
dinosaurs
K-T asteroid impact theory
turtles
lizards
snakes
crocodilians
birds
feathers
cloaca
amniote eggs

mammals	primates	opposable	*Homo habilis*
hair	tarsiers	hominoids	*Homo erectus*
mammary glands	prosimians	*Sahelanthropus tchadensis*	*Homo ergaster*
therapsids	anthropoids	*Ardipithecus ramidus*	*Homo sapiens*
monotremes	hominids	australopiths	multiregional model
marsupials	bipedalism	*Australopithecus afarensis*	African emergence
eutherians	culture	humans	model
placenta	prehensile	*Homo*	

Lecture Outline

Interpreting and Misinterpreting the Past
A. The absence of transitional forms was an early obstacle to Darwin's theory of evolution.
   1. The discovery of *Archaeopteryx* specimens, which display both reptilian and bird features, was significant.
   2. *Archaeopteryx* lived about 150 million years ago.
B. Such fossils are witness to the history of life.

16.1   Overview of the Animal Kingdom
A. Animals are defined by these characteristics:
   1. Animals are multicellular (diploid), with tissues arranged into organs and organ systems.
   2. Animals are aerobic and heterotrophic.
   3. Animals reproduce sexually, and in some cases asexually or both.
   4. Animal life cycles include a period of embryonic development; germ tissue layers (ectoderm, endoderm, and in most species, mesoderm) give rise to adult organs.
   5. Most animals are motile during at least part of their life cycle.
B. Animal Origins
   1. Animals probably arose from Ediacaran ancestors about 610 million years ago.
   2. Early animals were thin, flat-bodied, with a good surface-to-volume ratio for absorbing nutrients.
   3. During the Cambrian, animals underwent an enormous adaptive radiation resulting in all of the major groups of animals.
C. A Look at Body Plans
   1. Body Symmetry and Cephalization
     a. Animals show either radial (round) or bilateral (right and left sides) symmetry.
     b. Cephalization means having a definite head end, usually with feeding and sensory features.
   2. Type of Gut
     a. The place where food is digested is the gut; some are saclike with one opening—a mouth.
     b. "Complete" digestive tracts have two openings (mouth and anus) for continuous food processing, often through specialized regions.
       1) In protostomes the first embryonic opening becomes the mouth.
       2) In deuterostomes, the first opening becomes the anus, and the mouth develops from another opening.
   3. Body Cavities
     a. A coelom (lined with peritoneum) is a space between the gut and body wall that allows internal organs to expand and operate freely.

b. Some animals (flatworms) do not have a coelom but instead are packed solidly with tissue between the gut and body wall.

   c. Others, such as roundworms, have a "false" coelom (pseudocoel), not lined with peritoneum.

4. Segmentation

   a. A segmented animal is composed of repeating body units (for example, the earthworm).

   b. The segments may be grouped and modified for specialized tasks, as in insects.

16.2   Getting Along Well Without Organs

A. Sponges

   1. Sponges have an asymmetric body with no true tissues, no organs.

   2. Between two layers of body cells there is a semifluid matrix with needlelike spicules for support.

   3. Collar cells line the interior chambers.

      a. By means of their beating flagella, these cells move large volumes of water in through body pores and out through the large opening at the top of the body.

      b. They also trap suspended food particles in their collars and transfer the food to amoebalike cells in the matrix.

   4. Most sponges reproduce sexually.

      a. Sperm are released into the surrounding water to be picked up by a nearby sponge and directed to the egg within the matrix.

      b. The zygote develops into a free-swimming larva.

B. Cnidarians

   1. Cnidarians are radial, tentacled animals that include jellyfishes, sea anemones, corals, and hydras.

   2. Unique stinging devices called nematocysts discharge threads to capture prey and fend off predators.

   3. There are two common body plans:

      a. The medusa resembles an umbrella and floats like a tentacle-fringed bell in the water; oral arms surround the central mouth.

      b. The polyp is tubelike and is usually attached to some substrate; it may be solitary or part of a colony.

   4. The digestive cavity is saclike (only a mouth) and can accommodate prey larger than the cnidarian itself.

   5. An outer epidermis covers the body, and an inner gastrodermis lines the digestive cavity.

      a. A nerve net running through both layers coordinates the animal's response to stimuli.

      b. Some jellyfishes also have sensory cells and contractile cells.

   6. A jellylike mesoglea lies between the outer and inner body layers.

      a. Jellyfishes have abundant mesoglea, helpful in providing buoyancy and in swimming.

      b. Polyps have little mesoglea but use the water in their guts as a hydrostatic skeleton.

   7. The life cycle of a cnidarian may have a polyp and medusa stage, or it may have just the polyp.

      a. The medusa is usually the sexual form with gonads.

      b. The zygote develops into a swimming larva called a planula.

16.3   Flatworms—Introducing Organ Systems

A. Flatworms are the simplest animals to display organs—a grouping of tissues arranged in such a manner as to perform specialized functions.

1. These worms have a definite head end, are bilateral, and possess longitudinal and circular muscles in the body wall.
        2. The gut is saclike with a single (mouth) opening through which a pharynx extends for food gathering.
        3. Most flatworms are hermaphrodites (both sexes in one body).
    B. Turbellarians are free-living predators including the planarians of freshwater.
    C. Flukes and tapeworms are parasites.
        1. A definitive host harbors the mature parasitic stage; immature stages live in intermediate hosts.
        2. Tapeworms enter humans in undercooked meat and take up residence attached to the intestinal wall.
        3. Blood flukes cause schistosomiasis, a debilitating disease with a complex history.

16.4   Annelids—Segments Galore
    A. This phylum includes earthworms, polychaetes, and leeches.
        1. The body is bilateral with definite segmentation evidenced on the surface as "rings."
            a. A segmented body has great evolutionary potential, for individual parts can undergo modification and become highly adapted for specialized tasks.
            b. Leeches have suckers at both ends; polychaetes have fleshy, paddlelike parapods.
        2. Setae (bristles), which may be many or few in number, project directly from the body.
    B. Earthworms are typical annelids
        1. Their habit of ingesting dirt particles while scavenging for organic matter makes them valuable tillers of the soil.
        2. The outer body surface is covered with a cuticle; internal partitions define individual coelomic chambers filled with fluid to provide a hydrostatic skeleton against which the muscles act during movement.
        3. The circulatory system is closed (blood confined to hearts and vessels).
        4. Paired nerve cords extend from the brain to run the length of the body with a ganglion in each segment.

16.5   The Evolutionarily Pliable Mollusks
    A. Mollusks have a fleshy, soft, bilateral body with a small coelom.
        1. Some have a head with eyes and tentacles, some have a shell.
        2. All have a mantle, a skirtlike tissue covering the body.
    B. Hiding Out, or Not
        1. A bivalve not only has its two protected shells but can also burrow in the sand to disappear from sight of predators; water and suspended food are drawn in and waste voided through openings called siphons, by the action of the cilia on the gills.
        2. Nudibranchs (no shells) protect themselves by secreting toxic substances and incorporating nematocysts from the cnidarians they eat.
    C. On the Cephalopod Need for Speed
        1. The body of a squid is modified for a highly active predatory lifestyle; it has tentacles and beaklike jaws.
        2. They move by a type of jet propulsion caused by mantle contractions.
        3. To support greater activity, the circulatory system is a closed one; the nervous system is well developed with a large brain; the eyes form images; and learning and memory are possible.

16.6   Amazingly Abundant Roundworms

A. Roundworms are sometimes known as nematodes.
1. They are bilateral and possess a slender tapered body.
2. Reproductive organs lie in a false coelom filled with fluid.
3. A tough cuticle, covering and protecting the body, is shed periodically as the animal grows.

B. Most roundworms are small and free-living, but some are parasitic on plants and animals.
1. *Ascaris* is a very common intestinal parasite of humans and domestic animals.
2. In trichinosis, undercooked pork is the source of a roundworm that moves from the digestive tract of the host to encyst in the muscles.
3. Elephantiasis is a severe welling of the legs due to blockage of lymph flow by small roundworms deposited by a mosquito during feeding.

16.7 Arthropods—The Most Successful Animals

A. Keys to Success
1. Hardened exoskeleton:
   a. The arthropod covering is a combination of protein and chitin (plus calcium in some) that is flexible and lightweight, yet protective.
   b. It is a barrier to water loss and can support a body deprived of water's buoyancy.
   c. Exoskeletons restrict growth and so must be shed periodically (molting process).
2. Jointed appendages:
   a. Arthropod appendages are jointed.
   b. Appendages became specialized for feeding, sensing, locomotion, sperm transfer, and spinning silk.
3. Specialized segments and fused-together segments:
   a. Body segments became more specialized, reduced in number, and grouped together.
   b. In some lineages this has resulted in head, thorax, and abdomen regions.
4. Respiratory structures:
   a. Special tubes called tracheas supply oxygen directly to body tissues.
   b. This allows high metabolic rates and sustained activity, as in flight.
5. Specialized sensory structures:
   a. The compound eye provides a wide angle of vision.
   b. Many individual units of the eye allow motion perception.
6. Specialized developmental stages:
   a. Larval stages concentrate on feeding and growth.
   b. Adults specialize in dispersal and reproduction.
   c. The process of change from larva to adult is called metamorphosis.

B. Spiders and Their Relatives
1. Chelicerates include some marine species such as horseshoe crabs and the more familiar arachnids.
2. Arachnids include spiders, scorpions, ticks, and mites.
   a. Spiders are keen predators that trap insects in their webs, produced as silk strands from the abdomen; some are poisonous such as the brown recluse and black widow.
   b. Some mites are free-living, others are serious pests of plants and animals; ticks are notorious blood-suckers and disease-carriers (Lyme disease).

C. Crustaceans
1. Crustaceans—shrimps, lobsters, crabs, barnacles, and pillbugs—get their name from the "crusty" exoskeleton.
   a. These animals play important roles in food webs and serve as human food also.
   b. Like other arthropods, they repeatedly molt and shed the exoskeleton.

2. The crustacean body is divided into many segments, each of which bears paired specialized appendages including antennae, mandibles, maxillae, grasping claws, and legs.
　D. A Look at Insect Diversity
　　1. The body is divided into three regions: head (sensory and feeding), thorax (locomotion by six legs, two pairs of wings), and abdomen.
　　2. The complete digestive tract is divided into three regions: foregut, midgut (digestion and absorption), and hindgut (water reabsorption).
　　3. Unique small tubes attached to the gut and lying free in the abdominal cavity process metabolic waste (uric acid) and aid in water retention.
　　4. Insects display enormous diversity.
　　　a. Their ability to disperse by flight allows the utilization of widely ranging food sources.
　　　b. Their great success is due to their ability to exploit nature's resources during different stages of metamorphosis, such as larvae, nymphs, and pupae.

16.8　The Puzzling Echinoderms
　A. The name of this phylum, Echinodermata, refers to the "spiny skin" made of calcium carbonate.
　　1. Members include sea stars, sea urchins, brittle stars, and sea cucumbers.
　　2. Adults are radially symmetrical; larvae are bilateral.
　B. Internally, echinoderms are of simple design.
　　1. The nervous system is decentralized; there is no brain.
　　2. The unique water-vascular system operates the tube feet, which have suction disks that can be used in locomotion and to capture prey.
　　3. Sea stars can evert their stomachs when feeding.

16.9　Evolutionary Trends Among Vertebrates
　A. All chordates, at some time in their lives, have four distinctive features:
　　1. A *notochord* is a long rod of stiffened tissue that supports the body; later it changes to bony units in vertebrates.
　　2. A dorsal, tubular *nerve cord* lies above the notochord and gut.
　　3. Embryos have *gill slits* in the wall of the pharynx.
　　4. A *tail*, or rudiment thereof, exists near the anus.
　B. Early Craniates
　　1. Tunicates and lancelets do not have a cranium or vertebrae.
　　2. All other chordates are craniates.
　　　a. The earliest ones resembled lamprey—modern fishes without jaws.
　　　b. These were followed by ostracoderms—still jawless but with hardened external plates.
　　　c. Placoderms were the first fishes with jaws and paired fins; they were replaced by cartilaginous and bony fishes.
　C. The Key Innovations
　　1. The single, continuous notochord was replaced by a column of separate, hardened vertebrae, parts of which became modified near the head to form jaws.
　　2. Jaws allowed new feeding possibilities, coupled with better eyes for detecting both prey and predators.
　　3. The fins of fishes were the starting point for the legs, arms, and wings seen among higher vertebrates.

4. Gradually, there was less reliance on gills and more on lungs and the circulatory system (heart, blood vessels), which work in connection.

16.10 Major Groups of Jawed Fishes
A. Enormous numbers of fishes attest to their success in meeting the challenges of life in the water.
   1. Their streamlined bodies allow easy movement through the dense medium.
   2. Tail muscles are organized for powerful force.
   3. The swim bladder provides buoyancy.
B. Cartilaginous fishes possess a streamlined body with a cartilaginous endoskeleton, gill slits, fins, and small scales on the body surface.
   1. This group includes the sharks and rays.
   2. Sharks are formidable predators with their powerful jaws and teeth (replaceable).
C. Bony fishes are the most numerous and diverse vertebrates.
   1. Ray-finned fishes have highly maneuverable fins supported by rays that originate from the dermis.
   2. The lobe-finned fishes, such as the coelacanths, bear fleshy extensions on the body.
   3. Lungfishes have gills and one or a pair of "lungs" that are modified gut wall outpouchings.

16.11 Early Amphibious Tetrapods
A. Amphibians have a body plan and mode of reproduction somewhere between fishes and reptiles.
   1. Life on land presented new challenges to the emerging amphibians.
      a. Water availability was not reliable.
      b. Air temperatures were variable, and air itself was not the strong supporting medium that water was, but it was a richer source of oxygen.
      c. New habitats, including vast arrays of plants, necessitated keener sensory input.
   2. Existing amphibians share several common characteristics:
      a. All have bony endoskeletons and usually four legs.
      b. Depending on their habitat, amphibians can respire by use of gills, lungs, skin, and pharyngeal lining.
      c. The skin is usually thin and sometimes supplied with glands that produce toxins.
B. Even though most amphibians are aquatic, none has escaped the water entirely for they must return to it to lay eggs, which will produce larvae dependent on a watery environment.

16.12 The Rise of Amniotes
A. The "Reptiles"
   1. Four features were critical to amniotes' escape from water dependency:
      a. They produce amniote eggs with covering membranes and a shell, which allow the eggs to be laid in dry habitats.
      b. Amniotes have a toughened, dry, or scaly skin that is resistant to drying.
      c. They have a copulatory organ that permits internal fertilization.
      d. Their kidneys are good at conserving water.
   2. "Reptiles" demonstrate certain advantageous features compared to amphibians.
      a. Modification of limb bones, teeth, and jawbones allowed greater exploitation of the insect life emerging in the Late Carboniferous.
      b. Development of the cortex region of the cerebrum permitted greater integration of sensory input and motor response.

      c. A four-chambered heart and more efficient lungs allowed greater activity.

   3. Early "reptiles" gave rise to the dinosaurs.

      a. The first dinosaurs probably were small, warm-blooded creatures that thrived in the adaptive zones opened to them as the results of asteroid impacts about 213 million years ago.

      b. The monstrous dinosaurs that we all recognize in pictures and movies dominated life on Earth until the mass extinction, as proposed by the K-T asteroid impact theory, about 65 million years ago.

      c. Present-day crocodilians, turtles, tuataras, snakes, and lizards are what is left of this group.

B. Birds

   1. Birds can fly because of several adaptations:

      a. Feathers covering the wings make a good flight surface and conserve metabolic heat.

      b. Bones in the bird body are lightweight because of air cavities within them.

      c. The heart is four-chambered, and the lungs are highly efficient because of their "flow-through" design.

      d. Powerful muscles are attached at strategic places on the bones for maximum leverage.

   2. Birds are incredibly diverse in color, courtship, song, and size, including the very large flightless ones such as the ostrich.

C. Mammals

   1. Mammals are characterized by the following:

      a. Hair covers at least part of the body (whales are an exception).

      b. Milk-secreting glands nourish the young.

      c. Four different types of teeth (incisors, canines, premolars, and molars) in the mammalian mouth are specialized to meet dietary habits.

      d. Brain capacity is increased, allowing more capacity for memory, learning, conscious thought, and behavioral flexibility.

   2. Mammals evolved early in the Jurassic.

      a. Monotremes are the only egg-laying mammals.

      b. Marsupials are the pouched mammals, many peculiar to Australia and New Zealand.

      c. Placental mammals have a competitive edge afforded by higher metabolic rates, better body temperature regulation, and a more efficient method to nourish embryos.

16.13   From Early Primates to Humans

A. Primates include a wide variety of animals:

   1. Prosimians (literally: before apes) are small tree dwellers (arboreal) that use their large eyes to advantage during night hunting.

   2. Tarsiers (tarsioids) are small primates with features intermediate between prosimians and anthropoids.

   3. Anthropoids include monkeys, apes, and humans.

      a. Hominoids include apes and humans.

      b. Hominid refers to human lineages only.

B. Primate evolution displays key trends:

   1. Enhanced daytime vision:

      a. Early primates had an eye on each side of the head.

      b. Later ones had forward-directed eyes resulting in better depth perception and increased ability to discern shape, movement, color, and light intensity.

   2. Upright walking:

    a. Bipedalism is possible because of skeletal reorganization in primates ancestral to humans.

    b. A monkey skeleton is suitable for a life of climbing, leaping, and running along tree branches with palms down.

    c. An ape skeleton is suitable for climbing and using the arms for carrying some body weight; the shoulder blades allow the arms to swivel overhead.

    d. Humans have a shorter, S-shaped, and somewhat flexible backbone.

3. Power grip and precision grip:

    a. Prehensile movements allowed fingers to wrap around objects in a grasp.

    b. Opposable thumb and fingers allowed more refined use of the hand.

    c. The precision and power grip movements of the human hand allowed for tool-making.

4. Teeth for all occasions:

    a. Monkeys have rectangular jaws and long canines.

    b. Humans have a bow-shaped jaw and smaller teeth, reflecting the changes in diet.

5. Brains, behavior, and culture:

    a. Brain expansion and elaboration produced a brain of increased mass and complexity, especially for thought, language, and conscious movements.

    b. Human brain development led to patterns of human behavior known collectively as culture.

C. Origins and Early divergences

  1. The first primates that evolved from mammals about 60 million years ago (Paleocene) resembled small rodents or tree shrews; they had long snouts and were good foragers on the forest floor.

  2. By the Eocene, their descendants were living in trees, had larger brains, were active in the daytime, and possessed better grasping movements.

  3. By the time of the Oligocene, tree-dwelling ancestors of monkeys and apes had emerged.

  4. The first hominoids appeared between 23 and 5 million years ago (Miocene).

D. The First Hominids

  1. Most of the earliest known hominids lived in Central Africa.

    a. Cooler and drier weather encouraged the transition of hominids to mixed woodlands and grasslands.

    b. The plasticity of early hominids was the result of the capacity to learn to adapt.

  2. The first known hominids are designated australopiths (southern apes).

    a. Relationship of the australopithecine species is uncertain, but all shared several characteristics: improved dentition for grinding harder foods, upright walking, bipedalism (leaving footprints), and increased manual dexterity.

    b. *Australopithecus afarensis* is one of the species that walked across the African plane some 3.7 million years ago.

E. Emergence of Early Humans

  1. Which traits characterize humans?

    a. "Human" is mostly defined by the increased brain capacity, which allows analytical skills, complex social behavior, and technological innovation.

    b. The earliest human is designated *Homo habilis,* signifying "handy man."

      1) Hominids began to use stone tools about 2.5 million years ago to get marrow out of bone and to scrape flesh from bones.

      2) "Manufactured" tools have been found at Olduvai Gorge.

  2. The early form of *Homo* was twice as brainy as australopiths and ate well.

F. Emergence of Modern Humans

1. *H. erectus* migrated out of Africa into Europe and Asia.
2. Selection pressures triggered adaptive radiations, resulting in physical changes as well as cultural shifts.
   a. *Homo erectus* had a longer, chinless face, thick-walled skull, and heavy browridge but was narrow-hipped and long-legged.
   b. *Homo erectus* made advanced stone tools and used fire as they migrated out of Africa into Asia and Europe.
3. By about 100,000 years ago, *Homo sapiens* had evolved from *Homo erectus*.
   a. Early *H. sapiens* had smaller teeth, a chin, thinner facial bones, larger brain, and rounder, higher skull.
   b. Neanderthals were similar to modern humans but disappeared about 35,000 years ago.
   c. From about 40,000 years ago to today, human evolution has been cultural, not biological.
G. Where Did Modern Humans Originate?
1. All of the evidence points to the origin of humans in Africa.
2. Two models are used to interpret the evidence:
   a. In the multiregional model, *Homo sapiens* evolved from *H. erectus* in the various parts of the world to which it migrated many years before.
   b. In the African emergence model, *H. sapiens* originated in Africa and migrated out to replace the *H. erectus* populations already there.

Suggestions for Presenting the Material

- This chapter is as diverse as its name implies. It begins with definition of some basic terms used in describing the animal groups. Then the "march through the groups" begins. This can be a tedious and overwhelming experience unless you exercise special care to add those little extras that will hold student interest.

- Perhaps in previous biology courses, students have considered protozoans as animals. Recall that these one-celled organisms are now placed in the protistan group. Therefore, the present chapter begins with true multicellular animals—sponges—and proceeds on.

- This chapter contains a very useful table (Table 16.1) at the end of the chapter. It is a concise listing of the groups that are covered in this chapter.

- In a survey of animals that reduces volumes of information to just a few pages, there must be brevity that will certainly shortchange someone's favorite animal group. However, the authors have been fair in presenting the chief characteristics for each major group.

- If the instructor's background is primarily zoological, the chapter may seem oversimplified, but if the instructor is a botanist, quite the opposite may be true. No matter where you find yourself in this spectrum, remember the naive student and have compassion.

- One way to enliven your presentation is to relate the members of each group to the students' daily lives. This may be more difficult for sponges than arthropods, but with a little forethought it can be done. See samples in the Enrichment section.

- In contrast to the material on invertebrates, students should be more familiar with the vertebrates. In fact, they may be overly confident and not listen as attentively as they should.

- Interest can be sparked by use of films, slides, and videos to show exotic animals in their natural habitat.

- Additional interest can be generated by allowing any students that have cared for or studied vertebrates to share their experiences.

- The authors have gone to special lengths to present the vertebrates based on their evolution. This should be emphasized in lecture.

- Depending on the region of the country and your particular institution, the discussion of human origins may or may not spark some controversy in your class. Whether we acknowledge it or not, this is an area where religious beliefs and scientific explanations can conflict. It has been this author's experience that ridicule of a student's personal beliefs does very little to open the young mind to an alternative view. Therefore, I carefully craft my discussions to present the maximum amount of scientific evidence without deliberately being offensive.

- The origins of primates and the evolutionary trends that resulted in certain key characteristics are quite universally accepted.

- Be sure to distinguish "hominoid" from "hominid."

- Emphasize the fact that *Australopithecus* spp. and *Homo* spp. were contemporaries.

Classroom and Laboratory Enrichment

- There is no scarcity of visual material depicting the diversity of animal life. It ranges from professionally made slides, to single-phylum films, to full-length video surveys of the animal kingdom such as David Attenborough's *Life on Earth* (available at retail outlets).

- Perhaps your students will have an accompanying laboratory experience where they can see, touch, and dissect representatives of the various groups. If not, it will be even more crucial that you present adequate visual material—at least slides if you have to shoot them yourself.

- As mentioned in the Presentation section, relating animals to daily life will enhance your lectures. Below is a sampling that you can build upon:

  PORIFERA: Natural *sponges* (expensive) are still the best for some cleaning purposes and are used by artists for special effects.

  CNIDARIA: We wouldn't want to tangle with a *jellyfish,* but a valuable piece of *coral* on your ring finger is OK.

  PLATYHELMINTHES: The *tapeworms* and *flukes* have disgusting parasitic habits but are all a part of nature's balance.

  NEMATODA: Everyone is familiar with *roundworms* that may infect pets, but do you know that humans can get them too?

  ANNELIDA: The familiar *earthworm* is a very beneficial tiller of the soil, but is its relative the *leech* so well respected?

  ARTHROPODA: The largest phylum contains pesky *insects* as well as tasty *lobsters.*

  MOLLUSCA: *Snails* and *clams* are quite familiar—we even eat them! But what about *squid* and *octopus*?

  ECHINODERMATA: *Sea stars* seem exotic because they and their relatives are found only in the sea.

  CHORDATA: Finally, "familiar" animals, but they constitute less than 5 percent of all the animals on earth.

- If you are fortunate to live in or near a large city with a zoo, arrange a field trip, but this time with a difference. Prepare the students for note-taking on various topics such as classification, body symmetry and cavities, body system development, ecological niche, and so on. Comment on the lack of animal representatives from the invertebrate phyla (at least ones that are plainly visible).

- If any students have vertebrate pets suitable for showing in the laboratory, allow them to show the animals and describe any unusual aspects of their lives or habits.

- If you are fortunate to have an animal-rearing facility on your campus, arrange a visit to dispel the notion that animals are just warehoused in these places.

- Nearly every campus has some kind of vertebrate collection. Bring some of the specimens to the classroom or arrange for a tour of the museum.

- Because of the interest in the subject of human evolution, numerous videotapes and slide sets are available (check supply catalogs in your A/V center). Some may be more technical; others may be for the general public.

- If you are fortunate to have an expert in human evolution available, by all means arrange for an illustrated lecture on this complex subject.

- View museum displays depicting early human evolution and life.

Impacts, Issues Classroom Discussion Ideas

- Are all chordates, vertebrates? Are all vertebrates, chordates? Explain.

- Is the general public more concerned about the extinction of a vertebrate or an invertebrate? Why do you think there might be a difference in level of concern?

- Dating of fossil remains is critical to understanding human evolutionary sequence. How is the age of fossils determined?

- Rarely are entire fossil skeletons found in one geographical site. Rather, a skeleton is a composite of many "finds." How do scientists know what bones to group together?

- Why was *Archaeopteryx* such a hard fossil to characterize? Why did some people not believe it was possible for such an animal to exist?

Additional Ideas for Classroom Discussion

- Why are protozoans no longer included in the kingdom Animalia?

- Give the literal meaning of each group name in the chapter.

- Even if you cannot remember all the details concerning the members of each group, can you tell the major niches that each group seems to fill?

- The blood fluke, *Schistosoma,* is an important human parasite. What role do parasites play in nature? Are they necessarily villains, as we often think?

- When a pet owner says "My animal has worms," what worm is most likely present? How could you distinguish between a flatworm and a roundworm, other than by shape?

- Some people don't consider an organism as a true animal unless it bleeds red when injured. Which animals presented in this chapter would fit this definition?

- Arthropods as a group have more unique features than perhaps any other group. Name as many of these features as you can.

- Why do persons you know refuse to eat insects when close relatives such as crayfish and lobsters and near relatives such as snails and oysters are gourmet items?

- Organize a debate on the use of vertebrate animals as subjects of medical and scientific research. Are there alternatives to their use? Are these alternatives practical?

- Evaluate the extent to which humans should go when breeding unusual animals simply for "show." Are there any breeds that you know of that suffer anatomical or physiological anomalies just for the sake of a good show animal?
- What kinds of animals are the animal-rights movements concerned about? Which ones do they not see as worthy of their protests?
- What role do hunters and fishermen play in the ecological balance of nature? Is their contribution to game management significant?
- Why do you think it is that the unusual reptiles and mammals are found on islands and island continents?
- What characteristics define a "primate"?
- What characteristics distinguish *Australopithecus* from *Homo*?

How Would You Vote? Classroom Discussion Ideas

- Monitor the voting for the online question. In the United States, with its strong emphasis on individual land rights, it would be difficult to impose a sanction on landowners that would prohibit them from taking possession of the fossils found on their private property. Perhaps a compromise could be reached whereby the "owner" would share his finds with authorities but retain ownership. Certainly the advancement of science is aided by the finds of private collectors. It would be a shame to drive these persons "underground."

Term Paper Topics, Library Activities, and Special Projects

- In the early days of biological investigation, sponges and even some cnidarians were classified as plants. Search some older textbooks to see why scientists changed their minds.
- Prepare a report on the extent of platyhelminth parasitic infestation in humans. List the condition, number of cases, and economic loss to society.
- Prepare a report on the history of use of natural sponges including the present-day demand.
- Discover the facts about jellyfish stings including the numbers of humans affected each year.
- What are the risks in eating mollusks? How can the risk be reduced?
- Investigate the reports of intelligent feats performed by cephalopods, especially octopods.
- Research the extent to which insects are used as human food in countries around the world.
- The echinoderms do not possess any freshwater representatives. The reasons for this should be found in an invertebrate biology textbook; see if you can locate the details.
- Chordates dominate our thinking when the word *animal* is used. But they constitute about 3 percent of the total species (based on the numbers in Table 16.1). Relate this fact to the concept of pyramids (energy, biomass, numbers) as presented in Chapter 31.
- What is the extent of extinction of vertebrates compared with that of invertebrates?
- Evaluate the literature of the animal rights movement. Is it scientifically sound? Does it place emotion above the public good?
- Research the ethical basis (if there is any) of how we should treat animals. If you come to any conclusions about treatment of vertebrates, can you formulate as strong an argument for invertebrates?

- Prepare an analysis of the contribution that hunters and fishermen make to the management of animals.
- Research the creationists' arguments against evolution of humans, and rebut each one using scientific evidence and arguments.
- Prepare a report on the methods used by illustrators to reconstruct fossil humans. Assess the degree of freedom individual artists use in their reconstructions.
- Investigate the controversy surrounding the skeleton called "Lucy."

Possible Responses to *Critical Thinking* Questions

1. It is a reasonable hypothesis (and quite easily testable) to suspect that the same poisons used to kill mosquitoes could also kill lobsters. First, we know that the two organisms are related and are structurally similar, even to the anatomy and physiology of their nervous systems. Secondly, we know that the insecticide in question is most likely an organophosphate (OP) compound that targets the neuron synapse. Third, we know from other studies that the specific mechanism of OP action is the same in many invertebrates, and vertebrates as well.

2. Of course New Zealand is quite cut off from the remainder of the world's land areas. Something in the environment of the country's islands is conducive for the continued existence of the tuataras, enabling them to thrive. Furthermore, they have not had any competitors that would either kill them outright, or interbreed to change the gene pool.

3. It is easier for modern biologists to accept the idea that a mammal can have reptilelike traits because we have a lot more evidence of the links between reptiles, bird, and mammals. This would include more fossils and specimens as well as molecular data.

4. By the definition of a "species," which includes "the ability to interbreed and produce living, fertile offspring," it is obvious that we can perform breeding exercises to determine the success of producing the required offspring. This is obviously not possible with fossils, so we must put more emphasis on the less reliable morphological characteristics.

17

PLANTS AND ANIMALS: COMMON CHALLENGES

Chapter Outline

Objectives

1. Characterize the terms: tissue, organ, and organ system, and tell how they form a division of labor.
2. Distinguish between growth and development.
3. How does the body's internal environment help to maintain homeostasis?
4. Tell the difference(s) between short-term and long-term adaptation.
5. How is homeostasis maintained in plants and animals?

Key Terms

anatomy	internal environment	interstitial fluid	positive feedback
physiology	homeostasis	plasma	mechanism
division of labor	diffusion	sensory receptors	compartmentalization
tissue	surface-to-volume ratio	stimulus	circadian rhythm
organ	xylem	integrator	phytochrome
organ system	phloem	effectors	apoptosis
growth	active transport	negative feedback	
development	habitat	mechanism	

Lecture Outline

Too Hot To Handle

A. All organisms function best within a limited range of internal operating conditions.

   1. The human body operates best when the internal temperature is between 97°F and 100°F.

   2. Above 105°F the body's normal cooling mechanisms fail; heat stroke with its devastating denaturation of enzymes and death can occur.

B. Anatomy is the study of an organism's form; physiology is the study of function.

17.1 Levels of Structural Organization

A. From Cells to Multicelled Organisms

   1. The integrated parts of the body divide up the tasks—a division of labor.

   2. A *tissue* is a community of cells specialized for particular tasks.

   3. An *organ* consists of two or more tissues working together.

   4. An *organ system* consists of different organs working to accomplish a common task.

B. Growth Versus Development

   1. Growth (quantitative) is the increase in the number, size, and volume of the cells of a multicelled organism.

   2. Development (qualitative) refers to the successive stages in the formation of specialized tissues, organs, and organ systems.

C. Structural Organization Has a History

   1. As plants adapted to life on land they needed mechanisms to conserve and transport water.

   2. Animals that live outside a watery environment must also provide moist surfaces for gaseous diffusion.

D. The Body's Internal Environment

   1. Plant and animal cells must be bathed in a fluid that provides nutrients and carries away wastes.

   2. The internal environment—extracellular fluids—provides this stable environment.

E. How Do Parts Contribute to the Whole?

   1. Each plant and animal must provide its cells with key factors to ensure the survival of all.

   2. Homeostasis describes the relative constancy of the internal environment even when external conditions change.

17.2 Recurring Challenges to Survival

A. Requirements for Gas Exchange

   1. Animals take in oxygen and give off carbon dioxide; plants do mostly the reverse.

2. Diffusion down a concentration gradient drives these movements.
B. Requirements for Internal Transport
   1. The surface-to-volume ratio must be kept high so that there is sufficient surface to receive the nutrients and discharge the wastes for the cells and the organism as a whole.
   2. Substances must be transported within the organism also by vascular tissue: xylem and phloem in plants, arteries and veins in animals.
C. Maintaining a Solute-Water Balance
   1. Plants and animals constantly gain and lose water and solutes.
   2. Substances may follow the dictates of passive diffusion into and out of the body, but within the organism active transport pumps specific substances *against* the gradient.
D. Requirements for Integration and Control
   1. Cells of certain tissues release signaling molecules that coordinate and integrate activities for the whole body.
   2. There are different signaling mechanisms to meet specific body needs.
E. On Variations in Resources and Threats
   1. Resources and dangers differ among habitats—where the individuals of a species live.
   2. Besides the physical and chemical characteristics of the habitat, there are the biotic components.

17.3   Homeostasis in Animals
A. The trillions of cells in our bodies must draw nutrients from, and dump wastes into, the same fluid.
   1. The extracellular fluid consists of interstitial fluid (between the cells and tissues) and plasma (fluid of the blood).
   2. The component parts of an animal work together to maintain the stable fluid environment required by its living cells.
   3. Homeostatic control mechanisms require three components:
      a. *Sensory receptors* detect specific changes in the environment.
      b. *Integrators* (brain and spinal cord) act to direct impulses to the place where a response can be made.
      c. *Effectors* (muscles and glands) perform the appropriate response.
B. Negative Feedback
   1. It works by detecting a change in the internal environment that elicits a response that tends to return conditions to the original state.
   2. It is similar to the functioning of a thermostat in a heating/cooling system.
C. Positive Feedback
   1. *Positive feedback* mechanisms may intensify the original signal.
   2. The process of human birth is an example.

17.4   Does Homeostasis Occur in Plants?
A. Although plants grow only at the tips of their roots and shoots and do not have centralized mechanisms to maintain the internal environment, they do exhibit a sort of homeostasis.
B. Resisting Pathogens
   1. Trees respond to pathogen attack by setting in motion a mechanism called system acquired resistance, in which signaling molecules call for production of defensive compounds that make the plant less vulnerable.
   2. Compartmentalization isolates the threat from the remainder of the tree; examples include secretion of phenols and resins.

C. Sand, Wind, and the Yellow Bush Lupine
  1. The yellow bush lupine grows along the windswept, sandy shores of the Pacific Ocean.
  2. It responds to this harsh environment by folding its leaves to conserve water.
D. About Rhythmic Leaf Folding
  1. A bean plant will hold its leaves horizontally during the day and fold them closer to the stem at night.
  2. It will do this even if kept in the dark due to the innate circadian rhythm.

17.5 How Cells Receive and Respond to Signals
A. In living organisms molecular mechanisms allow cells to "talk" to one another.
  1. In general a signaling molecule binds to a receptor, initiating a transduction of the signal into a form that can operate inside the cell to cause a functional response.
  2. Most receptors are membrane proteins that can change shape and start signal transduction.
B. Cell suicide (apoptosis) is a natural part of life.
  1. Protease enzymes are the weapons of destruction that have been stockpiled inside the cells.
  2. Signs of suicide include: shrinkage of the cell, chromosomes are bunched up, the cell breaks apart, and phagocytic cells congregate to dispose of the remains.
C. In cancer cells the signal to die is ignored, allowing the cells to proliferate without control.

Suggestions for Presenting the Material

- This chapter brings together a variety of topics that introduce the units on plant and animal function.

- Because of its rather general, introductory nature, this may be one of those chapters that the lecturer will assign for reading only, not included in the formal lecture schedule.

- However, if a formal lecture is given it may be necessary to draw specific examples in the form of diagrams and illustrations from future chapters in order that chapter 17 not seem so abstract.

- It is important to remember that the lecturer knows more of what is to come in the next two units than does the student.

Classroom and Laboratory Enrichment

- Arrange for some kind of first-hand presentation of the challenges of life at severe altitudes.

- Present plant and animal examples of abnormalities in growth and/or development.

- Compare the maintenance of a constant environment in your home with that of the human body using homeostatic language.

- Give an example of circadian rhythms in humans who have been deprived of any time-keeping device for several days.

Impacts, Issues Classroom Discussion Ideas

- What physiological difficulties would a polar bear face if he wandered into a desert?
- What are the physiological signs and symptoms of heat stroke?

Additional Ideas for Classroom Discussion

- Why *do* people risk their lives to climb high mountains?
- How does the process of growth differ in plants from that in animals?
- Define illness in terms of homeostasis.
- What would be the effect on humans if the sex drive were controlled by *negative* rather than positive feedback?
- What would be the result to life if organisms were composed of just a few large cells, rather than many small cells?

How Would You Vote? Classroom Discussion Ideas

- Monitor the voting for the online question. Whether a coach should be held responsible for a player's death is a tough call. Perhaps the circumstances of the incident should determine the extent of responsibility. For instance, if the coach deliberately sent the suffering player back into play, this would be a clear case of neglect. However, if the coach were unaware of any difficulty even though environmental conditions were threatening, and the player suddenly and without warning "fell out," then there would be less responsibility on the coach.

Term Paper Topics, Library Activities, and Special Projects

- Investigate the advances in technology that have permitted more people at climb mountains safely.
- Select an animal or plant example of homeostasis and explain the molecular and physiological mechanisms that are in control.
- Research the development of the salt-tolerant tomatoes referred to in this chapter.
- In light of the discussion of "adaptation" in this chapter evaluate this statement: "Learn to adapt."
- Investigate the mechanisms of wound healing in trees.
- Prepare a table comparing plant hormones and animal hormones.

Possible Responses to *Critical Thinking* Questions

1. The complex interaction of plant, caterpillar pest, and parasitoid described in this research could serve as a premier example of the "design" built into nature—so say the creationists. Alas, their explanation is a bit too simplistic, for we realize natural interactions are far more complicated. What do we know? (1) The tobacco plant sits in the field at the mercy of the hungry *Heliothis* who dine seemingly without concern for their own safety. But (2) the plant, unbeknownst to the

caterpillars, is releasing a chemical that, while it has no effect on the diners, is attracting help ("calling" as the story suggests) in the form of a parasitoid (3) who will "do in" the caterpillar enemies. What other explanation could there be except "intelligent design"?

Let's rewind the video to a time "way back when" the tobacco plants may NOT have been releasing the attraction chemical. *Heliothis* caterpillars were eating their fill and the tobacco plants were barely surviving. Then by chance a few plants began secreting a strange new chemical, which just happened to attract parasitoids to plants that were infested with caterpillars. Of course, these parasitoids had been successful in finding caterpillars before—their existence depended on it—but never this feast! *Voila,* a threesome where everyone except the poor caterpillars are winners! Gradually, natural selection forces favored the "new, improved" tobacco plants and the more susceptible versions, eaten up by the caterpillars, faded to extinction.

2. Both the oryx and the thorn tree face the common challenge of survival in an environment that is too hot and too dry. As the textbook points out, all organisms have a tolerance range—especially when it comes to temperature and water requirements. Some simpler organisms such as bacteria and even insects have remarkably broad tolerance ranges. But in general more advanced organisms such as the two in this scenario have narrower tolerances.

Therefore, the oryx and the acacia must have mechanisms to conserve the valuable water needed for metabolic reactions and prevent buildup of excessive internal temperatures that could denature enzymes. Some possibilities are presented in the following table.

	Arabian oryx	Umbrella thorn tree
Morphological	• light skin color is reflective • heat-dissipating extremities • water acquired through eating of various grasses, shoots, and fruits	• leaves with minimal surface area • deep penetrating roots • thick protective cuticle
Physiological	• minimal sweating • use of fat for energy (more ATP per gram) • have unique ability to detect rainfall in distance and migrate to it • respiratory evaporation cools blood on its path to brain	• minimize transpiration
Behavioral	• stay out of direct sun by digging hollows to rest in shade • more active at night	• turn leaves away from direct sun • grow in groves to protect one another • grow near oasis

3. We will consider how four factors might interfere with the homeostatic controls over the body's internal temperature.

OBESITY: Obese persons tend to be more sedentary and have difficulty with breathing and getting sufficient oxygen; the fat could interfere with heat dissipation via the blood vessels; sweating could be reduced; these persons, feeling heavy already, may not like the additional "full" feeling caused by drinking extra fluids.

POOR CIRCULATION: Because dilated blood vessels and the blood running through them are the body's main mechanism for dissipating heat, reduced circulation would be a major hindrance to this action; this could be especially critical in the elderly, who are more sedentary and therefore not exercising the skeletal muscles (venous return) and the heart.

DEHYDRATION: Lack of sufficient water upsets the metabolic activities of the body; the hypothalamus may be less sensitive to temperature changes; excessive sweating, vomiting, and diarrhea will exacerbate the problem; the elderly or very young may not be able physically to obtain water.

ALCOHOL: Consumption of alcoholic beverages, although water based, actually have a dehydrating effect on body tissues because the alcohol inhibits ADH from the pituitary gland and causes the kidneys to effect more urine output.

18

PLANT FORM AND FUNCTION

Chapter Outline

Objectives

1. Describe the generalized body plan of a flowering plant.
2. Define and distinguish among the various types of tissues: ground, vascular, and dermal.
3. Explain how plant tissues develop from meristems.
4. Know the functions of stems, leaves, and roots.
5. Explain what is meant by *secondary growth* and describe how it occurs in woody eudicot roots and stems.
6. Know which elements are essential to plant health.
7. Explain how water is absorbed, transported, used, and lost by a plant.
8. Describe how the intake of carbon dioxide is connected with water loss.

9. Explain how essential mineral ions are taken up by a plant.
10. Know how translocation of organic substances occurs according to the pressure flow theory.

Key Terms

magnoliids
eudicots
monocots
shoots
stems
leaves
flowers
roots
ground tissue system
vascular tissue system
dermal tissue system
meristems
apical meristems
primary growth
secondary growth
lateral meristems
parenchyma
mesophyll
collenchyma
pectin
sclerenchyma
lignin
fibers
sclereids
xylem

vessel members
tracheids
phloem
sieve-tube members
companion cells
epidermis
cuticle
stoma, stomata
guard cells
cotyledons
vascular bundles
cortex
pith
leaf
blade
petiole
palisade mesophyll
spongy mesophyll
leaf veins
bud
terminal buds
lateral buds
taproot system
primary root
lateral roots

adventitious root
fibrous root system
vascular cylinder
pericycle
root hairs
annuals
herbaceous plants
biennials
perennials
woody plants
vascular cambium
cork cambium
periderm
bark
cork
heartwood
sapwood
early wood
late wood
growth rings
macronutrients
micronutrients
soil
humus
sand

silt
clay
loams
topsoil
leaching
soil erosion
root hairs
mycorrhiza, -ae
nitrogen fixation
root nodules
vascular cylinder
endodermis
Casparian strip
exodermis
transpiration
cohesion-tension theory
turgor pressure
guard cells
CAM plants
translocation
source regions
sink regions
pressure flow theory

Lecture Outline

Drought Versus Civilization
A. Severe droughts threaten the agricultural base of civilizations.
  1. The Akkadian civilization in Mesopotamia was brought down by a drought lasting 200 years.
  2. A drought of 150 years' duration contributed to the collapse of the Mayans.
B. Shorter drought periods can curtail food supplies to large numbers of people.
  1. The United States and Australia crop yields are down by 50 percent.
  2. Plants react to water shortages by closing their stomata, thus reducing photosynthesis.

18.1 Overview of the Plant Body
A. Although no one species of the 260,000 species of plants can be considered typical, the focus here is on angiosperms.
  1. Shoots consist of stems, leaves, and flowers (reproductive structures).
    a. Water, minerals, and organic substances are transported.

b. Stems are frameworks for upright growth and to display flowers.

c. Parts of the system store food.

2. Roots usually grow below ground.

a. A root system absorbs water and minerals from soil and conducts them upward.

b. Roots store food; they also anchor and support the plant.

B. Three Plant Tissue Systems

1. Plants consist of three basic tissue types:

a. The ground tissue system makes up the bulk of the plant body.

b. The vascular tissue system contains two kinds of conducting tissues that distribute water and solutes through the plant body.

c. The dermal tissue system covers and protects the plant's surfaces.

2. Plant tissues originate from meristems—localized regions of self-perpetuating, embryonic cells.

a. Apical meristem at the tips of roots and stems is responsible for growth and elongation.

1) Descendants of some of these cells will develop into the specialized tissues of the elongating root and stem.

2) Growth originating at root and shoot tips is labeled primary growth.

b. Lateral meristem tissues are responsible for the increase in diameter of older roots and stems—secondary growth.

C. Simple Tissues

1. Parenchyma makes up most of the soft, moist primary growth of plants.

a. Its thin-walled, pliable cells stay alive and retain the capacity to divide.

b. Various types participate in photosynthesis (mesophyll), storage, secretion, and other tasks.

2. Collenchyma cells are thickened and help strengthen the plant (for example, "strings" in celery).

a. It is commonly arranged at strands or cylinders beneath the dermal tissue of stems and stalks.

b. The primary cell walls of collenchyma become thickened with cellulose and pectin at maturity, often at their corners.

3. Sclerenchyma cells provide mechanical support and protection in mature plants.

a. The secondary walls are thick and often impregnated with lignin, which strengthens and waterproofs cell walls.

b. Sclerenchyma cells form *fibers* such as in hemp and flax; others called *sclereids* form strong coats around seeds as in a peach pit.

D. Complex Tissues

1. Vascular tissues function in the distribution of substances throughout the plant.

a. Xylem uses two kinds of cells (dead at maturity) to conduct water and minerals absorbed from the soil:

1) *Vessel members* are shorter cells joined end to end to form a vessel with perforation plates at the ends of each member.

2) *Tracheids* are long cells with tapered, overlapping ends.

b. Phloem transports sugars and other solutes throughout the plant body.

1) Phloem contains living conducting cells called *sieve tube members,* which bear clusters of pores in the walls through which the cytoplasm of adjacent cells is connected.

2) *Companion cells,* adjacent to the sieve tube members, help to load sugars produced in leaves and unload them in storage and growth regions.

2. A dermal tissue system called epidermis covers all primary plant parts.
   a. A waxy cuticle covers the external surfaces of the plant to restrict water loss and resist microbial attack.
   b. Stomata openings between pairs of guard cells permit water and gaseous exchange with the air.
   c. The periderm replaces the epidermis when roots and stems increase in diameter and become woody.

E. Eudicots and Monocots—Same Tissues, Different Features
   1. True dicots include common trees and shrubs (other than conifers).
   2. Monocots include grasses, lilies, irises, and palms.
   3. Monocot seeds have one cotyledon ("seed leaf"), and dicot seeds have two.

18.2 Primary Structure of Shoots
A. Internal Structure of Stems
   1. A vascular bundle is a multistranded cord of primary xylem and phloem running lengthwise through the ground tissue of shoots.
   2. The arrangement of vascular bundles is genetically different in dicots and monocots:
      a. The stems of most dicots have vascular bundles, arranged as a ring, that divide the ground tissue into the outer cortex and inner pith.
      b. In most monocots, the vascular bundles are scattered throughout the ground tissue.
B. Leaf Structure
   1. Leaves are metabolic factories equipped with photosynthetic cells.
      a. Most have a thin, flat blade that is attached to the stem by means of a stalk, or petiole.
      b. Leaves are adapted to local environmental conditions and can orient themselves for maximum exposure to the sun for photosynthesis.
   2. Mesophyll, consisting of photosynthetic parenchyma cells, extends throughout the interior of the leaf.
      a. Air spaces, which connect to the stomata, participate in gaseous exchange.
      b. Palisade mesophyll cells lie closer to the epidermis and are columnar in shape compared to the spongy mesophyll below them.
      c. The leaf's veins are vascular bundles of xylem and phloem that form a network for movement of water, solutes, and photosynthetic products.
   3. Epidermis covers every leaf surface exposed to air.
C. How Do Stems and Leaves Form?
   1. Buds are a shoot's main zone of primary growth.
      a. A bud is an undeveloped shoot of mostly meristematic tissue covered by modified leaves (bud scales).
      b. Terminal buds occur at the growing tips of shoots.
      c. Lateral buds form where leaves attach to the stems. They give rise to branches, leaves, or flowers.
   2. The cells of shoot apical meristem tissue divide continuously during the growing season.

18.3 Primary Structure of Roots
A. There are two types of root systems in plants:
   1. In most dicots, the primary root emerges from the seedling, increases in diameter, and grows downward.
      a. Lateral roots emerge sideways along its length.
      b. The primary root plus lateral roots form the taproot system.
   2. In monocots, adventitious roots arise from the stem.

    a. These roots and their branchings form a fibrous root system.

    b. Fibrous roots do not penetrate as deeply as taproots.

B. The root's structural organization is laid out in a seed.

  1. Cells in the apical meristem divide and then differentiate into root epidermis, ground tissues, and vascular tissues behind the meristematic region.

    a. The root cap protects the apical meristem and pushes through the soil.

    b. Cells are torn loose as the root grows.

  2. Vascular tissues form a vascular cylinder arranged as a central column.

    a. The column is surrounded by root cortex (ground tissue), which has abundant air spaces within it.

    b. Just inside the endodermis is the pericycle—it is meristematic and can give rise to lateral roots.

    c. Root hairs extend out from the epidermis to increase the absorptive surface area.

    d. The endodermis—the innermost layer of the cortex—surrounds the vascular cylinder and helps control water movement into it.

18.4   Secondary Growth—The Woody Plants

A. Seasonal growth cycles proceed from germination, to seed formation, to death.

  1. Annuals complete their life cycle in one season; they are nonwoody, or herbaceous, plants such as corn.

  2. Biennials, such as carrots, live two seasons: vegetative growth the first, flower and seed formation the second.

  3. Perennials live many years and have secondary growth (examples: roses, grape vines, apple trees).

B. Woody plants such as eudicots and gymnosperms show secondary growth by developing lateral meristems—vascular cambium and cork cambium.

  1. Vascular cambium is a cylinderlike lateral meristem.

    a. It produces secondary xylem on its inner face and secondary phloem on its outer.

    b. The secondary growth displaces the cells of the vascular cambium toward the stem surface.

  2. Periderm, formed from cork cambium, plus secondary phloem make up the bark.

  3. Cork cambium also produces cork.

    a. Cork contains suberin.

    b. Cork protects, insulates, and waterproofs the stem or root surfaces.

C. Wood's appearance changes as the stem grows older.

  1. Heartwood lies at the center of older stems and roots.

    a. It is a depository for resins, oils, gums, and tannins.

    b. It makes the tree strong and able to defy gravity.

  2. Sapwood is secondary growth located between heartwood and the vascular cambium.

    a. It is wet, pale in color, and not as strong.

    b. It is rich in the sugar-rich fluid of the phloem (for example, maple trees).

  3. In regions with cool winters or dry spells, the vascular cambium is inactive during part of the year.

    a. Early wood (start of growing season) contains xylem with large diameters and thin walls.

    b. Late wood contains xylem with small diameters and thick walls.

    c. Growth rings appear as alternating light bands of early wood and dark bands of late wood.

4. Hardwood (such as oak) has vessels, tracheids, and fibers in its xylem; softwood (such as conifers) has no vessels or fibers.

18.5 Plant Nutrients and Availability in Soil
A. Nutrients are essential for plant growth.
1. Nutrients are elements needed for growth and survival.
a. The "big three" elements are oxygen, hydrogen, and carbon.
b. Thirteen others are taken in water through the roots.
2. Nine elements have been deemed macronutrients (e.g. N, K, Ca); others are micronutrients (e.g. Cl, Fe, Zn).
B. Properties of Soil
1. Soil consists of particles of minerals mixed with humus (dead organisms and their litter).
a. Particles come in three sizes: sand, silt, and clay.
b. Clay, the smallest, holds onto nutrients as water percolates through the soil.
c. Plants do best in loams, soils with nearly equal proportions of the three particle types.
2. Layers of soil can be classified by profile properties; topsoil, the uppermost, is the most essential layer for plant growth.
C. Leaching and Erosion
1. Leaching refers to the removal of some of the nutrients from soil as water percolates through it.
2. Erosion is the movement of land under the force of wind, running water, and ice.

18.6 How Do Roots Absorb Water and Mineral Ions?
A. Specialized Absorptive Structures
1. Root hairs, extensions of the root epidermal cells, greatly increase the absorptive surface.
2. Mycorrhizae (fungi growing around plant roots) aid in absorbing minerals that are supplied to the plant in exchange for sugars, a symbiotic relationship that is beneficial to both.
3. Root nodules of legumes harbor bacteria that convert gaseous nitrogen to forms useful in the growth of the plants; this is a form of mutualism.
B. How Roots Control Water Uptake
1. Water moves from the soil across the root epidermis to the vascular cylinder, a column of vascular tissue in the center of the root.
a. A sheetlike layer of cells, the endodermis, surrounds the column.
b. The water-repellent Casparian strip forces water to move through the cytoplasm of the cells of the endodermis.
c. Therefore, membrane transport proteins help control the types of absorbed solutes that will become distributed throughout the plant.
2. Most flowering plants also have an exodermis, a layer of cells just inside the root epidermis, which also has a Casparian strip that functions just like the one next to the root vascular cylinder.

18.7 Water Transport through Plants
A. Transpiration Defined
1. Water moves from roots to stems and then to leaves.
2. Some water is used for growth and metabolism, but most evaporates into the air by transpiration.
B. Cohesion-Tension Theory

1. Water moves through pipelines called xylem, composed of cells (dead at maturity) called tracheids and vessel members.
2. The cohesion-tension theory of water transport explains water movement in plants:
   a. The drying power of air causes transpiration, which puts the water in the xylem in a state of tension leading from leaves, to stems, to roots.
   b. Unbroken, fluid columns of water show cohesion (aided by the hydrogen bonds); they resist rupturing as they are pulled upward under tension.
   c. As long as water molecules escape from the plant, molecules are pulled up to replace them.

18.8   How Do Stems and Leaves Conserve Water?
   A. The Water-Conserving Cuticle
       1. The cuticle is a translucent, water-impermeable layer secreted from epidermal cells.
       2. It coats the outer walls, which are exposed to air.
          a. Waxes are embedded in a matrix of cutin, a lipid polymer.
          b. The cuticle does not bar the entry of light rays, but does restrict water loss, the inward diffusion of CO_2, and the outward diffusion of oxygen.
   B. Controlled Water Loss at Stomata
       1. Stomata regulate the passage of water, carbon dioxide, and oxygen.
       2. A pair of guard cells defines each opening.
          a. In sunlight, a drop in carbon dioxide levels in the guard cells causes potassium and water to move into the guard cells, causing them to swell (turgor pressure); this creates an opening for carbon dioxide entry (a benefit) and water loss (a detriment).
          b. At night, potassium and water move out and the guard cells collapse to close the gap and conserve water.
       3. In CAM plants (cacti, for example), the stomata open at night when cells of these plants fix carbon dioxide; the stomata close during the day to conserve water in the arid habitats where these plants live.

18.9   How Organic Compounds Move through Plants
   A. Phloem distributes organic products of photosynthesis throughout the plant.
       1. Sieve tube cells are alive at maturity and are interconnected from leaf to root.
       2. Companion cells also participate in a supportive role.
       3. Storage forms of organic molecules (examples: starch, fats, proteins) are not easily transported throughout the plant body; therefore, they are converted to more soluble forms, such as sucrose.
   B. Translocation
       1. The term *translocation* is the technical name for the transport of sucrose and other compounds through phloem.
       2. Observations of aphids feeding show that sugars inside the sieve tubes are being moved under pressure.
       3. Movement of molecules through phloem is from sources (mostly leaves) to sinks (flowers and fruits).
       4. According to the pressure flow theory, translocation depends on pressure gradients.
          a. Solutes are loaded by active transport into the phloem from a source; water follows.
          b. As pressure builds in the tubes it pushes the sucrose-laden fluid out of the leaf, into the stem, and on to the sink.

Suggestions for Presenting the Material

- Help students to place the kinds of plants they will be hearing about in this chapter into perspective by briefly reviewing the terms *gymnosperm* and *angiosperm.*

- The information in this chapter is very visual in nature, so use overhead transparencies, slides, models, and diagrams whenever possible. Even if students may see these structures in a lab exercise, they will gain much reinforcement by seeing diagrams and photos of plant cells, tissues, and systems during the lecture.

- Emphasize the link between structure and function. Stress the differences between plants and animals, particularly in regard to growth. The concept of growth only at plant meristems, so different from the way in which animals grow, is initially puzzling to many students. Distinguish the terms *herbaceous* vs. *woody, apical* vs. *lateral, primary* vs. *secondary.* Remind students that the structures discussed in this chapter are vegetative structures (define this term); structures used for sexual reproduction will be covered in the next chapter.

- Introduce useful and familiar plant examples as you go through this chapter. Students are aware, of course, of the beauty plants provide in our day-to-day existence, but many forget the critical roles plants play in our lives. Use "grocery store" examples; students will be intrigued to hear more about the plants and plant parts that they have taken for granted. Bring in plants and fruits and vegetables whenever possible to demonstrate plant structures.

- Another area that is familiar to students, particularly those who have done woodworking, is wood. You can use many examples in this area to introduce points on plant structure and growth.

- Emphasize that plants are supported by a "skeleton" formed by a continuous column of water. Review, if necessary, some of the terms learned earlier, such as osmosis and turgor pressure, that relate to water movement.

- To help students understand the large surface area of a plant's root system, provide data on the surface areas of some typical plant root systems. Ask them to guess the ratio of shoot surface area to root surface area of a typical plant.

- This chapter provides many good opportunities to discuss the selective role of the environment in shaping such features as stomata and root systems.

Classroom and Laboratory Enrichment

- Distribute unusual types of plant tissues around the lecture classroom or lab room. Some possible examples include a fresh celery stalk cut in two (notice strands of collenchyma running along the "ribs" of the stalk), hemp used in making rope (fibers), cotton bolls (fibers), nutshells (sclereids).

- Obtain information about wood from lumber and paper companies. Several companies can supply posters and other materials about trees used for lumber and paper.

- In the lecture classroom, use an overhead transparency of a woody twig and ask students to point out structures such as nodes, internodes, apical meristem, terminal bud, axillary bud primordia, and terminal bud scale scars.

- Demonstrate dendrochronology. Using an overhead transparency (or, in small groups of students, an actual portion of a tree cross-section), discuss how interpretation of growth rings can reveal drought, fire, loss of trees due to disease, windfall, harvesting, and periods of normal growth. Show students a tree-boring device; let them interpret trunk samples obtained with it.

- Pass varied samples of leaves around the room. Ask students how leaf morphology varies with climate.

- If the number of students in the class permits it and the physical environment is suitable, take a short field trip to examine the plants and trees on your campus.

- Make ample use of plant structure models that will emphasize the 3-D quality lacking in flat photos. This is especially true of conducting tissue.

- Demonstrate the abundance and fragile nature of root hairs. Germinate radish seedlings in a petri dish lined with paper toweling. Pass the dish around the classroom, and allow each student to take a seedling and examine the root hairs. What happens to the root hairs minutes after the seedling is removed from the dish? Why?

- Demonstrate how species adapt to their surroundings by discussing the number, size, location, and distribution patterns of stomata in leaves of different species. Include some unusual examples, such as aquatic plants with stomata on upper leaf epidermis, conifers with sunken stomata, and plants with pubescent leaves.

- Examine tomato seedlings suffering from a deficiency of one of the macronutrients. This can be prepared as a lab experiment spanning several weeks, or a demonstration (or 35 mm slides) of the results can be shown instead.

- Use a simple soil-testing kit in lab to test samples of several different local soils. What are some steps that could be taken to improve each of the soils tested, if necessary?

- Set up demonstrations of root pressure or transpiration in lecture or lab.

- Sketch a diagram of a sieve tube of the phloem on the board or on an overhead transparency (your sketch can be similar to Figure 18.26 except that solute molecules and water molecules should be omitted). Begin to add water molecules and solute molecules at the source. Then ask your students to tell you what will happen next step-by-step as sugars move from the source (for example, leaf cells) to the sink (for example, root cells). Ask your students to think of an easy-to-see example of the result of the pressure flow theory (a potato is one answer).

- Show slides or transparencies of chloroplasts containing starch grains. Where did the starch come from? Would you be more likely to see such grains in the morning or in the afternoon? What will happen to the starch grains?

- In lab, provide prepared microscope slides of the undersides of plant species from different environments. In lecture, show slides or diagrams of the lower leaf epidermis.

- Compare the rates of recovery after wilting among three tomato seedlings that have each been cut off at the base of the main stem, as described below, and then placed in a beaker of water: (1) seedling is cut; (2) seedling is cut while plant is briefly submerged underwater; (3) seedling is cut, then allowed to sit on desktop for 15 minutes before being placed in water. Which seedling exhibits the least amount of wilting at the end of the lab period? The most? Why?

- Test slices of various fruits and vegetables for starch content by applying an iodine solution (should turn blue-black).

- Obtain a chart showing color photos of the symptoms of mineral deficiencies as listed in Table 18.2. Perhaps a plant nursery or fertilizer supplier can help you. If you cannot obtain a copy of some chart you would like, ask permission to photograph it for a slide.

Impacts, Issues Classroom Discussion Ideas

- Compare the lifestyles of plants and animals. In what ways does the nonmobility of plants influence their structure?

- In what ways are animals dependent on plants for survival?

- Desert plants must balance the need for carbon dioxide against the threat of desiccation. What are some adaptations of desert plants that allow them to open their stomata often enough to get the carbon dioxide sufficient for photosynthesis? Discuss how alternative photosynthetic pathways such as C4 and CAM photosynthesis have evolved in response to environmental pressures.

- What happens to transpiration rates on hot days? Dry days? Humid days? Breezy days?

- Reports of topsoil erosion and mineral leaching are numerous. Are there finite amounts of soil and soil nutrients? Will we ever completely exhaust our sources of plant sustenance?

Additional Ideas for Classroom Discussion

- How did companion cells acquire their name?

- How does growth in plants differ from growth in animals? What would humans look like if they grew like plants?

- What is the difference between primary growth and secondary growth? What kind(s) of growth occurs in a maple tree? Where would you look in the maple tree to find primary growth? Secondary growth? What is the difference between an apical meristem and a lateral meristem?

- What causes "growth rings" in wood? Does one ring always represent one growing season? Does some wood lack growth rings? Why or why not?

- What is girdling? Ask students to think of some examples of girdling that they might have seen (damage done to the bark of small trees by electric or gas-powered weed trimmers is one example). Ask how girdling might occur in nature (nibbling of bark by deer or porcupines is one possibility).

- What is the purpose of the root cap? Is there such a thing as a "shoot cap"? Why or why not? Is there any structure on the shoot tip that is analogous to the root cap?

- What plants have root systems and shoot systems that can be used as food? Many of these plants have modified structures such as roots (for example, carrots), stems (for example, ginger), or leaves (for example, celery, an enlarged petiole) that are eaten.

- Present some familiar examples of common and/or economically important plants such as corn, tomatoes, lettuce, rice, and wheat, and ask students to classify them as monocots or dicots.

- How useful are plant parts such as leaves, stems, and roots when one is attempting to identify a plant? Are such plant parts a reliable indicator of species?

- Ask your students if pines, firs, and spruces are monocots or dicots. (The answer, of course, is that conifers are gymnosperms and hence are not classified as either monocots or dicots.) The ensuing discussion will help students to learn the differences between gymnosperms and flowering plants.

- When you eat an apple, what ground tissue are you eating?

- What is the biggest monocot you can think of? (Some possible answers might be bamboo or palm.)

- What is cork? Where does the cork used in wine bottles come from?

- Plants are the source of many useful products including some insecticides. Do you know the source of pyrethrum? (Answer: mum flowers) Of nicotine? (Answer: tobacco leaves) Of rotenone? (Answer: *Derris* root)

- Why are plants "taken for granted" in our culture?
- How do the tracheids and vessel members found in xylem conduct water even though they are dead at maturity?
- Ask students who have raised tomatoes or other garden plants if they have ever observed "midday wilt," a phenomenon in which even well-watered plants temporarily wilt during the late afternoon. Ask them why this happens. (Midday wilt occurs when transpiration exceeds the rate of water uptake.)
- What are some crop plants that are particularly adept at storing sugars or starches?
- How do plants combat insect pests in nature? How do we help plants resist insect attack?

How Would You Vote? Classroom Discussion Ideas

- Monitor the voting for the online question. The idea of restricting the growth of cities to conserve resources such as water seems almost laughable in the United States. Maybe in a totalitarian country, but not here. Of course, limiting the growth of family size, as well as cities, would probably be a good idea. We are running out of resources. But the demand for housing (and the money it generates in our economy) shows no signs of slowing even though in our hearts we know the growth is not sustainable.

Term Paper Topics, Library Activities, and Special Projects

- What are some of the woody plant species used for lumber? Find the names of as many as you can; you may be surprised at the number! Describe some of these species and discuss their uses.
- Many plant parts provide dyes that can be used to color fabrics. Prepare a demonstration or an exhibit of plant species used as sources for dyes.
- Learn more about the history of paper making, and discuss how modern papers are made.
- Describe some of the morphological adaptations found among plants of extreme climates (for example, tundra, deserts, and bogs).
- Describe some of the plant species whose leaves, stems, and/or roots can be used as sources for drugs. Just a few of the many examples to include in your research are coca plant, marijuana, *Ephedra*, foxglove, and opium poppy.
- Describe the morphology, habitat, and geographic range of the insectivorous plant species found in the United States.
- Can plant parts such as leaves, roots, and stems be used to grow new plants? Discuss techniques of vegetative propagation; describe its role in commercial greenhouses and nurseries.
- Investigate the effects on plants that the gypsy moth has had in the northeastern United States.
- What factors make the vast majority of the United States suitable for intensive agriculture?
- Discuss the role of each of the macronutrients in plant metabolism and growth.
- What role has the fibrous root system of grasses played in the establishment and maintenance of prairies in the United States? What happens to the species composition of prairies if such areas are interrupted by roads, farming, or railroads? Discuss the history of the American prairies.
- Describe the role of mycorrhizae in successful seedling growth among species of gymnosperms. How do commercial lumber companies ensure that the proper mycorrhizal fungi will be present on the roots of their tree seedlings?

- Learn more about soil testing. Describe how a typical soil-testing kit works.

- Visit a nursery or garden center where lawn and garden fertilizers are sold. List the N-P-K ratio for each of the different fertilizers. Explain differences among N-P-K ratios of fertilizers for lawns, vegetables, and flowers. Why do fertilizers for different purposes have such different N-P-K ratios? Summarize the roles of nitrogen, phosphorus, and potassium in plant functioning and development.

- What are the effects of acid rain on plant functioning?

- Discuss the effects of extremely cold climates, such as Arctic tundra, on the ratio of shoot systems:root systems. Why is so much of the plant underground in such climates?

- Locate a report (USDA documents?) showing the decline in soil fertility in the United States in the past 100 years.

- Insects such as aphids can be controlled by insecticides introduced into the plant via uptake by the roots. They are called "systemic" insecticides. How do these chemicals accomplish their control? Give an example.

Possible Responses to *Critical Thinking* Questions

1. Insufficient nitrogen in a plant will have a negative impact on the synthesis of amino acids and the proteins from which they are assembled. This will in turn affect the structure of the plant, which is incorporating proteins, plus it will curtail the synthesis of enzymes needed for metabolic activities. Lack of nitrogen will also adversely affect the synthesis of nucleic acids needed for information storage (DNA) and decoding (RNA).

2. Wilted plants are always a disappointment. Fortunately, if the wilting has not been prolonged, a good drink of water should perk up the plant. Of course, what has happened is this: while you were on vacation (nice hot summer days at the beach) the plants continued to transpire and lose water to the air. For the first day or so, the molecules of water continued to move up the xylem columns due to their cohesion and tension properties. Alas, on about day three, there was insufficient water entering the roots to replace the water being lost and the column was broken, resulting in the wilting.

3. When moving a plant from one location to another, it is a good idea to take as much soil as practicable with the root mass. This will ensure that the mycorrhizae are substantially intact and can continue functioning in the new location, and the fragile root hairs so essential for water/mineral absorption are not stripped off.

4. In north Louisiana where I live, pine trees are the predominant species, with a few hardwoods thrown in for variety. Many of these pines are ornamental and therefore have escaped the logger's chainsaw. They may have a story—albeit a rather brief one, to tell. The pines in the managed tracts have considerably shorter tales. The hardwoods, if you can find them, would tell us more because they have been around so much longer.

19

PLANT REPRODUCTION AND DEVELOPMENT

Chapter Outline

Objectives

1. Describe the typical patterns of life cycles in flowering plants.
2. Draw and label the parts of a flower. Explain where gamete formation occurs in the male and female structures.
3. Define and distinguish between *pollination* and *fertilization*.
4. Trace embryonic development from zygote to seedling.
5. Describe the various styles presented by asexual reproduction in flowering plants.
6. Describe the general pattern of plant growth and list the factors that cause plants to germinate.

7. List the various chemical messengers that regulate growth and metabolism in plants.
8. Explain how plants respond to changes in their environment.
9. Know the factors that cause a plant to flower, to age, and to enter dormancy. Describe each process.

Key Terms

flowers	pollen grains	runners	gravitropism
sporophyte	microspores	tissue culture	phototropism
gametophyte	megaspores	propagation	long-day plants
receptacle	endosperm	germination	short-day plants
sepal	pollination	meristems	day-neutral plants
petal	pollen tube	plant hormones	night length
stamen	double fertilization	gibberellins	photoperiodism
anther	cotyledons	auxins	phytochrome
filament	seed	coleoptile	circadian rhythm
pollen sacs	fruit	indoleacetic acid (IAA)	abscission
carpels	simple fruit	2,4-D	senescence
stigma	aggregate fruit	herbicide	dormancy
germinate	multiple fruit	dioxin	vernalization
ovary	accessory fruit	cytokinins	
ovules	seed dispersal	ethylene	
pollinators	asexual reproduction	abscisic acid (ABA)	

Lecture Outline

Imperiled Sexual Partners
A. Many flowering plants need insect pollinators.
   1. The cacao tree from which chocolate is obtained requires a midge that will only live in tropical rain forests.
   2. Honeybees are very important pollinators of crops in the United States.
B. Hundreds of plant species are listed as endangered simply because of pollinator shortages.

19.1 Sexual Reproduction in Flowering Plants
A. Regarding the Flowers
   1. Flowers are specialized reproductive shoots of the sporophyte.
   2. Meiosis of cells within flowers produces the small haploid gametophytes, which in turn produce either sperm or eggs.
   3. Flower parts are arranged in whorls:
      a. Sepals are the outermost green, leaflike parts.
      b. Petals are the colored parts located between the reproductive structures and the sepals.
      c. Male parts consist of the stamens—a slender stalk (filament) capped with an anther, inside which pollen sacs enclose pollen grains.
      d. The female parts are the carpels, vessel-shaped structures with an expanded lower ovary (with ovules), a slender column (style), and an upper surface (stigma) for pollen landing.

B. Regarding the Pollinators
   1. Pollinators may be currents of wind, animals, or any other agent that transfers pollen grains from male to female reproductive structures of flowering plants.
   2. The structure, coloration, patterns, fragrances, and sugar-rich nectar of flowers coevolved with specific kinds of pollinators that could transfer pollen most effectively.
C. From Spores to Zygotes
   1. Pollen is produced by this method:
      a. In anthers, each diploid "mother" cell divides by meiosis to form four haploid *microspores.*
      b. Each microspore will divide to form pollen grains.
   2. Female cells are produced by this method:
      a. In the carpel, a mass of tissue forms ovules (potential seeds) enclosed by integuments.
      b. A diploid "mother" cell divides by meiosis to produce haploid megaspores, one of which will eventually produce the egg and others that will contribute to formation of the endosperm.
   3. When a pollen grain lands on a stigma, pollination has occurred.
      a. One cell in each pollen grain will produce the sperm; the other will form the pollen tube, which bores down through the carpel to deliver two sperm nuclei to an ovule.
      b. One sperm fuses with the egg nucleus to form a diploid zygote.
      c. The other sperm nucleus fuses with the two endosperm nuclei to yield a triploid endosperm, which will nourish the young sporophyte seedling.

19.2   From Zygotes to Seeds Packaged in Fruit
   A. The zygote undergoes repeated divisions to form an embryo sporophyte inside an ovule.
      1. Cotyledons (seed leaves) develop for the purpose of utilizing the endosperm during germination.
         a. From zygote to embryo, the plant supplies nutrition until the time when the connection between the ovule and ovary wall is broken.
         b. The mature ovule's integuments thicken into seed coats around the seed (a mature ovule containing embryo and food reserves).
      2. A fruit is a mature ovary with seeds (ovules) inside; they may be classified as simple, aggregate, multiple, or accessory.
   B. All fruits have a common function—seed dispersal.
      1. For example, the wall of maple seeds extends out like wings to catch the wind and be transported far from the parent tree.
      2. Winds can transport fruits as in the dandelion's pluming "parachute."
      3. Some fruits are dispersed by sticking on animal bodies or by passing through the digestive tract to be deposited in the feces.
      4. Specialized fruits with waxy coatings can disperse in water.
      5. Humans are perhaps the grand dispersing agents by virtue of the long distances to which they carry seeds, by design or accident.

19.3   Asexual Reproduction of Flowering Plants
   A. Asexual Reproduction in Nature
      1. Vegetative growth modes include: adventitious shoots and runners.
      2. In this mode of reproduction all of the plants are nearly identical.
   B. Induced Propagation.
      1. Tissue culture propagation can result in whole plants produced from a group of cells, as in the grafting of phylloxera-resistant grapevines.

2. This technique is used today to produce food crops that have desirable characteristics.

19.4   Patterns of Early Growth and Development
A. How Do Seeds Germinate?
1. Germination is the resumption of growth after a time of arrested embryonic development.
2. Environmental factors influence germination.
a. Often spring rains provide the water amounts necessary to swell and rupture the seed coat.
b. Oxygen moves in and allows the embryo to switch to aerobic metabolism.
c. Increased temperatures and number of daylight hours are also influential.
3. Repeated cell divisions produce a seedling with a primary root.
B. Genetic Programs, Environmental Cues
1. Patterns of germination and development have a heritable basis dictated by a plant's genes.
2. Early cell divisions may result in unequal distribution of cytoplasm.
a. Cytoplasmic differences trigger variable gene expression, which may result in variations in hormone synthesis.
b. Even though all cells have the same genes, it is the selective expression of those genes that results in cell differentiation.

19.5   Cell Communication in Plant Development
A. Growth and development are necessary for plants to survive.
1. Growth is defined as an increase in the number, size, and volume of cells.
2. Development is the emergence of specialized, morphologically different body parts.
B. Major Types of Plant Hormones
1. Plant hormones have central roles in the selective gene expression underlying cell differentiation and patterns of development.
2. *Gibberellins* promote stem elongation.
a. They also help buds and seeds break dormancy and resume growth in the spring.
b. In some species, they influence the flowering process.
3. *Auxins* affect the lengthening of stems and coleoptiles (the protective cylinder that covers and protects the tender leaves during germination).
a. Auxins also may participate in growth responses to light and gravity.
b. Indoleacetic acid (IAA) is applied to fruit trees to promote uniform flowering, set the fruit, and encourage synchronous development of fruit.
c. Synthetic auxins (such as 2,4-D) are used as herbicides.
4. *Cytokinins* stimulate cell division in root and shoot meristems, where they are most abundant; they are used commercially to prolong the life of stored vegetables and cut flowers.
5. *Ethylene* stimulates the ripening of fruit and is used commercially for this purpose.
6. *Abscisic acid* (ABA) inhibits cell growth, helps prevent water loss (by promoting stomata closure), and promotes seed and bud dormancy.

19.6   Adjusting Rates and Directions of Growth
A. A plant tropism is a growth response.
1. It is evidenced by a turning of a root or shoot toward or away from an environmental stimulus.
2. Hormones mediate the shifts in rates at which different cells grow and elongate to cause the overall responses.

B. Responses to Gravity
  1. *Gravitropism* is the growth response to gravity.
    a. No matter which way the plant is oriented to the Earth's surface, shoots grow up, roots grow down.
    b. Auxin, together with a growth-inhibiting hormone, may play a role in promoting or inhibiting growth in strategic regions.
  2. Statoliths, plant organelles filled with starch grains, settle downward, causing a redistribution of auxin.
C. Responses to Light
  1. *Phototropism* is a growth response to light.
    a. Flavoprotein, a pigment molecule, plays a role because of its capacity to absorb blue wavelengths of light.
    b. Bending toward the light is caused by elongation of cells (auxin stimulation) on the side of the plant *not* exposed to light.
  2. The difference in growth rates bends the plant *toward* the light.
D. Responses to Contact
  1. Hairs on the epidermal surfaces can detect contact.
  2. Redistribution of auxin and ethylene induces the plant cells to grow at unequal rates, causing the plant to curl around an object it contacts.
E. Responses to Mechanical Stress
  1. Mechanical stress, such as prevailing winds or grazing animals, inhibits stem lengthening.
  2. Even plants grown outdoors commonly have shorter stems than the same kinds of plants grown in a greenhouse.

19.7   Meanwhile, Back at the Flower . . .
  A. How Do Plants Know When to Flower?
    1. Biological clocks are internal time-measuring mechanisms that adjust daily and seasonal patterns of growth, development, and reproduction.
    2. The flowering process is keyed to changes in daylength throughout the year.
      a. "Short-day plants" flower in late summer or early autumn when daylength becomes *shorter* (example: poinsettias).
      b. "Long-day plants" flower in the spring as daylength becomes *longer* (example: spinach).
      c. "Day-neutral plants" flower when they are mature enough to do so.
    3. Photoperiodism is a biological response to a change in relative length of daylight and darkness in a 24-hour cycle; this resetting of the biological clocks is necessary to make seasonal adjustments.
      a. Phytochrome, a blue-green pigment, is the alarm button for some biological clocks in plants.
      b. Phytochrome can absorb both red and far-red wavelengths with different results.
    4. Circadian rhythms change with the seasons, causing leaf cells to transcribe more or less of a flowering gene, resulting in a meristem developing into a flower.

19.8   Life Cycles End, and Turn Again
  A. Changes in the environment bring changes in plants.
    1. The dropping of leaves, flowers, fruits, and so on is called abscission.

2. Senescence is the sum total of the processes leading to the death of plant parts or the whole plant.
   a. The recurring cue is a decrease in daylength that triggers a decrease in auxin production.
   b. Cells in abscission zones produce ethylene, which causes cells to deposit suberin in their walls.
   c. Simultaneously, enzymes digest cellulose and pectin in the middle lamella to weaken the abscission zone.
B. Plants may enter and break dormancy.
   1. Dormancy occurs in autumn when daylength shortens and growth stops in many trees and nonwoody perennials; it will not resume until spring.
      a. Strong cues for dormancy include short days, cold nights, and dry, nitrogen-deficient soil.
      b. Dormancy has great adaptive value in preventing plant growth on occasional warm autumn days only to be killed by later frost.
   2. Dormancy is broken by milder temperatures, rains, and nutrients; it probably involves gibberellins, abscisic acid, and environmental cues.
C. Vernalization is the stimulation of flowering only after plants have been exposed to low temperatures (winter).

19.9   Regarding the World's Most Nutritious Plant
A. *Chenopodium quinoa* (quinoa for short) is a remarkable plant.
   1. Its seeds provide valuable nutrition to South Americans.
   2. It contains about 16 percent protein and is a good source of iron and calcium.
   3. It is also highly resistant to drought, frost, and saline soils.
B. Quinoa has the potential to vastly reduce the incidence of kwashiorkor, a severe form of malnutrition caused by protein-deficient diets.

Suggestions for Presenting the Material

- Students frequently have trouble understanding the life cycle of a flowering plant because it is quite different from animal life cycles. Be sure to emphasize the importance of alternation of generations; spend plenty of time going over a diagram of the plant life cycle like the one shown in Figure 19.1b. Compare it to a drawing or diagram of the human life cycle to give students a familiar reference point.

- Give examples of a sporophyte and a gametophyte in the life cycles of some common plants. Explain the difference between a spore and a gamete. It may be necessary to briefly review meiosis I and II and terms such as *haploid* and *diploid*, especially if it has been a while since the students covered mitosis and meiosis.

- Students will find it easier to comprehend the development of male and female gametophytes if they have dissected a flower before this is discussed. If students wonder why the events of gamete formation and fertilization are so complicated, remind them that these are very advanced plants.

- Discuss with your students once again how growth in plants differs from growth in animals.

- Introduce the term *hormone* and discuss the need for growth-regulating hormones. There are many lab experiments designed to investigate the role of hormones in plant growth and development; many of them are available from biological supply houses in the form of kits. These can be prepared ahead of time and used as demonstrations or performed by the students.

- Videos are also effective ways to present plant growth and development.

Classroom and Laboratory Enrichment

- Show line drawings or color photos of flowers of any angiosperm, and ask students to point out the gametophyte and sporophyte portions of the plant.
- Use models, photos, and diagrams to present floral structure. Then dissect at least one type of flower, preferably one with large parts, in lab or lecture.
- Show time-lapse films of flower and fruit formation.
- Display some inflorescences of grasses (if available) in the lab or lecture classroom. Use diagrams or photos of corn inflorescences as examples of imperfect flowers; corn is a good choice because of the large "tassels" (staminate flowers) and because students are familiar with the ear of corn, the end product of many fertilization events.
- Learn the parts of a seed by dissecting bean and corn seeds after they have been softened in water for several hours.
- Use microscope slides and/or 35 mm slides of a lily to discuss microspore and megaspore development.
- View germinating pollen grains under the microscope in lab or with a microprojector in lecture.
- Prepare a demonstration of different kinds of fruits, or ask students to bring fruits to class or lab. Students will be fascinated to see the relationship between the parts of the flower before fertilization and the subsequent fruit parts.
- Use techniques of vegetative propagation or tissue culture to grow new plants. This can be done by the students in lab or can be prepared ahead of time as a demonstration, ideally with different stages of growth represented.
- Show scanning electron micrographs of the pollen grains of some familiar plants.
- Show close-up photos of bees and the pollen-carrying devices on their legs. Or if your group is small, place actual specimens of these insects under stereomicroscopes.
- Locate photos of flowers that are formed in various ways to lure insects to alight and feed.
- For a demonstration of growth at apical meristems, mark the root tips or shoot apical meristems of sturdy just-sprouted seedlings (beans or peas are fine) at measured intervals with India ink. Keep the seeds moist in a petri dish lined with paper toweling. Measure the rates of growth after one week. Exactly where along the root or shoot is the increase in length occurring?
- Determine if the food stored in sprouting seeds is starch or sugar by treating the seeds with tetrazolium solution and Lugol's solution.
- Design and implement experiments involving seed germination. Vary conditions such as temperature or light, and examine the effects on germination rate.
- In species with hard seed coats, examine the effects of seed scarification (the removal or breakage of seed coats) on germination rate. Students can use a seed scarifier, if available, or gently rub seeds between blocks covered with a fine grade of sandpaper. Compare germination rates between seeds that have been scarified and those left unscarified.
- How does soaking seeds in water overnight before sowing affect germination rate? Compare germination rates between presoaked seeds and unsoaked seeds.
- Compare the cotyledons of monocots and dicots by examining recently sprouted corn and bean seedlings.

- How does complete darkness affect seedling growth? Compare the lengths and weights of bean or pea seedlings raised in light with those raised in complete darkness. What is the adaptive value of etiolation?
- Examine the effects of auxins, gibberellins, and cytokinins on plant growth and development.
- Investigate the role of the intact shoot tip in inhibiting lateral bud development in *Coleus*. What happens to lateral buds if the shoot tip is removed? Design an experiment in which applications of IAA dissolved in lanolin paste mimic the effects of the intact shoot tip.
- Discover the effects of different wavelengths of light on phototropism.
- Examine the effects of ethylene on fruit ripening or abscission.
- Locate and show a segment of a movie or videotape depicting growth and development of a seedling.

Impacts, Issues Classroom Discussion Ideas

- Can you tell by a flower's appearance if it is wind-pollinated or insect-pollinated? What are some clues suggesting that a flower is wind-pollinated? What are some floral features suggestive of insect pollination?
- What is the difference between pollination and fertilization?
- Compare and contrast the advantages and disadvantages of sexual reproduction in flowering plants. What are some of the advantages and disadvantages that asexual reproduction offers to flowering plants? Why do so many species of flowering plants reproduce both sexually and asexually?
- After studying this chapter, do you see flowers as providing beauty to enhance the human experience or do you perceive them as more functional than that? Explain.

Additional Ideas for Classroom Discussion

- Why do botanists use flowers rather than leaves or stems as indicators of species identity?
- Distinguish between megaspores and microspores.
- What is included in an ovule of a flowering plant? What events take place inside the ovule? What are some of the changes that take place inside an ovule after fertilization has occurred?
- Is a pollen grain analogous to a human sperm cell? Why or why not?
- Discuss floral diversity. Ask students to name different kinds of flowers, and then discuss the shapes, types of parts, and pollination of each.
- What is double fertilization?
- Cut open apples, pears, green beans, strawberries, oranges, pineapples, and any other fruits or vegetables you have on hand in class or lab. Identify the floral origin of as many parts as you can. For example, which part of the fruit was the ovary wall? The carpel? The integument? The sepal? The stigma and style?
- Define the terms *fruit* and *vegetable.* What is the difference between these two terms? Why is it accurate to use the term *fruit* when we are talking about tomatoes and green beans? Ask students for examples of fruits, and use Figure 19.6 to classify each one.

- Why do many fruits change from green to red, yellow, or orange as they ripen? Of what adaptive value is the sweet smell produced by most fruits?

- Is there any truth to the disgusting allegation that honey is actually "bee vomit"?

- Why do you think there are poisonous seeds, berries, leaves, stems, and so on in the plant kingdom?

- How does growth in plants differ from growth in humans? Why can growth in plants be seen as a counterpart to movement in animals?

- How do hormone production and activity differ in plants and animals? What are some similarities shared by plants and animals? What are some differences?

- What is the adaptive value of seed dormancy?

- Why do grasses keep growing even after being repeatedly trimmed by lawn mowers or grazing animals? Where is the meristem located in shoots of grasses?

- What is "pinching back"? Why does it make plants bushier?

- What is "bolting"? Ask any of your students who have raised spinach or lettuce if they are familiar with this term. What can gardeners do to inhibit bolting?

- What is the biological reasoning behind the old saying "One bad apple spoils the whole bunch"? Discuss the role of ethylene in hastening fruit ripening.

- How could a sap-feeding insect actually stimulate plant growth? (Answer: the plant works harder to replace lost sap)

- How could a foliage-feeding insect increase growth of understory plants? (Answer: by increasing light penetration)

- How could irrigation of cotton plants increase insect damage? (Answer: more green leaves support more larvae)

How Would You Vote? Classroom Discussion Ideas

- Monitor the voting for the online question. Wow! What a dilemma. Here is a new, safer way to deliver pesticides that are needed to ensure our crops aren't overrun by pests, but it imperils the pollinators we need to ensure the development of our crops. Obviously much research needs to be done before we place such a load of these chemicals in the environment that we wipe out the vital little bees.

Term Paper Topics, Library Activities, and Special Projects

- Examine diversity among flowers. Describe the coevolution of flowering plants and insects.

- Identify as many of the flowering plants on campus as you can. If flowers are available, collect them, identify them, and bring them back to class or lab. One group of students could prepare a map of campus trees and plants and lead other groups on a campus plant walk.

- Select a well-known flowering plant species, and prepare a timetable showing when the reproductive events leading up to seed formation occur.

- Learn more about some of the reproductive isolating mechanisms that discourage self-pollination among many flowering plant species.

- Describe commercial uses of asexual reproduction in flowering plants.

- Describe the different uses of each part of the wheat grain. What is wheat germ? Wheat bran? How does white flour differ from whole wheat flour?

- Why are commercial bananas and many commercial varieties of grapes seedless? How are seedless varieties of normally "seedy" fruits such as watermelons created?

- Discuss the role of evolution in floral diversity. What is an example of a primitive flower? An advanced flower?

- Learn more about the role of pollen in human allergy. Collect daily and monthly information on the types and amounts of pollen found in your area. What species have the most pollen? What months of the year have the highest pollen counts? Should we regulate the planting of non-native ornamental vegetation in cities and towns in states such as Arizona where people have moved seeking low pollen counts?

- Discuss the use of pollen grains as indicators of the past vegetation history of an area.

- Describe different seed dispersal mechanisms used by flowering plants. Make a list of dispersal mechanisms found among local plants or plants on campus.

- Research the process by which bees make and store honey.

- Document the role of animals in seed dispersal and the extent to which this helps plants.

- Describe how insect infestations or plant diseases can affect plant growth.

- How long can most seeds remain viable? Learn more about documented cases of extreme seed longevity. What steps can be taken to increase seed viability? What are some of the actions taken by seed companies to ensure maximum seed viability?

- Why are seedlings raised in complete darkness white or yellow instead of green? Describe the role played by sunlight in chlorophyll synthesis.

- What are some species whose seeds require stratification (cold, moist conditions for several weeks prior to sowing) for successful germination? What is the survival value of such a requirement?

- How are auxins, gibberellins, cytokinins, and abscisic acid used by commercial growers? How is ethylene used to hasten fruit ripening?

- Look up the geographic distributions of several long-day plants, short-day plants, and day-neutral plants. How is the effect of daylength on flowering related to the geographic range of a particular plant species?

- Describe synthetic auxins used as herbicides. How do these compounds actually work? Why does 2,4-D kill dicot weeds but not grasses? How are these compounds manufactured? What is their impact on the environment?

- Discuss the use of Agent Orange during the Vietnam War. What are its side effects? Was its use justified?

- Look up and report on what factors limit growth of plants above certain altitudes and how these factors specifically affect plant growth and development.

- What effect(s) would petroleum-solvent insecticides have on plants if they were used instead of insecticides formulated in water?

Possible Responses to *Critical Thinking* Questions

1. The seedlings germinated in darkness evidently are experiencing greater amounts of hormones. These could be varying amounts of gibberellins and auxin.

2. Solar tracking whereby plants can "follow the sun" with their leaves oriented toward the sun is a response to auxin, which causes the cells on the shady side to lengthen and "push" the leaf in the direction of the sun.

3. A mutated gene in the water cress plant that produces excess auxin could have the following effects: a) cell division and plant growth, b) promotion of apical dominance by blocking lateral bud growth, c) blockage of abscission, and c) inhibition of growth of main roots but stimulation of adventitious root growth.

4. In the case of the kereru birds and their job as dispersing agents for seeds of the Puriri tree, things look grim. We can imagine that long ago there were several species of birds that could carry the large seeds far and wide, but human intervention has thwarted nature and reduced the dispersal agents to only one. Both natural and artificial agents will continue to place pressure on the sole surviving bird species. If its populations are not large enough to disperse the seeds in sufficient numbers, the Puriri tree will dwindle in numbers.

5. Hormones applied to plants could affect humans if the chemical structure of the plant hormone were similar enough to the human hormone that it could bind to the human cell receptors and cause its effects. Or possibly the plant hormone could be modified slightly upon entering the body to make it similar *enough* to the human hormone it resembles.

6. Any evolved mechanism that makes a plant part, such as flowers or fruits, more attractive and tasty to animals that visit to feed is going to have a selective advantage for the plant's survival and continued reproductive success.

20

ANIMAL TISSUES AND ORGAN SYSTEMS

Chapter Outline

Objectives

1. Understand the various levels of animal organization (cells, tissues, organs, and organ systems) and be familiar with the anatomical terms provided.
2. Know the characteristics of the various types of tissues. Know the types of cells that compose each tissue type and cite some examples of organs that contain significant amounts of each tissue type.
3. Characterize each of the major organ systems of the human body.
4. Describe how the four principal tissue types are organized into an organ such as the skin.

Key Terms

stem cells	simple epithelium	endocrine gland	collagen
tissue	stratified epithelium	tight junctions	fibers
organ	glandular epithelium	adhering junctions	"ground substance"
organ system	gland cells	gap junctions	loose connective tissue
homeostasis	glands	connective tissues	dense, irregular
epithelium, -ia	exocrine gland	fibroblasts	connective tissue

dense, regular connective tissue	involuntary	respiratory system	keratin
tendons	smooth muscle tissue	digestive system	melanocytes
ligaments	nervous tissue	urinary system	melanin
cartilage	neurons	reproductive system	mammary glands
bone tissue	neuroglial cells	germ cells	sweat glands
adipose tissue	vertebrates	somatic cells	oil glands
blood	integumentary system	ectoderm	vitamin D
muscle tissue	muscular system	mesoderm	folate
skeletal muscle tissue	skeletal system	endoderm	elastin fibers
striated	nervous system	skin	Langerhans cells
voluntary	endocrine system	epidermis	cold sores
cardiac muscle tissue	circulatory system	dermis	Herpes simplex
	lymphatic system	keratinocytes	

Lecture Outline

It's All About Potential
A. Stem cells form when a zygote first begins to divide.
  1. Stem cells can divide indefinitely without differentiating.
  2. They can be coaxed into forming many cell types.
B. The most pliable of stem cells comes from human embryos.
  1. These cells may be able to repair damaged nervous tissue.
  2. But ethical issues have been raised because of the source of the tissue.

20.1   Organization and Control in Animal Bodies
A. The cells of the body are organized into levels:
  1. A *tissue* is a group of cells that performs a common task.
  2. Each *organ* consists of different tissues working together for a common goal.
  3. *Organ systems* consist of two or more organs interacting for a common task.
B. Animals have an internal environment of blood and interstitial fluid.
  1. Homeostasis is the condition in which the body is "in balance."
  2. This coordination is maintained by signaling mechanisms and feedback controls.

20.2   Four Basic Types of Tissues
A. Epithelial Tissue
  1. Epithelial tissue is commonly called epithelium.
    a. One surface is free (may have cilia), and the other adheres to a noncellular basement membrane.
    b. *Simple epithelium* consists of a single layer of cells; example: wall of capillaries.
    c. *Stratified epithelium* consists of one or more layers of cells; example: skin.
    d. In epithelial tissues, cells are linked tightly together, with little intervening material.
  2. All animals have glandular epithelia with gland cells.
    a. Gland cells secrete products, unrelated to their own metabolism, that are to be used elsewhere.
    b. Glands are multicelled secretory structures.
      1) Exocrine glands often secrete through ducts to free surfaces; they secrete mucus, saliva, wax, milk, and so on.

2) Endocrine glands secrete hormones directly into intercellular fluid for distribution by the blood.
3. Epithelial cells have specialized junctions.
   a. In tight junctions, cells adhere to one another by means of special attachment sites; this prevents leakage (example: stomach acid).
   b. Adhering junctions are like spot welds that lock cells together.
   c. Gap junctions are channels that allow ions and molecules to flow between the cytoplasm of abutting cells.

B. Connective Tissues
1. Most connective tissue contains cells and fibers (collagen and/or elastin) secreted by fibroblasts, all scattered in a ground substance.
2. Soft Connective Tissues
   a. *Loose connective tissue* supports epithelia and organs and surrounds blood vessels and nerves; it contains fibroblast cells and fibers plus macrophages.
   b. *Dense, irregular connective tissue* has thicker fibers and more of them, but fewer cells; it forms protective capsules around organs.
   c. *Dense, regular connective tissue* has its fibers in parallel; this is the arrangement found in tendons (muscle to bone) and ligaments (bone to bone).
3. Specialized Connective Tissue
   a. *Cartilage* contains a dense array of fibers in a jellylike ground substance.
      1) It cushions and maintains the shape of body parts; it resists compression and is resilient.
      2) Locations include the ends of bones, parts of the nose, external ear, and disks between vertebrae.
   b. *Bone tissue* stores mineral salts, produces blood cells, and provides spaces for its own living osteocytes.
      1) Organized as flat plates and cylinders, bones support and protect body tissues and organs; some have sites for blood cell production.
      2) Bones work with muscles to perform movement.
   c. *Adipose tissue* cells are specialized for the storage of fat, which can be used as an energy reserve and as cushions to pad organs.
   d. *Blood* transports oxygen, wastes, hormones, and enzymes; it also contains clotting factors to protect against bleeding and components to protect against disease-causing agents.

C. Muscle Tissues
1. Muscle tissue contracts in response to stimulation then passively lengthens.
2. There are three varieties of muscle:
   a. *Skeletal* muscle tissue attaches to bones for voluntary movement; it contains striated, multinucleated, long cells.
   b. *Cardiac* (heart) muscle is composed of short, striated cells that can function in units.
   c. *Smooth* muscle tissue contains spindle-shaped cells; it lines the gut, blood vessels, and glands; its operation is involuntary.

D. Nervous Tissue
1. Nervous tissue exerts the greatest control over the body's responsiveness to changing conditions.
   a. Neurons are excitable cells, organized as lines of communication throughout the body.
   b. Neuroglia are diverse cells that protect and metabolically support the neurons.

2. Various neurons detect stimuli; others coordinate the body's responses; still others relay signals to muscles and glands for response.

20.3   Organ Systems Made From Tissues
A. Overview of the Major Organ Systems
1. Eleven organ systems are found in the vertebrate body: integumentary, muscular, skeletal, nervous, endocrine, circulatory, lymphatic, respiratory, digestive, urinary, and reproductive.
2. Each organ system contributes to the survival of all living cells of the animal body.
B. Tissue and Organ Formation
1. Germ cells in the parental gonads produce either sperm or eggs by meiosis; all other cells of the body are called somatic cells.
2. Fusion of gametes forms a zygote, which undergoes mitosis to form an embryo.
3. Cells in the embryo become arranged into three primary tissues:
   a. Ectoderm gives rise to skin and nervous system.
   b. Mesoderm gives rise to muscle, skeleton, and the organs of circulation, reproduction, and excretion.
   c. Endoderm gives rise to the lining of the gut and its associated organs.

20.4   Skin—Example of an Organ System
A. The outer covering of animal bodies is called the integument.
1. In vertebrates, the integument consists of skin and the structures derived from epidermal cells, such as scales, feathers, hair, beaks, horns, nails, and so forth.
2. The skin consists of an outer epidermis and an underlying dermis.
   a. Keratinocytes produce keratin, a tough, water-insoluble protein that accumulates in the cells.
   b. Melanocyte cells produce melanin pigment that darkens the skin and protects against the sun's rays; hemoglobin and carotene also contribute to skin color.
B. The skin has several functions:
1. The skin covers and protects the body from abrasion, bacterial attack, ultraviolet radiation, and dehydration.
2. It helps control internal temperature.
3. Its vessels serve as a blood reservoir for the body.
4. The skin produces vitamin D.
5. Its receptors are essential in detecting environmental stimuli.
C. The skin is layered.
1. Epidermis is a stratified epithelium, with an outermost layer (stratum corneum) consisting of flattened, dead cells filled with keratin.
2. The dermis lies beneath the epidermis.
   a. Its dense connective tissue cushions the body against everyday stretching and mechanical stresses.
   b. Blood vessels, lymph vessels, and receptors of sensory nerves are embedded in the tissue.
D. The skin harbors glands and hairs.
1. Sweat glands produce a fluid that is released in response to stress (overheating and fright, for example).
2. Oil glands (sebaceous) lubricate and soften the skin; plus they produce secretions that reduce bacterial populations on the skin.
3. Each hair is a flexible structure rooted in the skin and projecting above it.

    E. The Vitamin Connection
      1. Sunlight helps skin cells make vitamin D, which is necessary for calcium absorption from foods.
      2. Folate is also necessary for normal embryonic development.
    F. On Suntans and Shoe-Leather Skin
      1. Tanning helps to protect against UV radiation.
      2. But continued exposure to the sun's rays causes loss of elasticity and dwindling of glandular secretions—in short, aging.
    G. The Front Line of Defense
      1. Langerhans cells (phagocytes) engulf viruses and bacteria that they encounter in the skin.
      2. UV radiation damages these cells, triggering cold sores—a Herpes simplex infection.

Suggestions for Presenting the Material

- Although this chapter includes brief discussions of cell functions, embryonic tissues, and human organ systems, the main topic is *tissues*.

- The presentation of tissues will be more meaningful if slides are shown during your lecture.

- Even though bone tissue and the types of muscle tissue are introduced here, the skeletal system and muscle physiology are topics discussed more fully in Chapter 21.

- It is difficult for students to think of bone as a living tissue. What most of us have seen in the dog's mouth is the nonliving portion of a tissue one author has called "living reinforced concrete."

- The body systems listed in this chapter will be discussed more fully in later chapters.

- Skin structure and function is best presented by using an overhead transparency. This will allow the instructor to relate the layers of the integumentary system to the function of the structures in each layer.

Classroom and Laboratory Enrichment

- Select slides of various types of tissues for projection onto a large screen. Ask the students to identify the type of tissue and where it is found in the body.

- Invite an athlete who has suffered a knee injury and has had corrective surgery to describe the damage and reconstructive process.

- During the discussion of bone, pass a cleaned bone (from a meat market) around the classroom. Comment on the nonliving and living composition of the bone.

- To show that bone is hard but not indestructible, treat bone fragments with a variety of common laboratory acids and alkalis.

- Have prepared microscope slides of each tissue type available for student viewing.

- Use a model of bone to illustrate its structure.

- Exhibit a vertebrate embryonic or fetal skeleton that is specially stained to show the cartilage.

- Demonstrate that bone has both organic and mineral components by soaking one chicken bone in acetic acid (to remove minerals) and by heating another in an oven at a high temperature (to remove organic material).

Impacts, Issues Classroom Discussion Ideas

- Why are stem cells so valuable and sought after in embryological research?
- Why do some groups label stem cell research as unethical?
- What are the minimal tasks that a living cell and organism must perform to remain alive?

Additional Ideas for Classroom Discussion

- Why is blood—a liquid—considered a *connective* tissue?
- Is there any validity to the cynic's observation that "beauty queens are just exposing a lot of well-placed dead cells"?
- What is liposuction? Does it permanently remove adipose tissue from the treated areas? Why is there a limit to the amount of adipose tissue that can be safely removed from the body at one time?
- Astronauts who orbited the earth early in the space program experienced considerable loss of bone mass under gravity-free conditions. How was this remedied in subsequent flights?

How Would You Vote? Classroom Discussion Ideas

- Monitor the voting for the online question. This question of what source can or cannot be used for stem cell research is unfortunately clouded by political and religious stances. From a purely biological research standpoint, the value of these cells to the advancement of science outweighs the question of their source.

Term Paper Topics, Library Activities, and Special Projects

- Osteoporosis is a topic of current interest, especially to women. Can calcium supplements prevent, or do they simply delay, the stooped posture so prevalent in elderly women?
- What roles, if any, do estrogen replacement therapy and exercise play in the prevention of osteoporosis?

Possible Responses to *Critical Thinking* Questions

1. Porphyria is actually a group of uncommon inherited diseases caused by the accumulation in the body of substances called porphyrins. These chemicals are precursors in biosynthetic pathways leading to the formation of heme, a critical component of hemoglobin—the oxygen-carrying pigment in red blood cells. These porphyrins accumulate because the enzymes that would normally convert them to heme are either absent or not able to catalyze the reactions. This deficiency is due to a faulty gene that is inherited as an autosomal dominant; i.e., the affected individual need inherit only *one* copy of the gene to express the condition. Interestingly, when an affected individual with elevated levels of porphyrin in the blood and skin is exposed to sunlight, the porphyrins generate a form of oxygen that causes substantial damage to tissues and cells.

2. Blood and adipose tissues are classified as *connective* tissue perhaps because they fit most closely to that classification without the need for an entirely different class of tissues. However, they are atypical connective tissue in several ways: blood has no collagen or elastin as other connective tissues do; both blood and adipose have no fibers. The characteristic "ground substance" so familiar to connective tissue is redefined in blood and adipose: for blood it becomes the plasma in which the formed elements move; for adipose the ground substance (lipid molecules) is more prevalent *inside* the cells rather than surrounding them.

3. Because teratomas arise from more than one primary tissue they are able to produce a variety of tissues types, which might include the four basic ones—epithelial, connective, muscular, and nervous.

4. When deciding whether to test the safety of cosmetic products on laboratory grown tissues (LGTs) or on living animals, perhaps a two-phased approach should be envisioned. Why not *begin* with testing on LGTs? We know that these tissues are fairly close to the "real thing" or they would be rejected by the bodies onto which they are grafted. To some critics of testing on living animals, this might be sufficient. But can we always be sure that the LGTs are going to react in *exactly* the same way as tissues in the living animal will? Certainly it would be a tragedy to have to admit to a person suffering harm from a cosmetic, "Well, we never tested it on a *real human*." Perhaps the second phase of testing on live animals would require fewer animals based on the testing on LGTs, but I believe such trials will probably be necessary just to be sure.

5. The figure shows mucus-secreting and ciliated cells from an airway of the body. This is a type of epithelial tissue because it has a free surface that is covered with cilia.

21

HOW ANIMALS MOVE

Chapter Outline

Objectives

1. Compare invertebrate and vertebrate motor systems in terms of skeletal and muscular components and their interactions.
2. Give the details of bone construction.
3. Identify human bones by name and location.
4. Explain in detail the structure of muscles, from the molecular level to the organ systems level.
5. Explain how biochemical events occur in muscle contractions and how antagonistic muscle action refines movements.
6. Describe some of the muscle problems that are commonly encountered by people in exercise programs.

Key Terms

hydrostatic skeleton	pectoral girdle	intervertebral disks	osteoblasts
exoskeleton	pelvic girdle	herniate	osteocytes
endoskeleton	vertebrae	bones	osteoclasts

compact bone	strain	Z band	isotonically
spongy bone	sprain	myosin filament	isometrically
red marrow	osteoarthritis	actin filament	botulism
yellow marrow	rheumatoid arthritis	sliding-filament model	muscle fatigue
calcitonin	skeletal muscles	cross-bridge formation	muscle cramp
parathyroid hormone	tendons	creatine phosphate	muscular dystrophies
osteoporosis	smooth muscle	motor unit	aerobic exercise
joints	cardiac muscle	muscle twitch	strength training
ligaments	sarcomeres	tetanus	
cartilage	myofibrils	muscle tension	

Lecture Outline

Pumping Up Muscles
A. Androstenedione and creatine are dietary supplements used by athletes and body-builders.
  1. "Andro" can raise testosterone levels for a few hours, but controlled studies did not shown it to be effective in increasing muscle mass.
  2. Creatine can improve performance during brief, high-intensity exercise.
B. The long-term effects of these chemicals are not known because they have not been tested by the FDA; they don't have to be; they are not technically "drugs."

21.1 So What Is a Skeleton?
A. Types of Skeletons
  1. Animals move by the action of muscles, which need some medium or structural element against which the force of contraction can be applied.
  2. There are three main types of skeletons in animals:
    a. In *hydrostatic skeletons,* the force of contraction is applied against internal fluids; examples: sea anemones and earthworms.
    b. In an *exoskeleton,* the force is against rigid external body parts, such as shells or plates; example: arthropods.
    c. In an *endoskeleton,* the force is applied against rigid internal cartilage and bones; example: vertebrates.
B. Evolution of Vertebrate Skeletons
  1. The skeletons of vertebrates must support the body in terrestrial environments as well as aquatic.
    a. The pelvic and pectoral girdles are a stable base for the moving fins of fish and are conserved in four-legged vertebrates for supporting the limbs.
    b. Additional bones—jaws, ribs, breastbone, and vertebrae—are the legacy of ancient craniates.
  2. Vertebrae are the body segments of the backbone, serve as attachment sites for muscles and form a protective canal for the spinal cord. Intervertebral disks made of cartilage lie between individual vertebrae to act as shock absorbers.
C. Bone Structure and Function
  1. Bones have several roles:
    a. Bones interact with muscles to maintain or change the position of body parts.
    b. Bones support the skin and soft organs.
    c. Bones form compartments that enclose and protect soft internal organs.
    d. Bone tissue acts as a depository for calcium, phosphorus, and other ions.

e. Parts of some bones are sites of blood cell production.

2. Bone is a connective tissue with living cells (osteocytes) and collagen fibers distributed throughout a ground substance that is hardened by calcium salts.

   a. Compact bone tissue forms the bone's shaft and the outer portion of its two ends.

      1) Concentric layers form around canals that contain blood vessels and nerves (Haversian systems).

      2) The living bone cells reside in the ground substance.

   b. Spongy bone tissue has areas of red marrow that produces blood cells; cavities in most mature bones contain yellow marrow, which can be converted to red marrow if blood cell production needs to be increased.

3. Bones are constantly being remodeled.

   a. Osteoblasts are the bone-forming cells that secrete organic substances that become mineralized.

   b. Osteoclast cells digest the organic matrix of bone during the process of bone remodeling.

   c. Calcium levels in the blood are regulated by hormones.

      1) Calcitonin from the thyroid causes levels to decline by storing the excess calcium in bones.

      2) Parathyroid hormone detects low levels of calcium and pulls sufficient quantities out of storage.

D. Where Bones Meet—Skeletal Joints

1. Joints are areas of contact or near-contact between bones.

   a. Freely-movable joints are stabilized by ligaments—straps of dense connective tissue that attach bone.

   b. Cartilaginous joints, such as between the ribs, permit slight movement.

2. Joints are vulnerable to stress.

   a. Stretching or twisting a joint may result in a strain; tearing ligaments or tendons is a sprain.

   b. In osteoarthritis, the cartilage at the end of the bone has worn away.

   c. In rheumatoid arthritis, the membranes in the joints become inflamed, the cartilage degenerates, and bone is deposited into the joint.

21.2   How Do Bones and Muscles Interact?

A. Skeletal muscles are functional partners of bones.

1. Each skeletal muscle contains several bundles of hundreds or thousands of muscle cells (fibers).

   a. Tendons, cordlike straps of dense connective tissue, attach muscle to bone.

   b. Skeletal muscles, often arranged in antagonistic pairs, interact with one another and with bones.

2. There are nearly 700 skeletal muscles in the human body.

B. There are three types of muscle in the human body.

1. Only skeletal muscle is the functional partner of bone.

2. Smooth muscle is found in soft internal organs such as the digestive tract.

3. Cardiac muscle is found only in the heart wall.

21.3   How Does Skeletal Muscle Contract?

A. The basic units of contraction are the sarcomeres.

1. Muscle cells (fibers) are composed of myofibrils, which are composed of two kinds of parallel filaments: actin and myosin.

a. Actin is a thin filament composed of two beaded strands twisted together.

b. Myosin is thicker; each molecule has a bulbous head and long tail, making it resemble a golf club.

2. The actin filaments are anchored at each end by the Z band (or disk), surrounded by the myosin filaments.

B. Sliding-Filament Model for Contraction

1. Muscles shorten because the sarcomeres shorten within each cell by the sliding-filament model.

2. The mechanism "pulls" the Z disks of each sarcomere toward each other.

a. By forming cross-bridges, the myosin filaments slide along and pull the actin filaments toward the center of the sarcomere.

b. The cross-bridges are formed when the local concentration of calcium exposes binding sites.

c. ATP supplies the energy for both attachment and detachment.

C. Getting Energy for Contraction

1. During brief periods of intense muscle activity, creatine phosphate is the source of phosphate to remake ATP.

2. When muscle action is moderate, most of the ATP is provided by aerobic electron transport phosphorylation, which is dependent on oxygen supply and number of mitochondria present.

3. During intense and prolonged muscle action, anaerobic glycolysis produces low amounts of ATP, but this also results in an oxygen debt.

21.4   Properties of Whole Muscles

A. Muscle Tension

1. A motor neuron and all the muscle cells under its control are a *motor unit*.

a. A single, brief stimulus to a motor unit causes a brief contraction called a muscle twitch.

b. Repeated stimulation without sufficient interval causes a sustained contraction called tetanus.

2. When muscle tension is greater than the forces opposing it, contracting muscle cells shorten; when opposing forces are stronger, muscle cells lengthen.

a. Isotonically contracting muscles shorten and move a load.

b. Isometrically contracting muscle develops tension but does not shorten.

c. With lengthening contraction, a muscle lengthens when an external load is greater than its tension for the period of contraction, such as when you walk down stairs.

B. A Bad Case of Tetanic Contraction

1. Botulism is caused by a toxin from the bacterium *Clostridium botulinum*.

a. The organism usually enters the body by means of improperly preserved food.

b. Because it blocks the release of acetylcholine at the neuron synapse, it can shut down breathing and heartbeat.

2. Tetanus, more commonly called lockjaw, is caused by a toxin from *C. tetani*.

a. The bacteria live anaerobically in the soil, from which they can enter the body through a puncture wound.

b. The toxin has the unusual effect of causing motor neurons to continue their stimulation of skeletal muscles, which are then unable to relax.

C. What Is Muscle Fatigue?

1. When a muscle is kept in a state of tetanic contraction, there is a decline in the muscle's capacity to generate force—muscle fatigue.

2. The molecular mechanisms are unknown but glycogen depletion is a factor.
  D. What Are Muscular Dystrophies?
    1. Muscular dystrophies are a class of genetic disorders in which muscles progressively weaken and degenerate.
    2. A mutation on the X chromosome disrupts the normal action of dystrophin, one of the proteins of the T-tubule extensions that participate in contraction.
  E. Muscles, Exercise, and Aging
    1. With regular exercise, muscle cells do not increase in number; however, they do increase in size and metabolic activity and become resistant to fatigue.
      a. Aerobic exercise, not intense but long in duration, increases the number of mitochondria and blood capillaries.
      b. Strength training affects fast-acting muscle cells by forming more myofibrils and more enzymes of glycolysis.
    2. Muscle tension decreases as adult humans age, but exercise remains beneficial in improving blood circulation and preventing loss of muscle tissue.

Suggestions for Presenting the Material

- Although this chapter's title may imply that the content will be about muscles only, remind the students that muscles can move the body *only* in conjunction with the bones.

- Students, especially non-science majors, may question the value of learning the names of bones. However, with today's emphasis on the human body, the use of the anatomical names for body parts, including bones, is becoming more common.

- The formation, development, and replacement of bone is more meaningfully presented by referring briefly to the material on tissues in Chapter 20.

- It is nearly impossible to present the ultrastructure of muscle without a visual similar to Figure 21.7. Using the analogy of a rope (see the Enrichment section below) is very helpful.

- Don't miss the opportunity when discussing the sliding-filament model to emphasize the molecular explanation for the fact that individual muscles can only pull, not push. Again the rope analogy is helpful.

- The dual role of calcium as the provider of bone hardness and as muscle facilitator should be made clear.

- Emphasize that ATP is required for *both* muscle contraction and relaxation as well as for the active transport of calcium back into the sarcoplasmic reticulum.

Classroom and Laboratory Enrichment

- Ask a forensic pathologist to tell the class about the wealth of information that the skeletal remains can reveal about one's health and medical history at the time of death.

- Demonstrate the action of muscle by using a "muscle contraction kit" available from biological supply houses.

- If you have one available, the use of a real human skeleton rather than a transparency will stimulate better student interest and present a three-dimensional aspect to your lecture.

- Arrange for a body builder to appear before the class (more effective if unannounced). Describe the origin, insertion, and function of some major muscles as they are flexed.

- Students can visualize the ultrastructure of muscles more readily if the comparison to a large rope is made. The best is one used for boat anchorage because it is made of many subunits.
- If you can locate a ratchet mechanism (preferably not enclosed), your explanation of the actin/myosin cross-bridges (Figure 21.8) will be more comprehensible.
- Show a video of arthroscopic surgery. Many orthopedic surgeons routinely produce such videos and give them to their patients.
- Use models of freely movable joints to illustrate their structure.
- Obtain a fresh beef knee joint to demonstrate the structure and tissues of that joint.
- If available, use a model of a sarcomere to facilitate the students' comprehension of that microscopic structure.

Impacts, Issues Classroom Discussion Ideas

- Discuss the negative aspects of "self-medication" with supplements designed to enhance muscle performance.
- What motivates young athletes to take enhancing drugs?
- What could be bad about taking a chemical such as creatine, which is produced by the body normally?

Additional Ideas for Classroom Discussion

- Distinguish between hydrostatic skeleton, endoskeleton, and exoskeleton.
- The exoskeleton and muscle arrangement of ants allow them to accomplish extraordinary feats for their small size. Why are there not larger animals with similar motor system arrangements?
- Consider the present evolutionary state of the human knee. Is it sufficient for the punishment modern athletic activity places on it?
- Why is bone considered "nonliving" by those unfamiliar with its structure?
- What technological and research developments allowed the sliding-filament *theory* of the 1960s to become the sliding-filament *model* of the 1980s?
- Evaluate this statement: Muscles only pull. If this is true, how can you *push* a door open?
- Which muscles are collectively called the "hamstrings"? In which sports are they most likely to be injured and why?
- What is a "slipped" or herniated disk? What are its most common causes?

How Would You Vote? Classroom Discussion Ideas

- Monitor the voting for the online question. It is very unfortunate for the American consumer that dietary supplements are NOT regulated by the FDA. This loophole allows anyone to sell anything for any reason with no guarantee (by testing results) that the product is: (1) effective for the purposes listed on the label, and (2) safe taken as directed. I have little doubt that this oversight will have far reaching negative repercussions in future years.

Term Paper Topics, Library Activities, and Special Projects

- A challenging task is the assembly of a disarticulated skeleton. If your department has one, attempt to lay the bones out on a lab table in their approximate position and articulation. This is a good group project.
- Investigate the difference(s) in the development of muscles for power (weight) lifting versus development for body sculpting and exhibition.
- Document the development of the sliding-filament theory of muscle contraction and the research evidence that supports it.
- Report on the technique of arthroscopic surgery.
- Research the following spinal disorders: spina bifida, scoliosis, lordosis, and kyphosis.
- Investigate the use of electrical stimulation to accelerate the healing of bone fractures.
- Discuss the muscle disease called myasthenia gravis, its suspected cause, and the type of treatment currently used.

Possible Responses to *Critical Thinking* Questions

1. When encountering a child in the emergency room with multiple bone fractures or recurring incidents of fractures, many thoughts come to the healthcare worker. Unfortunately, osteogenesis imperfecta (OI) would not usually be one them because of its rarity. So the initial task of the handout announcement would be to reach as wide an audience with as simple an alert as possible. Perhaps the most effective way to do this would be in a daily email newsletter. Next best would be an in-house mailing. Points you would want to include:
    - Be aware that OI is easily confused with fractures associated with child abuse.
    - Research carefully the medical history of the child, both written and oral from the parents.
    - Check with siblings and relatives concerning the child's condition.
    - Search for other telltale markings of abuse.
    - Refer medical personnel to the OI website.

2. Creatine supplements are widely available in health food stores, a fact that most persons take as proof of their effectiveness and safety. Unfortunately, they have not been certified by the FDA as either. It *is* known that creatine is an intracellular source of phosphate for the regeneration of the ATP needed in muscle contraction. Research has shown that creatine will improve performance during brief, high-intensity exercise (marathons may not qualify here!). Some persons will accept this as reason enough to take the pills because "winning is everything." However, as with any exogenous compound taken into the body, the long-term effects must be evaluated. Again, because the FDA has not approved this "drug," the properly gathered data is not available. Lydia should be informed that she takes creatine "at her own risk."

3. As a long-distance runner, Lydia will need many skeletal muscle cells to power her through the distance. These cells will be packed with mitochondria, which are the location for the aerobic phase of cellular respiration. The importance of being able to obtain a dependable and abundant supply of ATP throughout the race is obvious. The third phase of cellular respiration (electron transport phosphorylation) yields 32 of the 36 ATPs produced from a single glucose molecule.

    By contrast, sprinters will need a supply of energy that can be obtained and used quickly. Their race will be over before the aerobic portion of cell respiration will be able to supply the needed

ATPs. So these speed demons will rely on glycolysis in the cytoplasm and phosphorylation of ADP from creatine to supply the energy for their muscle contractions.

4. The botulinum toxin causes a lack of muscle contraction by blocking ACh release. This may be desirable in certain small muscles that are contracting to form wrinkles on the face. However, the injected toxin can migrate to the muscles that control the eyelids and cause them to droop.

5. The advantage of having only a few fibers per motor unit would be that the motor units that control eye muscles would have a more precise degree of control when moving the eye. In the motor units of the arm, in which many muscle fibers are activated by a single motor unit, the activation would cause a more intense response such as might be needed to move a refrigerator.

22

CIRCULATION AND RESPIRATION

Chapter Outline

Objectives

1. Explain how the cardiovascular systems of vertebrates differ from those of invertebrates.
2. Describe the composition and functions of blood.
3. Be able to trace a drop of blood through the complete pulmonary and systemic circuits.
4. Explain what is happening during each portion of the cardiac cycle.
5. Explain the factors that cause blood to exist under different pressures.
6. Describe the composition of lymph and the functioning of the lymphatic system.
7. Understand the behavior of gases and the types of respiratory surfaces that participate in gas exchange.
8. Understand the mechanisms used by invertebrates and vertebrates for gas exchange.
9. Be able to trace the route of air into and out of the human lungs.
10. Understand how the human respiratory system is related to the circulatory system, to cellular respiration, and to the nervous system.
11. List some of the things that go awry with the respiratory system and describe the characteristics of the breakdown.

Key Terms

circulatory system
interstitial fluid
blood
heart
blood vessels
closed circulation
  system
open circulation system
capillaries
gills
lungs
capillary beds
pulmonary circuit
systemic circuit
lymphatic system
stem cells
plasma
erythrocytes
red blood cells
hemoglobin
leukocytes
white blood cells
neutrophils
basophils
macrophages
dendritic cells
lymphocytes
megakaryocytes

platelets
aorta
pericardium
myocardium
endothelium
coronary arteries
atrium, atria
ventricle
atrioventricular valve
semilunar valve
cardiac cycle
cardiac conduction
  system
sinoatrial node (= SA
  node)
atrioventricular node (=
  AV node)
cardiac pacemaker
arteries
arterioles
venules
veins
blood pressure
vasodilation
vasoconstriction
systolic pressure
diastolic pressure
ultrafiltration

reabsorption
edema
elephantiasis
hemostasis
fibrinogen
hypertension
arteriosclerosis
atherosclerosis
LDLs
HDLs
atherosclerotic plaque
thrombus
embolus
stroke
angina pectoris
coronary bypass
  surgery
laser angioplasty
respiration
partial pressure
  gradients
respiratory surface
surface-to-volume ratio
ventilation
hemoglobin
myoglobin
external gills
internal gills

countercurrent flow
lungs
alveolus, -oli
nasal cavities
pharynx
larynx
vocal cords
glottis
laryngitis
epiglottis
trachea
bronchus, -chi
diaphragm
pleurisy
bronchioles
respiratory cycle
inhalation
exhalation
heme groups
oxyhemoglobin, HbO_2
carbaminohemoglobin,
  $HbCO_2$
bicarbonate
carbonic anhydrase
bronchitis
secondhand smoke

Lecture Outline

Up In Smoke

A. The body reacts to tobacco smoke.

1. Immediately there is coughing, nausea, dizziness, even headaches.

2. Later, the cilia that line the respiratory tract are immobilized, white blood cells are killed, colds and bronchitis increase, and of course deadly cancer is a long-term reward.

B. The "active ingredient" in this scenario is of course nicotine.

1. It constricts the blood vessels and raises blood pressure.

2. It even raises the level of "bad" cholesterol.

C. Why would a seemingly intelligent person subject themselves to this? Social pressure!

22.1 The Nature of Blood Circulation

A. The circulatory system moves substances to and from cells.

1. Interstitial fluid "bathes" the cells of the body.

a. The volume, composition, and temperature of this fluid must be carefully maintained.

b. Exchanges between interstitial fluid and blood keep the internal environment tolerable.

2. A circulatory system is an internal transport system with three components:

a. Blood is a fluid tissue composed of water, solutes, and formed elements.

b. Blood vessels are tubes of various diameters through which the blood is transported.

c. The heart is a muscular pump that generates pressure to keep the blood flowing.

3. Arthropods and most mollusks have an open system:

a. Blood is pumped from a heart into large tissue spaces where organs are "bathed."

b. Blood is returned to the heart at a leisurely rate.

4. Vertebrates have a closed system.

a. All the vessels and the heart are connected so that blood remains enclosed.

b. Blood volume is constant and is equal to the heart's output at any time.

c. Flow rate slows as blood moves through the fine capillaries of the capillary beds

B. The Circulatory and Respiratory Systems of Vertebrates Evolved Together

1. Fishes have a single circuit plan, which includes flow to the gills.

2. Amphibians have two partially separated circuits with flow to the lungs.

3. Birds and mammals have two separate circuits of blood flow.

a. The right half of the heart receives deoxygenated blood and pumps it to the lungs of the pulmonary circuit.

b. The left half receives from the lungs and pumps the oxygen-rich blood to all of the tissues and organs in the systemic circuit.

C. Links with the Lymphatic System

1. The lymphatic system picks up excess fluids, solutes, and disease agents from the interstitial fluid.

2. This lymph is cleansed by exposure to the infection-fighting cells before being returned to the general circulation.

22.2 Characteristics of Human Blood

A. Blood serves several functions:

1. It carries oxygen and nutrients to cells, and it carries secretions and wastes away from them.

2. It contains phagocytic cells that fight infection.

3. It helps stabilize internal pH.

4. It equalizes body temperatures in birds and mammals.
B. The blood has a definite volume and composition.
   1. An average-sized adult has a blood volume of 4-5 quarts.
   2. Plasma is mostly water.
      a. Some plasma proteins transport lipids and vitamins; others function in immune responses and in blood clotting (fibrinogen).
      b. Plasma also contains ions, glucose, lipids, amino acids, vitamins, hormones, and dissolved gases.
   3. Red blood cells (erythrocytes) are biconcave disks.
      a. Red blood cells contain hemoglobin, an iron-containing protein that binds with oxygen.
      b. They form in the red bone marrow from stem cells.
      c. When mature they have no nuclei; they live about 120 days.
         1) Phagocytic cells remove the oldest cells from the bloodstream.
         2) Cell count remains at 5.4 million/cubic millimeter for males and 4.8 for females.
   4. White blood cells (leukocytes) come in many varieties.
      a. Leukocytes are derived from stem cells in the bone marrow.
      b. Leukocytes remove dead or worn-out cells and protect us against invading microbes and foreign agents.
      c. There are five types of white blood cells.
         1) Lymphocytes, the "B" and "T" cells, are involved in the immune responses.
         2) Macrophages and neutrophils are the "search-and-destroy" cells.
         3) Eosinophils and basophils have lesser roles in the system.
   5. Platelets are fragments of megakaryocytes produced by bone marrow stem cells; substances released from platelets initiate blood clotting.

22.3 Human Cardiovascular System
A. One Big Circuit and a Special Circuit to the Lungs
   1. "Cardiovascular" comes from the Greek words meaning "heart" and "vessel."
   2. Blood travel follows this route: heart — —> arteries — —> arterioles — —> capillaries — —> venules — —> veins — —> heart.
   3. The human heart is divided into right and left halves.
      a. Blood is transported from the right side of the heart to the lungs and back to the left side in the *pulmonary circuit.*
      b. Oxygenated blood is then pumped to the rest of the body in the *systemic circuit.*
   4. Usually a given volume of blood in either circuit passes through only one capillary bed; an exception is blood from the digestive tract, which passes through the liver before entering the general circulation.
B. The Heart Is a Lonely Pumper
   1. The heart is a durable pump made mostly of cardiac muscle (myocardium) and enclosed in a tough, fibrous sac (pericardium); its chambers are lined with connective tissue and endothelium.
      a. Each half of the heart consists of an atrium (receiving) chamber and a ventricle (pumping) chamber, separated by an atrioventricular (AV) valve.
      b. Blood exits each ventricle through a semilunar valve.
   2. Heart muscle cells are serviced by the coronary circulation, two arteries that branch directly off the aorta.
   3. The cardiac cycle consists of a sequence of contraction (systole) and relaxation (diastole).
      a. As the atria fill, the ventricles are relaxed.

b. Pressure of the blood in the atria forces the atrioventricular valves to open; the ventricles continue to fill as the atria contract.

c. The ventricles contract, the atrioventricular valves close, and blood flows out through the semilunar valves.

C. How Does Cardiac Muscle Contract?

1. Because of the close junctions of cardiac muscle cells, they contract in unison.

2. Excitation for a heartbeat is initiated in the sinoatrial (SA) node (also known as the cardiac pacemaker) then passes to the atrioventricular (AV) node for ventricular contraction; this is the cardiac conduction system.

3. The nervous system adjusts rate and strength.

22.4   Structure and Function of Blood Vessels

A. Blood is distributed by means of arteries, arterioles, capillaries, venules, and veins.

1. Two key factors influence the rate of flow through each type of blood vessel:

a. The flow rate is directly proportional to the pressure gradient between the start and end of the vessel.

b. The flow rate is inversely proportional to the vessel's resistance to flow.

2. Blood pressure drops along the way due to energy loss from resistance.

B. Rapid Transport in Arteries

1. Arteries are large diameter vessels that present low resistance to flow as they conduct blood *away from* the heart.

2. Because of their elastic walls, arteries tend to "smooth out" the pulsations associated with the discontinuous pumping cycle of the heart.

C. Adjusting Resistance at Arterioles

1. Arteries branch into smaller arterioles, which offer greater resistance to flow and thus the greatest drop in blood pressure.

2. Arterioles serve as control points where adjustments can be made in blood volume distribution.

3. Neural and endocrine signals cause changes in arteriole diameter by stimulating the muscle cells in the walls.

a. If the blood pressure increases, the arterioles are instructed to relax (vasodilation).

b. If the pressure decreases, the diameter of the arterioles decreases (vasoconstriction).

D. Measuring Blood Pressure

1. A special instrument with a cuff surrounding the upper arm is connected to a pressure measuring device.

2. The peak pressure (systolic) is recorded when the ventricles are contracting—120mm is typical.

3. The lowest pressure (diastolic) is reached when the ventricles are relaxing—80mm.

E. From Capillaries Back to the Heart

1. Capillaries are diffusion zones for *exchanges* between blood and interstitial fluid.

a. A capillary is the smallest tube (red blood cells travel single file) in the path of circulation.

b. Its wall consists of a single layer of endothelial cells, which facilitates diffusion to and from the interstitial fluid.

2. Movement across the capillary is by several modes: diffusion (of oxygen and carbon dioxide), endocytosis and exocytosis (of proteins), between the cells (of ions), and bulk flow (of water).

a. At the beginning of a capillary bed, there is a movement of plasma out into the interstitial fluid in a process known as ultrafiltration.

      b. Further on, some tissue fluid moves into the capillary through clefts between its endothelial walls in a process known as reabsorption.

   F. Venous Pressure

      1. Capillaries merge into venules then into veins.

         a. Blood pressure and resistance to flow are both low; valves prevent backflow.

         b. Veins are blood volume reservoirs (50-60 percent of blood volume) because their walls can distend or contract.

      2. The movement of skeletal muscles squeezes the veins and pushes the blood along against the forces of gravity.

22.5   Cardiovascular Disorders

   A. Good Clot, Bad Clot

      1. Hemostasis is the process that stops blood loss when a vessel is damaged and constructs a framework for repairs.

      2. There are several sequential steps:

         a. Spasm of the smooth muscle in the damaged blood vessel stops blood flow for a few minutes.

         b. Platelets clump to plug the rupture.

         c. The blood coagulates and forms a clot; the clot then retracts into a compact mass.

   B. A Silent Killer

      1. Hypertension (high blood pressure) can affect a person without outward symptoms.

      2. There is a gradual increase in resistance to flow in the smaller arteries.

         a. Heredity and/or diet may play roles.

         b. The heart may enlarge and fail; arterial walls may "harden."

   C. Atherosclerosis

      1. In this condition lipids such as cholesterol build up in the arterial wall.

         a. Low-density lipoproteins (LDLs) infiltrate the walls causing an atherosclerotic plaque to form.

         b. Platelets gather at the site and initiate clot formation.

      2. Enlarging plaques and blood clots narrow or block arteries.

         a. A clot that stays in place is a thrombus; a dislodged, traveling clot is an embolus.

         b. The tiny coronary arteries are the most vulnerable, leading to the familiar signs of a heart attack.

   D. Risk Factors

      1. Cardiovascular disorders are the leading cause of death in the United States.

      2. Risk factors include smoking, genetic predisposition, high levels of blood cholesterol, obesity, diabetes, age, and gender (until age 50, males).

22.6   The Nature of Respiration

   A. The Basis of Gas Exchange

      1. Respiration is the movement of oxygen into, and carbon dioxide out of, the internal environment of the animal body.

      2. Respiratory systems rely on the diffusion of gases down pressure gradients.

         a. Partial pressures for each gas in the atmosphere can be calculated; for example, oxygen's is 160 mm Hg.

         b. Gases will diffuse down a pressure gradient across a respiratory surface if it is permeable and moist.

   B. Which Factors Influence Gas Exchange?

      1. Surface-to-Volume Ratio

     a. As an animal grows, its surface area increases at a lesser rate than its volume, making diffusion of gases into the interior a problem.

     b. Therefore, animals either must have a body design that keeps internal cells close to the surface (flatworms) or must have a system to move the gases inward.

  2. Ventilation

     a. Animals have adaptations to move the air, or water, over the respiratory surfaces.

     b. Bony fish move the covers over the gills; sponges move the flagella on their collar cells; humans move the muscles of the thorax to expand and contract the chest cavity and move air in and out of the lungs.

  3. Transport Pigments

     a. Hemoglobin is the main transport pigment in the blood; it binds four molecules of oxygen in the lungs (high concentration) and releases them in the tissues where oxygen is low.

     b. Myoglobin is a similar pigment but with a higher oxygen-storing capacity; it is abundant in heart and skeletal muscle.

C. Gills of Fishes and Amphibians

  1. Gills of amphibian larvae are external.

  2. The internal gills of adult fishes are positioned where water can enter the mouth and then flow over them as it exits just behind the head.

     a. Water flows *over* the gills and blood circulates *through* them in OPPOSITE DIRECTIONS.

     b. This mechanism, called countercurrent flow, is highly efficient in extracting oxygen from water, whose oxygen content is lower than air.

D. Evolution of Paired Lungs

  1. Lungs contain internal respiratory surfaces in the shape of a cavity or sac.

  2. Simple lungs evolved about 450 million years ago to assist respiration in oxygen-poor habitats; some evolved into swim bladders, others into complex respiratory organs.

  3. Lungs provide a membrane for gaseous exchange with blood.

     a. Air moves by bulk flow into and out of the lungs.

     b. Gases diffuse across the inner respiratory surfaces of the lungs.

     c. Pulmonary circulation enhances the diffusion of dissolved gases into and out of lung capillaries.

     d. In body tissues, oxygen diffuses from blood ——> interstitial fluid ——> cells; carbon dioxide travels the route in reverse.

  4. Lungs also participate in sound production by forcing air to pass through the glottis opening, causing the vocal cords on either side to vibrate.

22.7   Human Respiratory System

A. The System's Many Functions

  1. Ventilation alternately moves air into and out of tiny air sacs of the lungs called alveoli, where gas exchange takes place.

  2. Breathing is necessary for speech.

  3. Limited amounts of excess heat and water are eliminated here.

  4. It also adjusts the body's acid-base balance.

  5. The respiratory system has mechanisms to deal with airborne foreign matter that enters the system.

B. From Airways into the Lungs

  1. Air enters or leaves the respiratory system through nasal cavities where hair and cilia filter out dust and particles; blood vessels warm, and mucus moistens the air.

2. Air moves via this route: pharynx ——> larynx (route blocked by epiglottis during swallowing) ——> vocal cords (space between is glottis) ——> trachea ——> bronchi ——> bronchioles ——> alveoli.

3. When air is exhaled through the glottis, the folds of the cords vibrate to produce sounds, which are under regulation by nerve commands to the elastic ligaments that regulate the glottal opening.

4. Human lungs are a pair of organs in the rib cage above the diaphragm.
   a. Each lung lies in a thin-walled pleural sac, which leaves a very thin intrapleural space between the membranes.
   b. A film of lubricating liquid cuts friction between the pleural membrane surfaces.

22.8. Moving Air and Transporting Gases
   A. The Respiratory Cycle
      1. In inhalation, the diaphragm contracts and flattens, muscles lift the rib cage upward and outward, the chest cavity volume increases, internal pressure decreases, and air rushes in.
      2. In exhalation, the actions listed above are reversed; the elastic lung tissue recoils passively.
      3. Exhalation becomes active and energy-demanding only when the body is vigorously exercising and so must expel more air.
   B. Exchanges at the Respiratory Membrane
      1. Each alveolus consists of a single layer of epithelial cells through which gases can readily diffuse to, and from interstitial fluid and blood capillaries.
      2. The partial pressure gradients are sufficient to move oxygen in and carbon dioxide out of the blood, passively.
   C. Oxygen and Carbon Dioxide Transport
      1. Blood cannot carry sufficient oxygen and carbon dioxide in *dissolved form* to satisfy the body's demands.
      2. Hemoglobin is a protein with four heme groups that bind oxygen.
         a. Oxygen diffuses down a pressure gradient into the blood plasma then into red blood cells, where it binds to hemoglobin (4 molecules of oxygen/hemoglobin to form oxyhemoglobin).
         b. Hemoglobin gives up its oxygen in tissues where partial pressure of oxygen is low, blood is warmer, partial pressure of carbon dioxide is higher, and pH is lower; all four conditions occur in tissues with high metabolism.
      3. Because the concentration of carbon dioxide is higher in the body tissues, it diffuses into the blood.
         a. Ten percent is dissolved in plasma, 30 percent binds with hemoglobin to form carbaminohemoglobin, and 60 percent is in bicarbonate form.
         b. Bicarbonate and carbonic acid formation is enhanced by the enzyme carbonic anhydrase, which is located in the red blood cells.
   D. Balancing Air and Blood Flow Rates
      1. Gas exchange in the alveoli is most efficient when air flow equals the rate of blood flow.
      2. The nervous system controls oxygen and carbon dioxide levels for the entire body by adjusting contraction rates of the diaphragm and chest wall muscles.
      3. The brain monitors input from carbon dioxide sensors in the bloodstream and from receptors sensitive to decreases in oxygen partial pressure (carotid bodies and aortic bodies).

22.9   When the Lungs Break Down
   A. Bronchitis and Emphysema
      1. The lining of the bronchioles can become irritated, say by cigarette smoke.
      2. Excessive mucus is secreted, which encourages bacterial growth.
      3. Chronic bronchitis leads to a condition known as emphysema, in which the alveoli become so damaged that adequate amounts of gas exchange cannot occur.
   B. Smoking's Impact
      1. Tobacco is the only legal consumer product that kills half of its regular users.
      2. Prolonged exposure to secondhand smoke, especially in the young, leads to allergies and lung problems.
      3. Marijuana smoke is even worse: more tars, more carcinogens, more dependency, more depression.

Suggestions for Presenting the Material

- This chapter begins with a discussion of closed and open circulatory systems. Students will be more familiar with a closed system because that is the type in the human body, but the open concept implies a great deal of "hemorrhaging," which sounds terminal but, in this context, is normal.

- When discussing the functions of blood, it may be helpful to anticipate future topics such as respiration, immunity, digestion, excretion, and hormones—all of which depend on the blood supply.

- Because of the complexity of the entire cardiovascular system, it might be good to skip to Figure 22.5 for an overview before dropping back to the material earlier in the chapter. The concept of oxygen-rich and oxygen-poor blood can be emphasized here. This can be followed by the heart pathways and contraction sequence.

- The heartbeat, pulse, and blood pressure are measurable quantities that should be of interest to students because they are indicators of good/poor health; therefore, these deserve a little extra lecture time.

- Capillary exchange is a topic that allows you to review previous lectures on diffusion and active transport.

- Usually students feel they have a fair grasp of circulation until the lymphatic system is introduced. Then it is a "What's this for?" expression. Stress the necessity for such a system and the *one-way return* of fluid to the general blood supply.

- The presentation of respiration can be effectively accomplished by following the sequence of the text. The outline begins with a survey of respiratory surfaces, then focuses on human respiratory organs and function, and concludes with mention of respiratory problems.

- When describing various respiratory surfaces, emphasize the one common feature they all share—moisture.

- Distinguish the arthropod *trachea* from other respiratory surfaces by its independence from the circulatory system.

- The most logical way to present the human respiratory system is to display Figure 22.21 and follow the pathway of an inhaled breath.

- The names of most of the structures in Figure 22.21 are familiar to students except the most critical structures—the *alveoli.* These deserve special attention.

- As you describe the *glottis* and *epiglottis,* you may wish to include a note on the *Heimlich maneuver,* which is the subject of question #1 of the *Critical Thinking.*

- Emphasize the correct pronunciation of *larynx* (lair—inks) and *pharynx* (fair—inks).

- Be sure to stress the passivity of the lungs (compare to balloon) during respiration, and emphasize the role of the diaphragm and rib muscles.

- Highlight the differences between the ways oxygen and carbon dioxide are transported in the blood.

- *Respiratory control* is a topic you may want to include in your presentation, even though it is not discussed in the text.

- Emphasize that the respiratory organs have some non-respiratory functions such as coughing, sneezing, speech, yawning, regulation of pH, and sense of smell.

Classroom and Laboratory Enrichment

- Ask a physician to demonstrate an artificial pacemaker; include comments on the limitations and usefulness of such an artificial device versus the natural SA node.

- Borrow a sphygmomanometer and ask a person skilled in its use to explain how blood pressure is determined; use members of the class as volunteers.

- Determine the resting and active pulse rates for a variety of body types in the class. Can you make any generalizations from your data?

- Obtain a recording of heart sounds as they would be heard through a stethoscope. Relate sounds to events of the normal and abnormal cardiac cycle.

- Show that measurement of oxygen consumption can be used to determine rate of metabolism by using a simple respirometer (see a biological supply catalog), or use a computer simulation of the experiment.

- Ask for volunteers to debate the "rights" of nonsmokers and smokers. Ask them to provide data rather than emotional attacks.

- Have a person who has visited a high altitude location report on the breathing discomforts she/he experienced.

- Construct or purchase a working model of the lungs, chest cavity, and diaphragm.

- Demonstrate the Heimlich maneuver on a class volunteer; then ask classmates to demonstrate (gently!) on one another.

- Have the students use a spirometer to measure respiratory air volumes. Compare the results of smokers and nonsmokers.

- Invite a scuba diver to discuss the special gas composition and gas exchange problems associated with deep dives.

- Use a chart or dissectible mannequin to locate major organs of the human respiratory system.

- Exhibit a model of a human larynx and trachea.

- Display a freeze-dried preparation of a sheep's lungs.

Impacts, Issues Classroom Discussion Ideas

- Using cigarette ads gathered from magazines published during the past 40 years, show the change in public attitude toward smoking.
- How does the experimental "smokeless" cigarette work? Why is the American Medical Association so adamantly opposed to its approval by the Food and Drug Administration?
- Why hasn't the message concerning the dangers of smoking reached teenagers and altered their taking up of the habit?
- Should smokers be subject to higher insurance rates (medical and automobile) due to the higher costs they incur, instead of forcing the insurance companies to pass the cost on to everyone?

Additional Ideas for Classroom Discussion

- How can a worker in a police crime lab determine if the blood found at a crime scene is human?
- How can you explain the fact that persons who die of heart attack (lack of oxygen to heart muscle) have perfectly adequate amounts of oxygenated blood in their heart chambers?
- The heart is really a "double pump." It is also, of course, divided into four chambers. Does this mean that one pump consists of atria, the other of ventricles, *or* does it mean the left and right sides are pumping to separate circulations? Explain your reasoning.
- Why is the lymph system such a "highway" for the spread of certain metastatic cancers?
- Why is hemophilia in *females* (although extremely rare) very often more fatal than in males?
- Evaluate the accuracy of the statement "I'm a blood relative." Is there a more accurate expression that could replace this one?
- Which of the following *respiratory surfaces* does not require participation of the blood for delivery of oxygen to the tissues: (a) integument, (b) gills, (c) tracheas (arthropods), (d) lungs?
- What is the singular advantage of the one-way flow of air in the *parabronchi* of the bird lung?
- What is happening in the condition we call "hiccups"? What causes it? What are the best short-term remedies? On what physiological principles (if any) are they based?
- Why is the *best* body position for public speaking and singing a standing, or "sitting tall," position?
- The air at high altitudes is sometimes described in everyday language as "thin." How does this translate in technical terms?
- Can you die from holding your breath? Explain the neural mechanisms that are operating here.
- What are the functions of the sinuses?
- "Respiratory distress syndrome" (hyaline membrane disease) is the primary cause of respiratory difficulty in immature newborns. What are its symptoms and cause? How is it treated?

How Would You Vote? Classroom Discussion Ideas

- Monitor the voting for the online question. If we assume that the goal of the tobacco companies is to make money, no matter what the health cost to individuals or society at large, then it would be a virtual necessity to compensate for sagging domestic sales by increasing global markets.

Term Paper Topics, Library Activities, and Special Projects

- Evaluate the reported links between lipids and cardiovascular diseases.

- Survey the various corrective surgical procedures that are routinely performed on the heart and its vessels. Select one or two for an in-depth report.

- It is often said that "the heart never rests." True, it does beat continuously from before birth until death, usually at old age. However, it does rest for 0.3 second after each beat. Assuming a steady pulse of 70 beats/minute, calculate the *total* amount of time the heart has rested in a person 75 years old.

- The Rh factor is named for the Rhesus monkey. Trace the historical discovery of this protein marker in primates and humans.

- Deaths of newborn babies from erythroblastosis fetalis (Rh factor related) have been virtually eliminated since the 1950s. How has this been accomplished?

- Blood typing is confusing to students. This is especially true because most believe that the ABO markers and the Rh markers are intimately connected since blood type is nearly always expressed that way, O^+ for example. Investigate how these two sets of markers were discovered independently.

- Vertebrate muscular activity is dependent on an oxygen supply carried by the blood (specifically red cells). When demand exceeds supply, an *oxygen debt* is incurred and activity slows or stops. Such is not the case with insects with their indefatigable flight muscles. Investigate why this difference exists.

- Certain woodwind musicians have perfected a breathing technique that allows the production of continuous sound from the instrument. Investigate reports of this technique, and interview a practitioner. Arrange a demonstration if possible.

- Check a book of world records for the longest continuous bout of hiccups. What is the "ultimate" cure for a persistent case?

- How many people in the United States die of simple choking each year? What age is most affected? What is the most commonly lodged object?

- How might the anatomy and physiology of persons who were born and raised at very high altitudes be different from those who were born and raised in the lowlands and have only recently become acclimated to high elevations?

- Investigate the effects of air pollution on respiratory functions.

Possible Responses to *Critical Thinking* Questions

1. There is no doubt that the simple Heimlich maneuver saves the lives of potential choking victims. (This writer used it on his young daughter choking on a piece of bacon.) Some restaurants even have posters explaining the technique. But would we be reluctant to take action, especially for a stranger, because grabbing someone around the middle is a bit "personal"? What is the alternative? Would we watch a person die, knowing we could have at least done something? Is this the time to think about being sued? I would opt for life!

2. Moving the leg muscles during a long airplane flight or during any other time of prolonged inactivity is a good idea. Why? Because blood in the veins of the legs is under practically zero pressure and can be moved upward in the body toward the heart only by the squeezing pressure of the skeletal muscle on the vessels. Moving about the cabin would be a good idea but in today's

smaller jets, this may be impractical (especially with that damnable beverage cart blocking the way). Nevertheless, you can move your legs while seated and attempt to exercise the muscles at least a little bit.

3. The lack of oxygen delivery to tissues due to competition from carbon monoxide at the binding sites of hemoglobin would have a direct impact on the respiratory chain (electron transport) in the mitochondria. The electrons in this chain are "pulled" by oxygen along a series of proteins on the inner membrane of the mitochondria, resulting in the generation of the large quantities of ATP needed by the cell for energy.

23

IMMUNITY

Chapter Outline

Objectives

1. Describe typical external barriers that organisms present to invading organisms.
2. Understand the process involved in the nonspecific inflammatory response.
3. Understand how vertebrates (especially mammals) recognize and discriminate between self and nonself tissues.
4. Distinguish between antibody-mediated and cell-mediated patterns of warfare.
5. Explain the mechanisms of immunological specificity and memory.
6. Explain the basis for immunization.

7. Describe some examples of immune failures and identify as specifically as you can which weapons in the immunity arsenal failed in each case.

Key Terms

immunity	acne	cytotoxic T cells	vaccine
antigen	plaque	lymph node	passive immunization
complement	periodontitis	spleen	allergens
innate immunity	attack complexes	antibodies	allergy
cytokines	acute inflammation	antibody variable	asthma
lymphocytes	histamine	region	hay fever
adaptive immunity	fibrin	antibody constant	anaphylactic shock
interleukins	clots	region	autoimmune response
interferons	fever	immunoglobulins: IgG,	Grave's disease
tumor necrosis factor	prostaglandins	IgA, IgE, IgM, IgD	multiple sclerosis
neutrophils	MHC markers	B cell receptors	primary immune
macrophages	T-cell receptors (TCRs)	exons	deficiencies
monocytes	self versus nonself	introns	secondary immune
dendritic cells	recognition	"naïve" B cell	deficiencies
basophils	specificity	thymus gland	acquired immune
mast cells	diversity	clonal selection	deficiency syndrome
eosinophils	memory	helper T cells	(AIDS)
B and T lymphocytes	effector cells	primary immune	human
natural killer (NK) cells	memory cells	response	immunodeficiency
intact skin	antibody-mediated	perforins	virus (HIV)
lysozymes	immune response	apoptosis	AZT
mucus	cell-mediated immune	immunization	
gastric fluid	response	active immunization	

Lecture Outline

The Face of AIDS
A. AIDS has had a devastating effect on Africa.
 1. Nearly 12 million children in Africa are orphaned by the disease.
 2. AIDS has claimed the lives of over 20 million people and another 40 million are now infected with HIV.
B. Why not a vaccine against AIDS?
 1. The experiments of Edward Jenner in 1796 led to the development of a vaccine that eventually eradicated smallpox.
 2. However, even though much effort has been spent to develop a vaccine for AIDS, it has not happened—yet.

23.1 Integrated Responses to Threats
A. Evolution of the Body's Defenses
 1. Immunity is the body's ability to resist and combat infections.
  a. The body must be able to distinguish *self* from *nonself*.
  b. Any molecule that is recognized as nonself is designated an antigen.

2. Evolutionarily, innate immunity—fast, preset responses to a fixed set of nonself cues—was the first to appear.

3. Adaptive immunity is specific, selective, remembered, and regulated using cytokines and lymphocytes.

B. Three Lines of Defense

1. Intact skin and linings of body tubes are effective barriers that exclude many pathogens; resident populations of microorganisms outcompete occasional intruders.

2. Innate immunity, the second line of defense, starts after antigen has been detected internally; it includes phagocytosis, complement activation, fever, and inflammation.

3. In the third line of defense, adaptive immunity, lymphocytes target immediate, specific threats and persist as memory cells in case of a re-infection.

C. Introducing the Defenders

1. White blood cells, produced from stem cells in bone marrow, not only circulate in blood and plasma, but also reside in lymph nodes, spleen, liver, kidneys, and other tissues where they stand ready to defend.

2. There are several kinds of white blood cells that are "first responders":
   a. *Neutrophils*, the most abundant, phagocytize bacteria.
   b. *Basophils* and *mast cells* secrete enzymes and cytokines in response to antigen.
   c. *Eosinophils* are specialized for control of parasites such as protozoa, fungi, and worms.
   d. Macrophages (formed from immature cells called monocytes) are slower to act but can engulf and digest just about any foreign agent or damaged tissue.
   e. Dendritic phagocytes alert the adaptive immune system to the presence of antigen.

3. B and T lymphocytes are central to adaptive immunity because of their ability to shuffle genes, allowing a response to many specific antigens.

4. Natural killer cells destroy body cells weakened by viral infection of cancer.

23.2 Surface Barriers

A. Intact Skin

1. *Intact skin* is an important barrier.
   a. The normal *microbial inhabitants* of the skin deter more insidious types from colonizing the surfaces.
   b. Vertebrate skin has tough surface layers of dead cells filled with keratin.

2. Damaged or weakened skin epithelial cells provide an entry point for pathogens.

B. Linings of Tubes and Cavities

1. Microbes inhabit the *outside surfaces* of tubes and cavities, including the eyes, nose, mouth, and urinary and genital openings.

2. Mucus and tears contain lysozyme, which destroys bacteria by cleaving the peptidoglycan in the cell walls.

3. Ciliated *mucous membranes* in the respiratory tract sweep out bacteria and particles.

4. Gastric fluid with its low pH and enzymes is hard on bacteria.

5. *Urine,* with its low pH and flushing action, keeps pathogens from the urinary tract.

C. An Uneasy Balance

1. Certain bacteria, such as those that cause tetanus, diphtheria, even strep, are normally on our external skin and cause us no problem unless there is a breakdown in defense mechanisms.

2. *Propionibacterium acnes* usually is no problem unless it gets trapped under excess sebum in hair follicles where it multiplies, causing the inflammatory condition we call acne.

3. Excessive numbers of *Streptococcus* bacteria can accumulate in the plaque that sticks to teeth, causing dental caries.

23.3   The Innate Immune Response
   A. Macrophages are usually first on the scene of an invasion.
       1. They engulf and digest anything other than undamaged body cells.
       2. If they bind a pathogen, cytokines are secreted that attract dendritic cells, neutrophils, and more macrophages.
   B. Complement proteins are also an important aspect of innate immunity.
       1. In a cascade effect, tremendous numbers of activated complement proteins accumulate locally.
       2. They are chemotactic, attracting phagocytes to the microbe that they have surrounded.
       3. Some complement proteins form membrane attack complexes that poke holes in a microbe's cell wall, causing death by lysis.
   C. Acute inflammation is a fast, nonspecific response to tissue invasion mediated by complement and cytokines.
       1. Outward symptoms include redness, swelling, warmth, and pain.
       2. Histamine (from mast cells) dilates arterioles for increased blood flow and also makes capillaries "leaky" to fluid as well as phagocytes.
       3. Clotting mechanisms help wall off the pathogen and promote repair of tissues.
       4. Cytokines released by macrophages cause the brain to release prostaglandins, which signal a rise in the hypothalamic thermostat and cause a fever (not necessarily a bad thing).

23.4   Tailoring Responses to Specific Antigens
   A. Features of Adaptive Immunity
       1. *Self versus nonself recognition* give each kind of cell (or virus) its unique identity.
           a. Located on the membranes of the body's cells are proteins called MHC markers.
           b. T cell receptors (TCRs) are antigen receptors at the surface of T cells that recognize MHC markers.
       2. *Specificity* means each new B cell or T cell makes receptors for only one kind of antigen.
       3. *Diversity* refers to the collection of antigen receptors on all B and T cells, numbering in the billions.
       4. *Memory* refers to the immune system's capacity to "remember" an antigen it has encountered and mount an even faster, heightened response if re-infection occurs.
   B. First Step—The Antigen Alert
       1. When antigens enter the body, they are engulfed and destroyed by macrophages, but not completely—the antigen becomes attached to the MHC marker to form an MHC-antigen complex, which is then displayed on the macrophage's surface.
       2. Any cell that displays antigen with a suitable MHC marker is known as an antigen-presenting cell and will be noticed by lymphocytes.
       3. At least one helper T cell will recognize a particular antigen-MHC complex and respond by secreting cytokines that promote the formation of large populations of effector and memory cells.
   C. Two Arms of Adaptive Immunity
       1. In the *antibody-mediated* response, B cells and their progeny (effector cells) produce antibodies, which tag bacteria, fungi, or toxins that are freely circulating in the blood or interstitial fluid.
       2. In the *cell-mediated response,* pathogens (viruses for example) that are attempting to hide out in body cells are detected by the antigens on the cell surface and are destroyed by phagocytes and cytotoxic T cells.

D. So Where Is Antigen Intercepted?
  1. Locations such as tonsils and lymph nodules allow antigen-presenting cells and lymphocytes to intercept invaders just after they penetrate surface barriers.
  2. Before antigen can reach the blood, it must trickle through lymph nodes, which are packed with defending cells.

23.5 Antibodies and Other Antigen Receptors
A. B Cell Weapons—The Antibodies
  1. Antibodies are Y-shaped proteins that are synthesized by B cells that encounter and bind antigen.
    a. An antibody molecule consists of four polypeptide chains—two "light" and two "heavy."
    b. Each chain has a constant region and a variable region, which is specific for binding a particular antigen.
  2. Each antibody binds only one kind of antigen—the one that prompted the B cell to make the antibody in the first place.
  3. B cells produce five classes of antibodies known as the immunoglobulins (Igs).
    a. IgG antibodies activate complement proteins and neutralize many toxins; they are long lasting and can cross the placenta to protect the fetus.
    b. IgA, present in saliva, tears, and mucus, helps repel invaders at the start of the respiratory, digestive, and reproductive tracts.
    c. IgE antibodies stimulate basophils and mast cells to secrete histamines and cytokines.
    d. IgM and IgD, the first to be secreted during immune response, cover the surface of B cells, where they function as antigen receptors for each cell.
B. The Making of Antigen Receptors
  1. The gene encoding the production of an antigen receptor (antibody) is assembled from several different segments (exons) selected at random from a pool inside the B cell developing in the bone marrow.
  2. T cells also form inside the bone marrow but mature in the thymus where they make receptors for MHC markers and begin to make TCRs—unique antigen receptors—by random gene splicing.
  3. These random assortments are the source of B and T cell receptor diversity.

23.6 Antibody-Mediated Immune Response
A. B cells use antibodies to liquidate an extracellular pathogen or toxin.
B. What happens when bacteria penetrate your skin?
  1. Complement coats the bacteria, which enter the lymph vessels to be paraded past naïve B cells in a lymph node.
    a. The B cell antigen receptors recognize the bacterial antigen and complement, thus triggering endocytosis of the bacterium into the B cell.
    b. At the same time a dendritic cell engulfs and digests some bacteria, displaying antigen fragments bound to MHC markers on the surface.
  2. Back in the lymph node, a TCR on a T cell binds the bacterial antigen-MHC complex residing on the dendritic cell surface.
    a. Interaction of the T cell with the dendritic cell has stimulated mitosis of the T cell.
    b. The clones differentiate into helper T cells, all with identical TCRs for the specific bacterial antigen.

3. Meanwhile, the original B cell is displaying bits of bacterial antigen bound to MHC markers on the cell surface.
   a. Fortunately, one of the helper T clones recognizes the bacterial antigen-MHC complexes on the B cell and binds to it.
   b. The helper T secretes interleukins, which stimulate the B cell to divide into huge numbers of clones.
   c. The effector clones secrete Igs, specific for the original antigen, that circulate throughout the body marking other bacteria of the same kind for destruction by phagocytes and complement.

23.7   The Cell-Mediated Immune Response
  A. The main targets of cell-mediated responses are cells infected with intracellular pathogens, tumor cells, and cells of organ transplants.
    1. Dendritic cells recognize, engulf, and digest the antigens displayed on the surface of infected body cells.
    2. The antigen-MHC complexes are presented to naïve helper T cells and cytotoxic T cells, which become activated.
    3. Effector helper T cells produce signals to activate cytotoxic T cells.
    4. The clones of mature cytotoxic T cells recognize the antigen-MHC complexes on infected cells and kill them by punching holes in their cell membranes with proteins called perforins.
  B. Helper T cell cytokines also stimulate cell divisions of NK cells, which will attack cells tagged for destruction by antibodies and also kill infected or cancerous cells with altered MHC markers.

23.8   Defenses Enhanced or Compromised
  A. Immunization
    1. Active immunization involves a deliberate production of memory cells by a vaccine that is made from killed or weakened bacteria or viruses.
    2. If a person has already been exposed to bacterial pathogens, passive immunity can be temporarily conferred by injecting antibodies.
  B. Allergies
    1. An allergy is a secondary immune response to a normally harmless substance, an allergen such as pollen or certain foods.
    2. Exposure triggers production of IgE antibodies, which cause the release of histamines and prostaglandins.
    3. A local inflammatory response results; death can even occur due to anaphylactic shock, a condition in which air passages leading to the lungs constrict, fluid escapes too rapidly from capillaries, and blood pressure drops.
  C. Autoimmune Disorders
    1. In autoimmune disorders, lymphocytes turn against the body's own cells.
    2. Grave' s disease is an overproduction of thyroid hormones, which elevate metabolic rates, heart fibrillations, nervousness, and weight loss.
    3. Multiple sclerosis arises when autoreactive T cells trigger inflammation of myelin sheaths, disrupting nerve transmission.
  D. Deficient Immune Responses
    1. Primary immune deficiencies are present at birth and result from altered genes or abnormal development.

2. Secondary immune deficiencies are losses of immune function after exposure to an agent, such as virus.
3. When immunity is weakened, infections that would normally not be serious become life-threatening.

23.9 AIDS: Immunity Lost
    A. AIDS is a group of disorders that follow infection by HIV.
        1. The virus cripples the immune system and makes the body highly susceptible to usually harmless infections.
        2. There is no cure for those already infected.
    B. HIV Infection—A Titanic Struggle Begins
        1. HIV only infects cells with CD4 receptors, such as helper T cells.
        2. The virus takes over the cell's machinery to produce massive quantities of new HIV particles.
        3. Many of the new virus particles are destroyed, but eventually the number of T cells destroyed exceeds the new T cells made and the battle tilts.
    C. How Is HIV Transmitted?
        1. The most common mode of transmission is by sex with an infected partner.
        2. Infected mothers can pass it to a newborn during vaginal birth.
        3. Small amounts of blood on shared needles can be passed among drug users.
    D. What About Drugs and Vaccines?
        1. AZT blocks reverse transcription to slow the production of new virus particles.
        2. Vaccines have been made and tested, most with disappointing results.

Suggestions for Presenting the Material

- The subject of immunity is a difficult one on any level, especially to students who may be hearing it for the first time. Proceeding slowly and making use of the excellent diagrams will help.

- The understanding of defense against foreign organisms by the human body is complicated by the fact that so many mechanisms and factors are operating *at the same time.*

- Draw your students' attention to the tables at the beginning of the chapter. These are useful to distinguish innate and adaptive immunity (23.1), chemical weapons of immunity (23.2), and examples of surface barriers (23.3).

- You may wish to organize your lectures around "lines of defense." For example, the "nonspecific defense responses" are sometimes referred to as the first and second lines of defense, i.e, the "barriers to invasion" would be a first line and "inflammation" (including phagocytes and complement) would be a second line.

- The third line of defense—the immune system itself—is more specific and more intricate. Because of this complexity, be sure to use the diagrams in the text.

- Students sometimes have difficulty distinguishing "antibody" from "antigen." This may help: antigen is short for *anti*body *gen*erator.

- The topics of *immunization* and *immune diseases* are always of interest to students and should be given sufficient time to allow for student discussion.

Classroom and Laboratory Enrichment

- The tragic suffering and death of a victim of AIDS (or a similar disease) will serve as an attention-getter for this topic—even more so if the victim was a personal acquaintance of the instructor.

- Tracking down the cause of an annoying allergy can involve some real detective work. Survey the class for such an experience, and ask for a brief oral report if the person is willing to share his/her experience.

- With the assistance of a microbiology student, prepare petri dishes onto which smears from the human mouth, nose, hands, head, as well as commonly touched surfaces are made. Identify the microorganisms present in each location.

- Are insect bodies filth carriers? Attempt to answer this by letting different insects including a cockroach, house fly, and cricket crawl over the surface of an agar-filled petri dish.

Impacts, Issues Classroom Discussion Ideas

- How is AIDS perceived as a disease in differing countries of the world? (Take into consideration attitudes about homosexuality, heterosexuality, prostitution, etc.)

- Could AIDS be the "grimmest" of the grim reapers Malthus wrote about in his essay (see bullet 3 in the section below)?

- What could be done to stem the epidemic of AIDS in African countries?

Additional Ideas for Classroom Discussion

- Where does our term *vaccination* derive its meaning? Was it first used as a medical term as it now is?

- Every year a small number of children die from diseases that develop as a result of vaccines received to protect them. It seems to be an inherent hazard associated with mass preventative inoculation. Is it worth the risk? Can you debate both sides of the issue?

- Thomas Malthus proposed three "grim reapers" that would restrain human population growth. One of these was "pestilence," or disease. How effective is disease as a population limiting factor in the developed countries versus the underdeveloped countries?

- If there are so many infectious people as patients in hospitals, why aren't doctors and nurses continuously ill?

How Would You Vote? Classroom Discussion Ideas

- Monitor the voting for the online question. The question of whether drug companies will ever supply AIDS drugs to poor countries at low cost depends on the humanitarian nature of the persons running the company. It is hard to believe that a huge pharmaceutical company would suffer economic damage by such a move. Surely the profits will dip; executives will not get their multi-million dollar bonuses, but the company will go on.

Term Paper Topics, Library Activities, and Special Projects

- Controversy still surrounds the polio vaccines—Salk and Sabin. Explore the details of how each of these vaccines is made and used. Include the advantages and disadvantages of each.

- Research on the cause and treatment of AIDS has been rapid and continues to progress. Report on the latest strategies.

- Although vaccines are available throughout the world for the prevention of measles, diphtheria, and polio, there are about 20 other infectious diseases for which vaccines could be developed, but there seems to be little incentive to do so. Report on the reasons why this is so.

- Polio and smallpox have been conquered by effective vaccination programs. Prepare a report on the development of the vaccine for either of these diseases; be sure to include the chronology of events leading up to the marketing of the vaccine.

Possible Responses to *Critical Thinking* Questions

1. Edward Jenner would never be able to perform his historic experiments today for several reasons, the greatest of which is the fact that he did not obtain informed consent from his subjects. But then how could he have, they were children!

2. Periodontitis would not cause heart attacks directly but could provide the entry point for nasty bacteria that would release toxins that could trigger the attacks.

3. Because of the shortage of organs for transplant, medical personnel are searching for alternative sources. Behold! The much-maligned pig seems to be the closest match to humans. But, of course, there is always the problem of rejection of porcine organs by the human body because they are not *self*. Therefore, it would seem necessary to insert into the pig some gene(s) that would trick the human leukocytes to NOT recognize the pig organs as foreign.

4. Lancelets cannot mount a specific immune response because they are not able to make the diverse antigen receptors that are the basis of pathogen-specific immune responses. Although the lancelets have the V-region genes of vertebrates they are not able to make the *rearrangements* of genes that are critical to producing the tremendous variety of proteins that would be able to specifically recognize virtually any antigen that enters the body.

5. Elena did not develop chicken pox when exposed to her infected children because her body retained memory cells (lymphocytes) that recognized the antigen and mounted a defensive action so quick and effective that she did not even realize it was occurring.

6. Even with a flu shot, you get a case of "the flu." What might have gone wrong here? One explanation is that the strain of flu you got was not the same as the vaccine was designed to combat. Another is that the flu shot was the correct one for the strain expected this season, but a mutation occurred and your flu virus was different. Perhaps you obtained a "bargain" flu shot that was not even a real vaccine.

7. The smallpox vaccine was effective because it targets a single type of virus. Cancer is a disease of great variation and thus a single vaccine is not feasible.

8. Monoclonal antibodies are proteins and as such would not be expected to remain in the body for long periods of time doing their work as memory cells do.

24

DIGESTION, NUTRITION, AND EXCRETION

Chapter Outline

Objectives

1. Know the various ways in which a digestive system can be structured. Realize the behavioral limitations of organisms with incomplete digestive systems.
2. Understand the structure and function of the human digestive system.
3. Summarize the daily nutritional requirement of a 25-year-old man who works at a desk job and exercises very little. State what he needs in energy, carbohydrates, proteins, and lipids and name at least six vitamins and six minerals that he needs to include in his diet every day.

4. Explain how the human body manages to meet the energy and nutritional needs of the various body parts even though the person may be feasting sometimes and fasting at other times.
5. Explain how the chemical composition of extracellular fluid is maintained by mammals.
6. Describe the process of urine formation.
7. Tell what mechanisms help to maintain the proper balance of acids and bases in body tissues.

Key Terms

digestive system	epiglottis	cholecystokinin, CCK	urethra
incomplete digestive system	esophagus	colon, large intestine	nephrons
complete digestive system	heartburn	feces	glomerular capillaries
	acid reflux	cecum	Bowman's capsule
motility	stomach	appendix	cortex
secretion	glandular epithelium	appendicitis	medulla
digestion	hydrochloric acid	constipation	proximal tubule
absorption	mucus	colon polyps	loop of Henle
elimination	gastric fluid	colon cancer	distal tubule
crop	chyme	colonoscopy	collecting duct
gizzard	gastrin	virtual colonoscopy	renal pelvis
cloaca	peptic ulcer	glycogen	peritubular capillaries
ruminants	duodenum	adipose tissue	glomerular filtration
lumen	jejunum	essential amino acids	tubular reabsorption
tooth	ileum	"food pyramid"	tubular secretion
enamel	liver	vitamins	countercurrent exchange system
dentin	gallbladder	minerals	thirst center
inner pulp	pancreas	body-mass index (BMI)	antidiuretic hormone, ADH
incisors	pepsin	kilocalorie	
canines	trypsin	interstitial fluid	aldosterone
premolars	chymotrypsin	blood	diabetes insipidus
molars	villi	extracellular fluid	hyperaldosteronism
tongue	microvilli	urinary excretion	kidney stones
saliva	bile	urea	renal failure
salivary glands	emulsification	urinary system	kidney dialysis machine
salivary amylase	micelle formation	kidneys	hemodialysis
mucins	chylomicrons	urine	peritoneal dialysis
pharynx	ghrelin	ureters	
	secretin	urinary bladder	

Lecture Outline

Hips and Hunger
A. Mammals store fat in their adipose cells in case food becomes scarce.
1. Adipose cells make a hormone, leptin, that suppresses appetite.
2. But there is also a hormone called ghrelin that makes you feel hungry.
B. A constant battle rages in the body between the amount of food *necessary* for survival and the amount *desired* to make us feel satisfied.

24.1   The Nature of Digestive Systems

A. A digestive system mechanically and chemically reduces food to particles and molecules small enough to be absorbed into the internal environment.

B. Incomplete and Complete Systems
1. An incomplete digestive system (for example, in a flatworm) has one opening.
    a. Food enters and waste leaves through the same opening.
    b. Digestive products are absorbed directly to the needy tissues.
2. A complete digestive system is a tube with two openings, allowing food to move in one direction through the lumen; it performs five tasks:
    a. *Mechanical processing and motility* is the breaking up, mixing, and transporting of food material.
    b. *Secretion* is the release of needed enzymes and other substances into the lumen.
    c. *Digestion* is the chemical breakdown of food matter to molecules small enough to cross the gut lining.
    d. *Absorption* is the passage of digested nutrients into the blood and lymph.
    e. *Elimination* is the expulsion of undigested and unabsorbed residues at the end of the gut.

C. Correlations with Feeding Behavior
1. The digestive system is an internal space or tube with specialized regions for food gathering, transport, processing, and storage.
2. Regional specializations correlate with feeding behavior.
    a. Birds store meals in a stretchable crop and grind the food in a gizzard.
    b. Ruminants (for example, cows) can eat grass almost continuously and have multiple stomachs to digest cellulose.

24.2   Human Digestive System

A. The human digestive system is a tube with two openings.
1. Stretched out, it would extend more than 20 feet.
2. An epithelium lines all the surfaces facing the lumen.

B. Into the Mouth, Down the Tube
1. Mechanical breakdown of food and its mixing with saliva begin in the mouth.
    a. Teeth chew the food.
        1) Each has an enamel coat, a dentine core, and an inner pulp.
        2) Incisors bite off chunks, canines tear, and premolars and molars grind food.
    b. Saliva (from salivary glands) contains salivary amylase to begin carbohydrate digestion, bicarbonate to neutralize acids, and mucins to lubricate.
2. The tongue pushes the ball of food into the pharynx where receptors initiate the swallowing reflex into the esophagus and then into the stomach; the epiglottis closes off the trachea to prevent choking.

C. The Stomach
1. The stomach is a muscular sac that stores and mixes food, secretes substances that dissolve and degrade food, and controls the rate at which food enters the small intestine.
2. Gastric fluid includes hydrochloric acid, pepsinogens, and mucus.
    a. HCl dissolves bits of food to form a soupy chyme; it also converts pepsinogen (inactive) to pepsin (active).
    b. Pepsin begins the digestion of proteins.
    c. Normally, mucus and bicarbonate ions protect the stomach lining; but if these are blocked, hydrogen ions stimulate the release of histamine, which in turn stimulates release of more HCl, which may result in a peptic ulcer.

3. Peristaltic contractions churn the chyme and keep the sphincter of the stomach's exit closed, but small amounts are released at regular intervals into the small intestine.

D. The Small Intestine

1. The three regions are: duodenum, jejunum, and ileum.
2. Secretions from the liver, gallbladder, and pancreas enter via a common duct.
3. Digestion is completed and most nutrients are absorbed in the small intestine.
   a. Trypsin and chymotrypsin digest proteins to peptide fragments.
   b. Carboxypeptidase and aminopeptidase degrade the fragments to amino acids.
   c. Bicarbonate from the pancreas buffers the acid from the stomach.
4. The intestinal wall consists of several layers:
   a. The mucosa is the epithelial lining that faces the lumen of the gut; connective tissue underlies it.
   b. The submucosa contains blood and lymph vessels plus nerve networks.
   c. A muscle layer (longitudinal and circular) is covered with the outermost serosa.
5. Absorptive surface area is increased by fingerlike projections of the intestinal lining called villi, the cells of which bear even smaller microvilli.

E. How Nutrients Are Absorbed

1. Repeated back and forth contractions create an oscillating movement that mixes the food and forces it against the wall's absorptive surface.
2. Monosaccharides (glucose) and amino acids cross the gut lining by active transport and enter the bloodstream.
3. The liver aids in fat digestion by the emulsification action of bile:
   a. First the fatty acids combine with bile salts to form micelles.
   b. Diffusion gradients favor movement of products out of the micelles and into the epithelial cells of the mucosa.
   c. Triglycerides combine to form chylomicrons, which leave the cell by exocytosis mainly to enter the lymph vessels.

F. Controls over Digestion

1. Distention of the gut wall after a meal stimulates mechanoreceptors and their neurons, which respond with muscle action and enzyme secretion.
2. Four gastrointestinal hormones play roles.
   a. *Gastrin,* produced by the stomach lining, stimulates secretion of acids into the stomach.
   b. *Secretin* from the intestinal lining stimulates insulin secretions from the pancreas.
   c. *Cholecystokinin* (CCK) enhances the actions of secretion and stimulates gallbladder contractions.

G. The Large Intestine (Colon)

1. The large intestine (colon) stores and concentrates feces—undigested and unabsorbed material, water, and bacteria.
   a. The large intestine begins as a cup-shaped pouch at its junction with the small intestine (appendix attached here).
   b. It is draped across the lower abdomen and ends in a rectum (feces storage) that opens to the outside through the anus.
2. Fiber ("bulk") in the diet is important in moving material in the feces through the large intestine at the proper speed.
   a. Delayed defecation can result in constipation.
   b. Fecal material lodged in the appendix can lead to the complications of appendicitis.
   c. Colon cancer is related to diet and the speed at which materials move through the colon.

24.3   Human Nutritional Requirements
   A. Carbohydrates
      1. Shortly after a meal, the level of carbohydrates rises; some are converted to fat for storage, and others are converted to glycogen in the liver and muscle tissue.
      2. Between meals, glucose levels are maintained by breakdown of glycogen reserves in the liver and amino acids are converted to glucose; fatty acids from fats can be used directly by cells for energy.
   B. Good Fat, Bad Fat
      1. Phospholipids and cholesterol are important components of membranes; fats are energy reserves and provide insulation and cushioning.
      2. The body needs very little polyunsaturated fat to supply the essential fatty acids, those not made by the body itself.
      3. Too many saturated fats and "trans fats" increase the risk of heart disease.
   C. Body-Building Proteins
      1. Of the 20 different amino acids in proteins, eight are essential (that is, must be supplied in the diet).
      2. Most proteins in animal tissues are labeled complete; those in plants are incomplete, that is, they lack one or more amino acids essential for human needs.
   D. Dietary Recommendations
      1. In January 2005, the United States Food and Drug Administration issued a set of nutritional guidelines to replace the earlier "food pyramid."
         a. In comparison with the diet of a typical American, the guidelines call for a lowered intake of refined sugars, saturated and trans fats, and added sugars.
         b. The guidelines suggest eating more whole grains, legumes, dark green and orange vegetables, fruits, and milk products.
      2. The long-term effects of the popular "low carb" diets are unknown at this time.
      3. Increased consumption of proteins produces more ammonia and urea, which must be processed by the liver and kidneys.
   E. Vitamins and Minerals
      1. Humans need small amounts of at least 13 organic molecules called vitamins to assist in cellular metabolism.
      2. Inorganic substances called minerals (Ca, Mg, K, Fe, for example) are also needed.
      3. A balanced diet will normally meet all requirements for these substances; excessive intake is at least wasteful, and at worst harmful.

24.4   Weighty Questions, Tantalizing Answers
   A. Obesity is a touchy subject.
      1. Partly, it is culturally defined.
      2. But medically it is a factor in many health problems: diabetes, heart disease, hypertension, cancers, gallstones, gout, and osteoarthritis.
   B. Body Mass Index (BMI) is a way to relate body weight to height.
      1. To maintain an acceptable BMI you must balance caloric intake with energy output.
      2. The number of calories you need per day can be calculated based on your daily activities, or lack thereof.

24.5   Urinary System of Mammals
   A. Shifts in Water and Solutes
       1. The volume and composition of extracellular fluid, which consists of the interstitial fluid
           surrounding living cells and blood in the vessels, is kept within tolerable ranges by the
           urinary system.
       2. Water Gains and Losses
           a. Water is gained by two processes:
               1) Absorption of water from liquids and solid foods occurs in the gastrointestinal
                   tract.
               2) Metabolism of nutrients yields water as a byproduct.
           b. Water is lost by at least four processes:
               1) Control over water loss is accomplished by urinary excretion.
               2) Evaporation occurs from respiratory surfaces and through the skin.
               3) Sweating occurs on the skin surface.
               4) Elimination of water in feces is a normal occurrence.
       3. Solute Gains and Losses
           a. Solutes are added to the internal environment by four processes:
               1) Nutrients, mineral ions, drugs, and food additives are absorbed by the
                   gastrointestinal tract.
               2) Secretion from endocrine glands adds hormones.
               3) Respiration puts oxygen into the blood.
               4) Metabolism reactions contribute waste products.
           b. Mineral ions and metabolic wastes are lost in these three ways:
               1) Urinary excretion disposes of ammonia (formed from amino acids), urea (formed
                   in the liver by joining two ammonias), and uric acid (from nucleic acids).
               2) Respiration disposes of carbon dioxide, the most abundant metabolic waste.
               3) Sweating results in the loss of mineral ions.
   B. Components of the Human Urinary System
       1. Each kidney is a bean-shaped structure about the size of a fist, with cortex and medulla
           regions covered by a tough coat of connective tissue.
           a. Kidneys filter a variety of substances from the blood.
           b. Most of the filtrate is returned to the blood; about 1 percent ends up as urine.
           c. The kidneys regulate the volume and solute concentrations of extracellular fluid.
       2. Urine flows from each kidney through a ureter to a urinary bladder (for storage) and then
           out of the body through the urethra.
       3. Urination is a reflex response but can be controlled by nervous and muscular actions.

24.6   How the Kidneys Make Urine
   A. Nephrons—Functional Units of Kidneys
       1. Each kidney has more than a million nephrons.
       2. Filtration occurs in the glomerulus—a ball of capillaries nestled in the Bowman's capsule.
       3. The Bowman's capsule collects the filtrate and directs it through the continuous nephron
           tubules: proximal ——> loop of Henle ——> distal ——> collecting duct.
       4. The capillaries exit the glomerulus, converge, then branch again into the peritubular
           capillaries around the nephron tubules where they participate in reclaiming water and
           essential solutes.

B. Filtration, Reabsorption, and Secretion
   1. In glomerular filtration, blood pressure forces filtrate out of the glomerular capillaries into Bowman's capsule, then into the proximal tubule.
      a. Blood cells, proteins, and other large solutes cannot pass the capillary wall into the capsule.
      b. Water, glucose, sodium, and urea are forced out.
   2. *Tubular reabsorption* takes place in the tubular parts of the nephron where water and solutes move across the tubular wall and out of the nephron and into the surrounding capillaries.
   3. *Tubular secretion* moves substances from the capillaries into the nephron walls.
      a. Capillaries surrounding the nephrons secrete excess amounts of hydrogen ions and potassium ions into the nephron tubules.
      b. This process also rids the body of drugs, uric acid, hemoglobin breakdown products, and other wastes.
C. Adjusting Urine Concentration
   1. Reabsorption mechanisms conserve water.
      a. Sodium ions are pumped out of the proximal tubule (filtrate) and into the interstitial fluid surrounding the peritubular capillaries.
      b. Significant amounts of water follow passively down the gradient that has been created.
      c. In the descending limb of the loop of Henle, water moves out by osmosis, but in the ascending portion sodium is pumped.
      d. This interaction of the limbs of the loop produces a very high solute concentration in the deeper parts of the kidney medulla and delivers a rather dilute urine to the distal tubule.
   2. There are hormone-induced adjustments.
      a. Antidiuretic hormone (ADH) from the posterior pituitary is secreted in response to a decrease in extracellular fluid; ADH causes the distal tubules and collecting ducts to become permeable to water, which moves back into the blood capillaries.
      b. When sodium levels fall so does the volume of extracellular fluid; this results in the release of *aldosterone,* which promotes sodium reabsorption.

24.7   When Kidneys Break Down
   A. Kidneys can fail for a number of reasons:
      1. Pathogens from the bloodstream may cause an infection.
      2. Toxins such as lead, arsenic, and pesticides may accumulate in kidney tissue.
      3. Kidney malfunction will lead to uremic toxicity.
   B. Several remedial actions are appropriate to the malady:
      1. Kidney stones, which can block the ureters or urethra, must be removed surgically or by lithotripsy.
      2. Dialysis (hemo- or peritoneal) is a process that uses a machine to remove certain solutes in the blood.

Suggestions for Presenting the Material

- The topics of *respiration* and *circulation,* which were covered previously, should be correlated with the present topics of *digestion* and *excretion.* Figure 24.16 at the end of the chapter will be very helpful; you may want to begin your lectures with this diagram.

- This chapter begins with a brief discussion of *incomplete* versus *complete* digestive systems, and then focuses on: (a) human digestive organs and function, and (b) human nutritional needs and metabolism. This is followed by a discussion of how the metabolic waste products of nutrients are excreted from the body.

- The traditional and most logical method of presentation of the digestive system is to follow a mouthful of food as it passes from mouth to anus. Along the way, you can be as detailed as your course requires. For example, you probably will ask students to know structures, general secretions, and main functions of digestion as presented in Figure 24.4 but not put undue emphasis on the numerous enzymes that attack each food group at various points along the way.

- Similarly, you will need to inform students as to the amount of material from Tables 24.2 (vitamins) and 24.3 (minerals) you require them to learn. Certainly, the authors of the text did not intend for these tables to be memorized entirely but provided them for reference and completeness.

- As each digestive organ is discussed, reference to the overhead transparency of Figure 24.4 (human digestive system) should be made.

- At some point in your discussion, be sure to emphasize that *digestion* and *absorption* are inseparable in the total function of providing nutrition to body cells.

- Students will enjoy your lectures more if you include brief notes on the various "problems along the way" that cause us minor, and occasionally major, distress.

- Nutrition is receiving increasingly more emphasis in our lives. You may wish to devote an entire lecture to this timely topic. This is also an excellent opportunity to review the contents of Chapter 2 (molecules of life).

- This is an ideal time to discuss some of the fad weight-loss diets as well as the more legitimate ones. Students are extremely interested in this topic, and it is a beneficial one for them to discuss.

- When discussing obesity, introduce the concept of body mass index (BMI) as an indicator of the degree of obesity. Consult a nutrition text for details.

- The Urinary System of Mammals section contains material that is less familiar to students, especially the intricacies of the kidney. Therefore, this section (sometimes referred as the "excretory system") will deserve some time and effort.

- The authors begin this section with an excellent prelude—water and solute gains and losses. These paragraphs make clear the necessity for the urinary system described next.

- Again the authors have presented the material in ever-increasing detail as the discussion progresses. Some instructors may find a few sections too detailed for their classes; others may enjoy these expanded explanations.

- If you use the word *excretion* in your lectures, clearly distinguish it from the word *elimination,* which is the voiding of undigested waste via the anus.

- Discussion of the nephron structure is entirely too abstract without constant reference to the transparencies of Figures 24.12 and 24.13. Be certain to distinguish between structures carrying *blood* and those carrying *filtrate.*

- An analogy to the common drip-type coffee brewing machine is helpful (see the Enrichment section).

- Reinforcement of ADH and aldosterone functions (Chapter 26) should be made during your presentation of kidney function.

- Large quantities of fluid are filtered from the blood, but nearly all of the fluid is replaced. Use the "storeroom-cleaning" analogy (see the Enrichment section) as a possible clue to why this is the body's method.

- In your lecture include some examples of larger desert mammals, such as the eland, and the special adaptations they have for conserving water and for regulating their body temperature.

Classroom and Laboratory Enrichment

- Because the digestive organs lie cramped in a small space, one upon the other, drawings such as Figure 24.4 are not as useful as life-size models. If your department has one, use it throughout your journey through the G-I tract.
- Demonstrate peristalsis by placing a ball of suitable size inside a flexible tube (such as a section of old bicycle tire inner tube) and squeezing to move it along.
- The action of a digestive enzyme (salivary amylase) can be demonstrated using the procedure outlined in the Enrichment section for Chapter 4 of this resource manual.
- Show a film depicting the consequences of vitamin and mineral deficiencies in the human diet.
- Ask if any volunteers from within the class, or outside, would be willing to tell the class about his/her digestive or eating disorder.
- Use molecular models to demonstrate the process of digestion.
- Mix oil and water together in a flask to show their immiscibility. Then add soap to the mixture to illustrate emulsification.
- The measurement of metabolic rate using a respirometer (see the Enrichment section of Chapter 22 in this manual) can be varied to show the effects of temperature on an endotherm (mouse) and an ectotherm (frog).
- To aid the students' conceptualization of the nephron function, the following comparison to a drip-type coffee maker is made:

Nephron Part	*Coffee Brewer Part*
a. Afferent arteriole carrying blood in	a. Hot water
b. Blood with wastes	b. Coffee grounds
c. Glomerulus	c. Filter paper
d. Bowman's capsule	d. Filter holder
e. Proximal and distal ducts, Henle's loop, collecting ducts	e. Carafe

- The storeroom-cleaning analogy reveals a possible explanation for why the kidney removes from the blood much more fluid than it will eventually excrete. Which of the following, (a) or (b), results in a more efficient cleaning of the storeroom?
    a. Carefully removing and disposing only those few selected items that are in plain view and identifiable as "no longer needed"
    b. Removing *all* items from the storeroom; then sweeping, dusting, mopping; finally replacing only those items selected as "still worth keeping"
- The complete analysis of urine can reveal a wealth of information concerning the status of body metabolism. Ask a clinical lab technician to speak on modern analysis techniques.
- If possible, invite a kidney transplant or dialysis patient to discuss his or her condition with the class. Some kidney centers have a speaker's bureau for just this purpose. They may also provide dialysis equipment for observation.
- Use a mannequin to show the locations of the urinary organs.
- Exhibit a model of a kidney to illustrate its parts and the blood vessels associated with it.
- Display a model of a nephron.

- Use a model of a renal corpuscle to illustrate its structure.

Impacts, Issues **Classroom Discussion Ideas**

- Millions of people around the world suffer from deficiencies in amount and nutritional composition of food. Surprisingly, dietary disorders of persons in affluent countries result from "too much of good things." What are the consequences of the American diet?

- Diet plans for weight reduction are numerous and proliferating daily. How can the wary consumer recognize a plan that could be dangerous?

- With the discovery of hormones that are influential in appetite, is it possible that overweight persons will dismiss their problem with "My hormones made me do it"?

Additional Ideas for Classroom Discussion

- What is meant by "heartburn"? Is its use in television antacid advertising misleading, especially for young viewers? What would you propose as a better term?

- In an incomplete digestive system, what types of foods would be avoided due to elimination difficulties?

- How is the stomach of a cow like the gut of a termite? How could antibiotics given to a ruminant animal for a blood infection interfere with digestive function?

- What do you think of the programs that call for regimens of fasting and "purification of body fluids"? Are they biologically sound?

- Give some of the reasons that dietary fiber, such as bran, is so important in our diet.

- Why do some adults, who could drink milk as infants without difficulty, experience intestinal pain (due to gas) and/or dehydrating diarrhea when they drink milk?

- Of these three processes—filtration, reabsorption, secretion—which is (are) accomplished by a kidney dialysis machine? Explain any limitations of the device.

- Why do high-protein diet supplements for increasing muscle mass or losing weight include warnings saying that water intake must be increased when consuming the product?

- In the storeroom-cleaning analogy (see the Enrichment section), which scenario do you think results in a better cleaning of the storeroom? Do you think the same would apply to kidney function?

- When asked what the kidney does, most people would probably respond that it "filters the blood." Why is this answer not a complete statement of kidney function?

- Obviously, humans can survive using only one kidney. Why then do we have two?

- Is it possible to overload our kidneys' capacity by excessive intake of water?

- Why does eating salty foods make you thirsty?

- Why does eating salty foods make you temporarily gain weight?

How Would You Vote? **Classroom Discussion Ideas**

- Monitor the voting for the online question. Fast foods carrying a warning label? Now that is ridiculous! Who would even read it? Even bigger question: who would heed it? Americans have been warning-labeled to sleep. Why don't we address the problem of the unhealthy fast food meal at its source, namely, the quality and quantity of the food? Of course, consumers will object to healthier food in smaller portions because they have become so accustomed to what is unhealthy. It is much like other bad habits (smoking, alcohol consumption); we know the risks but we crave the "forbidden fruit" anyway.

Term Paper Topics, Library Activities, and Special Projects

- Survey your class to collect data on height and weight as in Figure 24.10. What percent of your class members' data fall within the ranges given here?

- From the library, obtain a calorie chart. Monitor and record your caloric intake for a week. Prepare a report.

- Ulcers are regarded by most people as a badge of success for bank presidents and young stockbrokers. Investigate the serious nature of this medical problem including the ages of the sufferers and what treatments are prescribed.

- *Anorexia* and *bulimia* seem to have appeared only recently as eating disorders. Trace the history of what is known about these conditions.

- The role of vitamins in human health is a fascinating story. Select one or two vitamins and report on the history of discovery surrounding each.

- Investigate how the drug cimetidine (Zantac) suppresses the secretion of acid by the parietal cells of the stomach.

- Find out why drinking coffee or other caffeine-containing beverages increases the sensation of hunger.

- Investigate the workings of a kidney dialysis machine. Include historical perspectives and recent technological advances.

- Although Western cultures find the practice bizarre, the consumption of one's own urine is practiced in Eastern cultures (India, for example). Report on the supposed benefit of such actions and the possible dangers.

- What are "kidney stones"? What are some of the factors responsible for their formation?

- Investigate the reasons why humans cannot meet their water needs by drinking seawater exclusively.

Possible Responses to *Critical Thinking* Questions

1. The problems of bone loss and brittle bones indicate a calcium deficiency. It is reasonable to assume that both anorexics and persons who undergo stomach stapling would be vulnerable to these conditions because insufficient amounts of calcium-rich foods are being ingested, albeit for very different reasons. For the anorexic, the desire for food is diminished by emotional and psychological problems. For the person whose stomach is severely reduced in size, there is a feeling of satiation long before sufficient quantities of nutrients have been ingested. Perhaps some type of highly-concentrated calcium supplement could be administered.

2. Leptin, secreted by adipose cells, is a hormone secreted that suppresses appetite, thereby exerting some degree of control on food intake and subsequent weight gain. During normal kidney function, leptin is metabolized to prevent buildup in the blood. However, if the kidney

were malfunctioning, the leptin levels could remain high, thus depressing the appetite excessively, leading to unusual weight loss.

3. Of course, any holiday meal is usually *too much* of some very good food. The stretch receptors of the stomach tell us we have overdone it. Over the course of a few hours, the food will be liquefied in the stomach and begin to move in small amounts into the small intestine. However, a meal rich in fats will be digested rather slowly because chemical breakdown will not even begin until the lipids reach the small intestine. Then the long chains of fatty acids must be cleaved sequentially.

4. The breakdown of milk will be as follows:

Component	Broken down in...	By what enzyme?	To yield...
lactose	small intestine	lactase	glucose + galactose
proteins	stomach (begin); small intestine (continue)	proteases, peptidases	amino acids
butterfat	small intestine	lipases	fatty acids + glycerol
vitamins	absorbed as is in small intestine	not applicable	not applicable
minerals	absorbed as is in small intestine	not applicable	not applicable

5. The labels for the kidney on the left are (from top to bottom): renal capsule, renal cortex, renal medulla, renal pelvis, and ureter. The labels for the nephron on the right (from top to bottom): glomerulus in Bowman's capsule, distal tubule, proximal tubule, and loop of Henle.

25

NEURAL CONTROL AND THE SENSES

Chapter Outline

Objectives

1. Describe the visible structure of neurons, neuroglia, nerves, and ganglia, both separately and together as a system.
2. Describe the distribution of the invisible array of large proteins, ions, and other molecules in a neuron, both at rest and as a neuron experiences a change in potential.
3. Understand how a nerve impulse is received by a neuron, conducted along a neuron, and transmitted across a synapse to a neighboring neuron, muscle, or gland.
4. Outline some of the ways by which information flow is regulated and integrated in the human body.
5. Describe the organization of peripheral and central nervous systems.
6. Identify the parts of primitive brains; then tell how the human brain is advanced beyond the primitive types.
7. Describe how various drugs affect the nervous system.
8. Know what a sensory receptor is and list the various types of receptors.
9. Contrast the mechanism by which the chemical senses work with that by which the somatic senses work.
10. Describe how the sense of vision has evolved through time.
11. Understand how the senses of balance and hearing function.

Key Terms

nervous system
neurons
sensory neurons
stimulus
interneurons
motor neurons
cell body
dendrites
input zones
trigger zone
axon
conducting zone
output zones
resting membrane
  potential
sodium-potassium
  pumps
excitable cells
action potential
threshold potential
positive feedback
all-or-nothing event
chemical synapse
presynaptic cell
postsynaptic cell
neurotransmitter

excitatory signal
inhibitory signal
synaptic integration
acetylcholine
norepinephrine
epinephrine
dopamine
serotonin
GABA
Parkinson's disease
encephalins
endorphins
divergent circuits
convergent circuits
reverberating circuits
nerves
Schwann cells
neuroglia cells
myelin sheath
multiple sclerosis
reflexes
reflex arc
stretch reflex
muscle spindles
radial symmetry
nerve net

bilateral nervous system
ganglion, ganglia
cephalization
notochord
central nervous system
peripheral nervous
  system
afferent sensory fibers
efferent motor fibers
spinal nerves
cranial nerves
somatic nerves
autonomic nerves
sympathetic neurons
parasympathetic
  neurons
fight-flight response
white matter
gray matter
spinal cord
vertebral column
meninges
meningitis
paraplegia
tetraplegia
brain

forebrain
midbrain
hindbrain
brain stem
medulla oblongata
cerebellum
pons
cerebrum
thalamus
hypothalamus
pituitary gland
pineal gland
neural tube
cerebrospinal fluid
blood-brain barrier
cerebral hemispheres
cerebral cortex
corpus callosum
frontal lobe
occipital lobe
temporal lobe
parietal lobe
motor areas
Broca's area
premotor cortex
sensory areas

association areas	marijuana	sweet	macular degeneration
limbic system	sensory systems	sour	cataract
amygdala	stimulus	salty	glaucoma
hippocampus	thermoreceptors	bitter	hearing
cingulate gyrus	mechanoreceptors	umami	amplitude
psychoactive drugs	pain receptors	vision	frequency
drug addiction	chemoreceptors	eyes	outer ear
stimulants	osmoreceptors	photoreceptors	pinna
caffeine	photoreceptors	visual field	auditory canal
nicotine	sensory adaptation	lens	middle ear
cocaine	somatic sensations	retina	eardrum
amphetamines	special senses	sclera	hammer
MDMA	perception	cornea	anvil
crystal meth	sensation	choroid	stirrup
depressants	free nerve endings	ciliary body	oval window
alcohol	Meissner corpuscle	iris	inner ear
analgesics	bulb of Krause	pupil	cochlea
morphine	Ruffini endings	aqueous humor	vestibular apparatus
codeine	Pacinian corpuscle	vitreous body	scala vestibuli
heroin	pain	visual accommodation	scala tympani
fentanyl	somatic pain	nearsightedness	round window
oxycodone	visceral pain	farsightedness	cochlear duct
hallucinogens	smell	rod cells	basilar membrane
LSD	olfactory receptors	cone cells	organ of Corti
ketamine	pheromones	rhodopsin	tectorial membrane
PCP	taste receptors	fovea	semicircular canals

Lecture Outline

In Pursuit of Ecstasy
A. Ecstasy is a drug that can make you feel really good.
1. The active ingredient is MDMA, which interferes with the function of serotonin in the brain.
2. Too much serotonin can relieve anxiety, sharpen the senses, and make you feel socially accepted; it can also kill.
B. MDMA also damages neurons that secrete dopamine, the same chemical that is undersecreted in Parkinson's disease.

25.1   Neurons—The Great Communicators
A. Neurons and Their Functional Zones
1. The neuron, or nerve cell, is the basic unit of communication in all nervous systems.
   a. *Sensory* neurons are receptors for specific sensory stimuli.
   b. *Interneurons* in the brain and spinal cord integrate input and output signals.
   c. *Motor* neurons send information from integrator to muscle or gland cells (effectors).
2. Each neuron consists of three main parts:
   a. The *cell body* contains the nucleus and metabolic machinery for protein synthesis.
   b. *Dendrites* are numerous, usually short extensions that receive stimuli (input zones).

     c. An *axon* is usually a single, rather long extension (conducting zone) that transmits impulses to other cells at its branched endings (output zones); signals actually arise in trigger zones.

  B. Resting Membrane Potential

    1. A neuron at rest maintains a steady voltage difference across its plasma membrane.

      a. The inside is more negatively charged than the outside.

      b. This is called the *resting membrane potential.*

    2. The difference in charge between the outside and the inside of the neuron membrane is due to the greater number of Na^+ ions on the outside.

  C. The Action Potential

    1. When a neuron receives signals, an abrupt, temporary reversal in the polarity—the inside becomes more positive—is generated by the sodium ions rushing inward (an action potential).

      a. In an accelerating way, more and more gates open (example of positive feedback).

      b. At threshold, the opening of more gates no longer depends on the stimulus but is self-propagating.

    2. Action potentials are *all-or-nothing* events.

      a. When depolarization in one region is ended, the sodium gates close and potassium gates open.

      b. The sodium-potassium membrane pumps also become operational to fully restore the resting potential.

      c. The action potential is self-propagating and moves away from the stimulation site to adjacent regions of the membrane undiminished.

      d. A brief (refractory) period follows at each depolarization site—sodium gates shut, potassium gates open—during which the membrane is insensitive to stimulation.

25.2   How Messages Flow from Cell to Cell

  A. Chemical Synapses

    1. A chemical synapse is a junction between a neuron and an adjacent cell, separated by a synaptic cleft into which a neurotransmitter substance is released.

    2. The neuron that releases the neurotransmitter molecules into the cleft is called the *pre*synaptic cell.

      a. First, gated protein channels open to allow calcium ions to enter the neuron.

      b. Calcium causes the vesicles to fuse with the membrane and release the transmitter substance into the cleft.

    3. The neurotransmitter binds to receptors on the membrane of the *post*synaptic cell.

      a. Neurotransmitters may have excitatory effects if they drive a cell's membrane to the threshold of an action potential.

      b. Neurotransmitters may have inhibitory effects if they help drive the membrane away from the threshold.

  B. Synaptic Integration

    1. At any one moment thousands of communication lines reach a typical neuron in the brain.

    2. In *synaptic integration,* competing signals that reach the input zone are reinforced or dampened, sent on or suppressed.

  C. A Sampling of Signals

    1. There are various neurotransmitters depending on location within the nervous system.

      a. Acetylcholine is the transmitter at neuromuscular junctions.

b. Serotonin acts on brain cells to govern sleeping, sensory perception, temperature regulation, and emotional states.

c. Norepinephrine apparently affects brain regions concerned with emotions, dreaming, and awaking.

d. Dopamine is the specialty of neurons in brain regions dealing with emotions.

e. GABA is the most common inhibitory signal in the brain

2. Neurotransmitter molecules must be removed promptly from the synaptic cleft; acetylcholinesterase is one common method.

25.3   The Paths of Information Flow

A. Blocks and Cables of Neurons

1. Neuron circuits or pathways will determine the direction a signal will travel.

a. In the brain, neurons are organized into regional blocks that receive, integrate, and then send out signals.

b. The circuits may be divergent, convergent, or reverberating.

2. Signals between brain or spinal cord and body regions travel by nerves.

a. Axons of sensory neurons, motor neurons, or both, are bundled together in a nerve.

b. Within the brain and spinal cord, such bundles are called nerve pathways or "tracts."

3. Many axons are covered by a myelin sheath derived in part from Schwann cells.

a. Each section of the sheath is separated from adjacent ones by a node where the axon membrane (plentiful in gated sodium channels) is exposed.

b. The action potentials jump from node to node, which is fast and efficient.

B. Reflex Arcs

1. Reflexes are simple, stereotyped movements made in response to sensory stimuli.

2. In the simplest reflex (the reflex arc) sensory neurons synapse directly on motor neurons.

a. In the stretch reflex, receptors of sensory neurons (muscle spindles) transmit impulses to the spinal cord where direct synapses with motor neurons occur.

b. In the withdrawal reflex, interneurons in the spinal cord can activate or suppress motor neurons as necessary for a coordinated response.

25.4   Types of Nervous Systems

A. Regarding the Nerve Net

1. Nearly all animals have a nervous system, forming communication lines for detecting stimuli and responding in suitable ways.

2. The more complex the life-style of an animal, the more elaborate are its modes of receiving, integrating, and responding to information in the external and internal worlds.

3. The nerve net in the cnidarians reflects their radially symmetrical bodies.

4. Reflex pathways result in simple, stereotyped movements that provide the basic operating machinery of nervous systems such as the nerve net.

B. On the Importance of Having a Head

1. Flatworms are the simplest animals with bilateral symmetry, which is reflected in their arrangement of muscles and nerves.

a. The ladderlike nervous system includes two longitudinal nerve cords, associated ganglia, and nerves.

b. Some flatworms have a small brainlike clump of nervous tissue at the head end of the nerve cords (an example of cephalization).

2. Perhaps this arrangement evolved from the nerve net of cnidarian planula larvae.

3. Cephalization (formation of a head) is the evolutionary result of the layering of more and more nervous tissue over reflex pathways of ancient origin.

C. Evolution of the Spinal Cord and Brain
1. Early evolutionary forms of vertebrates relied more on the interaction of notochord and muscles to accomplish movement.
   a. Above the notochord a hollow, tubular nerve cord was evolving also.
   b. In early vertebrates, simple reflex pathways predominated.
   c. In existing vertebrates, the oldest parts of the brain deal with reflex coordination, other parts deal with storage of information, and most recent layerings are the basis of memory, learning, and reasoning.
2. The central nervous system includes the brain and spinal cord.
   a. The communication lines within the brain and spinal cord are called tracts; those in the *white matter* contain axons with glistening myelin sheaths and specialize in rapid transmission of impulses.
   b. *Gray matter* consists of unmyelinated axons, dendrites, nerve cell bodies, and neuroglia cells, which protect and support neurons.
3. The peripheral nervous system includes all of the nerves carrying signals to and from the brain and spinal cord.

25.5 The Peripheral Nervous System
A. Somatic and Autonomic Divisions
1. The human peripheral system has two types of nerves based on location:
   a. Spinal nerves (31 pairs) connect with the spinal cord and innervate most areas of the body.
   b. Cranial nerves (12 pairs) connect vital organs directly to the brain.
2. Spinal and cranial nerves can also be classified on the basis of function:
   a. The *somatic* nerves relay sensory information from receptors in the skin and muscles and motor commands to skeletal muscles (voluntary control).
   b. The *autonomic* nerves send signals to and from smooth muscles, cardiac muscle, and glands (involuntary control).
B. Subdivisions of the Autonomic System
1. *Sympathetic neurons* increase overall body activity during times of stress, excitement, or danger; they also call on the hormone epinephrine to increase the "fight-flight" response.
2. *Parasympathetic neurons* tend to slow down body activity when the body is not under stress.

25.6 The Central Nervous System
A. Spinal Cord
1. The spinal cord is a pathway for signal travel between the peripheral nervous system and the brain.
   a. The cord is also the center for controlling some reflex actions.
   b. The spinal cord (and also the brain) is covered with tough membranes—the meninges—and resides within the protection of the stacked vertebrae.
2. Signals move up and down the spinal cord in bundles of sheathed axons.
B. Regions of the Brain
1. The body's master control panel, the brain, is a continuation of the anterior end of the spinal cord, and is also protected by meninges and bones.
   a. The forebrain, midbrain, and hindbrain form from three successive portions of the neural tube.
   b. The most primitive of the tissue is the brain stem, which contains simple, basic reflex centers.

2. Regions of the brain include:
   a. The *medulla oblongata* has influence over respiration, blood circulation, motor response coordination, and sleep/wake responses.
   b. The *cerebellum* acts as reflex center for maintaining posture and coordinating limbs.
   c. The *pons* ("bridge") possesses bands of axons that pass between brain centers.
   d. The *midbrain* originally coordinated reflex responses to visual input; the *tectum* still integrates visual and auditory signals in vertebrates such as amphibians and reptiles.
   e. The large olfactory lobes dominated early vertebrate forebrains.
   f. The *cerebrum* integrates sensory input and selected motor responses.
   g. The *thalamus* (below cerebrum) relays and coordinates sensory signals.
   h. The *hypothalamus* monitors internal organs and influences responses to thirst, hunger, and sex.
3. The reticular formation is an ancient mesh of interneurons that extends from the uppermost part of the spinal cord, through the brain stem, and into the cerebral cortex.

C. The Blood-Brain Barrier
   1. The brain and spinal cord are bathed with cerebrospinal fluid, which exists within a system of cavities and canals.
   2. The fluid cushions vital nervous tissue from sudden, jarring movements.
   3. The blood-brain barrier operates at the plasma membranes of cells, forming the capillaries that service the brain.
      a. Tight junctions fuse the capillary cells together, forcing substances to move through the cells to reach the brain.
      b. Membrane transport proteins allow essential nutrients (glucose) to move through but bar wastes (urea) and certain toxins.

D. Focus on the Cerebral Cortex
   1. The human cerebrum is divided into left and right cerebral hemispheres.
      a. The left hemisphere deals with speech, math, and analytical skills; the right half controls nonverbal skills, such as music.
      b. The two halves communicate with each other by means of nerve tracts called the corpus callosum.
   2. Motor areas control voluntary motor activity.
      a. The *frontal* lobe includes the motor cortex, which coordinates instructions for motor responses.
      b. The frontal lobe also includes the premotor cortex (learned patterns of motor skills), Broca's area (speech), and the frontal eye field (voluntary eye movements).
   3. Sensory areas deal with the meaning of sensations.
      a. The *parietal* lobe contains the somatosensory cortex—the main receiving area for signals from the skin and joints.
      b. The *occipital* lobe, which is located in the rear, has centers for vision.
      c. The *temporal* lobe, near each temple, is a processing center for hearing and houses centers for influencing emotional behavior.
   4. Association areas—occupying all parts of the cortex except primary and sensory areas—integrate, analyze, and respond to many inputs.

E. Connections with the Limbic System
   1. The limbic system, located at the middle of the cerebral hemispheres, governs out emotions and has roles in memory.
   2. It is distantly related to olfactory lobes and still deals with the sense of smell, especially as it relates to memory.

3. Connections from the cerebral cortex pass through the limbic system, allowing us to correlate organ activities with self-gratifying behavior, such as eating and sex.

25.7　Drugging the Brain
A. A drug is a substance introduced into the body to provoke a specific physiological response.
  1. Habituation and tolerance are both signs of drug addiction: chemical dependence on a drug.
  2. Addicts abruptly deprived of their drugs undergo biochemical upheaval.
B. Effects of Some Psychoactive Drugs
  1. Stimulants:
    a. Caffeine increases alertness at low dosages, but induces clumsiness and mental incoherence at higher doses.
    b. Nicotine mimics Ach by directly stimulating diverse sensory receptors.
    c. Cocaine increases the sense of pleasure by blocking reabsorption of norepinephrine, dopamine, and other neurotransmitters.
    d. Amphetamines induce massive releases of dopamine and norepinephrine, with many negative effects on body physiology.
    e. MDMA in ecstasy is a "club" drug, which seems harmless as it enhances sex, trust, and calmness, but has a nasty side when it causes confusion, depression, anxiety, blurred vision, nausea, hypertension, and even death.
  2. Depressants, Hypnotics
    a. These drugs sedate and induce sleep.
    b. Alcohol is the most used, and abused, example.
  3. Analgesics
    a. Endorphins and enkephalins are natural pain killers secreted by the brain.
    b. Morphine, codeine, and heroin are the common addictive pain killers.
  4. Hallucinogens
    a. These drugs skew sensory perception by interfering with acetylcholine, norepinephrine, and serotonin.
    b. Marijuana acts like a mild depressant and gives mild euphoria, but it can also cause disorientation, anxiety, and hallucinations.

25.8　Overview of Sensory Pathways
A. Each sensory system has three component parts:
  1. Sensory receptors are the branched endings of sensory neurons, or specialized cells adjacent to them, that detect specific stimuli.
  2. Nerve pathways lead to the brain.
  3. Brain regions process the information into a sensation; later, perhaps, a perception (understanding) of the sensation will be made.
B. There are six main categories of sensory receptors:
  1. *Thermoreceptors:* detect heat energy.
  2. *Mechanoreceptors:* detect forms of mechanical energy (pressure, position, acceleration).
  3. *Pain receptors:* detect tissue damage.
  4. *Chemoreceptors:* detect chemical energy in specific substances dissolved in fluid.
  5. *Osmoreceptors:* detect changes in solute concentration (water volume).
  6. *Photoreceptors:* detect visible and UV light.
C. All sensory receptors convert stimulus energy to local, graded potentials, which may result in an action potential if the stimulus is intense or repeated fast enough.
  1. The brain assesses the nature of a given stimulus using three factors:

a. Genetically determined *pathways* of neurons in the brain can interpret incoming action potentials only in specific ways; for example, receptors from eyes see only light.

b. Strong stimulation of a receptor causes a greater *frequency* of action potentials.

c. Strong stimulation causes a greater *number* of neurons to fire.

2. In sensory adaptation the frequency of action potentials decreases or stops even when the stimulus is maintained; for example, clothing is no longer felt once it is put on for the day.

3. Sense organs in more than one location in the body contribute to the somatic sensations; receptors restricted to special locations or organs are the special senses.

25.9 Somatic Sensations

A. Each sensory pathway starts at receptors of sensory neurons that are sensitive to the same type of stimulus.

1. Sensory nerve pathways from different receptors lead to different parts of the somatosensory cortex of the brain.

2. Cells in this region are laid out like a map, with different regions corresponding to the functional importance of the different body parts.

B. Some receptors are located near the body surface.

1. Free nerve endings are simply branched endings of sensory neurons in the skin that function as mechanoreceptors, thermoreceptors, and pain receptors.

2. Encapsulated receptors are of several types:

a. Meissner corpuscles adapt slowly to vibrations of low frequencies.

b. The bulb of Krause is a thermoreceptor that is sensitive to temperatures below 10 degrees C.

c. Ruffini endings are sensitive to steady touching and pressure, and to temperatures above 45 degrees C.

d. Pacinian corpuscles are located both in the dermis and near joints; they are able to detect rapid pressure changes associated with touch and vibrations.

C. The muscle sense monitors limb motions and the body's position in space.

1. Mechanoreceptors in muscle joints, tendons, ligaments, and skin detect limb motions and the body's position in space.

2. Examples include the stretch receptors of muscle spindles.

D. Pain is the perception of injury to some region of the body.

1. Sensations of somatic pain come from receptors in the skin, skeletal muscles, joints, and tendons.

2. Sensations of visceral pain, which is associated with internal organs, are related to excessive chemical stimulation, muscle spasms and fatigue, and inadequate blood flow.

25.10 The Special Senses

A. Senses of Smell and Taste

1. Olfactory receptors detect water-soluble or volatile substances.

a. Some receptors respond to molecules from food or predators.

b. Others respond to pheromones, which are molecules released outside the body to elicit a social response in a member of the same species (example: bombykol in silkworm moths).

2. Taste receptors enable animals to distinguish nutritious from noxious substances.

a. Receptors of some animals are located on antennae, legs, tentacles, or fins.

b. In humans, taste receptors are often components of taste buds distributed mostly on the tongue, which has five primary sensations: sweet, sour, salty, bitter, and umami.

B. The Sense of Vision
  1. What Are the Requirements for Vision?
     a. Vision requires a complex system of photoreceptors and a neural program in the brain that can interpret the patterns of action potentials.
     b. All photoreceptors incorporate pigment molecules that can absorb photon energy, which can be converted into excitation energy in sensory neurons.
  2. Vertebrate Eyes
     a. The outer layer consists of a sclera ("white" of the eye), which covers most of the eye; the cornea covers the front.
     b. The middle layer consists of a dark-pigmented choroid and a lens with a pupil opening, as well as jellylike substances (aqueous humor on the lens, and vitreous body behind the lens).
     c. The pigmented iris controls the amount of light entering through the pupil.
     d. Because of the bending of the light rays by the cornea, visual accommodation must be made by the lens so that the image is in focus on the retina.
        1) In fish and reptiles, the lens is moved forward and back (like a camera lens) to focus.
        2) In birds and mammals, the ciliary muscle changes the shape of the lens to focus.
  3. Focus on the Retina
     a. Photoreceptors, linked to neurons, are located in the retina.
        1) Rods are sensitive to dim light and detect changes in light intensity.
        2) Cones respond to high-intensity light, contribute to sharp daytime vision, and detect colors.
     b. The sense of vision is the result of processing the information through levels of synapsing neurons.
        1) Stimulation begins in the rods and cones, then moves to bipolar sensory neurons, then to ganglion cells, whose axons form the optic nerves that lead to the brain's visual cortex.
        2) Before leaving the retina, signals flow among horizontal cells and amacrine cells, which dampen or enhance the signals.
     c. Each rod cell contains molecules of rhodopsin that can be altered by light, resulting in voltage changes in membranes.
        1) Cone cells each carry a different pigment for red, green, and blue colors; cone cells at the fovea (center of retina) provide the greatest visual acuity.
        2) Ganglion cells form restricted areas of the retinal surface called "receptive fields," which respond best to small spots of light.
     d. Axons of the two optic nerves end in the lateral geniculate nucleus of the brain, where the positions of the receptive fields correspond to those of the retina; final interpretation of sight occurs in the visual cortex.
C. The Sense of Hearing
  1. Properties of Sound
     a. Hearing is the perception of sounds, which are traveling vibrations of mechanical energy.
     b. These wavelike forms of mechanical energy show amplitude (loudness) and frequency (pitch).
  2. The Vertebrate Ear
     a. The middle ear contains small bones that amplify sounds before transmittal to the inner ear.
     b. The external ear in mammals has a pinna for collecting the sounds.

  c. In the cochlea of the inner ear, acoustical receptors in the form of hair cells respond to pressure waves transmitted through the surrounding fluid.

   1) Impulses are sent along the auditory nerve to the brain for interpretation.

   2) The hair cells in the organ of Corti of the human ear can be permanently damaged by prolonged exposure to intense sounds.

 D. The Sense of Balance

  1. The sense of balance depends on the organs of equilibrium located in the inner ear.

  2. The vestibular apparatus is a closed system of fluid-filled sacs and canals inside the ear.

   a. The *otolith organs* detect linear movements of the head (static equilibrium).

   b. Cristae located in the *semicircular canals* detect changing movements (dynamic equilibrium) when fluid bends hair cells attached to sensory neurons.

   c. Overstimulation of the hair cells of the vestibular apparatus can result in motion sickness.

Suggestions for Presenting the Material

- One of the most effective comparisons of the nervous system to anything made by humans is to the worldwide telephone network. Although the analogy is not perfect, it does convey the truth that billions of individual phone sets can send impulses that communicate with any other phone, or several phones at one time, via a connecting wire or microwave signal.

- Students ranging in scientific expertise from that of beginning freshman to third-year medical student all agree that the nervous system is one of the most difficult to comprehend at any level. Therefore, extra time and thorough explanations are especially needed for this topic.

- The function of the neuron membrane in permitting passage of Na^+ and K^+ ions is at first confusing. Initially you may wish to focus on sodium only, then briefly expand to the role of potassium.

- The changes in the membrane can be conveniently demonstrated using Figure 25.4 and the words *polarized* (no gates are open), *depolarized* (action potential is initiated), and *repolarized* (sodium gates are closed in preparation for another stimulation).

- The concept of "all-or-nothing" events and "thresholds" can be illustrated by describing the use of a firearm. When the trigger is pulled and reaches the critical point (threshold) at which the hammer is released, the bullet leaves the barrel and travels the expected distance. Of course, the bullet either goes or stays (all-or-nothing), and the manner by which the trigger is activated (slowly or quickly) should not influence the speed of bullet travel.

- Another device for illustrating "all-or-nothing" events (and certainly a lot safer than the one above) is an ordinary light switch. If your classroom has more than one switch, you can point out that each switch either turns a bank of lights ON or OFF; there is no such thing as "half-on." Furthermore, by moving more switches to ON, more lights are turned on (summation)

- Emphasize the temporary nature of the acetylcholine bridge across the synapse by comparing it to a pontoon bridge used by the military to cross small streams and rivers.

- If the students can recite the sequence of structures through which an impulse passes during a *reflex arc*, such as in Figure 25.9, they have a good grasp of the nerve conduction pathways. Add the ion flow across the membranes and the story is pretty well complete!

- Emphasize the difference between a neuron and a nerve. Students often have difficulty distinguishing between them.

- Prepare a transparency of an action potential recording. While projecting it on a screen, describe how the different regions of the tracing are related to the flow of sodium and potassium ions.

- Although Figure 25.10 does not present the body orientation sufficient to show it, you may wish to emphasize the difference between the *ventral* nerve cord of invertebrates and the *dorsal* one of vertebrates.

- Because both *notochord* and *nerve cord* are presented in this chapter, it is important to distinguish the former as a member of the support system of the body (notice spelling CHord as in CHORData).

- The division of the human nervous system into component parts, as presented in Figure 25.11 and accompanying text, is of course an arbitrary one. You should emphasize the "oneness" of the system. The divisions are really ones made by humans who need to study the interrelated functions.

- Some terms used to describe the divisions are not parallel. For example, *autonomic* (not a misspelling of "automatic," as some students think) is used to designate nerves NOT under voluntary control, and *somatic* is used to designate nerves under voluntary control.

- If this is your first use of the word *antagonistic,* you may want to remove any negative connotations students have attached to the word during regular conversational use. Tell them there are several instances where body homeostasis is maintained by antagonistic nerves, hormones, and muscles.

- You might be surprised at the number of students who cannot distinguish the backbone (vertebral or spinal column) from the spinal cord. Give them some assistance by referring to Figure 25.14.

- Emphasize the continuity of fiber tracts between brain and spinal cord. Stress the primary functions of the spinal cord as a reflex center versus the brain as a sense-interpretation and directed-response center.

- Students generally find it easier to distinguish between the sympathetic and parasympathetic divisions of the autonomic nervous system if they are told that the sympathetic division is involved in mobilizing "fight-or-flight" reaction, while the parasympathetic division produces a general "slowing-down" and "business as usual" response.

- The extent to which each instructor requires the students to delve into brain regions and functions will vary. Some instructors may want to select the major brain regions (cerebrum, hypothalamus/pituitary, cerebellum, and medulla) for special emphasis.

- The material on drugs is certainly timely but can be assigned for reading only, if time is short.

- The portion of the chapter covering sense organs presents information that your students will find more familiar because of previous exposure to the material. Most junior and senior high school health and biology classes provide a fair introduction to the sensory organs.

- Assuming your students do possess basic knowledge of the senses, it remains for you to emphasize two areas. The first is to relate the sense receptor and its interpretation within the brain. This is the subject of the initial portion of the chapter. The second is to provide some depth to the students' understanding of sensory receptor mechanisms.

- Two of the more difficult questions beginning students pose are: "How do I distinguish, say, sight from sound?" and "How do I perceive varying intensities of a stimulus?" Emphasize the role of the brain as an interpreter of impulses directed to specific regions by specialized receptors. Also point out that the frequency of action potentials and the number of axons that "fire" provide the quality we call "intensity" of stimulus.

- Each of the senses provides unique input. Try to draw distinctions between those that operate rather independently (for example, sight) and cooperatively (for example, taste and smell).

- As you describe each sense, you should describe the structure of the sense organ, the mechanism of stimulus reception, and the interpretation of that stimulus. For example, the eye perceives light by reaction with chemicals on the retina to give the sensation of degrees of light and color.

- Be sure to point out to the students that light coming into the eye must pass through several neuronal layers before it reaches the rods and cones. They generally get this backwards. Refer them to Figure 25.29.
- Students frequently have difficulty understanding how contraction of the ciliary muscles causes the suspensory ligaments to relax and the lens of the eye to thicken. It is the opposite of what they expect. Explain how the contraction of these muscles essentially lessens the circumference of the circle of processes to which the suspensory ligaments are attached. As a result the ligaments relax.

Classroom and Laboratory Enrichment

- The concept of thresholds and all-or-nothing events can be demonstrated by using dominoes (or for large classes, several audio cassette cases). Line up about 20 dominoes placed on end and spaced about one inch apart. Ask a student to gently touch one end domino to begin the progressive fall. Emphasize that the student's touch (threshold stimulus) caused a standing row (polarized) to begin falling (depolarization) at a constant speed (all-or-nothing event). Pose the following question (and demonstrate the answer): Would a greater and faster stimulus cause more rapid falling? To demonstrate *repolarization,* a second student could begin resetting the dominoes even before the falling is complete.
- Arrange with a physics student or an instructor for a demonstration of an action potential as recorded on an oscilloscope screen.
- Permit students to demonstrate the knee jerk reflex arc by use of percussion hammers. It is important to ask the subjects to close their eyes to prevent "cheating."
- Show a film or video of an animation of nerve impulse transmission.
- Exhibit models of neurons and neuroglial cells.
- Use models of *Hydra,* earthworm, grasshopper, and starfish to demonstrate nervous system development.
- Many laboratories have preserved specimens of the human or other vertebrate brain, which are valuable aids to comprehending the size and arrangement of brain parts.
- Using live *Hydra* and *Dugesia* (planaria), test for nervous response to touch, vibration, light, mild acid or alkali, and heat. Are there differences between the two species with respect to degree and speed of response?
- After obtaining the proper permission, if necessary, design a series of experiments to show the effects of beverage alcohol on mental function. Begin with a simple memory test using flash cards, or a before-and-after writing sample. Compare persons of different gender, body weight, and drinking habits.
- Use a dissectible model of the brain to illustrate the location of its parts.
- Exhibit a vertebral column/spinal cord/herniated disc model to demonstrate why so much pain and functional loss are associated with herniated discs.
- Show a film or video on brain function.
- Use a spinal cord/vertebral column cross-sectional model to illustrate the relation between the two structures.
- The simple detection of taste by a blindfolded person is still a student favorite. Ask volunteers to hold their nose and close their eyes while drops of various liquids (vinegar, onion, lemon, and so on) are placed on the tongue. Ask them to identify the substances, but without responding until you have repeated the experiment with the students using *both* smell and taste receptors.

- If your lecture room or laboratory can be sufficiently darkened, you can demonstrate the abilities of rods and cones by a simple demonstration. Pull the shades and turn out the lights, quickly pull a red cloth from your pocket, and ask students to identify the color. Substitute other colors, change the light intensity, and wait for iris accommodation as variations in the protocol.

- A very simple and dramatic example of sensory interpretation can be demonstrated by the following: Tell your students that the brain can be tricked into seeing *light* when in fact it is experiencing *pressure*. Simply have the students close their eyes and press gently on their eyelids. They should see small flashes of light (the so-called "stars" received from a bump on the noggin). Point out that they are not seeing actual light because their eyes are closed, but the brain interprets the signals coming in on the optic nerve as "light" because that is what is expected from the eye.

- Attempt to find film footage or photo stills of the highly successful evasive maneuvers that moths are able to make by detecting bat echolocation signals. It is truly a remarkable performance!

- One of the usual practices in optometrists' offices is to take instant photos of the retina. Ask for permission to make 2 x 2 transparencies of several photos, perhaps some exhibiting defects, and show them to the class. If the doctor will speak to the class, even better!

- A model of a cross-section through the organ of Corti is an excellent aid to comprehending this rather complex structure.

- Use dissectible models of the ear and eye to illustrate their structure.

- Use a Snellen chart to demonstrate the visual acuity test.

- If available, have the students use the Ishihara color charts for colorblindness. They enjoy this.

- Demonstrate the use of the ophthalmoscope for viewing the retina.

- Demonstrate the use of the otoscope for viewing the tympanic membrane.

Impacts, Issues Classroom Discussion Ideas

- Why are teenagers and young adults so susceptible to taking recreational drugs such as ecstasy?

- Do you think persons at a "rave" even know what drugs they might be taking?

- Would an education campaign about the dangers of ecstasy have any deterrent effect on young "ravers"?

Additional Ideas for Classroom Discussion

- What would be the result(s) of demyelination of axons such as occurs in multiple sclerosis?

- Upon hearing that salt was not good for him, a freshman college student began a fanatical program to eliminate all sodium chloride from his diet. By cooking his own meals, he was able to eliminate virtually all sodium. What complications could he expect as a result of his brash action?

- If neurons operate under the all-or-nothing principle, how are we able to distinguish soft sounds from loud sounds, or a gentle touch from a crushing blow?

- To most amateur musicians, the playing of 16th notes is a challenge, but to trumpet virtuoso Wynton Marsalis, 32nd and 64th notes are a breeze. Describe the action of nerves and tongue muscles that regulate the air flow through the mouthpiece.

- Why does a physician's tapping of the knee or elbow reveal the general status of the nervous system *in general*, not just the condition of those two joints?

- Why does saltatory ("jumping") conduction "afford the best possible conduction speed with the least metabolic effort by the cell"?
- Why does drinking large amounts of coffee or other caffeine-containing beverages tend to make a person "nervous" or "jittery"?
- Do invertebrates, such as the cockroach, feel pain?
- How do invertebrate nervous systems differ from vertebrate ones *structurally*?
- The central nervous system and closely associated ganglia house the cell bodies of neurons. As opposed to the peripheral axons and dendrites, the cell bodies are not regenerated after traumatic injury. What advantages and disadvantages does this structural arrangement pose for humans?
- Why does a small speck of food stuck between your teeth feel like a large chunk when rubbed with your tongue?
- The exact mode of action of the famous, and now banned, insecticide DDT has never been elucidated (after nearly 50 years of research). However, textbooks describe it as a "central nervous system" poison. What does this imply?
- Explain why elderly people may be unable to remember what they ate for breakfast but can relate the details of a teenage romance.
- Discuss the characteristics of brain disorders such as Parkinson's disease and Alzheimer's disease.
- Distinguish between flaccid and spastic paralysis. What are their causes?
- Why is it that the tastiest foods are bland and flat when eaten by a person with a bad head cold?
- It's trivia quiz time; name the sense that:
  a. is most easily fatigued (thank goodness!)
  b. cannot be shut out easily
  c. uses small bones
  d. can be dulled by smoking
  e. has more receptors in more places
  f. operates like a camera
- Sometimes musicians are said to have a "trained ear." What does this expression really mean?
- What is the advantage to an insect of having a compound eye?
- Why do many persons in their mid-forties need to use bifocal lenses?
- Is there any scientific basis to that "carrots are good for your eyes" slogan?
- What is "motion sickness"? How can it be controlled?
- In our "civilized" world, many people experience hearing loss as a result of aging, a condition called presbycusis. A study revealed that this condition did not exist in a primitive Sudanese tribe, the Mebans. This study suggests that some environmental factor of the civilized world is responsible for this type of deafness. What is that factor?

How Would You Vote? Classroom Discussion Ideas

- Monitor the voting for the online question. In many parts of the United States, there is tendency on the part of the general public to see jail as the solution to all of society's offenders. Logic should tell the person that is sensitive to reason that we cannot lock up everyone, and even if we could, is it a reasonable solution? Rehab programs for nonviolent drug offenders should be the first course of treatment. If successful, great, a life is saved. If not, then we could look at jail time.

Term Paper Topics, Library Activities, and Special Projects

- The neurons of the human body can communicate with one another much the same as telephones in your city can intercommunicate. In the telephone system, wires touch wires to pass the impulse, but neurons are not directly "wired." Investigate the effects on the body of the elimination of synapse function such as would be caused by organophosphate pesticides, which inhibit acetyl-cholinesterase.

- One of the most effective antidotes for the organophosphate poisoning referred to above is *atropine.* Investigate its mechanism of action. Based on what you find, could administration of atropine be harmful if OP poisoning *has not* occurred?

- Prepare a list of neurological disorders in which you focus on the specific cause of the difficulty in each case.

- Ask a resource person to explain the consequences of central nervous system damage as opposed to peripheral damage.

- Investigate some of the factors that determine the speed at which an impulse is conducted in a neuron.

- Why are injuries to the central nervous system, such as gunshot wounds, more permanently debilitating than those to the peripheral system?

- What is the basis for "healing" accomplished by the practice of chiropractic? What are its strengths and weaknesses?

- Using the mode of action of organophosphate insecticides as a tool, delve into the similarities and differences between the physiology of insect and human nerve function.

- Prepare an argument for the suppression of a presently readily-available drug, say, alcohol; or prepare an argument for the legalization of marijuana.

- Explore the research relating dreams to actual events—past and future. What do dreams tell us about ourselves?

- Discuss the basis for the use of acupuncture for relieving pain or providing anesthesia.

- Research the "gate theory" of pain transmission.

- Investigate the use of biofeedback for controlling pain, heart rate, and other autonomic functions.

- Scientists are gathering increasing amounts of evidence from laboratory studies and human testing that show gradual hearing loss caused by exposure to highly amplified music. Report on the dangers—are they real or imagined?

- One of the most intriguing subjects is the phenomenon of "phantom" pain. Explore its manifestations.

- Based on your library research, prepare an "awards" list for the animal group that exhibits the keenest of each of the five major senses (sight, hearing, smell, taste, touch).

- How do local anesthetics block the sensation of pain?

- Describe the various problems associated with vision that are correctable with lenses, surgery, drugs, or other means.

- How can animals such as fly larvae (maggots) respond to and move away from light when they have no eyes of any kind?

- How does a detector device that checks blood vessel patterns in the eye and compares them to known records provide a better security system for military installations than do fingerprints?

- Radial keratotomy, a surgical procedure for correcting myopia, is controversial. What does this procedure involve and what are the pros and cons of its use?

- Investigate the differences between sensorineural deafness and conductive deafness.

Possible Responses to *Critical Thinking* Questions

1. The argument against eating beef has some merit. Certainly one cannot be infected with the prions of vCJD, which might be in tainted beef, if one does NOT consume any such meat. Perhaps it is analogous to the arguments for abstinence from intercourse as a sure-fire way to prevent pregnancy. But in today's society avoiding beef is not easy, just as avoiding sex is not easy. So most persons just minimize the risks to the point where they have convinced themselves they can "live with it."

2. All too often we think of babies as miniature adults; they are not. The undeveloped blood-brain barrier is one good example. The adult body can process perfectly normal hormones, amino acids, ions, etc. even if their concentrations vary somewhat to the high side. Even the "baddies" such as alcohol, caffeine, and nicotine can be detoxified. But to the susceptible fetus and newborn, any of these substances could enter the brain in concentrations capable of causing damage. So a conscientious mother would limit her indulgences for the health of her unborn baby. And both parents would be careful in the foods they provide to their newborn.

3. The length of neuron cells, especially the axons, presents some challenges. The most obvious one is the inability of mature neurons to undergo mitosis. It is physically impossible for a cell that stretches several meters down a giraffe's neck to undergo the process of cell division. Other difficulty might be supplying nutrition to such a "strung out" cytoplasm, but this seems to have been overcome.

4. Evidently, birds of prey, such as owls and hawks, are better at seeing prey beneath them when flying because of the arrangement of the retina in the eye.

5. The toxin of this frog is similar in structure to acetylcholine, which means it could bind to the postsynaptic receptors in humans. However, it might not be degraded by acetylcholinesterase, which would cause continuous transmission of impulses across the synapse, leading to death.

26

ENDOCRINE CONTROL

Chapter Outline

Objectives

1. Know the general mechanisms by which molecules integrate and control the various metabolic activities in organisms.
2. Differentiate the modes of action of steroid and peptide hormones.
3. Understand how the neural-endocrine center controls secretion rates of other endocrine glands and responses in nerves and muscles.
4. Give classic examples of the effects of hyposecretion and hypersecretion of selected hormones.
5. Know how sugar levels are regulated by hormones.

Key Terms

signaling molecules
neurotransmitters
local signaling
  molecules
prostaglandins
nitric oxide
hormones
endocrine glands
endocrine system
steroid hormones
amine hormones
peptide hormones
protein hormones
androgen insensitivity
  syndrome
second messenger
cyclic AMP
hypothalamus
pituitary gland
posterior lobe
anterior lobe
antidiuretic hormone,
  ADH

oxytocin
releasers
inhibitors
adrenocorticotropin,
  ACTH
thyroid-stimulating
  hormone, TSH
follicle-stimulating
  hormone, FSH
luteinizing hormone,
  LH
prolactin, PRL
growth hormone, GH
  (somatotropin, STH)
pituitary gigantism
pituitary dwarfism
acromegaly
thymus
thymosins
thyroid gland
thyroxin
triiodothyronine
negative feedback

thyroid-releasing
  hormone (TRH)
goiter
hypothyroidism
parathyroid glands
parathyroid hormone,
  PTH
rickets
adrenal cortex
cortisol
aldosterone
corticotropin releasing
  hormone (CRH)
adrenal medulla
norepinephrine
epinephrine
Cushing syndrome
pancreas
exocrine
endocrine
pancreatic islet
alpha cells
glucagon

beta cells
insulin
delta cells
somatostatin
diabetes mellitus
type 1 diabetes
type 2 diabetes
gonads
testes
ovaries
estrogen
progesterone
testosterone
puberty
libido
pineal gland
melatonin
biological clock
seasonal affective
  disorder, SAD

Lecture Outline

Hormones in the Balance
A. Pesticides may be endocrine disrupters.
    1. In lab experiments the herbicide atrazine caused tadpoles to develop both male and female reproductive organs.
    2. Male alligators exposed to pesticide spilled into a Florida lake had reduced testosterone levels and small penises.
B. It is very controversial, but some investigators believe that chemicals in the environment are contributing to earlier onset of puberty and low sperm counts in humans.

26.1   Hormones and Other Signaling Molecules
A. Categories of Signaling Molecules
    1. Signaling molecules are hormones and secretions that can bind to target cells and elicit in them a response.
    2. There are four main types of signaling molecules:
        a. *Hormones* are secreted from endocrine sources and some neurons, and are then transported by the blood to remote targets.
        b. *Neurotransmitters* are secreted from neurons and act on immediately adjacent target cells for a short time.
        c. *Local signaling molecules* are secreted from cells of many different tissues; they act locally and are swiftly degraded.

d. *Pheromones,* which are secreted by exocrine glands, have targets outside the body; they integrate social activities between animals.
B. How Hormones Exert Their Effects
  1. Hormone action involves three steps:
    a. activation of a receptor as it reversibly binds the hormone,
    b. transduction, or conversion of a hormonal signal into a molecular form that can work inside the cell, and
    c. functional response of the target cell.
  2. Intracellular Receptors
    a. *Steroid hormones,* assembled from cholesterol, are lipid-soluble and therefore cross plasma membranes readily.
    b. Steroids stimulate or inhibit protein (especially enzyme) synthesis by switching certain genes on or off.
      1) They easily diffuse through the lipid bilayer of the plasma membrane, bind to chromosomal proteins in the nucleus, and then activate transcription.
      2) Testosterone is the male hormone, with receptors throughout the body; however, in androgen insensitivity syndrome, none of the target cells respond correctly, so the XY individual develops female characteristics.
  3. Plasma Membrane Receptors
    a. *Peptide hormones* include peptides, polypeptides, and glycoproteins.
    b. All peptide hormones issue signals at a receptor located on the target cell's membrane.
      1) First, the receptor binds to the peptide hormone because it cannot pass into the cell as steroid hormones do.
      2) The hormone-receptor complex stimulates the production of cyclic AMP, a "second messenger," which amplifies the signal by activating numerous enzymes.
C. Variations in Hormone Action
  1. The effect that any particular hormone has upon a cell depends on the blood concentration of that hormone, any interactions of this and other hormones, and the effect of other signaling molecules in the body.
  2. The effect of a hormone also depends on the receptors on the various cells it contacts.

26.2   The Hypothalamus and Pituitary Gland
A. The hypothalamus and pituitary gland work jointly to exert wide-ranging control over body functions.
  1. The hypothalamus is a portion of the brain that monitors internal conditions and emotional states.
  2. The pituitary is a pea-sized gland connected to the hypothalamus by a stalk.
    a. The posterior lobe of the pituitary consists of nervous tissue and releases two neuro-hormones made in the hypothalamus.
    b. The anterior lobe consists of glandular tissue and secretes six hormones and controls the release of others.
B. Posterior Pituitary Secretions
  1. The axons of neuron cell bodies in the hypothalamus extend down into the posterior lobe of the pituitary.
  2. Two hormones are released into the capillary bed:
    a. Antidiuretic hormone (ADH) acts on the walls of kidney tubules to control the body's water and solute levels.

b. Oxytocin triggers uterine muscle contractions to expel the fetus and acts on mammary glands to release milk.

C. Anterior Pituitary Secretions
   1. The anterior lobe releases six hormones that stimulate ("tropic") other endocrine glands:
      a. *Adrenocorticotropin* (ACTH) stimulates the adrenal cortex.
      b. *Thyroid-stimulating hormone* (TSH) stimulates the thyroid gland.
      c. *Follicle-stimulating hormone* (FSH) stimulates egg formation in females and sperm formation in males.
      d. *Luteinizing hormone* (LH) also acts on the ovary to release an egg and on the testes to release sperm.
      e. *Prolactin* acts on the mammary glands to sustain milk production.
      f. *Growth hormone* (GH), or *somatotropin* (STH), acts on body cells in general to promote growth.
   2. The hypothalamus produces releaser and inhibitor hormones that target the anterior pituitary.

D. Abnormal Pituitary Outputs
   1. The body does not produce large quantities of each hormone.
   2. But experience has shown that the amounts, no matter how tiny, are critical to normal body functioning.
      a. In childhood, too little STH can cause pituitary dwarfism, while too much causes gigantism.
      b. Oversecretion of STH in adulthood causes a thickening of skin and bones called acromegaly.

26.3   Thymus, Thyroid, and Parathyroid Glands
   A. The thymus gland lies beneath the sternum.
      1. Thymosins are necessary for the maturation of infection-fighting T cells.
      2. The thymus reaches its maximum size in adolescence, then shrinks, but continues to regulate immune function.
   B. Feedback Control of Thyroid Secretion
      1. The human thyroid gland lies at the base of the neck in front of the trachea.
      2. Its hormones, *thyroxine* and *triiodothyronine*, influence metabolic rates, growth, and development.
         a. Thyroid hormones are subject to negative feedback in which an increase or decrease in the concentration of a hormone triggers events that *inhibit* further secretion.
         b. If the amounts of iodine in the blood are too low, the pituitary responds by secreting too much TSH, causing the thyroid gland to enlarge abnormally in what we call a goiter.
         c. Thyroid deficiency, hypothyroidism, can disrupt development, slow growth, and delay sexual maturation.
   C. Parathyroid Glands and Calcium
      1. Four parathyroid glands are embedded in the thyroid gland and respond to the changing levels of calcium in the blood.
         a. A drop in calcium level causes *parathyroid hormone* (PTH) levels to rise, resulting in removal of calcium from bone and an activation of vitamin D (to help in calcium absorption from the gut).
         b. When calcium levels rise, the PTH levels are reduced.
      2. *Calcitonin* from the thyroid gland acts antagonistically to PTH and promotes deposition of calcium in bones.

26.4   Adrenal Glands and Stress Responses
    A. Negative feedback affects the adrenal cortex.
        1. One adrenal gland is located on top of each kidney.
        2. Among the secretions of the adrenal cortex are the glucocorticoids, such as cortisol, which
            help control blood glucose levels.
            a. When blood levels of glucose fall (as in hypoglycemia), the hypothalamus releases
                CRH — —> anterior pituitary — —> ACTH — —> adrenal cortex — —> cortisol, which
                helps maintain the blood level of glucose to fuel cellular respiration.
            b. When the body is stressed, as in painful injury, the nervous system provides an over-
                ride mechanism in which the levels of cortisol remain high to promote healing.
    B. The adrenal medulla responds to signals via the sympathetic nervous system.
        1. The inner medulla portion secretes *epinephrine* and *norepinephrine.*
        2. Its secretions mobilize the body during times of excitement or stress ("fight-or-flight"
            response).

26.5   The Pancreas and Glucose Homeostasis
    A. The pancreas is a dual function gland.
        1. Its exocrine function is to secrete digestive enzymes.
        2. Certain cells within the pancreas have an endocrine function:
            a. Alpha cells secrete *glucagon,* which causes glycogen stored in the liver to be converted
                to glucose, raising its levels in the blood.
            b. Beta cells secrete *insulin,* which stimulates the uptake of glucose by liver, muscle, and
                adipose to reduce glucose levels in the blood, especially after a meal.
            c. Delta cells secrete *somatostatin,* which can inhibit the secretion of glucagon and
                insulin.
    B. Diabetes Mellitus
        1. Diabetes mellitus is a disease resulting from imbalances of insulin; its effects include
            weight loss, ketone production, water-solute problems, and possible death.
        2. In type 1 diabetes, insulin is no longer produced because the beta cells have been
            destroyed by an autoimmune response; treatment is by insulin injection.
        3. In type 2 diabetes, the insulin levels are near normal but the target cells cannot respond to
            the hormone; controlling diet is an effective treatment.

26.6   Hormones and Reproductive Behavior
    A. The Gonads
        1. The ovaries and testes both produce these steroid hormones: estrogens, progesterone, and
            testosterone—albeit in varying amounts depending on gender.
        2. Synthesis of sex hormones increases during puberty to influence the development of
            secondary sexual characteristics and promote gamete production.
    B. The Pineal Gland
        1. The pineal gland is a photosensitive organ located in the brain.
        2. It secretes melatonin, which serves as part of the timing mechanism known as the
            biological clock.
            a. In the absence of light, melatonin is secreted; thus in winter, high levels of the
                hormone are instrumental in suppressing reproductive activity in hibernating
                animals.
            b. Decreased melatonin secretion in humans might help trigger the onset of puberty.
            c. Persons with seasonal affective disorder (SAD) have increased levels of melatonin.

Suggestions for Presenting the Material

- The core of this chapter is the section describing the various endocrine glands, their secretions and functions.

- Other important topics include: signaling molecules, signaling mechanisms, and feedback loops.

- When discussing signaling mechanisms (Figure 26.2) emphasize the chemical nature of steroids (lipid-bilayer soluble) versus proteins (not lipid soluble) and the need for a second messenger, namely cyclic AMP.

- After suitable introductions have been made, there is no practical way to escape a presentation of the major glands and their secretions. Unfortunately, students soon recognize the "cataloging" approach and become restless. One solution is indicated below.

- Because the chapter contains excellent figures of the human endocrine glands (Figure 26.1) and the pituitary (26.3 and 26.4), these can be used to great advantage. This textbook does have the familiar "table of the hormones" (Table 26.3) but it is located at the *end* of the chapter.

- This chapter presents an array of new words—hormone names that are long and unfamiliar. As an aid to learning, subdivide the name and give the literal meaning of each portion, for example: adreno (adrenals), cortico (cortex), and tropic (stimulate).

- "Antagonism" is often mentioned in connection with the autonomic nervous system to describe the interaction of the sympathetic and parasympathetic nerves. Take this opportunity to point out antagonistic hormone pairs: calcitonin/parathyroid hormone; insulin/glucagon.

- Emphasize the necessity of learning both the hormone name and the abbreviation, which is often more commonly used than the name itself.

- Notice that even though the gonadal hormones are introduced here they are not discussed in detail until Chapter 27.

- Emphasize that the posterior pituitary gland does not synthesize the hormones it secretes.

- Point out that some organs function as both endocrine and exocrine glands.

Classroom and Laboratory Enrichment

- Human nature is such that students are very interested in the abnormalities that hyper- and hyposecretion of human hormones cause. You can stimulate interest in the total area of hormone control by showing photos of the physical manifestations of such imbalances.

- Ask a local health scientist or practitioner to report on his/her experiences with hormone therapy.

- If a member of the class is willing to share his/her experiences as a diabetic, arrange for such a presentation before class begins and allow time for questions.

- Seek evidence of a class member who has experienced or witnessed an epinephrine-mediated "emergency response." Ask him/her to report.

- Survey local grocery stores to determine the relative stocks of iodized and non-iodized salt. Are there implications for the unwary consumer?

- Use a dissectible mannequin or a dissected fetal pig to show the location of the various endocrine glands.

Impacts, Issues Classroom Discussion Ideas

- Discuss the possibility that the current high incidences of cancer and other catastrophic diseases are the result of chemicals that pervade our lives.

- If humans of *today* are dying of cancer and heart disease, what were the major diseases of 100 years ago?

- Compare the average age of longevity in the United States today with that of 100 years ago.

Additional Ideas for Classroom Discussion

- Beverage alcohol inhibits the action of ADH. How is this unseen physiological event evidenced during a night of bar-hopping?

- Do hormones occur only in vertebrates? Have you ever heard of "ecdysone" in insects?

- Why does insulin have to be administered by injection rather than orally?

- Using knowledge gained in a freshman biology class, an athlete decided he might be able to raise his blood sugar quickly by injecting glucagon. This attempt is doomed for what reasons?

- What is the possible connection between the pineal gland and puberty?

- Some hormones seem to be doing another's duties, for example: sex hormones from the adrenals, blood sugar control by epinephrine, and thyroxine regulation of growth. Why is this so?

- What are anabolic steroids? Why do some athletes use them? What are the dangers associated with their use?

- Oxytocin is commonly used to induce labor. How does it work?

- Why do certain hypoglycemics, who regularly ingest excessive amounts of sugar, frequently develop diabetes later in life?

- Untreated diabetes mellitus victims tend to be very thirsty and yet produce large volumes of urine. Why is this so?

How Would You Vote? Classroom Discussion Ideas

- Monitor the voting for the online question. The question of whether to continue to use agricultural chemicals in light of their possible negative effects is a huge one. Certainly, the cessation of use would have massive repercussions on agriculture. Would farmers be able to control weeds at a cost that would still allow a profit to be made on the crop? Would increased prices for weed control be passed on to the consumer?

Term Paper Topics, Library Activities, and Special Projects

- Discuss the ethical issues of administering somatotropin to persons of normal stature who wish to become "super athletes."

- Investigate and report on the fascinating discovery of the role of insulin by researchers Banting and Best.

- Select a major hormone and prepare an in-depth report on the abnormalities that may result from hypo- and hypersecretion.

- The role of hormones in insect development has been elucidated only in the past 40 years. Check an insect physiology text and prepare a chronology of this research.
- Report on current research designed to correct type 1 diabetes, which is the result of autoimmune responses.
- Investigate which human hormones are now being produced using genetic engineering methods.
- Discuss the reason aspirin is effective as an analgesic, a fever reducer, and an anti-blood-clotting agent.
- Research the differences between diabetes mellitus and diabetes insipidus.
- As children many of us were told that "sleeping makes you grow." Is there any scientific basis for this statement?

Possible Responses to *Critical Thinking* Questions

1. As with all experimental designs involving human subjects, this one will not have clearly designated treatment and control groups as would be possible with caged laboratory animals. That is, we cannot randomly select one group of children to be exposed to phthalates and another to be the unexposed control. And even if this were theoretically possible, the children of the two groups would not be completely clear of phthalate exposure as would be, say, mice raised in a "sterile" setting. So the best we can do is find a group of girls who are as homogenous as possible but with high phthalate exposure and compare them with similarly situated girls who have not been exposed. Now, I am not sure of the conditions that expose girls to high phthalates. This would have to be investigated and accounted for in the design. Perhaps the experiment could be extended in such a way as to take the highly exposed group and remove them from exposure to see if there is any reversal of the breast development.

2. In these cases of dwarfism it is known that the somatotropin (growth) hormone itself is not defective, just insufficient to produce normal height. So it is reasonable to assume that there is a breakdown in the production. Sure enough, the releasing hormone from the hypothalamus is not being received properly by the anterior pituitary gland due to a mutation in the gene for the receptor protein. Therefore, the anterior pituitary, which normally would be stimulated to release the proper amount of somatotropin, *cannot* do so, resulting in short stature.

3. When Maya injected too much insulin, she caused the levels of sugar in the blood to drop to abnormal levels, bringing on the classic symptoms that could lead to coma, even death. First, she injected glucagon, which is the hormone antagonist to insulin. This would act to convert glycogen stored in the liver to glucose and begin the restoration of the correct blood glucose level. However, this is not instantaneous; therefore, the EMTs administered dextrose (glucose) intravenously to speed the recovery.

27

REPRODUCTION AND DEVELOPMENT

Chapter Outline

Objectives

1. Understand how asexual reproduction differs from sexual reproduction. Know the advantages and problems associated with having separate sexes.
2. Describe early embryonic development and distinguish each: oogenesis, fertilization, cleavage, gastrulation, and organ formation.
3. Explain how a spherical zygote becomes a multicellular adult with arms and legs.
4. Describe the structure and function of the male and female reproductive tracts.
5. Be able to put the simultaneous events of the menstrual cycle in proper sequence.
6. Outline the principal events of fertilization and prenatal development.
7. Know the principal means of controlling human fertility.
8. Discuss the hypotheses of aging.

Key Terms

sexual reproduction	master genes	oviduct	spermicidal foam
asexual reproduction	homeotic genes	uterus	spermicidal jelly
budding	testes (sing.: testis)	myometrium	diaphragm
fragmentation	secondary sexual traits	endometrium	condoms
transverse fission	scrotum	cervix	intrauterine device
parthenogenesis	epididymis	vagina	birth control pill
internal fertilization	ejaculation	labia majora	birth control patch
yolk	vas deferens	labia minora	Depo-Provera
sperm	ejaculatory ducts	clitoris	Norplant
oocyte	urethra	menstrual cycle	morning-after pills
fertilization	penis	menstruation	in vitro fertilization
cleavage	semen	progesterone	spontaneous abortion
blastual	seminal vesicles	estrogen	induced abortion
blastomeres	prostate gland	menopause	sexually transmitted
blastocoel	bulbourethral glands	follicular phase	diseases
cytoplasmic localization	prostate cancer	ovulation	pelvic inflammatory
gastrulation	testicular cancer	luteal phase	disease (PID)
gastrula	seminiferous tubules	GnRH	human
ectoderm	spermatogonia	primary oocyte	papillomaviruses
endoderm	primary spermatocytes	zona pellucida	genital warts
mesoderm	secondary	secondary oocyte	trichomoniasis
organ formation	spermatocytes	polar bodies	chlamydia
selective gene	spermatids	corpus luteum	genital herpes
expression	sperm	coitus	gonorrhea
cell differentiation	Sertoli cells	erection	syphilis
growth and tissue	Leydig cells	orgasm	HIV/AIDS
specialization	testosterone	ovum	embryonic period
morphogenesis	luteinizing hormone,	abstinence	fetus
neural tube	LH	rhythm method	trophoblast
apoptosis	follicle-stimulating	withdrawal	inner cell mass
embryonic induction	hormone, FSH	douching	implantation
pattern formation	ovaries	vasectomy	extraembryonic
morphogens	oocytes	tubal ligation	membranes

amniotic cavity	placenta	anti-acne drugs	telomeres
amnion	primitive streak	fetal alcohol syndrome	telomerase
yolk sac	neural tube	labor	Werner's syndrome
allantois	spina bifida	oxytocin	helicase
chorion	somites	postpartum depression	
HCG	rubella	lactation	
chorionic villi	thalidomide	prolactin	

Lecture Outline

Mind-Boggling Births
A. Multiple births are becoming more common.
    1. The incidence has increased almost 60 percent in the past two decades.
    2. Fertility drugs and assisted reproduction technologies are partly responsible.
B. Multiple births are a concern to doctors.
    1. There is a greater risk of miscarriage, premature delivery, and surgical delivery.
    2. Multiple newborns usually have lower birth weights and higher mortality rates.

27.1   Methods of Reproduction
A. Sexual Versus Asexual Reproduction
    1. Sexual reproduction permits adaptation through variation but is biologically costly because the sexes are separate; animals must produce gametes and must find each other (usually) for fertilization to occur.
    2. Asexual reproduction by budding (example: sponge) or fission (example: flatworm) results in offspring identical to the parents; this is a useful strategy in stable environments.
    3. Some species can switch between sexual and asexual.
        a. In the summer, female aphids give birth to daughters by parthenogenesis, the development of offspring from unfertilized eggs.
        b. In autumn, males are produced and sexual reproduction yields genetically variable females.
B. Costs of Sexual Reproduction
    1. Reproductive timing must allow for male and female gametes to be available at nearly the same time.
        a. Sensory structures and hormonal controls must be precise in both parents.
        b. Seasonal cues and behavioral patterns must evoke a suitable response in both sexes.
    2. It is a challenging task to find and recognize a potential mate of the same species.
        a. Chemical signals and body color/patterns are useful.
        b. Males spend much energy in performing elaborate courtship rituals.
    3. Fertilization also comes at a cost with separate sexes.
        a. External fertilization in water requires large numbers of gametes.
        b. Internal fertilization requires an investment in elaborate reproductive organs, including the penis, to transfer sperm to the female.
    4. Energy is set aside for nourishing some number of offspring.
        a. Those eggs with little yolk must develop larval stages quickly.
        b. Others, such as birds, have adequate food reserves for a more lengthy development within the shell.

c. Some eggs, such as those of humans, have no yolk; the embryo must be nourished with energy molecules drawn from the mother.

27.2   Processes of Animal Development
    A. There are six stages of animal reproduction and development:
        1. *Gamete formation* is the formation of eggs or sperm within each parent.
        2. *Fertilization* begins when a sperm penetrates an egg and is completed when the sperm nucleus fuses with the egg nucleus, resulting in formation of the zygote.
        3. Repeated mitotic divisions—*cleavage*—convert the zygote to numerous, small blastomeres whose fate is determined by cytoplasmic localization.
        4. *Gastrulation* results in three germ layers, or tissues:
            a. Ectoderm is the outer layer; it gives rise to the nervous system and the outer layers of the integument.
            b. Endoderm is the inner layer; it gives rise to the gut and organs derived from it.
            c. Mesoderm is the middle layer; muscle, organs of circulation, reproduction, excretion, and skeleton are derived from it.
        5. *Organ formation* begins as germ layers subdivide into populations of cells destined to become unique in structure and function.
        6. During *growth and tissue specialization*, organs acquire specialized chemical and physical properties.
    B. How Tissues and Organs Form
        1. Tissues and organs form in a programmed, orderly sequence called morphogenesis.
            a. Morphogenesis is the organization of differentiated cells into tissues and organs; it is the result of several events.
            b. Cells in various lineages divide, grow, migrate, and alter their size and shape.
        2. Some cells migrate along prescribed routes.
            a. When they reach their destination, the cells make connections with others already there.
            b. This is seen in the establishment of neural networks.
        3. Sheets of cells expand, and some fold inward and outward.
            a. Microtubules elongate and microfilaments constrict in ways that change cell size and shape.
            b. The neural tube, forerunner of the brain and spinal cord, is formed this way.
        4. Cell deaths help sculpt body parts.
            a. Controlled cell death, called apoptosis, is the genetically programmed elimination of tissues and cells that are used for only short periods in the embryo or adult.
            b. For example, humans develop with webs between the toes and fingers, but they are not born that way!
    C. Embryonic Induction
        1. During embryonic induction, the developmental fates of the embryonic cell lineages change when exposed to gene products from adjacent tissues.
            a. Clumps of cells develop into specialized tissues and organs in a process called pattern formation.
            b. Embryonic cells may produce and secrete signaling molecules that cause changes in the developmental fate of adjacent cells.
        2. Researchers have recently identified a class of signaling molecules called morphogens that serve as inducers as they diffuse from one group of cells to other cells, where they cause a developmental effect.

D. A Theory of Pattern Formation
  1. The formation of embryonic cells in ordered patterns starts with cytoplasmic localization and proceeds by gene-inspired cell-to-cell interactions.
  2. During development, classes of master genes are activated in orderly sequence at prescribed times.
  3. Products of homeotic genes and other master genes interact with control elements to map out the body plan.

27.3 Reproductive System of Human Males
  A. Human males have two testes, which produce sperm and sex hormones.
    1. The testes reside in the scrotum, which is a few degrees cooler than body temperature for proper sperm development.
    2. Sperm production begins during puberty, the stage when secondary sexual characteristics emerge.
  B. A Sperm's Journey
    1. Each testis contains many seminiferous tubules where sperm are continuously formed.
    2. Sperm move from a testis — —> epididymis (for maturation and storage) — —> vas deferens — —> ejaculatory ducts — — urethra (located inside the penis).
      a. The sperm-bearing fluid—semen—is formed by secretions from the seminal vesicles (fructose and prostaglandins) and the prostate (buffers against acidic vagina).
      b. The bulbourethral glands secrete a mucus-rich fluid into the vagina during sexual arousal.
  C. Cancers of the Prostate and Testes
    1. Prostate cancer is the second most common cancer among men.
      a. It is painless but can be detected early by a blood test for PSA.
      b. It can spread to other parts of the body.
    2. Testicular cancer is much less common but can also spread.
  D. How Sperm Form
    1. Diploid spermatogonia undergo mitosis — —> primary spermatocytes, which undergo meiosis I — —> haploid secondary spermatocytes, which undergo meiosis II — —> haploid spermatids — —> mature sperm.
      a. Sertoli cells in the tubule provide nourishment and chemical signals to the developing sperm.
      b. Each sperm has a head (nucleus and acrosome), midpiece (mitochondria), and tail (microtubules).
    2. Testosterone, produced by Leydig cells located between the lobes in the testes, stimulates spermatogenesis, the formation of reproductive organs and secondary sex characteristics, and helps to develop and maintain normal (or abnormal?) sexual behavior.
      a. Luteinizing hormone (LH) is released from the anterior pituitary (under prodding by GnRH from the hypothalamus) and stimulates testosterone production.
      b. GnRH also causes the pituitary to release FSH, which stimulates the production of sperm, beginning at puberty.

27.4 Reproductive System of Human Females
  A. The human female's primary reproductive organs are a pair of ovaries.
    1. The egg is released from the ovary — —> oviduct — —> uterus (zygote will implant in its lining, the endometrium).
    2. The lower part of the uterus is the cervix, which extends into the vagina, which in turn leads to the outer vulva (labia majora, labia minora, and clitoris).

B. Overview of the Menstrual Cycle
  1. Human females begin a recurring menstrual cycle at puberty.
  2. During each cycle an oocyte matures and escapes from the ovary, and (if it is fertilized) may implant in the endometrium; if there is no implantation, the uterine lining is sloughed at the end of each cycle of (approximately) 28 days.
  3. There are three major phases in the menstrual cycle:
     a. In the *follicular phase*, there is menstrual flow, endometrial breakdown and rebuilding, and maturation of the oocyte.
     b. *Ovulation* is the rather quick release of the oocyte from the ovary.
     c. During the *luteal phase*, the corpus luteum forms and the endometrium is primed for possible pregnancy.
C. Cyclic Changes in the Ovary
  1. At birth about 2 million immature eggs (primary oocytes) are already present and arrested in meiosis I.
  2. Of the approximately 300,000 oocytes still present at age seven, only about 400-500 will mature in a lifetime.
  3. The follicle consists of a layer of cells (granulosa) surrounding the primary oocyte; the granulosa cells gradually deposit a layer of material around the follicle.
  4. During the menstrual cycle, one oocyte resumes meiosis I to form a secondary oocyte and a polar body (both haploid).
  5. At about midcycle, there is a surge of LH that causes ovulation—the release of the secondary oocyte.
D. Cyclic Changes in the Uterus
  1. During the first half of the cycle, the hypothalamus signals the anterior pituitary to release LH and FSH, which in turn stimulate the ovary to secrete estrogen.
  2. The corpus luteum persists for about 12 days, secreting progesterone that inhibits further FSH and LH secretion.
  3. If fertilization does not occur, the corpus luteum degenerates, progesterone and estrogen levels fall, and FSH and LH are again secreted to begin another cycle.

27.5 How Pregnancy Happens
  A. Sexual Intercourse
    1. In male sexual arousal, the spongy tissue spaces inside the penis become filled with blood to cause an erection.
    2. During coitus, mechanical stimulation of the penis causes involuntary contractions that force semen out and into the vagina.
    3. Ejaculation of the male, and similar contractions in the female, are termed orgasm.
  B. Fertilization
    1. Of the 150 million to 350 million sperm deposited in the vagina during coitus, only a few hundred ever reach the upper region of the oviduct where fertilization occurs.
    2. Only one sperm will successfully enter the cytoplasm of the secondary oocyte after digesting its way through the zona pellucida.
       a. The arrival of that sperm stimulates the completion of meiosis II, which yields a mature ovum.
       b. The sperm nucleus fuses with the egg nucleus to restore the diploid chromosome number.
  C. Preventing Pregnancy
    1. Abstinence is most effective but probably unrealistic.

2. In the rhythm method, there is no intercourse during the days when an egg is capable of being fertilized.
3. Withdrawal before ejaculation would seem to be effective but is not.
4. Douching is similarly ineffective due to the speed with which sperm enter the uterus.
5. Surgery to cut and tie the oviducts (tubal ligation) or vas deferens (vasectomy) is effective and generally considered an irreversible method to prevent sperm and egg union.
6. Spermicidal foams and jellies are toxic to sperm but not reliable unless used in combination with a barrier device.
7. A diaphragm fits over the cervix and prevents entry of sperm into the uterus.
8. Condoms prevent sperm deposition in the vagina but must be used with care.
9. An intrauterine device (IUD) is implanted into the uterus, where it interferes with fertilization and implantation.
10. The birth control pill (and birth control patch) contains synthetic female hormones and prevents ovulation when taken faithfully according to directions.
11. Progestin injections (Depo-Provera) or implants (Norplant) inhibit ovulation over several months.
12. "Morning-after pills" intercept pregnancy by blocking fertilization or preventing implantation.

D. Seeking or Ending Pregnancy
1. In vitro fertilization is conception outside the body.
   a. Hormone injections prepare the ovaries for ovulation.
   b. The oocyte is withdrawn and a sperm injected into it.
   c. A few days later, a ball of cells is transferred to the woman's uterus for gestation.
2. Abortion is the termination of the development of an embryo, or fetus.
   a. A spontaneous abortion (miscarriage) occurs in about 10 percent of women who know they are pregnant and as many as 50 percent of eggs are aborted overall.
   b. Induced abortion is the deliberate termination of a pregnancy.

27.6 Sexually Transmitted Diseases
A. Consequences of Infection
1. Sexually transmitted diseases (STDs) infect about 15 million Americans each year.
2. The social consequences are enormous; women develop more complications (such as PID) than men.
B. Major Agents of STDs
1. HPV
   a. Human papillomavirus infection is the fastest growing STD in the U.S.
   b. Some strains cause genital warts; others can cause cervical cancer.
2. Trichomoniasis
   a. *Trichomonas vaginalis,* a protozoan, causes soreness and discharge from the vagina; males are usually symptom free.
   b. Untreated infections damage the urinary tract and invite HIV infection.
3. Chlamydia
   a. *Chlamydia trachomatis* causes the disease, with a particularly high incidence in teenagers—especially girls.
   b. It shows few symptoms but can lead to pelvic inflammatory disease.
4. Genital Herpes
   a. *Herpes simplex* virus can invade the mucous membranes of the mouth or genitals by direct contact.
   b. Blisters may form, disappear, and then reappear under stressful conditions.

5. Gonorrhea
   a. *Neisseria gonorrhoeae*, a bacterium, enters the body through mucous membranes during sexual intercourse.
   b. Because the initial symptoms are mild, treatment is often delayed, allowing the bacterium to multiply out of control.
6. Syphilis
   a. The spirochete *Treponema pallidum* enters the body from an infected sexual partner.
   b. Initially the spirochetes produce a localized ulcer that heals, but the organisms continue to multiply in the spinal cord, brain, eyes, bones, joints, and mucous membranes with serious consequences.
7. AIDS
   a. Infection by the human immunodeficiency virus (HIV) leads to AIDS, an incurable STD that leads to a complete breakdown of the immune system.
   b. Opportunistic infections are the eventual cause of death.
   c. HIV spreads by anal, vaginal, and oral intercourse as well as by intravenous drug use.

27.7   Human Prenatal Development
   A. Pregnancy lasts an average of 38 weeks.
      1. Blastocyst formation takes about two weeks.
      2. The embryonic period lasts from the third to the end of the eighth week.
      3. The fetal period extends from the ninth week until birth.
   B. Cleavage and Implantation
      1. During the first few days after fertilization, the zygote undergoes repeated cleavages as it travels down the oviduct.
      2. By the time it reaches the uterus, it is a solid ball of cells (morula), which is transformed into a blastocyst.
         a. The inner cell mass of the blastocyst is transformed into an embryonic disk that will develop into the embryo proper within the next week.
         b. Before the first week ends, the blastocyst contacts and adheres to the uterine lining; this is referred to as implantation.
   C. Extraembryonic Membranes
      1. The extraembryonic membranes inside a shelled egg (such as birds) are also formed in human development.
      2. The membranes and their functions are:
         a. The *amnion* is a fluid-filled sac that keeps the embryo from drying out and acts as a shock absorber.
         b. The *yolk sac* becomes a site for blood cell formation in humans.
         c. The *chorion,* a protective membrane around the embryo, forms a portion of the placenta and secretes a hormone (human chorionic gonadotropin) that maintains the uterine lining after implantation.
         d. The *allantois* does not function in waste storage (as it does in birds) but is active in blood vessel formation and formation of the urinary bladder.
   D. The Role of the Placenta
      1. The placenta is a combination of endometrial tissue and embryonic chorion.
      2. Materials are exchanged from blood capillaries of mother to fetus, and vice versa, by diffusion; the maternal blood and fetal bloods do not mix!

E. Emergence of the Vertebrate Body Plan
   1. By the third week of development, a two-layered disk consisting of ectoderm and endoderm has formed.
      a. The "primitive streak," a forerunner of the neural tube from which the brain and spinal cord will form, has appeared.
      b. Some cells also form the notochord, from which the vertebrae will form.
   2. Toward the end of the third week, mesoderm has developed and is giving rise to somites—segments of bones and skeletal muscles.
F. Emergence of Distinctly Human Features
   1. By the end of the fourth week the embryo has embarked on an intricate program of cell differentiation and morphogenesis, including development of limbs, circulation, and umbilical cord.
   2. The second trimester encompasses months four, five, and six; the individual is now called a fetus; the heart is beating; fuzzy hair (lanugo) covers the body.
   3. The third trimester extends from month seven until birth; the earliest delivery in which survival on its own is possible is the middle of this trimester.
G. Mother as Provider, Protector, Potential Threat
   1. Nutritional Considerations
      a. A well-balanced diet usually supplies the carbohydrates, lipids, and proteins that the embryo requires, but additional vitamins and minerals are required.
      b. Fetal organs are highly vulnerable to nutritional deficiencies.
   2. Risk of Infections
      a. IgG antibodies crossing the placenta from mother to child can protect against many bacterial infections.
      b. The viral disease rubella can cause improper organ development at certain critical periods in the fetus' life.
   3. Effects of Prescription Drugs
      a. Drugs must be carefully monitored during pregnancy.
      b. Tranquilizers, anti-acne drugs, even antibiotics cannot be taken.
   4. Effects of Alcohol
      a. Fetal alcohol syndrome symptoms include reduced brain size, mental impairment, slow growth, and heart defects.
      b. There is probably no "safe" drinking level.
   5. Effects of Cocaine
      a. Crack is especially disruptive to fetal brain development.
      b. The child may be of small stature and chronically irritated.
   6. Effects of Tobacco Smoking
      a. Toxic elements in tobacco smoke impair fetal growth, even if the smoke is secondhand.
      b. Infants of smokers have more heart abnormalities, are smaller, and have academic difficulty in school.

27.8   From Birth Onward
   A. The Process of Birth
      1. The birth process (labor) begins with contractions of the uterine muscles; the cervical canal dilates, and the amniotic sac ruptures.
         a. The hormone oxytocin induces powerful uterine contractions.
         b. The action of oxytocin on smooth muscles is an example of positive feedback.

2. The fetus is expelled accompanied by fluid and blood; the umbilical cord is severed; finally the placenta is expelled.

3. Corticotropin-releasing hormone affects the timing of labor and may contribute to postpartum depression.

B. Nourishing the Newborn

1. The mammary glands first produce a special fluid for the newborn; then, under the influence of prolactin, they produce milk.

2. Oxytocin is released in response to suckling and further increases the milk supply.

C. Postembryonic Development

1. The stages of postnatal development are: newborn (first 2 weeks) ——> infant (2 weeks to 15 months) ——> child (to 12 years) ——> pubescent (individual at puberty) ——> adolescent (from puberty to 3–4 years later) ——> adult.

2. Postnatal growth is most rapid between ages 13 and 19.

D. Why Do We Age and Die?

1. Perhaps genes regulate a "ticking clock" that indicates when the life of a cell is done.

a. One hypothesis is that cells can only divide a finite number of times.

b. Telomeres on the ends of chromosomes shorten during each round of mitosis, eventually signaling the end of a cell's life; cancer cells have an enzyme (telomerase) that causes telomeres to lengthen and thus continue cell division uncontrollably.

2. Another hypothesis is that the accumulation of damage at the molecular and cellular levels causes aging.

a. Perhaps aging is loss of the capacity for DNA to self-repair, or perhaps autoimmune responses intensify over time, producing increased vulnerability to disease and stress.

b. Environmental insults may play a powerful role.

Suggestions for Presenting the Material

- This chapter talks about development and the human reproductive system specifically. Although students will not be as familiar with the *general terms of reproduction* (sexual versus asexual), *development* (fertilization, cleavage, gastrulation, organogenesis, etc.), *growth, metamorphosis, differentiation, aging, and death,* they should have heard the names of most of the human reproductive structures. In fact many students may approach portions of this chapter with a sigh of relief and an attitude that says, "Finally, something I know everything about." The intuitive instructor will build upon what *accurate* information the students already know and will gently, but authoritatively, correct misinformation. This also prohibits any belittling of incomplete or inaccurate "folklore."

- Embryonic development is best demonstrated by use of a film or videotape (see the Enrichment section); but if these are not available, photos like those in Figure 27.5 can substitute, albeit not as well.

- The most abstract sections in this chapter include the topics of morphogenesis and pattern formation. These will require some inventive use of visual aids to convey the message.

- Aging is something your youthful class may not find of much interest now. But perhaps you can find some recent research tidbit on which to base your presentation of what is really a puzzling process.

- The sequence of topics concerning human reproduction is logically presented in the chapter: male and female structures, menstrual cycle, sexual union, fertility control, and prenatal development.

- The overhead transparencies of male and female reproductive systems should be in view of the students during your presentation.

- When comparing the male and female systems, it is helpful to note that the male produces and delivers sperm, much as the female produces and delivers eggs. However, the female also provides: (a) a site for fertilization, and (b) a site for embryonic and fetal development. This provides a convenient lead into the discussion of the menstrual cycle.

- The details of the menstrual cycle are of interest to both sexes but especially to females, of course. Because events are happening simultaneously in the pituitary, ovary, and uterus, it is almost a necessity to keep Figure 27.13 in constant view. The critical feature of this figure is the time line along the bottom, which puts all events into perspective.

- These points need emphasis in your lecture on female reproduction:
  a. Females are born with a finite number of eggs, which means eggs grow old (implications for causing genetic defects in offspring).
  b. Menstrual cycle can be defined as "the monthly release of an egg and all the preparations for it."
  c. Retention or sloughing of the endometrium is determined by progesterone levels at the end of the menstrual cycle.

- You may be able to surprise your students with the fact that only a few days of each month comprise the "fertile period." But hasten to inform your young "experimenters" that the fertile days can move around depending on a variety of nutritional, psychological, and health factors.

- Table 27.2 presents a good overview of human development. The specifics of each development in each time interval can lead to a "cataloging" approach, which can be alleviated by using the videotape referred to in the Enrichment section.

- The most practical aspect of the chapter is the section on control of human fertility. Students are eager for this information, especially when it can be presented with special reference to the mode of action of each device. It would probably be profitable for your students to have some indication of the relative effectiveness of the various methods.

- The topic of sexually transmitted diseases is also included in this chapter. Individual instructors may or may not wish to present this. But certainly some reference, even without details, should be made to the toll these diseases exact on society.

Classroom and Laboratory Enrichment

- If at all possible, show a videotape or film depicting development of some animal. Because of the dynamic nature of this process and the rapid changes, static photographs are woefully inadequate.

- Although it is not always convenient to do so, the demonstration of live chick embryos is a real attention-arresting sight. Don't neglect to place an embryo under a stereomicroscope to see the heartbeat and blood flow.

- The early development of sea urchin embryos is not as difficult to demonstrate as that of the chick. Biological supply houses sell demonstration kits. Timing is a critical factor for viewing all the stages, so you should plan to videotape the sequence.

- Because you probably teach students with a great range of sexual knowledge and experience, adjust your enrichment activities accordingly. For example, many students will appreciate observing birth control devices, or slide photos of them. Others may be intimately familiar with their use, or at least give that impression.

- The topic of prenatal development will be greatly enhanced by the use of a videotape such as *The Miracle of Life*, distributed by Crown Video through retail outlets.

- If you decide to present details of the physical manifestations of sexually transmitted diseases, use discretion in which slides you show.

- Students enjoy bragging about their sexual knowledge. Perhaps you can bring some perspective to this by preparing a true/false quiz of common facts and fallacies associated with human reproduction. Allowing the students to remain anonymous, administer the quiz prior to your lecture. Tabulate the results and report to the class as you give the accurate information.

Impacts, Issues Classroom Discussion Ideas

- Why do think the number of multiple births has increased so dramatically in the past 20 years?

- What are the risks of mothers in their forties and even fifties giving birth? Evaluate both the risk to the mother and the fetus/child.

- How many ways can you think of by which the increased number of multiple births results in increased costs to society?

- Will Americans ever agree to controls over fertility and reproduction as some other countries have?

Additional Ideas for Classroom Discussion

- What advantage(s) does asexual reproduction have over sexual union?

- Is there such a creature as a "female earthworm"? Explain your answer in anatomical terms.

- Some persons think the "yolk" of the chicken egg corresponds to the "nucleus." Is this true?

- Death is an unpleasant subject, but can you think for a moment about exactly what is death? How is death officially defined by doctors and coroners? Would their definition be different from that of a developmental biologist?

- The Old Testament records human life spans ranging in the hundreds of years. How can you rationally explain this?

- When an insect is in the pupal stage, seemingly there is no activity. Some people have even called it the "resting stage"—erroneously! Biochemically and histologically what is happening during the pupal stage?

- All animals reproduce at rates sufficient to maintain their populations. Humans are the only ones whose proliferation seems to be under very few limiting factors. Is this so? Why?

- The incidence of Down syndrome was said to increase with maternal age, especially for mothers over 40. Based on the information in the present chapter, can you present a possible reason why?

- Using anatomical terms, explain why men who have had a vasectomy operation are still able to expel normal amounts of semen, but containing no sperm.

- Explain the events that result in the production of identical and fraternal twins.

- What propels sperm from their point of origin to the opening where they exit the body?

- What mechanisms prevent the entry of more than a single sperm into the egg?

- The placenta supplements, or completely replaces, the activity of three organ systems in the fetus. What are they?

- Many communities, and even states, restrict or outright prohibit the teaching of human reproduction. Why do you think this body system is singled out over, say, digestion or respiration for such a prohibition?

How Would You Vote? Classroom Discussion Ideas

- Monitor the voting for the online question. As indicated in one of the questions in the *Impacts, Issues* section above, humans are very protective of their perceived right to reproduce. Of course, there is no such explicit right. Most persons just assume it is an unwritten, God-given right. But what if your right to have multiple children interferes with my right not to have to support them with my taxes and insurance premiums?

Term Paper Topics, Library Activities, and Special Projects

- Exciting progress is being made in research related to the aging process. Prepare a report on recent developments.

- Embryologists can transplant imaginal disks of insect larvae to produce *very* unusual adults, for example legs where antennae should be. Investigate the procedures used and the results produced. Could this be done in invertebrates?

- It is a curious, but real, fact that most sex crimes are committed by males. Investigate what psychologists and physicians say about the underlying cause(s) for this behavior.

- Sexual dysfunction is a frustrating situation for those involved, whether male or female. Prepare a list, based on your reading, of the most prevalent disorders and their treatment.

- We hear about "sperm banks" now and then. Do such repositories actually exist? Where are they? How do they function?

- Any interruption in the menstrual cycle, whether temporary or permanent, is cause for concern. Report on the causes and effects of the cessation of menstruation in females who drastically reduce their body weight (anorexia) or body fat (as in body building).

- Search for the physiological explanation for the cessation of menstruation (menopause)—usually when a woman is between the ages of 40 and 50. Is there any comparable phenomenon in men?

- It is known that overcrowding and stressful conditions reduce reproductive behavior in rodents. Is there any published evidence of such a phenomenon in humans?

Possible Responses to *Critical Thinking* Questions

1. The formation of somites is an indication of the segmentation that is to follow, especially the formation of the vertebrae and the enclosed spinal nerve cord.

2. As we can see from Figure 27.13, FSH from the pituitary gland stimulates the growth of follicles in the ovary, leading to the production of an ovum to be released mid-cycle. Usually the levels result in only *one* ovum in *one* ovary. But increased levels could cause more development leading to release of two ova, which if fertilized by sperm, could result in two zygotes—fraternal twins!

3. Wow, there are probably a number of factors that could explain male fertility decline, but I would guess that it lies in the age of the spermatogonial cells lining the seminiferous tubules. While it is true that the sperm produced from these cells are "fresh" (unlike the eggs), the spermatogonial cells that have been producing a continuous supply of sperm are the same ones that started producing during puberty.

4. There is good reason why rubella would cause so many of its effects on the fetus during the first trimester. It is during this time that the organs are developing; limbs form; toes and fingers are sculpted. Growth of the head surpasses that of other body regions.

5. The young armadillos are not identical to their parents because of sexual reproduction. The genes of one parent are not the same as those of the other parent and therefore the offspring are "recombinants." The fact that four of the siblings are genetically identical means that they had to come from the same zygote. Evidently, there was a separation of the blastomeres at an early stage into four separate groups, each of which developed into an individual organism.

28

POPULATION ECOLOGY

Chapter Outline

Objectives

1. Learn the language associated with the study of population ecology.
2. Understand the factors that affect population density, distribution, and dynamics.
3. Understand the meaning of the logistic growth equation and know how to calculate values for G by using the logistic growth equation. Understand the meaning of r_{max} and K.
4. Calculate a population growth rate (G); use values for natality, mortality, and number of individuals (N) that seem appropriate.
5. Use the equations for general population growth rate and the logistic growth equation.
6. Understand the significance and use of life tables; interpret survivorship curves.
7. Know the situation about the growth of human populations. Tell which factors have encouraged growth in some cultures and limited growth in others.

Key Terms

ecology
demographics
population size
age structure
pre-reproductive
reproductive
post-reproductive
reproductive base
population density
habitat
crude density
population distribution
clumped dispersion
nearly uniform
  dispersion

random dispersion
quadrats
capture-recapture
  method
births
immigration
deaths
emigration
migration
zero population growth
per capita
r, net reproduction per
  individual per unit of
  time
exponential growth

doubling time
J-shaped curve
biotic potential
limiting factor
carrying capacity
logistic growth
S-shaped curve
density-dependent
  controls
density-independent
  factors
life history pattern
cohort
life table
survivorship curves

family planning
  programs
total fertility rate
demographic transition
  model
preindustrial stage
transitional stage
industrial stage
post-industrial stage

Lecture Outline

The Human Touch

A. At one time as many as 15,000 people lived on Easter Island.

   1. The tiny island could not support this many people.
   2. Crop yields declined; soil nutrients were depleted.
   3. Large statues were erected to appease the gods.

B. The population dwindled as people turned against each other.

28.1 Characteristics of Populations

A. Ecology is the study of how organisms interact with one another and their physical environment.

B. Overview of the Demographics

   1. The *population size* is the number of individuals making up its gene pool.
   2. *Age structure* defines the relative proportions of individuals of each age—pre-reproductive years, reproductive, and post-reproductive.
   3. *Population density* is the number of individuals per unit of area or volume—the habitat.
   4. *Population distribution* refers to the general pattern by which the population members are dispersed through their habitat.
   5. The same area may be home to populations of a great number of different species, but these generally differ quite a bit in terms of their density.
      a. Crude density refers to the number of individuals in an area; it does not tell how the individuals are dispersed throughout the habitat.
      b. Variations in population density depend largely on ecological relationships among the species occupying the same area.
   6. Populations show three dispersion patterns.
      a. Members of a population living in clumps is very common for these reasons:
         1) Suitable physical, chemical, and biological conditions are patchy, not uniform.
         2) Many animals form social groups.
         3) Many offspring are not highly mobile and are forced to live "where they landed."

b. Uniform dispersion is rare in nature; when it does occur, it is usually the result of fierce competition for limited resources.

c. Random dispersion occurs in nature if environmental conditions are rather uniform in the habitat and members are neither attracting nor repelling each other.

C. Elusive Heads to Count

1. To determine the number of animals in a particular area you could try a full count to measure absolute density; this may be difficult especially with elusive animals such as deer.

2. You could divide up the area into smaller quadrats; count the number of deer in one quadrat and extrapolate the number for the whole area.

3. Because many animals migrate a lot, it may be better to use the capture-recapture method.

28.2 Population Size and Exponential Growth

A. From Zero to Exponential Growth

1. Population size is dependent on births, immigration, deaths, and emigration.

2. Population size may also change on a predictable basis as a result of daily or seasonal events called migrations.

3. *Zero population growth* designates a near balance of births and deaths.

4. Rate of increase (*r*) = net reproduction per individual per unit of time.

a. The growth rate formula is: $G = rN$.

b. A graphic plot of exponential growth results in a J-shaped curve that becomes steeper with advancing time.

c. As long as *r* is positive, the population will continue to increase at ever-increasing rates—easily measured by noting the "doubling time."

B. What Is the Biotic Potential?

1. The biotic potential of a population is its *maximum* rate of increase under ideal—nonlimiting—conditions.

2. The biotic potential varies from species to species because of three parameters:

a. at what age each generation starts reproducing,

b. how often reproduction occurs, and

c. how many offspring are born each time.

28.3 Limits on the Growth of Populations

A. What Are the Limiting Factors?

1. The *actual* rate of increase of a population is influenced by environmental conditions.

2. Limiting factors (nutrient supply, predation, competition for space, pollution, and metabolic wastes) are collectively known as the environmental resistance to population growth.

B. Carrying Capacity and Logistic Growth

1. The sustainable supply of resources defines the *carrying capacity* for a particular population in a given environment.

2. The carrying capacity can vary over time and is expressed graphically in the S-shaped curve pattern called *logistic growth*.

C. Density-Dependent Controls

1. The main density-dependent controls are competition for resources, predation, parasitism, and disease.

2. These factors exert their effects in proportion to the number of individuals present.

D. Density-Independent Factors
1. Some events, such as weather, tend to increase the death rate without respect to the number of individuals present.
2. Lightning, floods, snowstorms, and the like affect large populations as well as small groups.

28.4 Life History Patterns
A. Each species has a life history pattern that influences survival, fertility, and the age of first reproduction.
B. Life Tables
1. Life tables follow the fate of a group of newborn individuals (cohort) through their lives to calculate the survivorship schedule.
2. The number of offspring born to individuals in each age interval is also recorded.
C. Patterns of Survival and Reproduction
1. Survivorship curves are plots of the age-specific patterns of death for a given population in a given environment.
2. Most animals are characterized by one of these types of curves:
   a. *Type I* curve is typical of large mammals where few offspring are produced and cared for so that infant mortality is low; death usually comes after an extended life.
   b. *Type II* curve is typical of many animals where the chances of survival or death are about the same at any age.
   c. *Type III* curve indicates low survivorship, or conversely, high mortality in early life.
D. Evolution of Life History Traits
1. Reznick and Endler studied the differences in size and survival of guppies in Trinidad.
2. They discovered that the differences were genetically based and could change over time.

28.5 Human Population Growth
A. Notice these startling statistics:
1. The world population has surpassed 6.4 billion.
2. The annual rate of increase averaged 1.3 percent per year, which means that the birth rate continues to exceed the death rate, resulting in a larger absolute increase each year.
B. Why Have Human Populations Soared?
1. Humans expanded into new habitats and climate zones.
2. Agriculture increased the carrying capacity of the land to support humans and their animals.
3. Medical practice and improved sanitation conditions removed many population-limiting factors.
C. Fertility Rates and Family Planning
1. At the present rate of increase, the world human population should reach 8.9 billion by the year 2050.
2. The total fertility rate (TFR) is the average number of children born to women during their reproductive years, which is currently 2.8 children per female.
3. Even if the replacement level of fertility is achieved (about two children per woman), the human population will continue to grow for another 60 years.
4. Effective family planning programs can achieve a faster decline in birth rate than economic development alone.

D. Economics and Population Growth
   1. In the *demographic transition model,* changes in population growth are linked to four stages of economic development:
      a. In the *preindustrial stage,* living conditions are harsh, and birth and death rates are high; there is little increase in population size.
      b. In the *transitional stage,* living conditions improve, death rate drops, and birth rate remains high.
      c. In the *industrial stage,* growth slows.
      d. In the *post-industrial stage,* zero population growth is reached; birth rate falls below death rate.
   2. Some developed countries are in the industrial stage (examples: United States, Canada, Japan); some countries (example: Mexico) are in the transitional stage.
E. Environmental Impacts of Populations
   1. India has 15 percent of the world's human population; the United States only has 4.6 percent.
   2. But the U.S. uses 25 percent of the world's processed minerals and energy, and generates 25 percent of the global pollution and trash; India's numbers in these categories are a mere 3 percent.

Suggestions for Presenting the Material

- This is the second chapter in the book to discuss *populations.* Chapter 12 discussed the *genetics* of populations; the present one reports on the *ecology* of populations.

- It is time to return to Figure 1.1 for the "beginning of the end," as the individual cells and organisms are integrated into a complex natural order.

- The bulk of the chapter concerns general aspects of populations: density/distribution, dynamics, survival, and limits.

- Students will perhaps be most interested in studies of population as they affect human population growth, a subject well covered in this chapter. Examination of the changes in worldwide patterns of population growth since the turn of the century and in the last 20 years in particular will surprise students and highlight the overwhelming need for humans to find ways to control global population growth rate. The inclusion of human population growth studies in this chapter allows students to see that we are not exempt from the rules and limitations that govern all populations.

- Exploration of population ecology also sets the stage for interesting discussion of the socio-economic impacts of population growth and the ethical questions related to regulating population growth.

Classroom and Laboratory Enrichment

- Use flow charts on the board or on the overhead projector to show the relationships among the different components of an ecosystem.

- Select an ecosystem that consists of all or part of the campus or a nearby area. List as many of the biotic and abiotic components of that ecosystem as you can. Students could work in teams, with each team assigned to different ecosystem components.

- Graph the rates of population growth for several of the nations of the world. Discuss reasons for the differences between nations.

- Compare and contrast survivorship curves of different organisms. Ask students to first guess whether the organism you have named has a Type I, II, or III survivorship curve. Then use transparent overlays on the overhead projector to show survivorship curves for each species.

- Design and implement experiments examining the effects of resource availability, time lags, and competition on population densities of small organisms easily raised in the laboratory.

- Calculate population densities for a plant species in several small defined areas with varying environmental conditions. What pattern(s) of spatial distribution do you see? Identify factors that you believe might influence species distribution (some examples might be nutrient availability, amount of sunlight, moisture, and openings created by disturbance). Design experiments that would evaluate the role of each environmental factor in species distribution.

- Show overhead transparencies of age structure diagrams for human populations of different nations.

- If you review Figure 1.1, you may want to insert the concept of *biomes* as contained in Chapter 31.

- If you have a collection of slides, search for a scene that will include clearly visible examples of a population, the four participating groups in a community, an ecosystem, and the biosphere. As you project each slide, ask students to identify each element.

- Use the classroom and its occupants to illustrate density and distribution:
  - a. Head count......................................a. 50 students
  - b. Density..b. 50 students per room
  - c. Clumped distribution...................c. 50 students in rear half of room
  - d. Random distribution ....d. 50 students milling around before class begins
  - e. Uniform distribution ....e. 50 students in evenly spaced rows of chairs
  - f. Distribution over time ....f. 50 students disperse to all parts of campus after class

- Using the equations for expressing population dynamics, work through examples of problems gleaned from an ecology text.

- Show a copy of a life table as published in a modern entomology textbook. These are especially good examples because of the differential death rates in the various stages of metamorphosis.

- Stimulate interest in the future of HUMAN population dynamics by asking your class to vote on one of three possibilities (using Figure 28.6 as a guide):
  - a. The S-curve will not "flatten out" as it reaches a carrying capacity but will continue to climb indefinitely.
  - b. The curve will oscillate near the carrying capacity.
  - c. The curve will plunge downward in a "crash."

Impacts, Issues Classroom Discussion Ideas

- What factors *should* determine the carrying capacity of the planet Earth for humans? Do these actually operate? Do others operate instead?

- What *density-independent* factors influence the size of *insect* populations? Of these, which ones also limit *human* populations?

- Ask your students to think about the carrying capacity of the United States with regard to its human population. Do we know what that carrying capacity is? How much can we manipulate the environment to ensure that our nation will be able to support our population? What resources might be beyond our control?

- Discuss the pros and cons of government laws regulating family size. Do you think that nations with high rates of population growth should set a legal limit on the number of children a family may have? What are some of the consequences that can occur (for example, use of amniocentesis and abortion to ensure male children) when countries legislate family size?

- Why will the growth rate of the human population of Mexico continue to soar for many years to come, even if stringent birth control measures are started immediately?

Additional Ideas for Classroom Discussion

- Do you think the United States should play a role in disseminating birth control information and supplies to other nations?
- What is your opinion about the stance of the Roman Catholic Church against birth control?
- How has modern medical care changed the survivorship curve for humans since 1900?
- Some organisms (bamboo, cicadas) reproduce only at a single, very brief interlude during their life span but produce a large number of seeds or offspring during this short period of time. Can you think of some ways in which this pattern benefits a species?
- What is the relationship between the size of offspring and their number per reproductive event?
- Discuss the research by Reznick and Endler on the effects of different kinds of predation on the size, color, and rate of maturity among guppy populations as described in this chapter. Can you think of any parallels in the human population? What environmental factors might influence human characteristics? Can you think of any human characteristics that no longer have adaptive value in our society? What characteristics do you think might be useful in the future?
- What socioeconomic challenges will the current population structure in the United States someday pose to future generations?
- How might the current trend toward delayed childbearing change the population growth in the United States? Why would an increase in parental age change the population structure?
- What feature distinguishes each of the following categories from the others?

    a. community   b. population   c. ecosystem

How Would You Vote? Classroom Discussion Ideas

- Monitor the voting for the online question. The question of whether to encourage hunting of deer to reduce overpopulation will be answered very differently based on the acceptance of hunting in a particular geographical area. For instance, in southern states, hunting is nearly a sacred trust passed from one generation to the next and expected of all red-blooded Americans. Hunters would dearly love to be asked to thin a nearly-captive herd within the city limits. Why, the deer dined on my hanging pots of begonia plants just three nights ago! I'm ready to call in the artillery.

Term Paper Topics, Library Activities, and Special Projects

- Examine how the widespread wave of immigrants in the late 1800s and early 1900s changed the size and rate of growth in the U.S. population.

- Examine the effects of the 14th century bubonic plague on the subsequent size and growth of the human population in Europe. Was the effect the same as the reduction of the world population by the Spanish flu epidemic of 1918 when as many as 50 million perished? Why or why not?
- Look up information about organizations concerned with world overpopulation.
- Compare reproductive rates among different cultural and ethnic subgroups of people in the United States. Construct age structure diagrams for each subgroup.
- Look up information on population densities of several rural areas scattered randomly throughout the United States with population densities of several randomly located urban areas. Then find figures on the rates of alcoholism, crime, suicide, and divorce for each area. Is there a statistically significant correlation between population density and any one of these four types of pathology?
- Locate current data on human population growth in several countries around the world. Which countries are growing faster than the world average? Slower? Are any countries experiencing a *negative* population growth?
- Investigate the success of the world's most extensive human population limiting program—China's.
- Read several essays on human populations to learn the relationship between *numbers* of people and *rate* of consumption of nonrenewable resources. Which countries waste the most? The least?

Possible Responses to *Critical Thinking* Questions

1. The marking and recapture of the snails could provide information on: (a) how many snails survived/died in a period of time, (b) how far the snails migrated from the original capture site, (c) what possible predators or diseases affected the snails, (d) the rate of reproduction, and (e) any genetic variations that may not have been seen before.

2. The desert environment is supportive to both the saguaro and the poppies. The saguaro has a very long life history; therefore, it can endure the vagaries of desert life—heat, cold, lack of water—because it will grow slowly and not be affected by transient changes. On the other hand, the poppy takes advantage of the environment of the moment, grows rapidly, reproduces, and dies.

3. A large number of persons under the age of 15, especially females, would indicate a coming explosion in growth numbers. Most environmentalists have concluded that the Earth cannot sustain such numbers. Yet, the babies continue to be born. The simplest reason can be discovered by asking a group—say, a college biology class—"How many children do you plan to have?" The encouraging answer would be zero or one, but much more commonly it is two, three, four, or more! Their attitude is, "Let everyone cut back but me." Perhaps education is the answer, but what kind of education? Remember these are college students wanting large families; what about the rest of humanity? Perhaps a mandatory program like China's would be the answer; not in a democracy! Economics might limit families, but we know that the poorest families tend to have the largest number of children. Perhaps some catastrophe, such as AIDS, will limit population growth—and it has in small isolated pockets of our species—but its impact is not as great as we might think. Therefore, the human population continues to defy the natural laws governing all other species in which the J-shaped curve levels out to an S-shaped one. Perhaps human population growth is like a run-away freight train: you know it will crash, you just don't know when and how great the destruction will be.

29

COMMUNITY STRUCTURE AND BIODIVERSITY

Chapter Outline

Objectives

1. Define the following ecological terms: habitat, niche, community, symbiotic, competition, predation, parasitism, and mutualism.
2. List and distinguish among the several types of species interactions.
3. Discuss the positive aspects and the negative aspects of predation on prey populations.
4. Describe how communities are organized, how they develop, and how they diversify.
5. Explain how species become "endangered."
6. Be able to distinguish the various aspects of "habitat."
7. List the endeavors of conservation biology.
8. Propose some reasonable reconciliations of species diversity with human demands.

Key Terms

habitat	intraspecific	biological controls	distance effect
community	competition	ecological succession	area effect
niche	interference competition	primary succession	K-T boundary
fundamental	exploitative competition	pioneer species	biodiversity
realized	competitive exclusion	secondary succession	endangered species
indirect interactions	resource partitioning	climax community	habitat loss
commensalism	predators	intermediate	indicator species
mutualism	prey	disturbance hypothesis	conservation biology
interspecific	warning coloration	tolerance	hot spots
competition	mimicry	inhibition	ecoregion
predation	camouflage	facilitation	strip logging
parasitism	parasites	keystone species	riparian zone
symbiosis	parasitoids	geographic dispersal	
coevolution	social parasites	exotic species	

Lecture Outline

Fire Ants in the Pants
A. Fire ants have invaded the United States.
  1. Two species entered from Argentina in the 1930s.
  2. Both inflict very painful bites on humans and other animals.
B. Ecologists are using biological controls.
  1. Inside the fire ant, a parasitoid lays her eggs, which hatch to a larva that consumes the ant's vital tissues.
  2. Another idea is to use microbes that will infect fire ants but not native species.

29.1 Which Factors Shape Community Structure?
  A. A habitat is a place where an organism lives; it is characterized by distinctive physical features, vegetation, and the array of species living in it.
    1. A community is an association of interacting populations of different species living in a particular habitat.

2. Five factors shape the structure of the community:
   a. Interactions between climate and topography dictate rainfall, temperature, soil composition, and so on.
   b. Availability of food and resources affects inhabitants.
   c. Adaptive traits enable individuals to exploit specific resources.
   d. Interactions of various kinds occur among the inhabitants; these include competition, predation, and mutualism.
   e. The overall pattern of population sizes affects community structure.
B. The Niche
   1. The niche of each species is defined by the sum of activities and relationships in which it engages to secure and use the resources necessary for its survival and reproduction.
   2. The *fundamental niche* is the one that could prevail in the absence of competition; the *realized niche* results from shifts in large and small ways over time as individuals of the species respond to a mosaic of changes.
C. Categories of Species Interactions
   1. Interactions can occur between any two species in a community and between entire communities.
   2. There are several types of species interactions:
      a. *Indirect interactions:* neither species <u>directly</u> affects the other (example: eagles and grass).
      b. *Commensalism:* one species benefits while the other is not affected (example: bird's nest in a tree).
      c. *Mutualism:* there is a symbiotic relationship where both species benefit.
      d. *Interspecific competition:* both species are harmed by the interaction.
      e. *Predation and parasitism:* one species (predator or parasite) benefits while the other (prey or host) is harmed.
   3. Commensalism, mutualism, and parasitism are all types of symbiosis, the biological term for "living together."
   4. Close interactions between species, whether beneficial or harmful, can lead to coevolution.

29.2   Mutually Beneficial Interactions
A. The yucca moth feeds only on the yucca plant, which is completely dependent on the moth for pollination—a classic example of mutualism.
B. This example is also a form of symbiosis, which implies an intimate and rather permanent interdependence of the two species on one another for survival and reproduction.

29.3   Competitive Interactions
A. There are two major categories of competition:
   1. Competition within a population of the same species (intraspecific) is usually fierce and may result in depletion of a resource.
   2. Interspecific competition is less intense because requirements are less similar between the competitors.
   3. There are two types of competitive interactions regardless of whether they are inter- or intraspecific:
      a. In *interference competition,* some individuals limit others' access to the resource.
      b. In *exploitative competition,* all individuals have equal access to a resource but differ in their ability (speed or efficiency) to exploit that resource.

B. Competitive Exclusion
   1. Competitive exclusion suggests that complete competitors cannot coexist indefinitely.
   2. When competitors' niches do not overlap quite as much, the coexistence is more probable.
   3. Differences in adaptive traits will give certain species the competitive edge.
C. Coexisting Competitors
   1. Similar species share the same resource in different ways.
   2. Resource partitioning arises in two ways:
      a. Ecological differences between established and competing populations may increase through natural selection.
      b. Only species that are dissimilar from established ones can succeed in joining an existing community.

29.4   Predator-Prey Interactions
   A. Predators get their food from prey, but they do not take up residence on or in the prey.
   B. Models for Predator–Prey Interactions
      1. By the type I model, each individual predator will consume a constant number of prey individuals over time, regardless of prey abundance.
      2. In the type II model, the consumption of prey by each predator increases, but not as fast as increases in prey density.
      3. By the type III model, a predator response is lowest when prey density is at its lowest level, and predation pressure lessens.
   C. The Canadian Lynx and Snowshoe Hare
      1. Stable coexistence results when predators prevent prey from overshooting the carrying capacity.
      2. Fluctuations in population density tend to occur when predators do not reproduce as fast as their prey, when they can eat only so many prey, and when carrying capacity for prey is high.
   D. An Evolutionary Arms Race
      1. *Warning coloration* in toxic prey offer bright colors or bold patterns that serve as a warning to predators.
      2. In *mimicry*, prey not equipped with defenses may escape predators by resembling toxic prey.
      3. *Camouflage* is any adaptation in form, color, patterning, or behavior that allows a prey or predator to blend with its surroundings.
      4. *Moment-of-truth defenses* allow prey animals to defend themselves by startling or intimidating the predator with *display behavior*.
      5. *Predator responses to prey* are adaptations used by predators to counter prey defenses.

29.5   Parasites and Parasitoids
   A. Parasites have wide-reaching ecological impacts.
      1. Natural selection tends to favor parasite and host adaptations that promote some level of mutual tolerance and less-than-lethal effects.
      2. Usually death results only when a parasite attacks a novel host or when the number of parasites overwhelms the host's defenses.
      3. There are many kinds of parasites:
         a. Parasites may live on the surface of the host or within the host's body.
         b. Examples include viruses, bacteria, protists, fungi, flatworms, roundworms, and small arthropods.
      4. Parasitoids are insect larvae that develop inside the body of a host and devour it as they grow.

5. Social parasites depend on the social behavior of another to complete the life cycle; for example, cowbirds lay their eggs in the nest of other birds, which unknowingly incubate and hatch the cowbirds' eggs

B. Biological Control Agents
1. Parasites and parasitoids have five attributes that make them good control agents:
   a. They are well adapted to the host species and their habitat.
   b. They are exceptionally good at searching for hosts.
   c. Their growth rate is high relative to that of the host species.
   d. They are mobile enough for adequate dispersal.
   e. The lag time between responses to changes in the numbers of the host population is minimal.
2. Care must be taken in releasing more that one kind of control agent in a given area due to the possibility of triggering competition among them and lessening their overall level of effectiveness.

29.6   Changes in Community Structure over Time
A. Ecological Succession
1. Ecological succession is the transformational sequence of species in a community.
   a. Pioneer species are the first to colonize an area, followed by more competitive species.
   b. A climax community is the most persistent array of species that results after some lapse of time.
2. Primary succession happens in an area that was devoid of life.
   a. Pioneer species help to improve soil fertility; they are usually small, low-growing plants with a short life cycle and an abundance of seeds.
   b. Gradually other, usually larger, species join or replace the pioneer species.
3. In secondary succession, a community reestablishes itself after a disturbance that allows sunlight to penetrate.

B. Intermediate Disturbance Hypothesis
1. It was once thought that the same general type of community would always develop in a given region because of constraints imposed by typography, climate, and soil.
2. According to the intermediate disturbance hypothesis, the number of species in a community is influenced by the frequency and severity of disturbances.
3. Ecologists now regard communities as dynamic entities that are rarely, if ever, in a stable state.

C. Species Interactions in Succession
1. In cases of *tolerance*, an early colonizer has no effect on which species will colonize the habitat after it.
2. In *inhibition,* an early colonizer alters the habitat in some way that discourages other species from colonizing.
3. In *facilitation,* early colonizers improve conditions for later ones.

29.7   Forces Contributing to Community Instability
A. The Role of Keystone Species
1. A keystone species is a dominant species that can dictate community structure.
2. For example, when sea stars (keystone predator on mussels) were removed from a habitat, mussels increased in number and in turn preyed on enough other species to reduce the community from 15 to 8.

B. How Species Introductions Tip the Balance
  1. Geographic dispersal of species can occur in three ways:
     a. A population might expand its home range by slowly moving into outlying regions that prove hospitable.
     b. During the course of a lifetime, individuals may be rapidly transported across great distances (jump dispersal), as in bilge water of large ships.
     c. A population may move out from its home range over geologic time, as by continental drift.
  2. Some introduced species have proved beneficial: soybeans, rice, wheat, corn, and potatoes; others are notoriously bad: water hyacinth, kudzu in the southern United States, the green alga *Caulerpa* in the Mediterranean; and rabbits in Australia.

29.8   Patterns of Species Diversity
  A. Mainland and Marine Patterns
     1. The number of species increases from the Arctic regions, to the temperate zones, to the tropics.
     2. Diversity is favored in the tropics for three reasons:
        a. More rainfall and sunlight provides more food reserves.
        b. Tropical communities have been evolving for a longer time than temperate zones.
        c. Species diversity is self-reinforcing from herbivores to predators and parasites.
  B. Island Patterns
     1. Islands distant from source areas receive fewer colonizing species (distance effect).
     2. Larger islands tend to support more species (area effect).
     3. Species numbers increase on new islands and reach a stable number that is a balance between immigration rate for species new to the island and the extinction rate for established species.

29.9   Conservation Biology
  A. Even though extinctions have occurred, biodiversity is still very great.
     1. Prokaryotes dominated until the Cambrian period when abundant oxygen favored emergence of eukaryotes.
     2. Extinctions have occurred rapidly, but recovery is measured in millions of years.
  B. About the Newly Endangered Species
     1. Another major extinction event is under way.
        a. About 300 mammals are on the endangered species list.
        b. These endangered species are endemic to only one geographic region and thus are very vulnerable to human encroachment activities.
     2. As humans, we are threatening other species with habitat losses, species introductions, and illegal wildlife trading.
  C. The Major Threats
     1. Habitat loss may be a *physical* reduction of suitable places to live as well as a loss of habitat due to *chemical* pollution.
     2. Habitats may also be chopped into isolated patches (habitat fragmentation), which has three effects:
        a. It increases the habitats boundaries, making species more vulnerable to predators, environmental factors, and disease.
        b. The patches may not be large enough to support the population numbers needed for breeding.
        c. There may not be enough food to sustain the population.

3. The extinction patterns on oceanic islands can be used to model what could happen to land-based habitat islands (parks, reserves) that are surrounded by destructive human activities (logging, urbanization).
4. Indicator species, such as birds, provide warning of changes in habitat and impending loss of diversity.
5. Exotic species that move into a new habitat are responsible for almost 70 percent of the cases where endemic species are driven to extinction.
6. Overharvesting also reduces biodiversity.

D. Emergence of Conservation Biology
1. There are three goals:
    a. It involves a systematic survey of the full range of biological diversity.
    b. It attempts to decipher the evolutionary and ecological origins of diversity.
    c. It attempts to identify methods that might maintain and use biodiversity for the good of the human population.
2. The Role of Systematics
    a. Because it is impossible to make a global survey of all species, scientists have identified hot spots where habitats with the greatest number of species found nowhere else are in danger of extinction.
    b. Various hot spot inventories can be combined to define an ecoregion.
3. Bioeconomic Analysis
    a. Species inventories can lead to assigning an economic value to ecoregions.
    b. The goal is to convince individuals, and governments, that sustaining biodiversity has more value than destroying it.
    c. Biodiversity will be best protected when its species can be used over the long term for the good of local economies.
4. Sustainable Development
    a. Strip logging is a proposal that would provide for a profitable, yet sustainable, way to harvest trees for wood; it would be used in sloped terrain with a number of streams, providing for regrowth of new saplings.
    b. Ranching can be done in riparian zones.
        1) Riparian zones are valuable strips of vegetation along a stream or river.
        2) Cattle destroy riparian zones, but restricting cattle from these areas is costly.
        3) Rotation of cattle into and out of the zones, combined with raising different breeds, is a way of managing the riparian zones.

Suggestions for Presenting the Material

- While the previous chapter covered population structure and growth, this chapter discusses the interactions among the species of a community.
- The elaborate, finely tuned species interactions described here offer another excellent opportunity to discuss coevolution. Examples such as the array of yucca species in Colorado, each pollinated exclusively by one kind of yucca moth species, emphasize the point that individuals don't evolve, populations do. Students will see many good examples of adaptive traits in this chapter.
- The coevolution of predator and prey (or would-be prey) is also another good example of the impact of one species upon the evolution of another. After reading and discussing this chapter, students should understand that communities are shaped by a complex web of many different factors.
- Perhaps one of the best ways to maintain student interest in biodiversity is to pepper your lectures with examples, preferably illustrated with visual material.

Classroom and Laboratory Enrichment

- Identify examples of exploitation, competition, and interference competition among local plant and animal communities.
- Design an experiment to be carried out in the lab or in the field that would test Gause's principle of competitive exclusion.
- Develop a method of graphing habitat usage and habitat overlap among two or more species living in the same habitat.
- Examine a vegetated area on campus or in an area nearby. How are the plants in the area competing for resources? Suggest some ways in which competition has shaped the plant community.
- Show slides and/or films of examples of camouflage; ask students to distinguish the camouflaged organism.
- Select any ecosystem and look for examples of resource partitioning.
- Design and implement a study of succession. This can be done on a small scale in the lab or on a larger scale in the field. List the species and their approximate densities at the beginning of the study, then follow the changes in species composition and density as the study progresses. Students may establish a baseline study to be followed in later semesters by other students.
- Examine road cuts, construction sites, flooded river banks, plowed fields, and other places that have recently been disturbed. Can you find several plant species that you would describe as pioneer species?
- Describe patterns of succession at edges of stream beds, rivers, or coastlines.
- Ask your students to classify each of the items below as belonging to a human "habitat" or "niche":
    a. President
    b. Dorm room
    c. Secretary
    d. Lounge
    e. Counselor
    f. Student
- As each topic in the chapter is discussed, 2 x 2 transparencies should be in view because these topics are best taught and remembered by the *examples* given.
- Show the graphs (Figure 29.5) of the classic experiments of *Paramecium* growth that Gause performed. Why did *P. caudatum* decrease to near extinction in the containers but thrive in nature?
- Using the observation that grass quickly establishes itself in the cracks in the pavement of a highway on which traffic has been blocked for some time, describe what is happening using terms from the chapter.
- The stories of the statues on Easter Island and the disappearance of the dodo bird make for interesting "extras" to this material.
- If you are fortunate to have an expert in biodiversity available, by all means arrange for an illustrated lecture.
- Invite a guest speaker who would disagree with the thesis of this chapter.
- Choose a local example of the destruction of habitat (a new shopping center) and evaluate the positive and negative aspects.
- If possible, arrange a field trip to the site of some local habitat destruction.

Impacts, Issues Classroom Discussion Ideas

- How do parasites help to regulate host populations in nature?

- Why do insects introduced into the United States become such pests when they were not so in their native country?

- Are certain plants "born" to be weeds? Or do they achieve that status by human condemnation?

- Is it true that all decisions regarding habitat preservation have to be economic? Is esthetics worth anything?

Additional Ideas for Classroom Discussion

- Would you expect competition between two finches of different species to be less intense or more intense than competition between two finches of the same species? Explain your answer.

- How does a shift in niche benefit competing species sharing the same environment?

- Distinguish between "habitat" and "niche."

- Discuss predator-prey interactions. What do you think a predator would do if deprived of its primary prey item? Examine the actual diets of several predatory species; how do these diets change from one month to the next throughout the year? How can environmental disturbances such as fires, floods, climate fluctuations, and insect outbreaks influence the predator-prey cycle? What are some of the other variables that may be overlooked in predator-prey interactions?

- What is the difference between parasites and parasitoids? Between true parasitism and social parasitism?

- Why is resource partitioning essential for groups of functionally similar species living together?

- What characteristics distinguish a pioneer species? Are pioneer species good competitors against later successional species? Why are pioneer species dependent on the frequent advent of open, disturbed places?

- Do you think that fires in national parks should be allowed to proceed without human intervention? Why or why not?

- What is a weed? What characteristics distinguish weeds from other plants? Are there biological features that weeds tend to share?

- In the classic graph of lynx and hare populations (Figure 29.9), what was the basis of the numerical count on the x-axis? How valid was this compared to actual field counts of these two animals?

- What do you think a "hyperparasitoid" insect is?

- The *monarch* butterfly is orange and black and tastes bad (birds eating them spit them out immediately); *viceroy* butterflies are almost indistinguishable from monarchs but taste good. Which of these is the model; which is the mimic?

- "In primary succession," according to your text, "changes begin when pioneer species colonize a barren habitat." Are there any uninhabited places left on earth for pioneer plants and animals to colonize? What would create such a setting?

- Arrange a debate on "bioeconomic analysis." Try to answer the question: "Is the preservation of nature more important than preservation of humans?"

- In reference to the item above, discuss how the preservation of nature is in the best *long-term* interests of humans.

- Illustrate with examples how the short-term interests of humans are usually given preference over the long-term needs.
- Evaluate the possible scenarios of human life as the world population expands to 8 or 9 billion.

How Would You Vote? Classroom Discussion Ideas

- Monitor the voting for the online question. The answer to the question of more extensive inspection programs of imported containers gets an affirmative nod until we read the trailer: "…even if it means increasing the cost of imported goods?" Nobody likes to pay more for something, especially when they see no direct result or benefit in the purchased product. Most persons would not even realize the danger involved with the importation of exotic species.

Term Paper Topics, Library Activities, and Special Projects

- Summarize several of the classic studies involving predator-prey interactions.
- Describe several species of parasites commonly found among humans in the United States earlier in this century, prior to the advent of improved hygiene and widespread medical care. What parasites are still commonly found among human populations today? What are some of the steps that can be taken to reduce parasitic infections?
- Write a report on the effects of interspecific competition on a native species whose populations have been adversely affected by an introduced species.
- Describe succession as it has occurred following a major disaster such as a flood, debris slide, fire, or volcanic eruption.
- Discuss examples of mutualism among plants and animals.
- Discuss the role of fire in regenerating plant communities in Yellowstone National Park.
- How did disturbance by human intervention help to initiate secondary succession in American prairies?
- At what point will the growing number of plant species in a previously disturbed area stop increasing? What factors will halt the rise in species composition? Examine studies of island ecology that seek to answer this question.
- Select a group of related species for which distribution data are available, and construct a graph of patterns of species diversity corresponding to latitude.
- Discuss the discovery, history, and causes of the greenhouse effect. Summarize some of the steps recommended by scientists today to combat the greenhouse effect.
- Search for specific examples of insects that are parasitoids of other insects. Are the parasitoids "effective" controls?
- Report on the succession that has occurred since the eruption of Mount Saint Helens in Washington in 1980.
- From a book on insect pest management, report on the successful control of the cottony-cushion scale by ladybugs in California.
- Investigate more of the details of the Easter Island statues.
- Prepare a report on the details of the extinction of the dodo bird.
- List the job opportunities in the area of conservation biology.

- Prepare the projection of the effects on diversity of the expansion of the world population from 6 to 10 billion.

Possible Responses to *Critical Thinking* Questions

1. In this scenario in which beneficial bacteria out-compete harmful bacteria, the principle of competitive exclusion is operating. The massive quantities of beneficial bacteria in the cattle, coupled with the extremely rapid reproduction rate, make it unlikely that the harmful bacteria will thrive.

2. The phasmids, walkingsticks, have been remarkably successful by simply remaining very quiet, motionless, and stick-like. That would seem to be an easy task, but they pull it off better than most imitators. A simple experiment to show the adaptive value of the walkingstick's little bag of tricks would involve countering the camouflage effect. For example, we could apply some non-toxic paint of various colors ranging from bright to dull to several phasmids and record the reaction of potential predators.

3. In this item, the question is asked about human concern for regions of low species diversity. The example given is the coniferous forests of the Northern Hemisphere. Certainly this biome is one of the most lush and beautiful (looking like acres and acres of Christmas trees) on the planet. But to the casual observer it is one of the most boring—looking too much the same for too long. To the non-biologist this might indicate a degree of unimportance. This is misdirected because the reality is that the forest is removing vast quantities of carbon dioxide *from* the air and putting vast quantities of oxygen *into* the air. This is a critical component to the overall global cycling of carbon.

4. In this scenario, the poverty-stricken inhabitant of the rain forest is credited with knowing that the "brilliantly feathered parrot" is rare. But to him *rare* just means he can't lay his eyes on one very often. He is not educated enough to know that *rare* really indicates *endangered* to the point of near extinction. But even if he were told the facts, would he forgo the handsome financial reward for himself and his desperate family just to preserve environmental stability? It is doubtful!

5. There is little doubt that the "burial" described here is ecologically friendly. But it is also a bit creepy. Many folks don't warm to the idea of cremation in the first place, but are comforted that Grandma's ashes are in an urn on the mantle if we wish to turn our eyes in her direction to pay our respects on Memorial Day. But to have the ashes incorporated into concrete to be eventually covered with crusty marine life at the bottom of the ocean; that takes some real ecological dedication!

30

ECOSYSTEMS

Chapter Outline

Objectives

1. Understand how materials and energy enter, pass through, and exit an ecosystem.
2. Describe an important study that determined the annual pattern of energy flow in an aquatic ecosystem.
3. Understand the various trophic roles and levels.
4. Describe the movement of materials through the biogeochemical cycles.

Key Terms

photoautotrophs	carnivores	omnivores	food chain
primary producers	parasites	scavengers	food webs
consumers	detritivores	ecosystem	grazing food webs
herbivores	decomposers	trophic levels	detrital food webs

biological magnification	biogeochemical cycles	groundwater	nitrogen fixation
biomass pyramid	hydrologic cycle	desalinization	ammonification
energy pyramid	atmospheric cycles	carbon cycle	denitrification
primary productivity	sedimentary cycles	greenhouse effect	ion exchange
net ecosystem production	watershed	global warming	phosphorus cycle
	salinization	nitrogen cycle	eutrophication

Lecture Outline

Bye-Bye Bayou

A. Louisiana is losing its wetlands.
   1. Ocean levels are rising and sediments are being held back by dams and levees rather than flowing into the sea to replace those washed away.
   2. The shellfish, fish, and migratory birds will have no place to survive.

B. Warmer temperatures will also have effects on Louisiana.
   1. Algal blooms will cause fish kills; bacteria will make animals sick.
   2. Mosquitoes will thrive and transmit diseases, like West Nile virus.
   3. Weather patterns may be affected; floods will alternate with drought.

30.1 The Nature of Ecosystems

A. Overview of the Participants
   1. Regions of the earth function as systems running on energy from the sun, processed through various organisms.
      a. *Photoautotrophs* (primary producers) can capture sunlight energy and incorporate it into organic compounds.
      b. *Consumers* are heterotrophs that feed on tissues of other organisms.
         1) *Herbivores* eat plants.
         2) *Carnivores* eat animals.
         3) *Omnivores* eat a variety of organisms.
         4) *Parasites* reside in or on living hosts and extract energy from them.
      c. *Detritivores* include small invertebrates that feed on partly decomposed particles of organic matter (detritus).
      d. *Decomposers* are also heterotrophs and include fungi and bacteria that extract energy from the remains or products of organisms.
   2. An *ecosystem* is a complex of organisms interacting with one another *and* with the physical environment.
      a. Ecosystems are open systems through which energy *flows* and materials are cycled.
      b. Ecosystems require energy and nutrient *input* and generate energy (usually as heat) and nutrient *output*.

B. Trophic Interactions
   1. Trophic ("feeding") levels are a hierarchy of energy transfers, or bluntly stated, "who eats whom."
      a. Level 1 (closest to the energy source) consists of producers; level 2 comprises herbivores; and levels 3 and above are carnivores.
      b. Decomposers feed on organisms from all levels.
   2. Organisms interact with one another at various feeding levels.
      a. A simple sequence of who eats whom is called a *food chain*.

      b. Interconnected food chains comprise *food webs* in which the same food resource is often part of more than one food chain.

  C. Food Webs

    1. How many energy transfers can there be?

      a. In a simple food chain (for example: grass —> cutworm —> garter snake —> plover —> hawk), the energy initially captured by the producers passes through no more than four or five trophic levels.

      b. This is because energy is lost (as heat) at each level, making the amount of energy gained less than that expended in capturing the prey.

    2. There are two categories of food webs.

      a. Energy flows into ecosystems from the sun.

        1) Energy flows through ecosystems by way of *grazing food webs*, in which energy flows from plants to herbivores and then to carnivores.

        2) In *detrital food webs* it flows mainly from plants through decomposers and detritivores.

      b. Energy leaves ecosystems through heat losses generated by metabolism.

30.2   Biological Magnification in Food Webs

  A. DDT, which was an effective chemical to kill mosquitoes, accumulates in fatty tissues and results in biological magnification and unexpected nontarget effects.

  B. Even though DDT has been banned since the 1970s, the chemical is very persistent in certain sections of the environment, namely sediments.

30.3   Studying Energy Flow through Ecosystems

  A. Ecological Pyramids

    1. Ecologists represent the trophic structure as an ecological pyramid in which producers form a base for successive tiers of consumers above them.

    2. A *biomass pyramid* makes provision for differences in size of organisms by using the weight of the members in each trophic level.

    3. An *energy pyramid* reflects trophic structure most accurately because it is based on energy losses at each level.

  B. Primary Productivity

    1. Primary productivity is the rate at which producers get and store energy in their tissues.

      a. *Gross* primary productivity is the total rate of photosynthesis for the ecosystem during a specified interval.

      b. *Net* ecosystem production is the energy left over after that which is used by the plants and soil organisms is subtracted from the gross primary production.

    2. Many factors interact to influence net production.

30.4   Global Cycling of Water and Nutrients

  A. Biogeochemical cycles influence the availability of essential elements in ecosystems.

    1. Elements are available in the form of mineral ions.

    2. Nutrient reserves are maintained by environmental inputs and recycling activities.

    3. The amount of nutrients being cycled is greater than the amount entering or leaving.

    4. Environment inputs are by precipitation, metabolism, and weathering. Outputs are by runoff and evaporation.

    5. There are three categories of biogeochemical cycles:

      a. In the *hydrologic cycle,* oxygen and hydrogen move as water molecules.

      b. In the *atmospheric cycles,* elements can move in the gaseous phase; examples include carbon and nitrogen.

      c. In *sedimentary cycles,* the element does not have a gaseous phase; an example is phosphorus.

B. Hydrologic Cycle

  1. Water is moved or stored by evaporation, precipitation, retention, and transportation.

  2. Water moves other nutrients in or out of ecosystems.

      a. A watershed funnels rain or snow into a single river.

      b. Nutrients are absorbed by plants to prevent their loss by leaching.

C. The Water Crisis

  1. Most of the earth's water is too salty for human consumption or for agriculture.

  2. Agriculture accounts for two-thirds of our water usage for irrigation, which of course grows crops but also leads to salt buildup (salinization).

  3. About one-half of the United States population depends on groundwater for drinking water, but groundwater is being polluted by toxic chemicals leached from landfills and waste dumps.

      a. Human waste, insecticides, herbicides, chemicals, radioactive materials, and heat can pollute water.

      b. In the past decade, 33 nations have engaged in conflicts over reductions in water flow, pollution, and silt buildup.

  4. Could desalinization be the answer?

      a. Salt removal processes are available and can be used when absolutely necessary.

      b. However, desalinization is not cost effective in most locales, and it uses valuable fuel reserves to provide the energy for the desalination equipment.

30.5   Carbon Cycle

A. Carbon enters the atmosphere (where it exists as carbon dioxide) by aerobic respiration, fossil-fuel burning, and volcanic eruptions.

  1. Carbon is removed from the atmosphere (and bodies of water) by photosynthesizers and shelled organisms.

  2. Decomposition of carbon compounds buried millions of years ago led to the formation of fossil fuels.

  3. Burning of fossil fuels puts extra amounts of carbon dioxide into the atmosphere, an occurrence that may lead to global warming—the greenhouse effect.

B. Most researchers think the carbon buildup in the atmosphere is amplifying the greenhouse effect.

30.6   Greenhouse Gases, Global Warming

A. Greenhouse Effect

  1. The greenhouse gases (carbon dioxide, water vapor, ozone, methane, nitrous oxide, and CFCs) trap heat, preventing its escape from the Earth back into space.

  2. Heat builds in the lower atmosphere—the greenhouse effect.

B. Global Warming and Climate Change

  1. Temperatures have risen by one degree F since 1861.

  2. Nine of the ten hottest years have occurred since 1990.

  3. Pollutants are substances with which ecosystems have no prior evolutionary experience, and they therefore cannot deal with them.

      a. Air pollutants include carbon dioxide, oxides of nitrogen and sulfur, and chlorofluorocarbons.

b. Most of the pollutants come from emissions generated in the "developed" countries.

30.7   Nitrogen Cycle
       A. Nitrogen is a part of several steps in a cycling process:
           1. In *nitrogen fixation*, bacteria convert N_2 to NH_3, which is then used in the synthesis of proteins and nucleic acids.
           2. By *ammonification*, bacteria and fungi breakdown nitrogenous compounds found in the wastes and bodies of dead organisms.
           3. *Nitrification* is a type of chemosynthesis where NH_3 or NH_4^+ is converted to NO_2^-; other nitrifying bacteria use the nitrite for energy and release NO_3^-.
           4. *Denitrification* is the release of nitrogen gas to the atmosphere by the action of bacteria (NO_2^- and NO_3^- ——> N_2).
       B. Human Impact on the Nitrogen Cycle
           1. Nitrogen losses can occur through deforestation and loss of grasslands, but are partly remedied by crop rotation, especially with legume crops.
           2. Heavy applications of commercial fertilizers are not only costly but lead to extensive runoff into waterways.
           3. Nitrogen-rich sewage flows into rivers, lakes, and estuaries; nitrogen oxides are released into the atmosphere from the burning of fossil fuels.

30.8   Phosphorus Cycle
       A. Phosphorus moves from land, to sediments in the seas, and back to the land in its long-term geochemical phase of the cycle.
           1. In the ecosystem phase, plants take up the phosphorus from the soil; it is then transferred to herbivores and carnivores, which excrete it in wastes and their own decomposing bodies.
           2. Of all minerals, phosphorus is the most limiting factor in all natural ecosystems.
       B. Runoff from agricultural applications of fertilizers adds large amounts of phosphorus to aquatic ecosystems; this is called eutrophication.

Suggestions for Presenting the Material

- The material presented in this chapter will help students understand that any ecosystem is comprised of many interdependent parts. After learning about ecosystems described in terms of their food webs, trophic levels, and biogeochemical cycles, students will be aware of the unity that joins all organisms.

- Use as many *local* examples of ecosystems as possible in discussions, demonstrations, and lab work. Describing the different levels of an ecosystem should help the students understand the functioning of an ecosystem as a whole. Such ecosystem descriptions provide a valuable baseline against which we can measure the effects of change.

- In various sections of the chapter, the author shows how humans have altered the natural ecosystems and their functioning.

Classroom and Laboratory Enrichment

- Choose a community, list its species, and categorize them as producers, consumers, decomposers, or detritivores.

- Working individually or in teams, students should select an ecosystem in a laboratory or a field setting and identify which organisms comprise each trophic level of the ecosystem.

- Devise an experiment in which one of the trophic levels of an ecosystem is removed or disrupted and the effects are measured and described.

- Set up aquatic ecosystems in the lab, and monitor them throughout the semester. Identify the trophic levels of the ecosystem, and analyze the cycling of minerals and nutrients within it. In what ways are the aquatic ecosystems in the lab similar to/different from real aquatic ecosystems?

- Discuss the primary productivities of different regions of the United States. How can human intervention change primary productivity?

- Construct a detrital food web for a typical forest or open field ecosystem. Students can list the decomposers and detritivores one might find in such areas (or identify as many of the detritivores as possible in lab) and then find out how each organism would be arranged in a food web.

- Use overhead transparencies to present the biogeochemical cycles.

- Analyze local soils to determine the mineral and organic contents.

- Use Figure 30.3 (food web in tallgrass prairie) to clarify the *trophic levels* and *consumer designations*. What group of organisms necessary for nutrient recycling is not indicated in this figure?

- Assuming that a flat 10 percent of the energy in one trophic level is conserved to the next and the producer level represents 100 percent, calculate what percent is received by the marsh hawk in Figure 30.3.

- Using the overhead transparencies for the major biogeochemical cycles (nitrogen, carbon, phosphorus, and water) indicate where humans are active or passive participants. How have human activities altered the "natural" cycles?

- Assess public understanding of environmental pollution issues by designing a brief questionnaire. Divide the public into several different groups, and compare the levels of understanding among the groups. Some possible groupings are: students in this course, past students of the course, university or college students at large, university employees, different age groups, local residents not employed by the college or university, and groups created on the basis of differences in factors such as socioeconomic status, political affiliation, age, and education. How well informed are the different groups? Did they know more or less about environmental issues than you thought they would? Can you identify any myths about environmental pollution that appear to be widely held?

- Monitor the quality of air in your area. What has been the impact of humans on the air in your community?

- What happens to your trash? Trace the fate of the garbage that leaves your campus daily. What about wastes containing dangerous chemicals from research labs or medical wastes from the campus infirmary or university hospital? Does your institution have a set of rules and guidelines governing waste disposal?

- Visit a sewage treatment plant. Discuss the biological steps involved in the treatment of your local sewage. In what ways could sewage treatment be improved?

- Collect water samples from your classroom building and have the samples analyzed. Discuss the results with your class.

- Working in small groups, debate the pros and cons of different energy sources. Each group should be prepared to discuss the merits and drawbacks of one of the following energy sources: oil, coal, natural gas, hydropower, solar power, nuclear power, and other alternatives.
- Ask a representative from a local environmental group to address the class.
- Prepare a list of environmental concerns in your area and state. Ask students what *should* be done, then ask them what realistically *can* be done.
- Obtain a map of the United States showing the areas of highest cancer rates. Ask students to speculate as to why certain areas are more at risk than others.

Impacts, Issues Classroom Discussion Ideas

- Why do you think relatively little has been done to eliminate the greenhouse effect? What do you think is required before governments such as our own will pass laws regulating the types of human activities responsible for phenomena such as the greenhouse effect?
- Do you think that our current environmental pollution problems reflect a fundamental shift in human values over the past 50 years? Why or why not?
- Collect articles on the greenhouse effect from popular magazines and newspapers published in the past year. Compare and contrast the coverage of this issue provided by these publications.
- One of the highest concentrations of industrial chemical plants is along the lower Mississippi River, mainly in Louisiana. The effects of these plants on the environment are not hard to document. Why then are they allowed to continue to operate?

Additional Ideas for Classroom Discussion

- Discuss what would happen to an ecosystem if all of the producers disappeared. What would happen to the ecosystem if all of the consumers, decomposers, or detritivores disappeared? Can you think of examples of ecosystems in which any of these events has occurred? How can an ecosystem recover from such a disturbance?
- Describe several trophic levels of a typical ecosystem, and ask students to arrange them in the correct order.
- What is the one ingredient required by all ecosystems that cannot be recycled?
- Why is the term *food chain* rarely used when describing *actual* ecosystems?
- What do you think were the first producers to evolve on earth?
- How (and where) do humans fit into food webs?
- Does the loss of tropical forests throughout South America affect us? How?
- Why is a pyramid of biomass a more accurate representation of an ecosystem than a pyramid of numbers?
- Why does a pyramid of energy narrow as it goes up?
- Tropical forests are highly productive ecosystems, incorporating extremely large amounts of carbon and other nutrients into plant material. Yet, when cleared of vegetation, such areas make very poor farmlands. Why?
- Is it environmentally wise to rely on large quantities of nitrogen-rich fertilizers for crop production? What are some alternatives? Discuss the pros and cons of commercial fertilizers.

- The pesticide DDT is just one example of a substance that undergoes biological magnification as it travels through an ecosystem. Can you think of others? (One possible example is the movement of strontium 90, a byproduct of nuclear testing in the 1950s, through the food web.)

- Why do most food chains have only three or four consumer links?

- Why is it nearly impossible to study a single food chain?

- Why are humans at the top of nearly every food web of which they are a part? Are they ever at any other level?

- What would the personal and ecological advantages be to humans if they were to eat "lower down" on the energy pyramid?

- Analyze each of the segments of the following expression: "bio—geo—chemical cycle."

- In each of the biogeochemical cycles indicate the route each component takes in recycling. What "invisible" component is not recyclable?

- How have coal-burning power plants changed in the past 20 years?

- What is a "clean" energy source? Can you think of an example?

- Why is the ozone layer of the earth's atmosphere shrinking at the same time that excessive amounts of ozone at the earth's surface are present in photochemical smog?

- Do you think our laws regarding air pollution are too lenient? What changes would you make in the laws or their enforcement?

- Why does normal rainwater have a pH of around 5.6?

- Where does the tap water in your classroom building come from?

- Why would it be unwise to clear tropical forests and irrigate arid lands for conversion to agriculture?

- What are some examples of renewable energy sources?

- How many students in the class recycle their aluminum cans? Newspapers? Glass? Take a hand count. Ask students for reasons why they do (or do not) recycle these materials.

- Ask students to make a list of ways in which they could modify their own lifestyles and behaviors to reduce environmental pollution.

- What do you think will be the most important areas of science in the next decade? In 50 years?

- How would *you* rate as a "pioneer" in a setting where there was no electricity, stores, or running water?

- List the ways in which a city, especially a large one, represents one of the least stable of ecosystems.

- Your text lists several "excesses of outputs." These constitute important environmental problems, but what is the root problem in each case? (Answer: too many people)

- Does it seem wasteful to you that billions of gallons of pure drinking water are used to flush toilets and wash cars? Can you propose an alternative? Could you convince the city managers to adopt it?

- About 500,000 trees are needed for all of the Sunday newspapers for Americans. Is this necessary? When will we no longer be able to afford such extravagance? Will it be too late to reverse the ecological damage?

How Would You Vote? Classroom Discussion Ideas

- Monitor the voting for the online question. Of course it would be a good idea to raise the standards for fuel efficiency and emissions for motor vehicles. But the average driver is not concerned with the long-term effects of pollution, but rather the additional dollars added to the selling price.

Term Paper Topics, Library Activities, and Special Projects

- Write a report on ecosystems deep on the ocean floor at depths impenetrable by light. What kinds of organisms make up the first trophic level in such ecosystems? How are these organisms obtaining energy?
- What happens to an ecosystem if any one of its levels is removed? Find descriptions of ecosystems in which this has happened and describe the results.
- Describe the biochemical steps used by chemosynthetic autotrophs to produce energy.
- List and describe some of the primary producers in an open ocean ecosystem off the U.S. coast.
- Discuss the primary productivities of various regions around the world. Which areas have the highest and lowest primary productivities? Why?
- Look up the root/shoot ratios of several plant species, and graph these values against the latitudes of their geographic ranges.
- Describe nitrogen fixation. What kinds of organisms can perform nitrogen fixation? Discuss genetic engineering research in this area.
- Discuss farming techniques designed to minimize nitrogen loss in the soil.
- Describe the effects of strip-mining on biogeochemical cycles.
- Describe the history of the use and subsequent banning of DDT in the United States.
- Consult several geography texts to see where people from different countries of the world are located in the food webs of their areas.
- Obtain records of the yearly average temperatures and rainfall amounts from your local weather bureau. Graph the data. Are there any trends?
- The spectacular rise and fall of the most famous of all insecticides—DDT—occurred roughly during the years 1943 to 1973. Prepare a chronology of the significant events in its "life story."
- Describe the actual contents of industrial smog or photochemical smog in the nearest city with an air pollution problem. Describe the ways in which the air pollution affects the health of area residents.
- What are the biological effects of acid rain on fish populations?
- Examine the statistical link between air quality and rates of respiratory disease.
- Describe successful community recycling programs. List the features of successful programs, and describe obstacles that must be overcome to ensure success.
- Discuss the success of recycling programs in states (such as New Jersey) with laws requiring mandatory recycling.
- Write a report describing the discovery and use of new plastics that will degrade when exposed to sunlight or can be decomposed by microorganisms.
- Summarize the federal laws against pollution.
- Who are your local polluters? Find out which industries release pollutants into the atmosphere. List the pollutants and describe what steps the companies have taken to reduce emission of pollutants.

- Describe the process of illegal dumping. Why is it done? Has it been done in your area? What are the penalties for illegal dumping?
- Make a list of the contents of a toxic waste dump, and describe the potential hazards posed by such compounds.
- Discuss the environmental effects of strip-mining.
- What are the current alternatives for storing nuclear waste? What are some proposed methods that might be used to store nuclear waste in the future?
- Just a handful of states have mandatory refundable deposits on drink containers. The highest (10 cents per container) is in Michigan. Investigate the effect this law has had on the soft drink industry, the retailers, and the environment.
- Tap water in all metropolitan areas is certified as "safe," but that doesn't necessarily mean you would want to drink it. In your library find the yellow pages listings for suppliers of bottled water for these cities: New York, Chicago, Los Angeles, New Orleans, and Atlanta. Compare the number of these suppliers with the population to obtain a ratio. Did you find any surprises?

Possible Responses to *Critical Thinking* Questions

1. The assumption and worry would be this: if there is enough global warming to melt ice in Antarctica, then there is probably some global warming going on elsewhere but without such dramatic effects. We should all take heed.

2. The levels of mercury can vary among species living in the same habitat because of where a particular animal is situated in the food chain. If the species is one of the top carnivores, then by the concept of biological magnification that carnivore is literally taking on all of the pollutants that have accumulated in the organisms lower in the food chain.

3. There are many factors that influence the growth of plants no matter where they are growing, but in Maine the factors may be a bit more limited than, say, in the semitropics. These factors would include: the soil nutrients (may be rocky); sunlight (shorter growing season); water (could be lots if a few nor'easters blow ashore); and temperature (kind of cool up there).

4. Global warming is in part due to the increased levels of carbon dioxide in the atmosphere. So anything we use that necessitated combustion would be a problem. Perhaps plastics would be one. Of course, the use of automobiles would be also. We could walk or ride bicycles to reduce our use of plastics, but no one wants to be inconvenienced and, besides, *no one else* is conserving.

5. Nitrogen in fertilizers is necessary for the making of proteins and nucleic acids. Phosphorus is needed for phospholipids, ATP, NADPH, and nucleic acids. All of these molecules are absolutely essential to life, both to the plants and to the animals that will eventually eat the plants. But we homeowners (of lawns) and farmers (of fields) cannot put the *precise* amount of fertilizer necessary for growth, without getting a little extra in there. So the excess runs off into our streams, ponds, lakes, rivers, etc. where it provides for luxuriant growth of algae and other "weedy" plants that choke our waterways.

6. The four molecules of life are carbohydrates, lipids, proteins, and nucleic acids. Of course, carbon is central to building all of these. Nitrogen is particularly abundant in the amino acids of proteins, but also is a part of the nucleotide bases of nucleic acids. Phosphorus is found in the nucleic acids and also in the phospholipids of membranes.

31

THE BIOSPHERE

Chapter Outline

Objectives

1. Describe the ways in which climate affects the biomes of Earth and influences how organisms are shaped and how they behave.
2. Characterize each of the world's major biomes with respect to climate, plant life, and animal life.
3. Contrast life in lake ecosystems with that in oceans and estuaries.

Key Terms

biosphere
climate
temperature zones
atmosphere
ozone layer
ozone thinning
CFCs
thermal inversion
industrial smog
photochemical smog
acid rain
solar-hydrogen energy
wind farms
ocean
currents
topography
rain shadow
monsoons
biogeographic realms
biomes
ecoregions

hot spots
deserts
desertification
dry shrublands
dry woodlands
grasslands
shortgrass prairie
tallgrass prairie
savanna
monsoon grasslands
evergreen broadleafs
deciduous broadleafs
evergreen conifers
tropical rain forest
monsoon forests
temperate deciduous
  forest
conifers
coniferous forest
boreal forest
taiga

montane coniferous
  forest
temperate rain forest
southern pine forests
tundra
arctic tundra
permafrost
alpine tundra
lake
littoral zone
limnetic zone
profundal zone
phytoplankton
zooplankton
spring overturn
thermocline
fall overturn
eutrophication
oligotrophic
eutrophic
estuaries

mangrove wetland
rocky coastlines
sandy coastlines
upper littoral
midlittoral
lower littoral
sandy shores
coral reefs
coral bleaching
pelagic province
neritic zone
oceanic zone
marine snow
hydrothermal vents
upwelling
downwelling
El Niño
La Niña
ENSO

Lecture Outline

Surfers, Seals, and the Sea
A. El Niño can have drastic effects.
   1. In 1997-1998 half of the sea lions disappeared in the Galapagos Islands.
   2. The number of Northern fur seals plummeted in California.
B. In that winter a massive volume of warm water from the southwestern Pacific moved east.
   1. Currents that would have churned up nutrients were displaced.
   2. Violent storms affected sea life and coastal human dwellings.
   3. Monster hurricanes, ice storms, flooding, and drought were in the news.

31.1   Air Circulation and Climates
    A. Global Air Circulation Patterns
      1. Climate means average weather conditions, such as temperature, humidity, wind speed, cloud cover, and rainfall, over time.
        a. Ultraviolet radiation is absorbed by ozone and oxygen in the upper atmosphere.
        b. Clouds, dust, and water vapor in the atmosphere absorb and reflect solar radiation.
        c. Radiation warms the Earth's surface and generates heat that drives the Earth's weather systems.
      2. The sun differentially heats equatorial and polar regions, creating the world's major temperature zones.
        a. Warm equatorial air rises, cools, releases its moisture, and spreads northward and southward where it descends at $30°$ latitudes as very dry air (results in deserts).

     b. The air is warmed again and ascends at 60° latitudes; as it moves toward the poles, regional areas receive varying amounts of rainfall that in turn influence ecosystems.

   3. Seasonal variations in climate result from the Earth's revolution around the sun.

     a. The amount of solar radiation reaching the Earth's surface changes in the Northern and Southern hemispheres; this results in seasonal changes in climate.

     b. In temperate regions, organisms respond most to changes in daylength and temperature; in deserts and tropical regions, they respond more to seasonal changes in rainfall.

   4. Latitudinal and seasonal variations in solar heating cause ocean water to warm and cool on a vast scale.

     a. Surface waters tend to move from the equator to the poles, warming the air above.

     b. Currents form because of the earth's rotation, winds, variations in temperature, and distribution of land masses.

     c. Immense circular water movements in the Atlantic and Pacific Oceans influence the distribution of ecosystems.

B. A Fence of Wind and Ozone Thinning

   1. Ozone in the lower stratosphere absorbs most of the ultraviolet radiation from the sun.

     a. Seasonal ozone thinning occurs over Antarctica.

     b. With less ozone, more UV radiation reaches the Earth causing more skin cancers, cataracts, and weakened immune systems.

   2. Chlorofluorocarbons (CFCs) seem to be the cause—one chlorine atom can convert 10,000 ozone molecules to oxygen.

     a. Winds rotate around the poles for most of the winter like a dynamic fence.

     b. Chlorine molecules are split apart on "platforms" of ice crystals in fenced-in clouds.

C. No Wind, Lots of Pollutants, and Smog

   1. Thermal inversions can trap pollutants close to the ground.

   2. Industrial smog is gray air found in industrial cities that burn fossil fuel.

   3. Photochemical smog is brown air found in large cities in warm climates; the key culprit is nitric oxide.

D. Winds and Acid Rain

   1. Burning coal in power plants produces sulfur dioxides.

   2. Burning fossil fuels and using nitrogen-rich fertilizers results in nitrogen oxides.

   3. Tiny particles of these oxides can fall to the earth in two forms: dry acid deposition or acid rain.

E. Harnessing Solar and Wind Energy

   1. Solar-hydrogen energy is an attractive technology because it depends on a renewable energy source—the sun.

   2. Photovoltaic cells produce an electric current that splits water into oxygen and hydrogen gas, which can be used directly as fuel or to produce electricity.

   3. Where winds travel faster than 7.5 meters per second, wind turbines are cost-effective producers of electricity.

   4. Because winds do not blow on a regular schedule, wind turbines cannot be the exclusive source of energy.

31.2   The Ocean, Landforms, and Climates

A. Ocean Currents and Their Effects

   1. Ocean water covers almost three-fourths of the earth's surface.

   2. Latitudinal and seasonal variations in solar heating cause ocean water to warm and cool on a vast scale.

a. Surface waters tend to move from the equator to the poles, warming the air above.

b. Currents form because of the earth's rotation, winds, variations in temperature, and distribution of land masses.

c. Immense circular water movements in the Atlantic and Pacific Oceans influence the distribution of ecosystems.

B. Rain Shadows and Monsoons

1. Topography refers to physical features of a region, such as elevation.

2. Mountains, valleys, and other features influence regional climates.

a. The mountains of the western United States cause the winds from the ocean to rise, cool, and lose their moisture.

b. As the winds descend on the leeward (eastern) slopes, they gain moisture from the earth and its vegetation causing a rain shadow effect.

c. Monsoon rains occur when warm winds pick up ocean moisture and release it over the cooler landmasses of Asia and Africa.

31.3 Realms of Biodiversity

A. *Biogeographic realms* are broad land regions with characteristic types of plants and animals, which can be subdivided into biomes.

1. *Biomes* are broad vegetational subdivisions including all animals and other organisms.

a. Biome distribution corresponds with climate, topography, and soil type.

b. The form of the dominant plants tells us something of the weather conditions.

2. *Ecoregions* are portions of biomes that have been identified as possessing species vulnerable to extinction.

B. Deserts, Natural and Man-Made

1. Most deserts lie between 30° north and south latitudes.

a. Annual rainfall is less than 10 centimeters.

b. Vegetation is scarce but there is some diversity; day/night temperatures fluctuate widely.

2. Desertification is the conversion of grasslands and croplands to desertlike conditions.

a. Large-scale desertification is caused by overgrazing of cattle (non-native) on marginal lands.

b. Far-reaching ecological effects of dust storms moving off the African coast may be contributing to the decline of coral reefs in the Caribbean.

C. Dry Shrublands, Dry Woodlands, and Grasslands

1. Dry shrublands prevail when rainfall is less than 25–60 cm (example: the highly flammable California chaparral).

a. The climate is semiarid.

b. Rains occur during mild winter months; summers are long, hot, and dry; dominant plants have tough, evergreen leaves.

2. Dry woodlands occur when rainfall is about 40–100 cm; there are trees but not in dense forests.

3. Grasslands sweep across much of the interior of continents in the zones between deserts and temperate forests.

a. Grassland characteristics include: flat or rolling land, high rates of evaporation, limited rainfall, grazing and burrowing animals, and few forests.

b. There are three basic types in North America:

1) *Shortgrass prairie* of the American Midwest is typified by short, drought-resistant grasses, which have been replaced by grains that require irrigation.

2) *Tallgrass prairie* was originally found in the American West where water was more plentiful.

  c. *Savannas* such as the African *savanna* are hot, dry, and bear small bushes among the grass.

  d. The *monsoon grasslands* of southern Asia experience seasons of torrential rain alternating with near drought.

D. Broadleaf Forests

1. Three forest biomes differ in their types of trees, partly influenced by the distance from the equator.

  a. Evergreen broadleafs dominate between 20° N and S latitude.

  b. Deciduous broadleaf forests lie farther from the equator; the regions are milder in temperature with moderate rainfall.

  c. Evergreen conifers are dominant in high, cold latitudes and high mountains.

2. *Tropical rain forests* occur where high temperatures, rainfall, and humidity promote luxuriant plant growth, competing vines, and incredible animal diversity.

3. In the *tropical deciduous forest,* many trees drop some or all of their leaves during the pronounced dry season.

4. The *monsoon forests* of Southeast Asia also have such trees.

5. In the *temperate deciduous forests* of North America, conditions of temperature and rainfall do not favor rapid decomposition; thus, nutrients are conserved to provide fertile soil.

E. Coniferous Forests

1. The typical "tree" in these forests is some variety of evergreen cone-bearer with needlelike leaves.

2. These forests are found in widely divergent geographic areas:

  a. *Boreal forests* (or *taiga*) are found in the cool to cold northern regions of North America, Europe, and Asia; spruce and balsam fir are dominant.

  b. *Montane coniferous forests* extend southward through the great mountain ranges; fir and pine dominate.

  c. *Temperate rain forest* parallels the west coast of North America and features sequoias and redwoods.

  d. *Southern pine forests* grow in the sandy soil of several Atlantic and Gulf coast states.

F. Arctic and Alpine Tundra

1. *Arctic tundra* lies to the north of the boreal forests; it is a vast treeless plain, very cold, with low moisture; it is characterized by *permafrost,* which prevents growth of large trees.

2. *Alpine tundra* occurs at high elevations in mountains throughout the world.

31.4   The Water Provinces

A. Lake Ecosystems

1. A lake is a body of standing freshwater produced by geologic processes, as when an advancing glacier carves a basin in the Earth.

  a. The *littoral zone* extends from the shore to where rooted plants stop growing.

  b. The *limnetic zone* includes open, sunlit waters beyond the littoral to a depth where photosynthesis is no longer significant; plankton life is abundant.

  c. The *profundal zone* is the deep, open water below the depth of light penetration; detritus sinks from the limnetic and is acted upon by decomposers.

2. Seasonal Changes in Lakes

  a. In temperate regions, lakes undergo changes in density and temperature.

  b. In winter, ice (less dense) forms on the surface over water that is warmer, much of it at $4°$ C (greatest density), and heavier.

    c. During the *spring overturn,* warming and winds cause oxygen to be carried downward and nutrients up to the surface.

    d. By midsummer a *thermocline* between the upper, warmer layers and lower, cooler layers prevents vertical warming.

    e. During autumn, the upper layers cool and sink, causing a *fall overturn.*

  3. Trophic Nature of Lakes

    a. Glaciers carve out basins, which become filled with water to form lakes.

    b. Interactions of soils, basin shape, and climate produce a continuum of trophic structure.

    c. *Oligotrophic* lakes are deep, nutrient-poor, and low in primary productivity.

    d. *Eutrophic* lakes are shallow and nutrient-rich, often due to agricultural and urban runoff wastes.

B. Estuaries and Mangrove Wetlands

  1. Estuaries are partially enclosed regions where fresh and salt water meet.

    a. Estuaries are incredibly productive feeding and breeding grounds for many animals.

    b. Many estuaries are declining because of upstream diversion of the freshwater that is necessary for their maintenance.

  2. "Mangrove" refers to forests in sheltered regions along tropical coasts.

    a. Ocean waves cannot reach these regions, so anaerobic sediments and mud accumulate.

    b. Salt-tolerant plants with shallow, spreading roots abound here.

    c. The net primary productivity of mangrove wetlands depends on the volume and flow rate of the water moving in and out with the tides.

C. Rocky and Sandy Coastlines

  1. The inhabitants of the intertidal-zone are alternately exposed and submerged; existence is difficult.

  2. Rocky shores have three vertically arranged zones:

    a. The *upper littoral* is submerged only during the highest possible lunar tide; it is sparsely populated.

    b. The *mid-littoral* is submerged during the regular tide and exposed at the lowest tide of the day.

    c. The *lower littoral* is exposed only during the lowest lunar tide.

  3. Sandy and muddy shores are rather unstable stretches of loose sediments; detrital food webs occur; invertebrates are plentiful.

D. Coral Reefs

  1. Coral reefs are wave-resistant formations that consist of accumulated remains of marine organisms.

  2. Corals, dinoflagellates, fishes, algae, and many other organisms live in a delicate balance.

  3. If the reef is stressed and the living organism dies, only the white, hardened chambers remain—coral bleaching.

E. The Open Ocean

  1. The *benthic province* includes all the sediments and rocky formations of the ocean bottom; its zones begin with the continental shelf and extend downward to the deep-sea trenches.

  2. The *pelagic province* includes the entire volume of ocean water and is subdivided into two zones:

    a. The *neritic zone* constitutes the relatively shallow water overlying the continental shelves.

      b. The *oceanic zone* is the water over the ocean basins; photosynthetic activity is restricted to the surface; deeper food webs are dependent on marine snow—bits of organic matter that float downward.

  F. Hydrothermal Vents

    1. Hydrothermal vents occur on the ocean floor.

      a. Here very cold water at the ocean bottom seeps into fissures, is heated, and then is spewed forth mixed with minerals.

      b. Chemoautotrophic bacteria provide the starting point for complex communities of tube worms, crustaceans, clams, and fishes.

    2. By one hypothesis, life may have originated near such nutrient-rich places on the seafloor.

  G. Upwelling Along Coasts

    1. Upwelling is the upward movement of deep, nutrient-rich colder water along the margins of continents.

    2. Under the influence of northern winds and the Earth's rotation, water along the western coasts of the Northern Hemisphere move westward where cold, deep water moves in vertically to replace it.

31.5   Applying Knowledge of the Biosphere

  A. Every three to seven years, the warm surface waters of the western equatorial Pacific move eastward to the coasts of South and Central America to cause "downwelling"—a phenomenon known as El Niño, which can affect weather patterns over land.

    1. El Niño episodes last about 6 to 18 months.

    2. Another oscillation known as La Niña replaces it (the ENSO).

  B. During the 1997-1998 El Niño episode, the number of cases of cholera in Peru increased dramatically.

    1. But where was the bacterial cause, *Vibrio cholerae,* reservoired before the outbreak?

    2. Rita Colwell discovered the answer: copepods, tiny crustaceans that live on phytoplankton, which increase/decrease with the warming/cooling of the ocean water.

Suggestions for Presenting the Material

- Reference to Figure 1.1 should be made for one last time. You can use this figure to put a good "wrap" to the course.

- Many of the subjects discussed in this chapter can be presented very effectively with the aid of slides, films, and videos. Many of the biomes are unfamiliar to most students, but they can be made memorable by use of slides illustrating their different features.

- After reading about ecosystems in the previous chapter, students will be able to identify ecosystem components in the biomes and aquatic ecosystems discussed here. Use familiar examples related to local weather patterns, if possible, when discussing climate.

- Students will be interested in learning more about tropical deforestation, El Niño, the depletion of the ozone layer, and ocean pollution—subjects that have recently been in the news.

- Several aspects of human impact on the biosphere are discussed in the next chapter; you and your students may wish to wait until then before exploring some of the topics and activities suggested here.

Classroom and Laboratory Enrichment

- Use overhead transparencies to show worldwide patterns of climate distribution and biome distribution.

- Use a globe and the information you have learned about global patterns of air circulation to explain the reasons for your latest weather conditions. Explain why your region has the weather it does.

- Discuss the latest advances in meteorology. Describe the role of satellites in assisting weather prediction.

- Select an example of a high elevation mountaintop ecosystem, and examine the plant and animal communities that are found at different elevational ranges. Examine the effects of elevation on plant community composition by taking a field trip, if possible, to an area with variations in elevation.

- Prepare a diagram showing how the effects of increasing elevation are similar to those of decreasing latitude.

- Examine changes in terrestrial plant community composition along moisture gradients.

- Study zonation in a local pond or lake. List the plants, animals, protists, and other microorganisms you find in each zone. Students in subsequent semesters could sample the lake again and describe what changes occur from season to season.

- Design and implement a study of lake stratification. Measure the temperature, dissolved oxygen, and nutrients in each layer of the lake.

- Examine zonation in a marine ecosystem. Visit a coastline area to observe shoreline species, if possible, or look at slides or films, or visit a marine aquarium.

- Construct small-scale replications of freshwater or marine ecosystems in the lab.

- Ask a weather specialist to speak to the class concerning global and local weather and trends in climate change.

- If you do not feel qualified to present the climatological information, secure a film or videotape that will explain it fully and concisely.

- If you are located near an intergrade between biomes (such as temperate deciduous forest to grassland), draw this to the students' attention. Remind them to observe the changes in plant life as they drive through the area and note some highway marker or nearby town for reference.

- To most people the American desert is viewed as a vast wasteland of sand and cactus to be bypassed, as the early settlers did, to reach the promise of the west coast. Gather information on how weekend revelers are destroying this fragile biome that "heals" itself very slowly.

- Prepare a table listing: (a) each biome, (b) its principal location, and (c) its chief plant and animal life.

- Assess public understanding of environmental pollution issues by designing a brief questionnaire. Divide the public into several different groups, and compare the levels of understanding among the groups. Some possible groupings are: students in this course, past students of the course, university or college students at large, university employees, different age groups, local residents not employed by the college or university, and groups created on the basis of differences in factors such as socioeconomic status, political affiliation, age, and education. How well informed are the different groups? Did they know more or less about environmental issues than you thought they would? Can you identify any myths about environmental pollution that appear to be widely held?

- Monitor the quality of air in your area. What has been the impact of humans on the air in your community?

- Collect water samples from your classroom building and have the samples analyzed. Discuss the results with your class.
- Working in small groups, debate the pros and cons of different energy sources. Each group should be prepared to discuss the merits and drawbacks of one of the following energy sources: oil, coal, natural gas, hydropower, solar power, nuclear power, and other alternatives.
- Ask a representative from a local environmental group to address the class.
- Prepare a list of environmental concerns in your area and state. Ask students what *should* be done, then ask them what realistically *can* be done.
- Obtain a map of the United States showing the areas of highest cancer rates. Ask students to speculate as to why certain areas are more at risk than others.

Impacts, Issues Classroom Discussion Ideas

- What impact have human activities had on the weather in the last century?
- Relate the movement of hurricanes through the Caribbean and Gulf of Mexico to the ocean currents you see drawn in Figure 31.7.
- What effect will the rising of ocean waters have on estuarine areas if the greenhouse effect melts the polar ice masses?

Additional Ideas for Classroom Discussion

- As each biome is discussed, ask students who have visited that biome to share their observations with the class.
- Discuss some of the ways to improve soils considered too poor for agriculture. What are some of the characteristics of desert soils and tropical soils that make them poorly suited for long-term agriculture?
- Discuss the ways in which animal morphology might differ from one biome to the next. What role does annual mean temperature play in determining animal morphology? What differences in plant morphology can you see among the different biomes?
- What is a prairie? What happened to the American prairies? Are there still patches of prairie in the United States?
- Why is species diversity so high in tropical rain forests?
- Describe the rates of nutrient cycling in the tundra and in the tropical forest. How can you explain the different rates of nutrient cycling in these two biomes?
- What is meant when a lake is described as "dead"? How does such a condition come about? How can a "dead" lake be rejuvenated?
- What is the most readily observable feature that distinguishes one biome from another?
- As a child you may have believed that if you could leave the Earth's surface and fly toward the sun, you would get warmer and warmer. But of course just the opposite is true; why?
- Should modern technology change desert habitats such as Palm Springs, California, where lawns are green only because they are maintained by artificial means?
- What is "low sulfur" coal?
- How have coal-burning power plants changed in the past 20 years?

- What is a "clean" energy source? Can you think of an example?

- Why is the ozone layer of the earth's atmosphere shrinking at the same time that excessive amounts of ozone at the Earth's surface are present in photochemical smog?

- What is thermal pollution? What are its effects?

- Do you think our laws regarding air pollution are too lenient? What changes would you make in the laws or their enforcement?

- Why do you think relatively little has been done to eliminate the greenhouse effect? What do you think is required before governments such as our own will pass laws regulating the types of human activities responsible for phenomena such as the greenhouse effect?

- Why does normal rainwater have a pH of around 5.6?

- Where does the tap water in your classroom building come from?

- Why would it be unwise to clear tropical forests and irrigate arid lands for conversion to agriculture?

- What are some examples of renewable energy sources?

- How many students in the class recycle their aluminum cans? Newspapers? Glass? Take a hand count. Ask students for reasons why they do (or do not) recycle these materials.

- Ask students to make a list of ways in which they could modify their own lifestyles and behaviors to reduce environmental pollution.

- Do you think that our current environmental pollution problems reflect a fundamental shift in human values over the past 50 years? Why or why not?

- What do you think will be the most important areas of science in the next decade? In 50 years?

- How would *you* rate as a "pioneer" in a setting where there was no electricity, stores, or running water?

- List the ways in which a city, especially a large one, represents one of the least stable of ecosystems.

How Would You Vote? Classroom Discussion Ideas

- Monitor the voting for the online question. Gee, the government wants still more of my hard-earned money. This time it is to fund research on something that might occur every eight to ten years, and might affect me here in a small town in the Midwest. Aren't there more pressing problems?

Term Paper Topics, Library Activities, and Special Projects

- Describe plant and animal features that are influenced by climate.

- Write a description of your local climate. List and describe all of the factors responsible for your local climate.

- Write a report about desertification.

- Describe where prairie remnants are found today in the United States. Prepare plant species lists for the shortgrass prairie and the tallgrass prairie.

- Write a report about historical descriptions of the Dust Bowl.

- What changes in plant species composition would you see among deciduous forests as you traveled from the eastern United States to the western coast?

- Describe the latest efforts made by governments around the world to slow the rate of tropical deforestation.

- What happens to the arctic tundra when the permafrost becomes damaged? Discuss the effects of human habitation on the arctic tundra.

- Describe what happens when a lake undergoes eutrophication. Discuss examples of situations in which eutrophication was reversed. What changes in aquatic species composition will occur as a result of eutrophication?

- Discuss the rejuvenation of lake ecosystems that were formerly polluted.

- Describe the role of estuaries in commercial fisheries. Discuss the ecology of one of the commercially important estuaries in the United States.

- Learn more about the recent research suggesting that the ozone layer may be shrinking.

- In the Northern Hemisphere we experience warm summer temperatures when the Earth is tilted *toward* the sun. In winter the tilt is just the opposite. But during which season is the Earth slightly closer to the sun? Don't assume you know this one—look it up!

- Irrigation has brought "bloom to the deserts." But is there a negative side to this practice? Search for a balanced perspective.

- Prepare a colored map of the United States showing which areas of the nation provide the most food and least food; superimpose shading to show the areas of densest consumer (human) populations.

- Describe the actual contents of industrial smog or photochemical smog in the nearest city with an air pollution problem. Describe the ways in which the air pollution affects the health of area residents.

- Look up historical records of thermal air inversions that resulted in significant numbers of deaths due to air pollution.

- What are the biological effects of acid rain on fish populations?

- Examine the statistical link between air quality and rates of respiratory disease.

- Describe successful community recycling programs. List the features of successful programs, and describe obstacles that must be overcome to ensure success.

- Discuss the success of recycling programs in states (such as New Jersey) with laws requiring mandatory recycling.

- Summarize the federal laws against pollution.

- Who are your local polluters? Find out which industries release pollutants into the atmosphere. List the pollutants and describe what steps the companies have taken to reduce emission of pollutants.

- Describe the process of illegal dumping. Why is it done? Has it been done in your area? What are the penalties for illegal dumping?

- Make a list of the contents of a toxic waste dump, and describe the potential hazards posed by such compounds.

- Discuss the environmental effects of strip-mining.

Possible Responses to *Critical Thinking* Questions

1. If the oak woodlands disappear, that would remove a canopy of leaves that is blocking a significant amount of sunlight from reaching the understory. With the influx of sunlight, small bushes should begin to grow, possibly resulting in a highly combustible undergrowth.

2. Boreal forests stretch around the globe at latitudes where the weather is generally cool to very cold year round. The fact that they can maintain a high rate of photosynthesis in these temperatures and not form bubbles in their vascular tissue as the sap thaws have permitted them to survive the pressures of natural selection and thrive.

3. At first glance, nuclear power plants generating electricity appear very clean and environmentally friendly. However, when we consider the deeper issues we become less enthusiastic. First, there is the building of the power plant, which is very expensive because of the containment of the radioactivity. Secondly, there is always the danger of an explosion and the spread of radioactive materials. Finally, there is the huge problem of what to do with the radioactive wastes. Not seen for many years is another pesky little fact: the whole plant will have to be decommissioned and dismantled, often at more cost (due to inflation) than it took to build it. Who would want one of these in their vicinity? Not many people. But if the thing were way off somewhere and the nice, dependable electricity arrived in my home via unseen, underground wires, ah shoot, let somebody else worry about, right? Wrong!

4. To most people there is nothing more desolate and useless than a desert. It just seems to be lying there waiting for "terror-tourists" on ATVs. Perhaps it is not their fault, it is ours—the biologists—for not educating them on the fragility of the desert biome. Most sad, however, are the long periods of time necessary to undo the damage these vehicles cause, and to restore the ecosystem.

5. If global warming increased the overall air temperature over the Minnesota lakes, then there might not be as much freezing of the lake surface, it any at all. That would mean less of a spring thaw and less differential of the temperatures in the water as the sun began to warm the air, moving toward summer. Thus there would be less of a spring overturn and less mixing of the nutrients that support the animal life.

6. Wetlands, to many people, are probably in the same category of usefulness as the deserts mentioned in #4 above. To most people wetlands are just a swampy, mosquitoey, snakey bunch of water. Even if the value to wildlife and ecosystem balance is pointed out, most people would reply "Of what value is that to *me*?" In the United States we have a strong sense of rugged individualism, which includes land ownership. And furthermore, if we own the land, we feel we have the right to do what we want with it. The idea of the federal or state government seizing land, even if reparations are given, is just so "communist." Perhaps in some ways our strong democracy heritage will not serve us well as we become more crowded on this precarious planet and more dependent on the good will and good actions of all others.

32

BEHAVIORAL ECOLOGY

Chapter Outline

Objectives

1. Understand the components of behavior that have a genetic and/or hormonal basis.
2. Distinguish behavior that is primarily instinctive from behavior that is learned.
3. Know the aspects of behavior that have an adaptive value.
4. Describe how forms of communication organize social behavior.
5. List the costs and benefits of social life.
6. Explain the roles of self-sacrifice and altruism in social life.

Key Terms

pheromone	natural selection	composite signal	dominance hierarchies
animal behavior	reproductive success	communication display	cost-benefit approach
hormones	adaptive behavior	threat display	indirect selection theory
oxytocin	social behavior	tactile displays	inclusive fitness
instinctive behavior	selfish behavior	illegitimate receiver	vomeronasal organ
sign stimuli	altruism	illegitimate signalers	autism
fixed action pattern	communication signals	courtship displays	
learned behavior	signaling pheromones	selfish herd	
imprinting	priming pheromones	cooperative hunting	

Lecture Outline

My Pheromones Made Me Do It
  A. Africanized honeybees are more aggressive in their stinging attacks.
    1. Isopentyl acetate functions as an alarm pheromone.
    2. Africanized bees respond faster and in greater numbers than their European cousins.
  B. This is an example of differences in animal behavior—coordinated responses that animal species make to stimuli.

32.1 So Where Does Behavior Start?
  A. Genes and Behavior
    1. Behavioral responses depend on neural patterns, which are determined by genes.
    2. Illustration: Two populations of garter snakes in California show different feeding preferences from birth.
      a. The feeding preferences differ by geographical location and are the result of natural selection of genes for taste and smell.
      b. When snakes from the two locations are crossbred, the hybrids have an intermediate response to the stimuli.
  B. Hormones and Behavior
    1. Hormones are signaling molecules that can affect a series of behavioral responses.
    2. Illustration: The hormone oxytocin in mammals can affect social behavior.
      a. If oxytocin is injected into a female, she becomes quickly receptive to the male.
      b. If a female is given an oxytocin-blocking drug, she promptly dumps her partners.
  C. Regarding Instinct and Learning
    1. In *instinctive behavior*, components of the nervous system allow an animal to make a stereotyped response to a first-time encounter with environmental cues.
      a. Each of these instinctive responses is triggered by a sign stimulus, which sets in motion a *fixed action pattern*.
      b. Illustrations: Newly hatched cuckoos respond to the shape of eggs in the nest by pushing them out; tongue-flicking, orientation, and strike of a newborn garter snake are instinctive; and human infants smile at a face-sized mask with two eyelike spots.
    2. In *learned behavior*, an animal processes and integrates information gained from specific experiences in order to vary or change responses to stimuli.

3. In *imprinting*, learning requires exposure to key stimuli in the environment during a sensitive period in the young animal's life.
    a. White-crowned sparrows learn the specific dialect of their songs by listening to other males in their population.
    b. The period for this learning is a sensitive time between 10 and 50 days after hatching.
    c. Sparrows can learn some of the dialect from recordings, but do better if they have a social experience with a live "tutor."

D. The Adaptive Value of Behavior
    1. *Natural selection* is the outcome of differences in survival and reproduction that has occurred among individuals that show variation in their heritable traits.
    2. Definitions used in describing behavioral evolution:
        a. *Reproductive success* refers to the survival and production of offspring.
        b. *Adaptive behavior* promotes the propagation of an individual's genes and tends to occur at increased frequency in successive generations.
        c. *Social behavior* defines the cooperative, interdependent relationships among individuals of the species.
        d. *Selfish behavior* occurs when an individual increases its own chances of producing offspring.
        e. *Altruism* is self-sacrificing behavior that helps others and decreases the individual's own chance to reproduce.
    3. When behaviorists speak of "selfish" or "altruistic" behavior, they do not mean that the individual is consciously aware of what it is doing or of the ultimate goal of its behavior.
        a. Do lemmings commit suicide to remove "excess" lemmings? Or did some just die through starvation, predation, or drowning?
        b. Do starlings "decorate" their nests with sprigs of wild carrot greenery just because it looks nice? No, experiments show that these sprigs repel mites and thus contribute to the health of the birds.

32.2   Communication Signals
  A. The Nature of Communication Signals
    1. Social behavior is the tendency of individual animals to enter into cooperative, interdependent relationships with others of their kind.
        a. Communication signals are actions or cues that have a beneficial effect on the signaler and receiver during an exchange of information.
        b. Natural selection tends to favor communication signals that promote the reproductive success of both the signaler and the receiver.
    2. Pheromones are powerful chemicals released into the air to attract members of the opposite sex.
        a. *Signaling* pheromones induce a receiver to respond fast, such as the alarm pheromone of honeybees.
        b. *Priming* pheromones elicit generalized physiological responses; an example would be the volatile odor of male mice urine, which triggers and enhances estrus in female mice.
    3. Several types of signals, including chemical, acoustical, and visual, can combine to produce a composite signal.
  B. Examples of Communication Displays
    1. Visual signals may be used by animals as a threat display; for example, male baboons may threaten a rival with a "yawn" that exposes the canine teeth.

2. Visual signals may be a vital part of more obviously cooperative interactions, as in the courtship displays of birds, which often involve contorted posturing.
3. Tactile signals are used to communicate by some means of bodily contact.
   a. When a foraging honeybee finds food relatively close to the hive, it returns and performs a "round dance" on the honeycomb with several bees in close contact.
   b. If the forager is to communicate more precise information about the location of the food source, she performs a "waggle dance," which pinpoints the location of the food relative to the position of the sun.
C. Illegitimate Signalers and Receivers
1. Termites can be the illegitimate receivers of signals intended to be sent from one ant to another ant.
2. Certain predatory female fireflies can be illegitimate signalers when they lure a male, not for sex, but as a tasty meal.

32.3 Mates, Offspring, and Reproductive Success
A. Sexual Selection and Mating Behavior
1. *Sexual selection* is the evolutionary outcome of competition for mates and selectivity among potential mates.
   a. Males produce large numbers of small gametes; therefore, reproductive success is measured in terms of how many females the male can inseminate.
   b. Because females produce limited numbers of eggs and can only care for a small number of offspring, it is the *quality* of a mate that is important.
2. The following are some examples of selection procedures:
   a. Male hangingflies kill a moth, which they then present as a gift to females, who will mate only so long as the food holds out.
   b. Male sage grouse gather on a communal display ground (a lek) to strut their stuff, hoping to attract the attention of the females gathered around.
3. In these examples and many other species, it is the females that dictate the rules of male competition, with males employing tactics that will help them fertilize as many eggs as possible.
B. Parental Care
1. Parental behavior drains time and energy that might be allocated to improving the parents' own chances of living to reproduce at another time.
2. Yet parental behavior benefits the individual by improving the likelihood that the current generation of offspring will survive.

32.4 Costs and Benefits of Social Groups
A. Cooperative Predator Avoidance
1. All actions within a social group can be analyzed on a *cost-benefit approach* that considers the individual's success in contributing genes to the next generation.
2. In a large group, a prey animal is less likely to become a victim.
3. Social animals are better able to repel a predator through group defense.
B. The Selfish Herd
1. Some animals live in groups simply to "use" others as a shield against predators.
2. Bluegill sunfish near the center of nesting sites are safer from attacks by largemouth bass than those at the periphery.
C. Cooperative Hunting
1. Group hunts are not necessarily more successful than solitary hunting because the captured prey must be shared.

2. Hunting in groups may have other benefits such as fending off scavengers, caring for one another's young, and protection of the common territory.
    D. Dominance Hierarchies
        1. Some animals show self-sacrificing behavior that enhances the continuity of their particular genetic lineage.
        2. Why do individuals sacrifice some of their own reproductive success for the good of the group?
            a. Sacrifice may be the cost of belonging to the group.
            b. Individuals may cooperate against predators, even though the opportunities to reproduce may not be theirs.
            c. Dominance hierarchies tend to minimize aggression within the society, and dominant members leave more offspring than subordinates, who may move up if they patiently wait.
    E. Regarding the Costs
        1. Animals living in close association may increase their hunting success to such an extent that they deplete the local resources more rapidly than if they were spread out.
        2. Sociality may also increase vulnerability to predators, parasites, and disease.

32.5   Why Sacrifice Yourself?
    A. In altruistic behavior, the "helper" reduces its own reproductive potential while the "helped" enjoys increased reproductive success.
    B. Social Insects.
        1. In insect societies such as bees, sterile guards may protect the queen by stinging an intruder and thereby committing suicide.
        2. By their self-sacrificing behavior, bees increase the number of genetically similar offspring produced.
    C. Termites live in enormous family groups.
        1. Soldier termites defend the colony by secreting substances to attract other defenders and battling the invaders themselves.
        2. Worker termites cultivate a fungus to provide food for the next mates.
        3. Soldiers and workers are sterile and dedicate their lives to provide for the fertile king(s) and queen.
    D. Social Mole-Rats
        1. The only eusocial mammals are the African mole-rats, who live in excavated burrows.
        2. One reproducing female dominates the clan and mates with one to three males; other non-breeders tend the "queen" and "king(s)" and their offspring.
        3. Digger mole-rats even provide food to "loafers" who lie around doing practically nothing.
    E. Indirect Selection Theory
        1. The theory of *inclusive fitness* holds that individuals can indirectly pass on their genes by helping relatives survive and reproduce.
        2. All individuals of the insect colonies are members of an extended family.

32.6   A Look at Primate Social Behavior
    A. Sex is the premier binding force in the social life of chimpanzees.
        1. Female chimps have strong physiological and physical adaptations to attract several males.
        2. The males spend their lives in the group into which they are born and form strong social bonds; but they also may attack and kill infants.

B. Bonobos reveal contrasting sexual behavior.
  1. The females in a group form strong bonds and are receptive to sex at any time.
  2. Males display less social cohesion than male chimps and have never been observed committing infanticide.

32.7 Human Social Behavior
  A. Human Pheromones
    1. Studies have shown that women living together in a college dormitory can become synchronized in their menstrual cycles.
    2. Is it possible that female humans have a vomeronasal organ to detect pheromones in one another's sweat?
  B. Hormones and Bonding Behavior
    1. Oxytocin influences human social attachment; not surprisingly, autistic individuals—lacking in normal behavioral and social skills—have lowered oxytocin levels.
    2. Researchers are studying oxytocin's role in the formation of bonds between mother and infant and between sexual partners.
  C. Evolutionary Questions
    1. "Adaptive" does not mean the same thing as "moral right"; it does mean that the behavior is valuable in the transmission of an individual's genes.
    2. Infanticide is morally repugnant but it is not unnatural; the absence of a biological father and the presence of an unrelated male increases the risk to an American child under age two by 70 times.

Suggestions for Presenting the Material

- This chapter deals with topics that are not *strictly* biological but rather encompass the realm of social interaction.

- One approach to presenting the material is the inclusion of representative examples (with slides) that illustrate each principle of learning.

- Stress the "interpretative" aspect of studying behavior; that is, rarely do two investigators give exactly the same interpretation of the behavior they see.

- Many of the principles of animal behavior are difficult to demonstrate in the lab, although behavior textbooks and lab manuals contain possibilities for classroom lab experiments that can be used to accompany this chapter or the following chapter on social behavior.

- Films of such aspects of animal behavior as instinctive behaviors and learned behaviors make an excellent addition to the classroom. Students can also read and report on animal behavior experiments performed by others or the careers of famous animal behaviorists.

- The topic of animal behavior can serve as an opening for discussing the challenges of experimental design, especially with regard to experiments conducted in the field.

- If you feel capable of commenting on the relationship between behavior as viewed by a biologist and as viewed by a sociologist, your students would no doubt appreciate this "bridging" of the disciplines.

- Emphasize the evolutionary value of each of the social behaviors described in the text. Students have seen many examples of adaptive traits by this point in their study of introductory biology and will be fascinated to think of behaviors as yet another example.

- Students will ask questions about aspects of human behavior that will serve as the focal points of some interesting discussions.

- Because many social behaviors are difficult to describe or demonstrate in class, films can be effectively used to present many of the more complex examples of social behavior, such as communication among honeybees.

Classroom and Laboratory Enrichment

- Design an animal behavior experiment that can be performed outdoors in your campus environment. Begin by listing animal species found on campus, and then design methods of observing their behaviors.
- Learn more about experiments investigating instinctive behaviors in newly hatched chicks.
- Design experiments to test the ability of rats to learn mazes.
- Can zoos or aquaria be used as laboratories for animal behavior research? Visit a nearby zoo or aquarium to observe animal behavior. What types of behaviors do you see that are a product of captivity?
- Develop lab experiments investigating territoriality among fishes or small vertebrates.
- The most reliable sources of visual enhancement for these lectures are films and videotapes (the Disney series is excellent) because they are edited to show the critical behavior that may have occurred only after patient waiting.
- Although this chapter focuses on behavior in general using a variety of animals, you may want to prepare a listing of human examples for each topic and ask students to evaluate your list and supplement it.
- Survey the class opinion on whether each of the topics below is controlled more by *heredity* or *environment*, or equally:
    a. Intelligence
    b. Body size
    c. Beauty
    d. Speech patterns
    e. Health
- Design and implement a lab experiment involving schooling behavior among tropical fish species. How many fish must swim together before a lone fish will recognize them as a school and join them? Will fish school selectively with members of their own species?
- Look up information about body language and visual cues used by humans. Design experiments to be performed on campus that will allow you to observe these and other forms of nonverbal human communication. Is nonverbal communication different in males and females? Do students use different types of body language in different campus locations (classrooms, library, cafeteria, dormitories)?
- Design and perform a lab experiment investigating maternal behaviors in white mice. Is a mother able to quickly retrieve her pups if they are removed from the nest? Why is this an adaptive trait? What signals does she use to find her pups?
- What kinds of acoustical signaling can you hear in your area on a spring or summer evening? What kinds of acoustical signaling can you hear during the daytime hours? Determine the species responsible for the sounds you hear, and analyze the meaning of their calls.
- The best example of highly social insect behavior is the waggle dance of the honeybee. There are several sources of videotape and film; check your biological supply house catalogs.

- If the opportunity is available, consider a demonstration of firefly signaling. This may be overly ambitious but might be of interest to an honors group as a special project.
- To stimulate interest in this material, try to include a human behavior example for each of the topics discussed in the text.

Impacts, Issues Classroom Discussion Ideas

- What are some of the difficulties in designing research experiments in animal behavior? Discuss problems that must be overcome when performing animal behavior research.
- Can you think of some reasons why displays of aggression between males of the same species rarely result in actual bloodshed?
- What part has natural selection played in the behaviors we observe in animals today?
- Explain the benefits that accrue to the young vertebrate "helpers" who forego reproduction to assist in the rearing of their siblings.
- Why do you think true social behavior has evolved in only a few insect species?
- What aspects of bee behavior are "learned"; which are innate?

Additional Ideas for Classroom Discussion

- Can avoidance behavior in *Paramecium* be considered learning?
- What is the link between environment and behavior?
- What are the characteristics of innate behaviors? What are the characteristics of learned behaviors?
- Distinguish among associative learning, latent learning, and insight learning.
- Give an example of a sign stimulus.
- How much of the animal behavior we see and interpret is the result of what "we want to see"?
- What kinds of methods are used to alter animal behavior (for example, training dogs)? Are these the same methods as used for altering behavior in children?
- In what ways is human behavior altered by prison incarceration?
- Discuss the ways in which elaborate mating displays benefit a species.
- In what ways do elements of sociality such as schooling benefit a species? What are the drawbacks of sociality?
- How do dominance hierarchies benefit those species that use them?
- What is meant by the term *selfish herd*?
- How much of our human behavior is determined by our culture? What behaviors seem to be universal among all cultures? Can you think of unusual behaviors that seem to be found only among one culture?
- Can you think of some selection pressures that are responsible for the evolution of many human traits? (Some examples include selection for capturing large prey, coping with carnivorous competitors, and caring for infants.)
- Is child abuse a human behavior of modern times in Western cultures? Can you think of some reasons why this might be so?

- In what respects are countries that describe themselves as "socialist" similar to truly social insects? How do they differ?

How Would You Vote? Classroom Discussion Ideas

- Monitor the voting for the online question. It seems a reasonable request that there be increased funding for research on bees—both European and Africanized. These insects are extremely valuable participants in the balance of nature. We have got to learn how to live with them.

Term Paper Topics, Library Activities, and Special Projects

- Describe the role of environmental cues in determining migratory behaviors in birds. Do biologists understand the physiology underlying the navigational senses of birds?
- Discuss the annual migration of salmon to spawning grounds.
- How are green sea turtles able to find their way from their home in ocean waters off Brazil to their breeding grounds hundreds of miles away on Ascension Island? Describe the latest research efforts attempting to answer this question.
- Describe the mood-altering effects of the steroid drugs sometimes taken by athletes to increase muscle mass.
- Examine the effects of any one of the so-called recreational drugs (alcohol, nicotine, marijuana, cocaine, LSD, amphetamines, barbiturates) on human behavior.
- Describe the role of melatonin in vertebrate behavior.
- Examine the role of sex in determining human behavior. Are there some behaviors that occur with significantly greater frequency among individuals of one sex than among individuals of the opposite sex?
- Station yourself in a variety of busy spots on campus. Record the usual and unusual behaviors you see. Make note of the day of the week, time of day, gender of participants, race, weather conditions, and so on. Compare your observations with others in the class.
- What is unusual about monarch butterfly migrations compared to bird migrations? (Hint: Investigate the migration of the offspring.)
- Describe the chemical nature, distribution, and role of pheromones in animal behavior.
- Describe the visual communication system of fireflies.
- Make a list of altruistic behaviors among humans.
- Describe behavioral studies of human infants.
- How can human behaviors change as a result of brain surgery (such as a lobotomy) or injury? Describe the relationship between the different areas of the brain and human behavior.
- Discuss research in primate behavior. What have such experiments taught us about human behavior?
- What examples of nonverbal communication (for example, certain gestures and facial displays) seem to be universally understood? What are some examples of nonverbal communication that exist only within a particular culture or have different meanings among different cultures?
- Examine the growing commercial use of pheromones to control insect pests. How do pheromones work? How are they produced?

- Why do humans universally regard infants as "cute"? Are there facial features present only among infants that elicit a characteristic loving, nurturing response from adults?

- Discuss behaviorists' views on war as a human behavior. Why do humans fight wars with one another?

- Read about Diane Fosse's research on the societies of primates in Africa.

- E. O. Wilson is well known for his synthesis of biology and sociology as presented in his book on "sociobiology." Prepare a brief synopsis of his ideas.

Possible Responses to *Critical Thinking* Questions

1. Evidently this rooster had an experience early in its life in which it took up company with some ducks and now doesn't know it is a rooster. This is often seen in other animals including family pets that are supposed to be enemies but lie next to each other, even grooming one another.

2. At first glance it might seem that the booby parents *know* that two eggs must be laid if one chick is to be killed. But this is not so. Rather, over the course of evolution the laying of two eggs by some boobies was adaptive in terms of survival. Alternatively, perhaps a single egg could be laid, which would hatch to a single chick with no rival. Perhaps an experiment could be performed in which the second egg is removed to see if the lone egg and its chick would make it.

3. The rise of a mutated gene that permitted the throat muscles and vocal cords to form language was critical to the development of social behavior and learning. While it is true that non-language animals do develop forms of social behavior and certainly "learn" to perform many tasks, they do not have the broad range of behaviors and learning that communication through spoken language affords. Think of the school classroom. What difficulty would occur if the teacher and students could not communicate the thoughts that originate in each group?

4. First, a researcher would collect some of the cheetah's exocrine gland secretions and attempt to identify the chemical(s) present. Once this was accomplished, one could place the isolated compound on various items in the territory and note the response by cheetahs, male and female. One could also perform variations such as dilution of the extract to test potency or make derivatives of the extract to pinpoint the exact part of the chemical that is eliciting the response. This could lead to a proposed mechanism of action.

5. The data would seem to indicate that large testicles in males would be correlated with multiple matings with females (promiscuity). This is seen in the chimps but is not the case in gorillas, where the male (possessing small testicles) mates with few females. The human testicle size is somewhere in between that of gorillas and chimps. Perhaps humans are supposed to be more promiscuous *biologically* but our social customs dictate against this.

6. A gene mutation that affects the synthesis of fatty acids could produce pheromone derivatives that are not recognizable by mates. Because these pheromones are species-specific, they are critical for the process of finding a mate of the same species, which is the only mate that will lead to successful breeding. If the mutations prevent the successful location of a mate, then the whole courtship and breeding processes are short-circuited.

WRITING ESSAYS AND TERM PAPERS

A term paper is really just a long essay, its greater length reflecting more extensive treatment of a broader issue. Both assignments present critical evaluations of what you have read. In preparing an essay, you synthesize information, explore relationships, analyze, compare, contrast, evaluate, and organize your own arguments clearly, logically, and persuasively—gradually leading up to an assessment of your own. A good term paper or short essay is a creative work; you must interpret thoughtfully what you have read and come up with something that goes beyond what is presented in any single article or book consulted.

Getting Started

You must first decide on a general subject of interest. Often your instructor will suggest topics that former students have successfully exploited. Use these suggestions as guides, but do not feel compelled to select one of these topics unless so instructed. Be sure to choose or develop a subject that interests you. It is much easier to write successfully about something of interest than about something that bores you. All you need for getting started is a general subject, not a specific topic. Stay flexible. As you research your selected subject, you usually will find that you must narrow your focus to a particular topic because you encounter an unmanageable number of references pertinent to your original idea. You cannot, for instance, write about the entire field of primate behavior because the field has many different facets, each associated with a large and growing literature. In such a case, you will find a smaller topic, such as the social significance of primate grooming behavior, to be more appropriate; as you continue your literature search, you may even find it necessary to restrict your attention to a few primate species. Alternatively, you may find that the topic originally selected is too narrow and that you cannot find enough information on which to base a substantial paper. You must then broaden your topic, or switch topics entirely, so that you will end up with something to discuss. Don't be afraid to discard a topic on which you cannot find much information. Choose a topic you can understand fully. You can't possibly write clearly and convincingly on something beyond your grasp. Don't set out to impress your instructor with complexity; instead, dazzle your instructor with clarity and understanding. Simple topics often make the best ones for essays.

Researching Your Topic

Begin by carefully reading the appropriate section of your textbook to get an overview of the general subject of which your topic is a part. It is usually wise to then consult one or two additional textbooks before venturing into the recent literature; a solid construction requires a firm foundation. Your instructor may have placed a number of pertinent textbooks on reserve in your college library.

This section is adapted from *A Short Guide to Writing About Biology* by Jan A. Pechenik. Copyright ©1987 by Jan A. Pechenik. Reprinted by permission of Scott, Foresman and Company.

Alternatively, you can consult your librarian, or the library card file or computer system, looking for books listed under the topic you have chosen to investigate.

Plagiarism and Note Taking

The essay or term paper you submit for evaluation must be original work: yours. Submitting anyone else's work under your name is plagiarism and can get you expelled from college. Presenting someone else's ideas as your own is also plagiarism. Consider the following two paragraphs.

> Smith (1981) suggests that this discrepancy in feeding rates may reflect differences in light levels used in the two different experiments. Jones (1984), however, found that light level did not influence the feeding rates of these animals and suggested that the rate differences reflect differences in the density at which the animals were held during the two experiments.

> This discrepancy in feeding rates might reflect differences in light levels. Jones (1984), however, found that light level did not influence feeding rates. Perhaps the difference in rates reflects differences in the density at which the animals were held during the two experiments.

The first example is fine. In the second example, however, the writer takes credit for the ideas of Smith and Jones; the writer has plagiarized.

Plagiarism sometimes occurs unintentionally through faulty note taking. Photocopying an article or book chapter does not constitute note taking; neither does copying a passage by hand, occasionally substituting a synonym for a word used by the source's author. Take notes using your own words; you must get away from being awed by other people's words and move toward building confidence in your own thoughts and phrasings. Note taking involves critical evaluation; as you read, you must decide either that particular facts or ideas are relevant to your topic or that they are irrelevant. As Sylvan Barnet says in *A Short Guide to Writing About Art* (1981. Little, Brown and Company, second edition, p. 142), "You are not doing stenography; rather, you are assimilating knowledge and you are thinking, and so for the most part your source should be digested rather than engorged whole." If an idea is relevant, you should jot down a summary using your own words. Avoid writing complete sentences as you take notes; this will help prevent unintentional plagiarism later and will encourage you to see through to the essence of a statement while note taking.

Sometimes the authors' words seem so perfect that you cannot see how they might be revised to best advantage for your paper. In this case, you may wish to copy a phrase or a sentence or two verbatim, but be sure to enclose this material in quotation marks as you write, and clearly indicate the source and page number from which the quotation derives. If you modify the original wording slightly as you take notes, you should indicate this as well, perhaps by using modified quotation marks: ". . .". If your notes on a particular passage are in your own words, you should also indicate this as you write. I precede such notes, reflecting my own ideas or my own choice of words, with the word *Me* and a colon; my wife, who is also a biologist, uses her initials. If you take notes in this manner you will avoid the unintentional plagiarism that occurs when you later forget who is actually responsible for the wording of your notes or who is really responsible for the origin of an idea.

You probably cannot take notes in your own words if you do not understand what you are reading. Similarly, it is also difficult to be selective in your note taking until you have achieved a general understanding of the material. I suggest that you first consult at least one general reference text and read the material carefully, as recommended earlier. Once you have located a particularly promising scientific article, read the entire paper through at least once without taking any notes. Resist the (strong) temptation to annotate and take notes during this first reading, even though you may feel that without a pen in your hand you are accomplishing nothing. Put your pencils, pens, and notecards or paper away and read. Read slowly and with care. Read to understand. Study the illustrations, figure captions, tables, and graphs carefully, and try to develop your own interpretations before reading those of the author(s). Don't be frustrated by not understanding the paper at the first reading; understanding scientific literature takes time and patience.

By the time you have completed your first reading of the paper, you may find that the article is not really relevant to your topic after all, or is of little help in developing your theme. If so, the preliminary read-through will have saved you from wasted note taking.

Some people suggest taking notes on index cards, with one idea per card so that the notes can be sorted readily into categories at a later stage of the paper's development. If you prefer to take notes on full-sized paper, beginning a separate page for each new source and writing on only one side of each page will facilitate sorting later.

As you take notes, be sure to make a complete record of each source used: author(s), year of publication, volume and page numbers (if consulting a scientific journal), title of article or book, publisher, and total number of pages (if consulting a book). It is not always easy to relocate a source once returned to the library stacks; the source you forget to record completely is always the one that vanishes as soon as you realize that you need it again. Also, before you finish with a source, it is good practice to read the source through one last time to be sure that your notes accurately reflect the content of what you have read.

Writing the Paper

Begin by reading all your notes. Again, do this without pen or pencil in hand. Having completed a reading of your notes to get an overview of what you have accomplished, reread them, this time with the intention of sorting your ideas into categories. Notes taken on index cards are particularly easy to sort, provided that you have not written many different ideas on a single card; one idea per card is a good rule to follow. To arrange notes written on full-sized sheets of paper, some people suggest annotating the notes with pens of different colors or using a variety of symbols, with each color or symbol representing a particular aspect of the topic. Still other people simply use scissors to snip out sections of the notes and then group the resulting scraps of paper into piles of related ideas. You should experiment to find a system that works well for you.

At this point you must eliminate those notes that are irrelevant to the specific topic you have finally decided to write about. No matter how interesting a fact or an idea is, it has no place in your paper unless it clearly relates to the rest of the paper and therefore helps you develop your argument. Some of the notes you took early on in your exploration of the literature are especially likely to be irrelevant to your essay, since these notes were taken before you had developed a firm focus. Put these irrelevant notes in a safe place for later use; don't let them coax their way into your paper.

You must next decide how best to arrange your categorized notes, so that your essay or term paper progresses toward some conclusion. The direction your paper will take should be clearly and specifically indicated in the opening paragraph, as in the following example written by Student A:

Most shelled molluscs, including clams, oysters, muscles, snails, and chitons, are sedentary; they live either attached to hard substrate (like rock) or in soft-substrate burrows. A few bivalve species, however, can actually swim, by expelling water from their mantle cavities. One such swimming mollusc is the scallop *Pecten maximus*. This paper will describe the morphological features that make swimming possible in P. *maximus* and will consider some of the evolutionary pressures that might have selected for these adaptations.

The nature of the problem being addressed is clearly indicated in this first paragraph, and Student A tells us clearly why the problem is of interest: (1) the typical bivalve doesn't move and certainly doesn't swim; (2) a few bivalves can swim; (3) what is there about these exceptional species that enables them to do what other species can't? and (4) why might this swimming ability have evolved? Note that use of the pronoun "I" is now perfectly acceptable in scientific writing.

The first paragraph of your paper must state clearly what you are setting out to accomplish and why. Every paragraph that follows the first paragraph should advance your argument clearly and logically toward the stated goal.

State your case, and build it carefully. Use your information and ideas to build an argument, to develop a point, to synthesize. Avoid the tendency to simply summarize papers one by one: They did this, then they did that, and then they suggested the following explanation. Instead, set out to compare, to contrast, to illustrate, and to discuss.

In referring to specific experiments, don't simply state that a particular experiment supports some particular hypothesis; describe the relevant parts of the experiment and explain how the results relate to the hypothesis under question.

In all writing, avoid quotations unless they are absolutely necessary; use your own words whenever possible. At the end of your essay, summarize the problem addressed and the major points you have made so that the reader will remember the key elements of your paper.

Never introduce any new information in your summary paragraph.

Citing Sources

Unless you are told otherwise, do not footnote. Instead, cite references directly in the text by author and date of publication. For example: Landscapes can be classified according to the dominant plant species (Slobodkin, 1988). Jones (1981), for example, refers to white oak forests.

At the end of your paper, include a section entitled Literature Cited, listing all references you have referred to in your paper. Do not include any references you have not actually read. Each reference listed must give author(s), date of publication, title of article, title of journal, and volume and page numbers. If the reference is a book, the citation must include the publisher, place of publication, and total number of pages in the book, or the page numbers pertinent to the citation. Your instructor may specify a particular format for preparing this section of your paper.

Creating a Title

By the time you have finished writing, you should be ready to title your creation. Give the essay or term paper a title that is appropriate and interesting, one that conveys significant information about the specific topic of your paper.

Good title: Behavioral and Chemical Defense Mechanisms of Gastropods and Bivalves

Poor title: Molluscan Defenses

Good title: The Effects of Spilled Fuel Oil on the Breeding of Shorebirds

Poor title: Pollutants and Birds

The following are good sources of information for developing essays and term papers:

General biology textbooks

Specialized textbooks, such as general texts on human physiology, invertebrate zoology, marine biology, and ecology

Science sections of major newspapers, such as the *Boston Globe*, the *New York Times*, and the *Los Angeles Times*. Most major daily newspapers have a science section once each week.

BioScience

The New England Journal of Medicine

Oceans

Science News

Scientific American

Sea Frontiers